Psychology as a
Social Science

Psychology as a Social Science

Albert A. Harrison

University of California at Davis

BROOKS/COLE PUBLISHING COMPANY
MONTEREY, CALIFORNIA

A Division of Wadsworth Publishing Company, Inc.
Belmont, California

Photographs by Michael H. Kellicutt
University of California at Davis

ISBN: 0-8185-0028-X
L.C. Cat. Card No.: 75-187500
Printed in the United States of America

1 2 3 4 5 6 7 8 9 10—76 75 74 73 72

This book was edited by Micky Stay and designed by Linda Marcetti. It was typeset by Continental Graphics, Inc., Los Angeles, California, and printed and bound by Kingsport Press, Kingsport, Tennessee.

To E. A. H., C. B. H., and R. H., who helped me become a passive spectator of psychology.

To C. G. McC., R. B. Z., and the anonymous subjects who helped me become an active participant in psychology.

Preface

Psychology textbooks, like television shows, never really begin without a commercial, waivers and disclaimers, and a careful assignment of credits. If you already know that this book is an introductory psychology text for use in courses with a strong emphasis on personality and social psychology, if you do not have to be warned that you might stumble across an error or shortcoming somewhere within these pages, and if you recognize that this book was made possible only by the efforts of many wonderful people, then go on to page 1 and let the effort speak for itself. Otherwise, pause with me for these brief messages.

One Commercial

As a result of rapid growth in the field, many psychology departments have split their introductory course into two or more courses that can be taken alone, concurrently, or sequentially. Typically, one such course stresses personality and social psychology. This book is precisely geared for that course—and for any other introductory psychology course whose instructor chooses to emphasize such topics as personality, human development, and interpersonal relations.

Because this text was written for instructors with a particular orientation, it omits some material traditionally associated with introductory texts. Such topics as physiological psychology, psychophysics, and memory-drum experiments receive little or no emphasis. However, in this text you will find extended discussions of such topics as interpersonal processes, the concept of self, psychoanalysis, humanistic psychology, personality assessment, and the ways in which psychologists attempt to deal with salient social issues. In other words, this book is not a compendium of facts about all kinds of behavior. But within the treated topics, selected issues are dealt with in somewhat more depth than is common. By discussing these topics in a direct, conversational style, I hope to give the reader an appreciation of the psychologist's perspective and how he studies people in a scientific way.

Let there be no confusion. The topics covered are considered by some to represent the "softer" fields of psychology. I, personally, am an experimental social psychologist with an emphasis on "experimental." You will find in this book a strong accent on controlled observation. Where feasible, studies of interesting content are featured, but no experiments have been cited simply because they are "fun" or "cute." Similarly, certain classic studies with important results have not been excluded because their content is drab or dry.

The main dilemma I faced in preparing this somewhat specialized but nonetheless introductory text was the same one I encounter in teaching the somewhat specialized but nonetheless introductory course. For some students the material provides a first contact with psychology; others have already completed an introductory course stressing the biological bases of behavior. I chose to assume that the student opening this text is completely unacquainted with psychology. But when I deal with topics most likely to coincide with those covered in other introductory courses (such as certain issues within perception, learning, and motivation), I stress examples that I consider unlikely to overlap with those previously encountered. Thus this text does not contain extended references to Pavlov's dogs, but it does explain how principles of classical conditioning can produce or modify significant human behavior.

One Thousand Pardons

Now, it may be that this book is not entirely perfect. In fact, it contains some known errors of omission and, quite likely, some unknown errors of commission. As for errors of omission, even within the relatively constrained limits of the social science orientation, vast quantities of worthwhile material had to be excluded. Some readers are sure to feel that some alien-sounding topics received overemphasis, whereas pet topics were underplayed. I have not attempted to give equal coverage to all positions. Instead, for most issues, space is devoted to one or two explanations, either because I consider them unusually promising or interesting or because they integrate the material with that presented elsewhere in the text. As for sins of commission, suffice it to say that any resemblance between the present work and fiction is purely accidental.

One Million Thanks

It gives me great pleasure to make public and explicit my warm personal regards for the many people who have helped with this project. My own teachers, from Santa Barbara City College, the University of California at Santa Barbara, and the University of Michigan, have contributed both directly and indirectly. Especially prominent in my own intellectual career have been Drs. Robert Zajonc and Charles G. McClintock; those of you who are familiar with their work are sure to detect their influence at certain points in this text.

The faculty and students of the psychology department at U.C. Davis have been particularly supportive. For the most part, to single out specific people for acknowledgment would only do the others an injustice. However, very special help has come from three people: my colleague Mike Kellicutt, who did the photography, and former students Rick Crandall and Carolyn Quirici, who served as student reviewers and general assistants and, most importantly, helped straighten out the references and glossary.

Brooks/Cole has been really great. I have enjoyed working closely with Bonnie Fitzwater, Terry Hendrix, and Jack Thornton from general headquarters and with local drummers Pat Farrant and Gary Greene. Brooks/Cole gave me the best tools that an author could hope for: themselves, consulting editor Ed Walker, and a panel of prepublication reviewers representing a variety of colleges, universities, and orientations. Frank Blume, of San Bernardino Valley College, Don Johnson, of West Valley College, Marty Rogers, of Sacramento State College, Jim Geiwitz, of the University of California at Santa Barbara, and Bob Eichinger, Management Consultant, put tremendous efforts into their reviews, making them both motivational and informative. Linda Marcetti, Konrad Kerst, and the other people on the production staff have been entirely helpful. In a class by herself is Micky Stay, who, like me, had the pleasure of agonizing over each and every word.

Albert A. Harrison

Contents

xii

xiv

xvi

xviii

Psychology as a Social Science

1

An Orientation to Psychology

Hearing a person in distress, a young woman angrily grumbled "Why does everything have to happen to me?"

Tell me, child. Why do Americans plant trees?
For shade and beauty.
And why do Russians plant trees?
To block the view and to make work for the prisoners.

"Oh, God. I shouldn't be hurting this man," the middle-aged businessman taking part in an experiment moaned—and then continued with his task of inflicting painful electric shocks on another participant.

Fiction? Not at all, although the complexity and variety of human thoughts and actions as reflected in the above true examples can stretch the imagination. But surprising or not, anger at seeing someone else hurt, assigning Americans and Russians different motives for their landscaping, and acting in violation of the stern dictates of the conscience are not accidental events.

1

There are underlying *regularities* between cause and effect, and under appropriate conditions any one of us is likely to act in similar ways.

In this text, I will discuss the psychologists' search for regularities in actions and reactions and the theories they have evolved to account for the regularities thus far uncovered. Sometimes you will read of psychologists' pronouncements about the startling or unusual things people say and do, but mostly you will read of their probes into forms of activity that we think of as common and natural. You may find your attention drawn to some human activities you never noticed before, and perhaps you will come to discard some of your favorite notions.

Chapter One gives a brief idea of what psychology encompasses, what the different kinds of psychologists do, and how to distinguish psychologists from other professionals with similar-sounding titles.

After these initial bearings, Chapter Two starts right off with a hard look at the scientific tools psychologists use for making the observations on which they base their contentions. The word *science* has been used to dignify everything from gasolines to bowling balls, and as a result the term has lost much impact. But by calling my book *Psychology as a Social Science,* I show that many psychologists choose to follow the rules of science. In Chapter Two these rules will be made explicit within the framework of psychology. Remember, though, that neither God nor the American Psychological Association has decreed that psychologists must be scientific. So, from time to time throughout the text, you will read of interesting speculations that are clearly identified as such.

Many factors have been identified that help us to understand regularities in human conduct. Some of these factors come from inside the person and some from without. Some, like cells, are very small, whereas others, like societies, are very large. In Chapter Three I will describe some of these contributants to behavior, ways of classifying and relating them, and how they interplay with one another. Part One, then, is intended to give you an orientation to the field of psychology, to the rules of scientific psychology, and to the forces that act on man.

1.
Psychology and Psychologists

Wherever we find people, we find activity. Sometimes the activity draws the immediate interest of all present. In a living room, a small child takes his first step, and his family's attention is undivided. During the last few seconds of play, a football team wins the big game of the year, bringing forth wild screams and moans. Two men argue loudly, and a small crowd gathers around.

At other times human activity is far less spectacular, but, if you are not too preoccupied with your own concerns, it is still easy to observe. In a supermarket, for instance, you might find an attractive young woman carefully comparing two jars of instant coffee. Nearby stands a bewildered man, his gaze shifting between a shopping list and a display of canned tomato sauce. An older, heavy-set woman ambles by, snatches one brand from the shelf, and, with relief, the man does the same. From somewhere, out of sight, comes the wail of a child demanding a treat.

At still other times human activity is difficult to observe politely. But it is there, for people are not lifeless like statues. An old man on a park bench stares off into space. If you interrupt his train of thought, he might tell you of glorious days long gone. A small girl is asleep. There is moisture on her brow; she twists, thrashes, and groans. If you are curious enough to awaken her at that instant, she would probably tell you of an unpleasant dream.

Psychologists study activity. They are concerned, among other things, with what people think, feel, and do. Since at some point psychologists, as scientists, must deal with observables, descriptions of psychology frequently stress its concern with what humans and other living animals do. The action and reaction of living things constitute **behavior**, and **psychology** is typically

3

defined as *the study of behavior.* Yet observed behavior provides a basis for making inferences about thoughts and feelings, too.

Wherever we find people, we find activity.

We live in a crowded and complicated society. As members of this society, each of us must know quite a bit about behavior; otherwise we could not coordinate our activities and survive. When you approach an intersection and hear the scream of a siren, you are likely to stop because you know that the driver of the bright-red vehicle has no intention of doing so. You can, in fact, make hundreds of useful predictions about how people are likely to act under different conditions. Moreover, you can put this knowledge to use and have some influence on what others do. Perhaps you have noticed that, by acting warm and friendly, you can maintain an enjoyable conversation, whereas, by acting cold and aloof, you can silence unpleasant or boring people. If we all know so much about people, what makes the psychologist different?

To survive in society, it is only necessary to know principles of behavior that seem to work well enough to get us by from day to day. To be a psychologist, it is necessary to go a little deeper than this. The psychologist must systematically ask questions and probe. As a result of his systematic probing, the psychologist has found that matters are not always so simple as they appear on the surface.

PSYCHOLOGY, COMMON SENSE, AND
THE OBVIOUS

There are a number of **"common-sense"** principles of behavior. Although they can be used to make specific predictions, they are more often pointed to to account for something that has already happened. The psychologist is not willing to accept common sense on faith. The principle may be right, but it may also be wrong, and one of the jobs of the psychologist is to find out.

Common-sense principles are frequently violated by human behavior. "Opposites attract," for example. When the discussion turns to friendship, you will find that people who like each other tend to come from similar backgrounds and have similar personalities, tastes, and attitudes.

"Two heads are better than one." It all depends. Under some conditions people working together are less efficient, make more mistakes, and take longer to accomplish a task than people working alone. Yet we cannot conclude that "Too many cooks spoil the soup." Although I know of no study that has compared soup made by one or two chefs with soup made by an army of chefs, I will later describe conditions under which people working together are known to do a better job than people working alone.

"Aha," you say. "So there are conditions under which some common-sense principles hold true!" But such common-sense principles are worthless unless you specify the conditions under which they apply; once you do this, you are moving away from the realm of common sense and toward the realm of science.

To most psychologists the statement that something is obvious is as worthless as the statement that it is common sense. For the most part, something is "obvious" only to the beholder.

In the late 1940s several volumes of books reported the results of more than half a million interviews of American soldiers in World War II. Historians, commentators, and social critics, who had been eagerly awaiting the reports, were disappointed. They bitterly complained that the reports stated only obvious things that everybody already knew.

However, a man by the name of Lazarsfeld (1949)[1] gave the critics some interesting second thoughts. First he cited some representative "obvious findings," such as the following:

1. Southern soldiers, compared to Northern soldiers, adapted better to the climate of the South Seas Islands. (Obviously, Southern men were more used to hot weather.)

2. Country boys adapted to army life better than did city boys. (Obviously, country boys should have had more experience at roughing it and camping out.)

3. While the war in Europe continued, the soldiers wanted very desperately to come home. But when victory was achieved, they wanted to remain in Europe as conquering heroes. (Obviously, living the life of a victor is more attractive than being shot at.)

After citing a number of such "obvious findings," Lazarsfeld confessed that he had played a trick. In point of fact, the studies of the American soldier had *really* discovered exactly the opposite. Thus Northern men fared better in tropical climates than did Southern men; city boys adapted to army life more readily than did country boys; while the war raged, men were willing to fight, but they wanted to return home immediately after peace was gained.

If Lazarsfeld had stated these true findings, they, too, would have seemed obvious. Because the range and variety of human behavior are so great, it is possible to find examples to support any claim. The important question for the psychologist is: "What *typically* happens under the stated conditions?"

PSYCHOLOGISTS AND MORE PSYCHOLOGISTS

There are many kinds of animal life and many kinds of behavior. As a result, there are many kinds of psychologists, who specialize in different areas. In a sense, psychology has its own eye-ear-nose-and-throat men. The sheer size of the field encourages and supports such specialization.

[1] In psychology it is customary to cite references by author's *name* and *year of publication*. Then you can look up the reference at the end of the text. This system tells you *who* found or said something and *when* he found or said it, so you don't have to look at the bottom of the page like this. This procedure keeps both author and reader from becoming entangled in a web of *ibids*, *op cits*, and similar terms.

Psychology is an enormous field, and its products infiltrate all spheres of living. Virtually all Americans have had their lives affected in some way by psychologists. If you are reading this book as a student in a college or university, you are probably only too well aware of psychologists' tests. It is likely, too, that you or some of your friends have received some form of psychological counseling. Psychologists' efforts often go unrecognized, however, such as when they engineer telephones, design packages for commercial products, or assist with the instrumentation of a space capsule.

At present the leading professional organization for psychologists, the American Psychological Association, has about 30,000 members, and it is estimated that twice that many Americans might be called professional psychologists. In our universities more than half a million students take introductory psychology courses each year.

Psychologists tend to write a lot—probably in accordance with the rule that science is, in part, a body of publicly available knowledge. There is on the market an overwhelming number of psychology books aimed at both laymen and professionals; there are at least two psychology book clubs; the number of professional journals is increasing; there is even a monthly magazine (*Psychology Today*) geared to the literate public.

The growth of psychology over the last four or five decades is perhaps best reflected in the *Psychological Abstracts,* a journal published by the American Psychological Association that presents capsule summaries of recent books and articles of interest to psychologists. (*Psychological Abstracts,* you should note, is well indexed and provides a wonderful tool for finding material for a term paper.)

In 1927 the *Abstracts* summarized 2730 books and articles; in 1970, 21,722. The number of books and articles abstracted over the years is presented in Figure 1-1, which suggests that psychology's growth has been great, if a bit uneven. The more than 340,000 articles summarized should give you some idea of why this journal is published.

Certainly all this writing reflects a wide variety of interests. Although, like anyone else, most psychologists would object to being placed into a particular mold, there do seem to be some more or less systematic differences in the kinds of interests they typically express. Bringing order into these different fields is not easy. *The best I can tell you is that different psychologists ask different questions about behavior.*

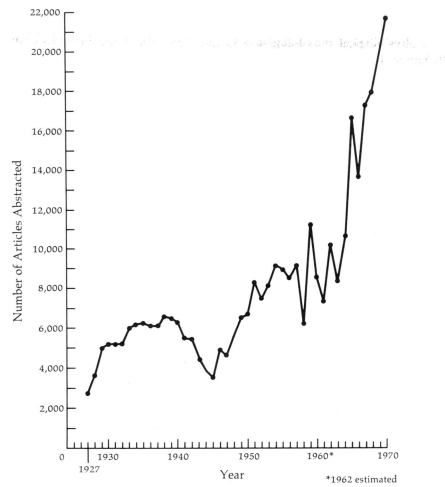

Figure 1-1. Abstracts from Psychological Books and Journals

First we will consider psychologists whose questions typically center around selected aspects of the individual, then psychologists who phrase their questions in terms of the whole individual, and then psychologists who move beyond the individual and ask questions about groups. Since there are some extra comments to make about the psychologists you might think of as bearded types with thick glasses and penetrating, hypnotic eyes, I will save them for last.

*Asking Questions about Selected Aspects
of the Individual*

Physiological Psychology

The **physiological psychologist** asks questions about the biological bases of behavior. Why in some cases are people given to violent, uncontrollable seizures? What behavior changes will occur if a certain part of the brain is injured? What are the physiological states producing tremendous amounts of food or water consumption?

The physiological psychologist asks questions about the ~~biological bases of behavior.~~

To answer such questions about the relationship between anatomical structures or physiological processes and behavioral regularities, the physiological psychologist may stimulate or remove certain parts of his **subject's**[2] brain, or he may examine the effects of nutritional, hormonal, or endocrinal imbalances. Or, he may introduce certain chemical substances such as drugs or alcohol into the subject's body and observe their effects on behavior.

[2] The term *subject* is used in psychology to indicate the human or animal under observation.

Closely related to the physiological psychologist is the comparative psychologist, who also asks questions about the biological bases of behavior. He asks why much behavior is seemingly related to membership in a biological class or species. Why does the sleeping arctic wolf rise every few minutes, walk around in a tight circle, and then go back to sleep, whereas the sleeping swallow does not? Why do many swallows annually venture to a place known as Capistrano, whereas arctic wolves never do? To answer his questions, the comparative psychologist examines different species with similar and different biological "givens" and requirements.

Motivation

The psychologist interested in **motivation** asks questions about the forces that instigate or impel behavior and give it direction, strength, and persistence. Why will one child choose to try a game of skill, such as ringtoss or beanbag, in such a way that he is sure to succeed, another in such a way that he is sure to fail, and a third in such a way that he is about equally likely to succeed or

The psychologist interested in motivation asks questions about the forces that instigate or impel behavior and give it direction, strength, and persistence.

fail? Why is the hungry raccoon more energetic than the fed raccoon? What packaging or merchandising techniques will lead to greater sales of this product? To find his answers, the psychologist asking questions about motivation examines possible contributing causes, which range from fairly simple biological states, such as hunger, to intangibles, such as the desire for success or self-knowledge.

Note that already there is an overlapping of interests. A psychologist who is interested in the effects of the drug cortisone on activity and who expects that it will make his subjects respond more energetically could be a physiological psychologist—in that he asks questions about internal biological processes—or a motivation psychologist—in that he is asking about the strength of behavior.

Perception

The psychologist who asks questions about how the organism receives, structures, and interprets information is interested in perception. He thus asks questions about seeing, hearing, smelling, and feeling. Why do people recognize things from different angles and under different conditions of illumination (such as night and day), even though the objective conditions differ tremendously? How little does a person need to hear in order to recognize a sound? Why do people see things as three dimensional instead of flat, like a pancake? To answer his questions, this type of psychologist varies the quantity and quality of information he gives to his subjects.

Learning

In the theorizing characteristic of American, British, and Russian psychologists, much behavior is believed to be a product of past experience. That is, as a result of changing environmental conditions, we abandon old ways of behavior and acquire new ones.

The psychologist who asks questions about regularities in behavior that result from past experience is interested in learning. He asks why and how new ways of behaving are acquired and strengthened and old ways abandoned. What accounts for the differences in how well we know things? What conditions encourage or discourage learning? To find answers to his questions, he studies everything from the choices an insect makes when it is winding its way through a **maze** (a series of interconnecting corridors) to the way humans solve complex, abstract problems.

Industrial Psychology

Industrial psychologists ask questions about human performance in the man-machine setting. How can we select the right man for this job? What conditions of lighting are best for people doing this kind of work? How can we better arrange the controls in this submarine to minimize the chances that a crew member will make a fatal mistake? To answer his questions, the industrial psychologist measures interests and abilities that he believes are related to successful performance or varies working conditions to see which ones elicit the best performance.

Other types of psychologists also work in the industrial setting but specialize in asking questions about the social environment of the work setting. They are described later as *organizational psychologists*.

Asking Questions about the Whole Individual

Developmental Psychology

The **child**, or **developmental**, **psychologist** asks questions about the systematic forces acting on the person as he or she progresses throughout life. Although many such psychologists do in fact study children, the label *developmental psychologist* is more appropriate, because important age-related changes in adolescence, maturity, and old age have been identified.

The developmental psychologist may ask: At what ages and in what sequence do children acquire specific skills, such as walking and talking? What are the differences in reasoning abilities among children, and how are they to be understood? What are the special problems of adolescents and of the elderly? To answer his questions, the developmental psychologist, like all psychologists who seek to understand the whole individual, must examine a multitude of contributants to behavior; he typically draws on genetics, biology, and all fields of psychology.

Personality

Personality is something that provides an overall coherence and continuity
to the individual's behavior and sense of self. According to Murray, it accounts
for why each person is in some ways like all other people, in some ways like
some other people, and in some ways like no other person. The psychologist
who is interested in personality thus asks questions about the similarities and
differences between people. Why is one woman happy, confident, and outgoing, whereas another is shy and retiring? What causes certain people to be
domineering and others submissive? The number of questions that can be
asked about personality is limited only by the number of personality differences
that can be distinguished. In one survey (Allport & Odbert, 1936) it was found
that in the English language there are about 18,000 words that describe human
attributes.

*Personality . . . accounts for why each person is in some ways like all
other people, in some ways like some other people, and in some ways
like no other person.*

*Asking Questions about the Interrelationships
of People*

The favored object for inquiry in psychology is the individual. But it is nonsense to claim the individual can be fully understood if his relationships with
other people are not taken into account.

Social Psychology

The **social psychologist** asks questions about the relationships among individuals and between individuals and groups. Although others, such as sociologists, are also interested in groups, the social psychologist differs in that he remains sensitive to the behavior of each individual.

According to Zajonc (1966)—whose name rhymes with *science*—social psychologists ask questions about behavioral dependence and interdependence. **Behavioral dependence** refers to the fact that each individual's behavior is influenced by the behavior of other people. **Behavioral interdependence** refers to the fact that this influence is both mutual and reciprocal. Thus the social psychologist examines the effects of individuals on one another.

The social psychologist asks questions about the relationships among individuals and between individuals and groups.

The social psychologist may ask: What happens to the person's performance when he is cheered or jeered by others? How do groups solve the problems posed by nonconformists? What are the results of watching someone engage in aggressive activity? To answer his questions, the social psychologist's procedures include eliciting social behavior from one person and then observing its effects on another.

Organizational Psychology

The **organizational psychologist** asks questions about human satisfaction and performance within such organizations as a large business firm or the military. Why are the people in this department of the firm demoralized and totally inefficient? What can we do to provide more responsive and effective leadership? How can we attract new people to replace those who are leaving? The organizational psychologist's concerns center around fitting together all the human pieces in such a fashion that the whole functions in a smooth and happy way. To answer his questions, the organizational psychologist may draw heavily on the work of other psychologists, but he has also developed his own concepts and techniques.

*Psychologists We All Know about and People
with Similar-Sounding Titles*

And now—at long last—some words about those psychologists who work directly with people and try to help them cope with their personal problems. This kind of psychologist is the **counseling**, or **clinical, psychologist**. He asks questions about the whole person and deals with people (whom he refers to as **clients** rather than subjects) one by one.

The clinical psychologist asks questions about **diagnosis** (the nature of the client's problem) and **prognosis** (what is likely to happen to the client under various conditions). He also asks questions about **psychotherapy**—that is, the procedures he should employ to induce more effective behavior on the part of his client. To answer his questions, the clinical psychologist draws heavily on all areas of psychology.

Because of the nature of his work, and because of his large number of contacts outside the academic or industrial community, the clinical psychologist is likely to be the most widely known type of psychologist. He is frequently confused with **psychiatrists** and **psychoanalysts,** who also deal directly with clients. Yet there are subtle differences in areas of competence and significant differences in training.

The psychiatrist and psychoanalyst both have Doctor of Medicine degrees. Up to a point, they receive the same training as all physicians, but they choose **psychiatry** as a medical specialty—much as their associates choose surgery or internal medicine. Following medical school and internship, they enter into residency for three to five years and receive specialized training in the diagnosis and treatment of emotional and behavioral disturbances.

Some psychiatrists go on to study **psychoanalysis,** the theory of personality and method of treatment originated by Sigmund Freud. (You will read about Freud's theory in Chapter Eight.) As a result of this additional, specialized training, they receive the title of psychoanalyst and the right to practice the psychoanalytic method. Psychoanalysts, then, are psychiatrists with additional, specialized training in a particular theory of personality and method of treatment. A few psychologists and others are also accredited to practice psychoanalysis, even though they have not attended medical school. However, in the United States the number of such nonmedical or "lay" analysts is quite small.

Psychiatrists and psychoanalysts, because of their training, tend to adopt a **medical model** for viewing emotional or behavioral disturbances. In extreme form, this model states that disturbed people are "patients" suffering from an "illness" that reflects an underlying "mental disease." They are "treated," sometimes in a "mental hospital," and may perhaps be "cured." This model is not necessarily a bad one, but some of its limitations will become apparent in the course of this book.

The clinical psychologist, on the other hand, has not attended medical school. But he generally has a Doctor of Philosophy degree in **clinical psychology** and spends enough years in internship and supervised training so that he is not likely to get a much earlier professional start than the psychiatrist. To be accredited and licensed, the clinical psychologist must meet high standards, since almost all states have stringent examinations for those who wish to practice psychotherapy.

The clinical psychologist, whose training emphasizes behavior, seeks the antecedents of emotional and behavioral disturbances in the client's present and past environment rather than in an illness in the client's mind. To be sure, the medical model has left a clear mark on contemporary clinical psychology; yet many clinical psychologists today emphasize behavior problems rather than mental illnesses and personal growth and new learning experiences rather than cures. This is not merely a substitution of words. Later you will see how the medical model has one set of implications and the behavioral model another. Contrasting predictions can be derived from each one, and the evidence is becoming pretty lopsided in favor of one of the two alternatives, but for now I'll keep you guessing.

PSYCHOLOGY: ART OR SCIENCE?

Is psychology an **art,** whereby the psychologist attempts to creatively solve the unique problems of specific individuals and groups? Or is psychology a **science,** in which efforts are devoted to seeking out underlying regularities in behavior and relating them to their causes? In a sense, since psychology is so large, it is both. In this book, though, it is treated as a science, for three reasons. (1) This happens to be *my* orientation (shared with a large number of others). (2) If you have but one brush with psychology, you might find it most valuable if you discover how psychologists support their claims scientifically. (3) Even if your goal is to become an artful practitioner, it is unlikely that you could do so without first knowing about some of the more or less demonstrated principles of behavior, how they were found, and how they are explained.

Is psychology an art, whereby the psychologist attempts to creatively solve the unique problems of specific individuals and groups?

Or is psychology a science, in which efforts are devoted to seeking out underlying regularities in behavior and relating them to their causes?

Those of you who are addicted to physics and chemistry may be inclined to emit roars of disbelief when I tell you that psychology is a science. So let's put it this way: science has certain rules, and many psychologists follow these rules. In doing so, they have collected observations and developed theories to explain **them.**

Physical, natural, and social sciences are alike in that they attempt to identify and explain regularities in the universe. The physical scientist seeks systematic regularities in nonliving things. The natural scientist seeks regularities in living things. The social scientist also seeks regularities in living things, but his emphasis is on how these regularities are caused by and affect other, similar living things.

Almost a century ago, during psychology's early days, great emphasis was placed on **introspection,** the conscious analysis of experience. For example, if you were introspecting, you would be handed something, such as a card of a certain color, and told to report your thoughts and feelings about it in the greatest possible detail. In this way early psychologists collected lengthy and intricate reports of what it was like to see a color, hear a tone, or lift a small weight. The subjective experiences thus studied were relatively simple ones.

In the United States, during the first decades of the twentieth century, there was a strong reaction against the introspective approach. The leader of this revolution was a rather colorful individual by the name of John B. Watson, who, among other things, is rumored to be responsible for suggesting flavored toothpaste.

Watson and his followers declared that, since science is *public,* all scientists must be convincing when they tell others about their findings. The best way to be convincing is to talk about observables, since statements about observables can be verified. If psychologists are to study "mental life" scientifically, they, too, must deal with observables. Experience is subjective, unobservable, and private, but behavior is objective, observable, and public. This line of reasoning by Watson and other early **behaviorists** has prompted the scientific definition of psychology as "the study of behavior."

Today many psychologists consider themselves scientists but not behaviorists—at least not in the same sense that Watson and his associates were considered behaviorists. There are several reasons why they avoid the label. First of all, psychologists do not like to be assigned to "camps," and Watson and his group clearly formed a camp. Second, the public image of the behaviorist is that of a tall, thin, heartless wretch who wears a white lab coat and carries a bag of rat chow; nobody wants to assume that image. Third, the present-day student of behavior is a much more sophisticated fellow, with broader interests and a more imposing social conscience than his predecessors of the early 1900s. In short, more than fifty years of attitudes of "If it can't be seen, it doesn't exist" and "If it doesn't move, it can't be understood" have been replaced by positions of greater moderation.

At present some psychologists are again seeking to study subjective feelings and experiences in ways that they suggest do not involve emphasizing behavior. These psychologists believe that an important part of understanding an individual lies in discovering how things seem to him subjectively. Unlike the early introspectionists, they try to study very complicated types of experiences. This "phenomenological" emphasis on dealing as directly as possible with the subjective and the experiential will be explored later in the discussion of *Third Force* or **humanistic** psychology. Here, however, you might note that some psychologists with this phenomenological orientation argue that, ultimately, everything is reducible to experience. Even the behaviorist reporting a study is dealing with experience: his experience of his study.

Advocating either the behavioral or the phenomenological orientation requires certain philosophical assumptions—assumptions of such a nature that they can be neither proven nor disproven.

Some assumptions of science are that: (1) a real world exists independent of our experience of it; (2) there are regularities in this world in terms of cause and effect; (3) this world and its regularities are knowable; (4) this knowledge may be discovered and then verified by ourselves or by others. The assumptions of the behavioral orientation are in closest accord with these assumptions made by scientists in general. Since I can neither prove nor disprove these assumptions, I will merely point out that I tended to follow them while writing this book.

CONCLUSIONS

Like other people, psychologists are interested in what individuals think, feel, and do. Since psychologists often deal with observables, definitions of psychology typically stress the study of behavior. Behavior, however, encompasses a great deal, and with effort and ingenuity the study of behavior allows the psychologist to make plausible inferences about thoughts and feelings.

As members of society, we all know quite a bit about behavior. However, most people tend to exercise this knowledge in an automatic and uncritical way. The psychologist, who is professionally interested in behavior, is more questioning, and this characteristic has led him to reject many common-sense and "obvious" explanations of behavior.

Psychology is an enormous enterprise. Within the field different psychologists have different specialties. They can best be distinguished from one another on the basis of the kinds of questions they ask. Physiological psychologists, comparative psychologists, and psychologists interested in motivation, perception, and learning ask questions about selected aspects of the individual. Those interested in developmental psychology and personality ask questions about the whole individual. Social psychologists and organizational psychologists ask questions about individuals' relationships to one another.

The clinical psychologist deals directly with persons who come to him because they find their behavior unacceptable. He can be distinguished from professionals with similar-sounding titles largely on the basis of training and orientation.

Psychology may be viewed as either an art or a science. This text emphasizes psychology as a science, particularly as a social science. Calling psychology a science implies that psychologists seek systematic and verifiable regularities in behavior. Calling psychology a social science draws attention to the effects people have on one another.

Now let us turn to the rules of the game.

2.
The Rules of the Game

The psychologist, in his attempts to describe and understand behavior, typically follows certain established procedures. Let us now consider some of these procedures and why they are favored.

THE OBSERVATION OF BEHAVIOR

The simplest method used by the psychologist to obtain the **data** that provide the raw materials of his science involves making casual observations. However, "just looking" has serious limitations, as I found out firsthand.

It was the summer of 1967. The gentleman in the suit leaned forward expectantly. Anxiously I fingered my collar and gulped. "Well," I began, "the lady was coming out of the store into the parking lot. A blue '54 Plymouth was backing up and a blue '56—no, yellow '56 Chev. . . ."

Thus began my testimony concerning an accident in which a woman was knocked down by a car. My account was a little bit garbled, but I thought it was basically correct. But then the questioning began.

"Was the woman carrying anything?"

"Yes, some packages."

"How many?"

I wasn't sure if it was two or three.

"But she wasn't carrying a purse?"

21

I didn't know.

And so the questioning continued.

"Did she appear pregnant to you?" . . .

Other witnesses gave conflicting reports, even on the points I was sure of. Fortunately in this case, the "prosecutor" was Kent Marquis, a social psychologist, and the accident had been staged for the benefit of a movie camera. Kent was dealing with a problem that had been identified more than a hundred years earlier: inconsistent and conflicting eyewitness accounts. We find it routinely, such as in inconsistent and conflicting legal testimony or when police officials and protesters describe a confrontation to television interviewers. The reason for such confusion is that it is very difficult to keep personal prejudices and biases from influencing what people "see" and report. Honesty, sincerity, interest, ability, and training help people to become better observers and reporters. But, for the most part, simple observations often prove deficient in terms of accepted scientific criteria.

Other witnesses gave conflicting reports.

First simple observations are likely to have less **reliability** than do observations collected by other means. *An observation is reliable if it is the same when made* *by different people or on different occasions.* If two people can agree on what they observe, and if still other people can make the same observation, then that observation can be considered reliable.

Procedures aimed at minimizing subjectivity serve to make an observation reliable. One technique is to use some sort of standard or assessment device that is *external* to the observer. In the physical sciences, thermometers or rulers would be such devices. If something is 10 inches long, as measured by a ruler, everyone who can use a ruler could arrive at a similar answer. In psychology such items as questionnaires, interview forms, rating sheets, and psychological tests function as rulers, as does anything else that carefully specifies and measures responses.

Does this mean that to obtain reliable information it is necessary to have eyewitnesses fill out forms or answer specific questions? Not necessarily. Eyewitness reports of such events are reliable *if* a group of independent judges witness the event and then draw the same conclusions. (By *independent* I mean that they are not personally involved in the action and that they do not influence one another while making their observations.) If a number of such judges are in agreement, it is less likely that the observation is the result of personal prejudices.

The question of validity also must be confronted in observing behavior. *If an observation is valid, then it is truthful.* Again, because of inabilities and prejudices, simple observations made by single observers are less likely to be valid than are observations based on measures external to the observer or observations verified by a group of independent judges.

A lack of validity becomes particularly striking when the "observation" is second- or thirdhand. Allport and Postman (1947) presented subjects with slides of semidramatic scenes containing a great deal of detail. After observing a slide, the subject described what he saw to a second subject. The second subject described it to a third subject, who in turn told it to a fourth, and so on, until a total of five subjects had described the scene. The first omitted about 35 percent of the details. By the time the report reached the last subject, about 75 percent of the details had been lost. Even more discouraging, the facts of the story got twisted. One slide pictured the interior of an elevated railroad car carrying a number of people, including a black man dressed in a business suit and a white man dressed in laborer's clothes and carrying an open straight razor. Somehow, in the telling, the white man ended up wearing the neat suit and the black man wearing laborer's clothes and carrying the razor.

A report may be reliable—in that everyone can agree on it—yet not necessarily valid. A series of reports that the black man carried the razor could be agreed upon, even if it were not true. Furthermore, a report can be valid but not reliable. Copernicus, the fifteenth-century Polish astronomer, was among the first persons to report that the earth and the planets revolved around the sun. But other observers of that day quite reliably reported that the sun and the planets revolved around the earth. What is needed, clearly, are observations that are *both* reliable and valid.

One other observational problem stems from the tendency of eyewitnesses to have their attention drawn to the unusual, atypical, and surprising (Berlyne, 1960, 1966), a tendency that may distract them from more typical or representative events. Television cameramen, for example, may concentrate on the troublemakers at a demonstration and ignore thousands of peaceful protesters. Although scientists do not preclude the unusual, the infrequent, or the exciting, there is a certain usefulness in studying events that are more representative and hence more likely to recur. Observation of typical behavior leads to findings that are of greater applicability.

The need for reliable, valid, and representative observations puts the psychologist to a great deal of trouble. In evaluating psychological theories and having to choose between observations based on one man's reports and those based on techniques of demonstrated reliability and validity, most psychologists I know have a pronounced tendency to choose the latter. But, under certain conditions, "just looking" still plays an important part in psychology, for the use of external assessment devices or the assembly of a panel of impartial judges is not always possible.

RELATING VARIABLES

Reliability, validity, and representativeness are important factors in *describing* behavior. However, description is only one of the aims of psychology. Other aims are *prediction, explanation,* and *control,* which move us into the realm of correlational and experimental techniques.

Correlations

The subject matter of psychology is not static or stationary. Both behavior and its antecedents are dynamic and ongoing. Thus the psychologist deals with

variables—that is, with conditions that vary and change. The exciting part of psychology lies not in obtaining frozen snapshots of behavior but in discovering how two or more variables are related.

Here is a simple example. When people are asked to describe themselves, they tend to do so in rosy, glowing terms. Edwards (1957) referred to this tendency as the social desirability response bias (see Chapter Nine). I became interested in this problem and decided to study it. I first selected 127 adjectives that could apply to people. One group of subjects rated these adjectives in terms of the extent to which each represented something good, favorable, or positive. Another group indicated the extent to which they thought each adjective described themselves. The two variables in this study were thus (1) *desirability,* or the extent to which each adjective represented something good, favorable, or positive, and (2) *endorsement,* or the extent to which the subjects claimed the adjective applied to themselves. Following Edwards and many others, I expected that the greater the desirability of the adjective, the greater its endorsement would be.

There are several ways to report my findings to you. One possibility would be to show you a huge table that tells the desirability rating of each adjective and the extent to which people endorsed it. But this method would require tremendous space, and it might be hard for you to detect any relationship.

On the other hand, I could show you a **scatterplot** (Figure 2-1), which is simply a graph on which pairs of observations are presented as data points or "spots." In this case, one arm or axis of the graph stands for desirability and the other axis for endorsement. Each point represents an adjective. By looking at the axis below each point, you can discover the associated adjective's desirability, and by looking at the axis to the left, you can see the extent to which it was endorsed. The scatterplot provides the same information as a table of numbers, but the overall pattern is easier to see. Figure 2-1 shows that, in general, the more socially desirable the adjective, the more people claimed that it applied to themselves.

Figure 2-1 shows a direct or **positive relationship,** which is defined by the following rule: *as the value or magnitude of one variable increases, the magnitude of the related variable increases; as the magnitude of one variable decreases, the magnitude of the related variable decreases.* If the relationship were perfect, all the observations or data points would fall on a straight line (Figure 2-2). But, as the saying goes, nothing is perfect. Thus *no* science obtains perfect relationships; they are always a matter of degree. In the social desirability study, some adjectives were endorsed more or less than would be

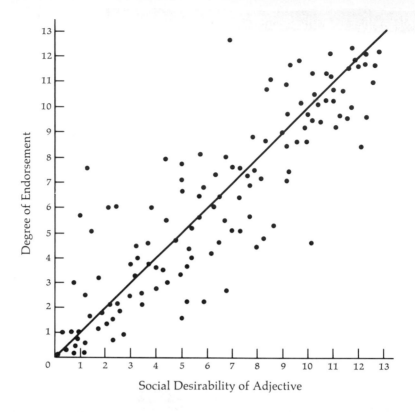

Figure 2-1. Item Endorsement as a Function of Social Desirability (drawn from data presented by Harrison, 1968a).

expected if there were a perfect correspondence between desirability and endorsement.

There are also **negative relationships**. In a negative relationship the two variables are related in such a way that *as the magnitude or value of one variable increases, the magnitude or value of the related variable decreases.* Figure 2-3 shows a perfect negative relationship.

Figure 2-4 shows a *realistic* negative relationship—again, a bit less attractive than the perfect relationship of all scientists' dreams. In the study that produced this relationship (Harrison, 1969), subjects were asked (1) how much they liked different religious faiths and (2) how curious they were to find out about people who adhered to these faiths. Figure 2-4 suggests that the college students I

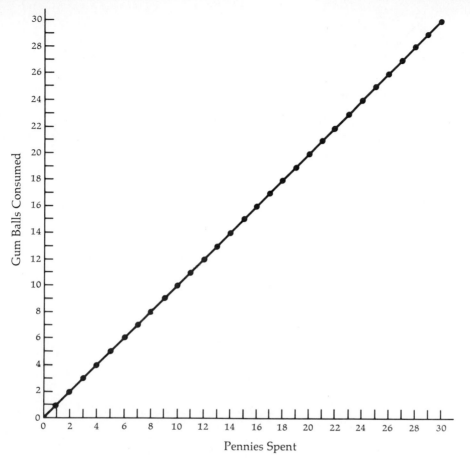

Figure 2-2. A Perfect Positive Relationship.

interviewed were more curious about members of the *less*-liked faiths. Why? The interpretation is based on other findings. Many Americans have frequent contact with members of common religious faiths. As a result, they feel comfortable in the presence of members of these faiths and describe the faiths as likable. Many Americans do not have frequent contact with members of uncommon faiths. They feel a bit worried or nervous in the presence of known representatives of these faiths and hence describe the faiths as less likable. However, this same nervousness may lead to curiosity, which would represent an attempt to get to know and feel comfortable with members of these statistically rare faiths.

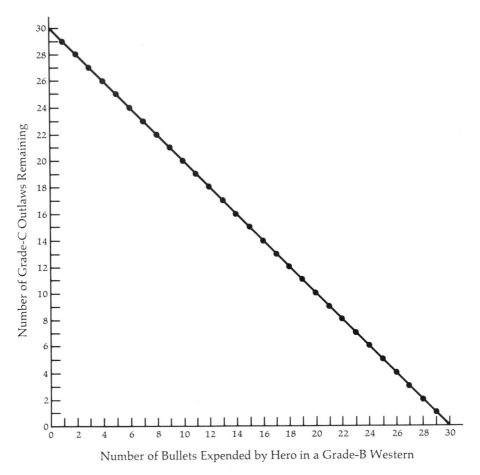

Figure 2-3. A Perfect Negative Relationship.

Scatterplots such as those in Figures 2-1 through 2-4 do more than provide an instant overview of the relationship between two variables. When the relationship is clear, it is possible to make a **prediction**—that is, a statement about the value of one variable if the value of the second variable is known. In the case of the results presented in Figure 2-4, if you knew something about the likability of a given faith, you could make an educated guess concerning the extent to which it would elicit curiosity.

The precision or accuracy of the prediction will depend on how closely the two variables are related—that is, how closely the data points approximate a straight line, such as in Figures 2-2 and 2-3. Hays (1963) has reported data showing a

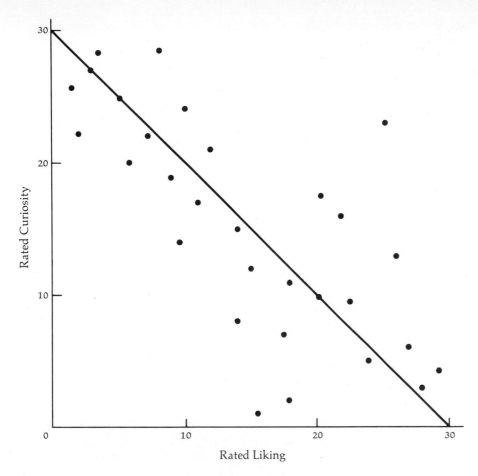

Figure 2-4. Rated Curiosity about Members of Different Religious Groups as a Function of Rated Liking of that Faith (drawn from data presented by Harrison, 1969).

positive relationship between the heights of husbands and the heights of wives. Even though, *on the whole,* interviewees tended to have spouses of similar heights, there remained a few cases in which a midget married a giantess. Therefore, how can one feel confident making a prediction about the height of a husband given the height of his wife?

The answer is simple: it is impossible to be certain that a prediction will be accurate. Predictions are to some extent guesses. But they can be sophisticated guesses, and there are ways of estimating the likelihood that they will be accurate. When we know the chances that a prediction will be accurate, we know how much confidence to put into it.

Daily we operate with varying amounts of confidence in our predictions about other people's behavior. Flying in a commercial airliner from coast to coast, you would most likely have confidence in your prediction that the flight crew had both ability and training and would perform in such a way as to safely take you to your destination. On the other hand, if you decide to depart with a novice pilot for an across-mountain flight on a cloudy night, you might choose to take two tranquilizers and a parachute, since that pilot's level of performance is not quite so predictable. Like the traveler, the psychologist feels more confident about some of his predictions than about others.

Daily we operate with varying amounts of confidence in our predictions about other people's behavior.

How to Get Out of Drawing Scatterplots

The psychologist, in describing the relationship between two variables, speaks of **correlations.** When two variables are correlated, they are related in such a way that, given information about one, you can make a statement about the other, exactly as in the examples above. A positive correlation (+) refers to a direct or positive relationship (Figures 2-1 and 2-2), and a negative correlation (−) refers to an inverse or negative relationship (Figures 2-3 and 2-4).

A **coefficient of correlation** (or "correlation" for short) is a numerical statement summarizing such a relationship. It is much more succinct than a scatterplot. In a quarter of an inch or so, it tells both the direction and the degree of the relationship (that is, how closely the data points approximate a straight line). Coefficients of correlation theoretically range from +1.00 to −1.00. A correlation of +1.00 represents a perfect positive relationship, whereas a correlation of −1.00 stands for a perfect negative relationship.

The larger the *absolute value*[1] of the correlation, the closer the relationship between the two variables and the more closely the data points approximate a straight line. As the absolute value of the correlation becomes small, there is little linearity. That is, a correlation of .00 would indicate no approximation of a straight line at all.

One way to get a feel for correlations is to think of a spotted balloon with the spots standing for data points. The balloon can be inflated to any degree and pointed either upward or downward. Partially inflated, the spots or data points are closely packed in, and the correlation is large. More inflation spreads out the data points, lowering the correlation. Figure 2-5 illustrates this idea and summarizes the last few paragraphs. Following convention, the correlation for each example is expressed as an *r*.

Regression Equations

Unfortunately, knowing a correlation does not give all the information necessary to attempt a precise prediction. This is because correlations do not provide bearings with respect to the arms or axes of the scatterplot. But there are formulas that make it possible to make predictions without having to draw scatterplots. These formulas are known as **regression equations**, the specifics of which need not concern us here.

[1] That is, the number disregarding the plus or minus sign. Thus the absolute value of −.78 is greater than the absolute value of +.55.

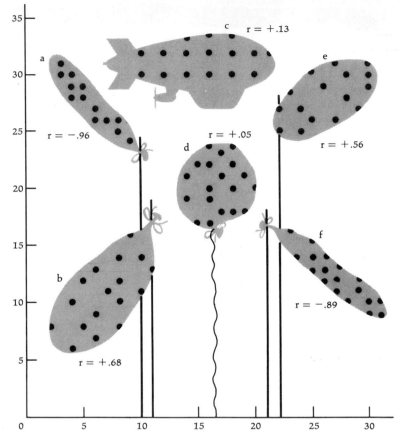

Figure 2-5. Correlations: The Balloon Summary.

Uses of Correlations and Regression Equations

Correlations and regression equations have three main uses in psychology. First, they aid with making predictions about behavior. Second, they aid with the evaluation of observations. Third, they assist with the evaluation of psychological tests.

One business of science is to make predictions. Psychologists want to make predictions about behavior, and from the preceding discussion, you should see that correlations and regression equations help them to do so. For example, the psychologist working in a prison setting may wonder which prisoners would be good parole risks. Since quality of work record and probability of successful adjustment on the "outside" are positively correlated, he can predict that, in general, prisoners with better work records prior to their imprisonment are better parole risks. He would then make recommendations accordingly.

A second business of science is to continually evaluate its own success. Correlational techniques are very useful for appraising the reliability and validity of psychological observations, particularly those made by means of psychological tests. For example, a person's ability to perceive and understand mechanical relationships is believed to remain fairly stable over time (Cronbach, 1960). There should be a fair amount of consistency among the scores a man obtains if he takes the same test of mechanical ability several times. That test can be considered reliable to the extent that his scores are correlated, for higher correlations suggest a greater repeatability of measurement. On the other hand, the test would seem unreliable if it suggested that the man had the ability of Thomas Edison on Monday but was unable to understand how to operate a pair of scissors on Tuesday. To evaluate the validity of the same test, the scores could be correlated with some accepted indicator of performance. For example, if success as a mechanic or engineer were an acceptable indicator of mechanical ability, one could correlate test scores and performance on the job. The higher the correlation, the more valid the test.

A third business of science is to construct and evaluate theories. Correlational techniques are helpful for this evaluation. If a theory suggests that two variables are related in a certain way, correlational techniques can provide evidence as to whether or not this is indeed the case.

The Experiment

To satisfactorily explain behavior, it is necessary to understand its causes. To understand the relationship between cause and effect, it is necessary to turn to the experimental method. Psychologists distinguish between cause and effect in terms of independent and dependent variables. **Independent variables** are those responsible for behavior. Changes in independent variables are changes in the antecedents, or believed *causes*, of behavior. **Dependent variables** are forms of behavior. Changes in dependent variables are thus the consequences, or *effects*, of changes in independent variables. It is the measure of the dependent variables that provides the psychologist with his data.

The nature of causality has been debated for centuries. However, in daily life and in science we are generally satisfied that a cause-effect relationship has been demonstrated if three conditions are satisfied: (1) correlation, (2) cause before effect, and (3) the elimination of alternative possibilities.

1. *The suspected cause and effect must systematically correlate in such a way that changes in the suspected cause are associated with changes in the suspected effect.* For example, suppose you suspect that stomach contractions cause feelings of hunger. The first requirement is to show that, when stomach contractions are absent, there are no reports of hunger and that, to the extent stomach contractions are present, so are reports of hunger.

2. *The suspected cause must precede the effect.* If stomach contractions are correlated with reports of hunger, it may be that the contractions caused the report of hunger or that the report "I am hungry" constituted a signal from the brain that caused the stomach to contract. If stomach contractions precede the reports of hunger, the reports could not have caused the contractions.

3. *Alternative possibilities must be eliminated.* Discovering that two variables are correlated and that changes in one preceded changes in the other is not sufficient evidence for assuming a cause-effect relationship. Some other factor could have produced changes in both variables, perhaps in such a sequence that it appeared as if changes in one caused changes in the other. For example, to continue with the hunger study, perhaps a lemon meringue pie brought into the laboratory (to celebrate the beginning of a great experiment) triggered off sensations of hunger, as reflected in *both* reports of hunger and stomach contractions. And perhaps the stomach contractions appeared to come first because the subject was salivating so copiously that he could not promptly report his feelings of hunger. Thus the third condition to be satisfied for demonstrating a cause-effect relationship is the elimination of possible alternative causes of the behavior in question. Unfortunately, these alternatives are not always so obvious as a lemon meringue pie.

Logic of the Experimental Method

The experimental method, when properly applied, satisfies all three conditions for showing causality. In the **experiment** the psychologist tries to actually produce changes in behavior by manipulating a suspected independent variable. This procedure satisfies the conditions of correlation and cause before effect. But to ensure that his manipulations are responsible for the observed changes in behavior, he must still eliminate alternative explanations. There should be no changes in other independent variables that might account for the observed effects. Thus these other independent variables should be held constant.

On the surface, it might seem easy to produce changes in one independent variable while holding other contributants to behavior constant. (For a starter, don't bring lemon meringue pies in the laboratory!) But the world is characterized by flux and change, and it is impossible to identify and hold constant all but the manipulated independent variable. For example, what if the experimenter wears a light-yellow chiffon dress that reminds the subject of a lemon meringue pie?

Experimental and Control Conditions

Although the experimenter can never feel confident that all independent variables except the one he deliberately manipulates have remained constant in the course of his experiment, he can discover if these variables influenced the behavior under study. To do so, he compares behavior under different conditions: **experimental conditions** and **control conditions.** Under both conditions subjects receive the exact same treatment, except that under experimental conditions something is applied or manipulated. For example, under experimental conditions elderly people may be given a drug, whereas under control conditions they are not given the drug.[2] Systematic differences in behavior under the different conditions are seen as a result of the experimental manipulation.

The Effects of Vision on Pin-the-Tail-on-the-Donkey. Since the experiment is so important in so much of psychology, let us pause now to consider a very simple application of experimental procedures.

A **hypothesis** is an assertion that is usually derived from a theory. To be worth anything, a hypothesis must be capable of proof or disproof.

Let us hypothesize that the availability of vision will improve performance at a task known as pin-the-tail-on-the-donkey. This, if you do not know, is a game in which blindfolded children attempt to pin a cut-out tail on a large picture of a tail-less donkey. Success is assessed in terms of how far the tail is placed from a dime-sized spot or "target," which indicates the tail's proper location.

The subject in this experiment, Brian, was 9 years old. The *independent variable* was the presence or absence of vision. The *dependent variable* was Brian's

[2] My favorite definition of a drug: anything that, fed or injected into an animal, results in a scientific paper.

accuracy, as determined by measuring the distance between Brian's placing of the tail and the location of the target.

Under *experimental* conditions Brian was allowed full use of all senses and given five opportunities to pin-the-tail-on-the-donkey. Under *control* conditions he was again given five such opportunities, but this time he was blindfolded.

Under experimental conditions Brian was allowed full use of all senses and given five opportunities to pin-the-tail-on-the-donkey.

Under control conditions he was again given five such opportunities, but this time he was blindfolded.

Under control conditions, Brian missed the target by 1, 6, 9, 15, and 22 inches. Very importantly, these measures provide a yardstick by which to gauge

Brian's performance under the experimental conditions. Without the blindfold Brian missed the dime-sized target by 0, 0, 0, 0, and .5 inch.

Brian very definitely performed better under the experimental conditions. Since he was treated the same under the two conditions (with the exception, of course, of the presence or absence of the blindfold), we can conclude that some support was obtained for the hypothesis that the availability of vision enhances performance at pin-the-tail-on-the-donkey. Note that the same conclusion could *not* be drawn if there were hornets in the room under control conditions, if Brian had been promised a new bicycle for good performance under experimental conditions, or if an earthquake had struck under either of the two conditions; any of these other events could have contributed to different performances under the two conditions.

In this experiment the subject was tested under two conditions. In other experiments the use of the same subject under the two conditions may not be possible or feasible. Often, different subjects are assigned to **experimental groups** and **control groups,** and comparisons are then made of the performance typical of the two groups. Groups are required because a given subject's unique personality and abilities contribute heavily to his performance. From observing one subject alone, it is not possible to discover the behavior that is *typical* under the examined conditions.

Planning an experiment to investigate causal relationships is called *designing an experiment.* An experimental design may be very complex and can tax the most clever psychologist's ingenuity. Many different experimental designs contribute to the findings reported in this text. A good design is a prerequisite for a good experiment, but, without the hard work of actually conducting the experiment, designs remain intellectual games.

When Is a Result a Result?

The effect of vision on Brian's performance was very clear. His *worst* performance without the blindfold was better than his *best* performance with the blindfold. Although he missed the target by an average of 10.6 inches under control conditions, he missed it by an average of only .1 inch under the experimental conditions.

But suppose the difference in his performance under the two conditions was very small? Would the results still support the hypothesis? Or would they reflect something else, such as coincidence or chance?

Sometimes chance seems to provide a plausible explanation of an observation. For example, suppose I told you that I had tremendous ESP powers and that by willpower alone could cause coins to come up heads. I then produced 50 pennies and threw them in the air, and 26 came up heads. I claimed that this result proved my ESP powers. I doubt that you'd believe me, for you would think that *chance alone* could account for the results of my demonstration.

At other times, attributing something to chance seems far less plausible. Suppose I pulled a perfectly functioning typewriter out of a washing machine. Then I told you that some time ago I had placed all the typewriter's parts into the washing machine and turned it on and kept it running until, due to chance alone, all the parts jiggled into place and formed a perfect typewriter. I doubt that you'd believe me, for you would suspect that something *other than chance* accounted for the typewriter assembly.

However, you must admit that the coins coming up heads *could* reflect the powers of my mind and that the typewriter *could* have been produced by chance. One can never be sure.

Whenever there is a psychological result (such as a difference in the behavior under experimental and control conditions), there are two possible explanations. One is that the result is due to the treatment accorded the two groups. The other is that it is due to chance.

The alternative that a result is due to chance can never be ruled out. *However, it is possible to calculate the likelihood of this alternative.* If it is likely that a result is due to chance, we must discount it, for it tells us nothing. This is exemplified in the case of the pennies, for it is very likely that chance alone could produce 26 heads given 50 coins.

By convention, when the likelihood that a result or difference is due to chance is 1 in 20 or less (such as 1 in 100), chance is ruled out as an alternative. Under these conditions results are then called **significant results,** and it is significant results that are reported in this text.

Hazards of the Experimental Approach

The psychological experiment is useful because it allows statements to be made about the causes of behavior. There are, however, some potential hazards associated with psychological experiments. The extent to which these hazards raise serious doubts about an experiment depends largely on the competence of the experimenter.

The Experiment as Artificial. Experiments often involve participation in strange and unusual activities that seem to bear little resemblance to anything the subjects usually do. (Whoever heard of playing pin-the-tail-on-the-donkey without a blindfold?) These activities often take place in a laboratory room unlike rooms usually encountered, and this room may be packed with strange and foreboding equipment. Furthermore, performance is closely scrutinized by one or more trained professionals.

Considerations such as these have led to the charge that the psychological experiment is unnatural or artificial. Critics of the experiment thus suggest that, although psychologists want to understand how people usually behave, they study them under conditions very different from those of everyday life. As a result, people behave in ways that do not closely correspond to their typical behavior.

Experiments vary in terms of the fidelity with which they reflect real-world conditions. Some experiments are conducted in the *field*, or natural setting. In other cases, experiments are conducted in the laboratory but are such marvels of stagemanship and engineering that the subjects may be unaware of the experimentation. Centers (1963), for example, made observations while his subjects thought they were still waiting for the experiment to begin.

It remains true, however, that there is a large number of experiments that involve highly contrived situations and tasks. What about them?

First, the experimenter may be studying psychological processes that are known not to change appreciably with the nature of the setting. The degree to which one sound must be louder than another in order for a difference to be detected is the same at home or in the laboratory. Second, the experimenter may have no reason *not* to believe that his subjects are behaving in ways that reflect their everyday behavior.

In a sense, the psychological experimenter may be compared to a foreign-language examiner, who also tests behavior in a contrived situation. During a language exam, the passages selected for translation are likely to be contrived, since the instructor wants selections that involve complex grammar rules and a large vocabulary. From this contrivance he obtains a score he believes *reflects* the student's typical level of proficiency outside the classroom. By the same token, the experimental psychologist examines behavior that be believes *reflects* behavior outside his laboratory. Both the foreign-language examiner and the experimental psychologist can make mistakes, but if they continually check the validity of their methods, the number of mistakes can be quite low.

The Overuse of Rats and College Students. If you are going to start a zoo, buy a monkey first. As zoo animals go, they are very inexpensive. But they still cost about a hundred times as much to purchase and at least 20 times as much to maintain as rats. Rats are cheap and convenient, and partly for this reason many studies of "animals" are studies of rats.

...generalizing from one group of sub-jects...   *...to another group of subjects is always a risky business.*

Humans also differ in terms of the ease and convenience with which they may be studied. In most research settings, college students are in generous supply. Partly for this reason, many studies of human behavior are studies of the behavior of college students, which has led some critics to suggest that the experimental approach has produced a "psychology of the college sophomore" that is not applicable to other people.

It is true that generalizing from one group of subjects (such as nuns) to another group of subjects (such as U. S. Marines) is always a risky business. But the general applicability of findings of studies using college students as subjects depends to a large extent on the topic under investigation. A study involving the ability to tell the difference between two colors is one thing; a study whose results are likely to be influenced by intelligence, interests, social class, and educational level is another. Perhaps the best procedure is to be cautious when generalizing results from one group to another but not unduly alarmed in the absence of evidence that the two groups differ in important, relevant ways.

Experimenter Bias as a Cause of Results.   Naturally, an experimenter hopes that his study will produce results that reflect favorably on his ideas and procedures. Consequently, he may unwittingly influence his subjects to perform the way he wants or "see" them as behaving in a way that will prove flattering to his ideas. This is the problem of **experimenter bias.**

Experimenter bias is a problem but, perhaps, one that has been dramatically overplayed in recent years. The experimenter inadvertently influences his subjects' behavior only if he departs from the logic of the experimental method by not treating experimental and control subjects alike except for the manipulation of the independent variable. Moreover, he can "see" his subjects as behaving in the way he wants them to behave only if his observational techniques allow considerable latitude for error. I believe most experiments simply aren't that bad. Care and proper safeguards can minimize the effects of experimenter bias.

Experimental Results as the Hard Facts of Life.

> The car hummed past one of the great light-reflecting signs that dominated the highway edge at every hundred yards. "Science is Truth" glinted the sign. Behind it ran a perspective line of other boards.
>
> > *"If Science Says No—No!"*
> > *"All is patterned."*
> > *"Our order is the true order."*
>
> "It's as you say, Harry," Ralph said over his shoulder. "After a while you take the words for granted."

This excerpt is from a provocative short story (Matheson, 1970, p. 46) that depicts a society based on science alone. What the scientist says is, literally, law. The story capitalizes on a conception of the scientist as one who offers ultimate truth, which everyone else is supposed to accept.

Yet what is fact today is fiction tomorrow. Proven principles come and go. The *very best* the experimental approach can accomplish is to provide *adequate*

The story capitalizes on a conception of the scientist as one who offers ultimate truth, which everyone else is supposed to accept.

information at that point in time. Never lose your skepticism. Psychologists have never lost theirs.

All these hazards of the experimental approach must be taken seriously. Reading a study, you might ask the following questions. (1) Is it likely that the behavior studied reflected the subjects' typical behavior outside the laboratory? (2) Does the author try to generalize his findings to a group of very different subjects whom he has not studied? (3) Is it likely that the experimenter somehow biased his results? Using these criteria, there is a wide variety in the acceptability of studies. Hazards of experimentation are something to be aware of and sensitive to, but they need not be considered overwhelming.

PSYCHOLOGICAL THEORIES

A psychological **theory** provides descriptions and explanations of the relationships among variables. Like numbers, theories provide summary statements about things and events. Although theories are based on a relatively limited number of observations, they can, if successful, generate many new propositions.

Suppose a psychologist interested in motivation observes that people who have not eaten for 6 hours are more active than people who have just been fed. He also notes that people who have not eaten for 12 hours are more active than people who have gone unfed for only 6 hours. Later he might notice that the same changes in level of activity can be noted for thirsty individuals: people who have not had a drink for 6 hours are more active than people who have just had a drink, and people who have not had a drink for 12 hours are more active than those who had water 6 hours earlier. He might speculate that the hungrier and thirstier people have two things in common: they have been more *deprived*, and they are more *active*.

On the basis of a few such observations, he can begin formulating a theory. The hungrier and thirstier subjects have something in common, which he chooses to call *drive*. The theory (which you will read about in Chapter Four) is then stated as: *Deprivation leads to increased drive, which is characterized by greater activity*. Note that this proposition is more general than the statement that hungry people are more active than fed people and thirsty people more active than nonthirsty people. The psychologist can use this theory to derive other propositions concerning the activity level of people who have been deprived for different lengths of time or deprived of commodities other than food or water. In each case greater deprivation should be associated with more vigorous activity. A theory therefore provides a summary of statements about the observed and expected relationships of many different independent and dependent variables.

Going beyond Observables

In describing relationships among variables, theories typically invoke things or processes that are not directly observable but that are believed to link the variables together. Such inferred mediators or links are usually called **hypothetical constructs**. Drive is an example of a hypothetical construct. Deprivation produces *drive*, and *drive* produces greater activity. That is, deprivation affects activity level through drive. Both deprivation and activity level are observable, but drive is not. The concept of drive is useful, however, because it relates different deprivations and different activity increases that might otherwise seem unconnected.

The list of hypothetical constructs—things that we cannot directly see, hear, taste, smell, or touch but that have proven to be useful inferences—is extensive. Examples from psychology are instincts, intelligence, habits, attitudes, and personality. Occasionally, something whose existence is initially inferred later becomes observable. In physics the planet Pluto and the atom are examples. But for the most part, hypothetical constructs remain *ideas* and are not to be confused with things. The temptation to regard them as tangible is highly discouraged. When viewed as "real" in the same sense as a turnip or a shoelace, they become less flexible and hence less subject to change. As ideas, hypothetical constructs should be subject to modification and abandonment as new evidence gathers.

The Interplay of Theory and Data

Psychological theories describe and explain data. Therefore theory and data must interplay. Theorizing is usually prompted by some relationship that the psychologist believes he has observed. Thus the interplay begins with the initial formulation of a theory.

After a theory has been formulated, it is necessary to test it by discovering whether new observations can be made that will conform to the theory. If there is another theory that also tries to explain the same behavior, it becomes a challenge to collect observations showing the merits of one theory compared to the other. The second way theory and data interplay, then, is in the evaluation of the theory.

The testing of different theories provides much of the excitement in psychology. When observations do not conform to a theory, lively controversies develop: those making the observations may claim that the theory is inadequate, and proponents of the theory may charge that the observations were faulty or wrong. In most cases, people following these lively issues must carefully weigh very complicated evidence.

Evaluating Psychological Theories

There are so many different and conflicting theories in psychology that it is useful to have some way of choosing among them. Certainly, the degree to which a theory is supported by data is important. However, there are other considerations as well. The following are some additional standards for evaluating psychological theories, as summarized by F. H. Allport (1955).

1. A theory should be logically consistent within itself.
2. A theory must be subject to confirmation or disconfirmation. That is, the hypotheses derived from the theory must be testable.
3. A theory should offer an explanation. In Allport's (1955, p. 9) words: "It should provide more in the nature of an accounting than a mere analogy. There should be a feeling of inevitability about its explanations once its postulates have been accepted and its rationale understood, and the explanations given should be sufficiently clear and detailed to be convincing."
4. All other considerations being equal, favor should be given the theory that is more general, in the sense that it accounts for the wider range of behavior.
5. All other considerations being equal, favor should be given the less complicated, more *parsimonious* theory.

Let us try to keep these considerations in mind. Unfortunately, most theories do not live up to all these high standards, and the theory that is most promising one year is not so promising the next. No matter how clever the theorist, with time evidence accumulates suggesting that his theory needs reworking or abandonment. Does this mean that theory construction is a fruitless enterprise?

A very few psychologists suggest that more data should be required before psychological theories can be constructed (despite the 340,000+ articles reported in the *Psychological Abstracts*), whereas others suggest that elaborate theorizing is a waste of time, since all that is really needed are very simple statements about the relationships between independent and dependent variables. Still others counter that, although theories are imperfect, they do much to advance knowledge: many unexpected and interesting findings have been produced during the tests of different theories. My own position is that psychological theories provide imperfect, impermanent, but useful tools that assist with the job of understanding behavior.

CONCLUSIONS

Psychologists observe and analyze a vast panorama of behavior. Although many techniques aid in this task, the favored procedures are those that are known to be reliable and valid, for they can then be verified by other people.

Behavior and its antecedents are in a continual state of flux and change. To understand behavior, it is thus necessary to discover the dynamic relationships among variables. Correlational techniques are useful for describing such relationships, making predictions, testing theories, and evaluating various psychological procedures. However, correlations are not sufficient for proving cause-effect relationships, because if two or more variables are correlated, it is not possible to distinguish antecedents from consequences. For this task, it is necessary to turn to the experimental method, which involves comparing behavior under experimental and control conditions. Subjects under the two conditions are treated in identical ways, except that under experimental conditions there is a manipulation that is not present under control conditions. Systematic differences in the behavior of subjects under the two conditions are presumed to be caused by the manipulation.

The experimental approach is useful, but certain potential drawbacks are associated with it. Critics argue that the experiment may not accurately reflect real-world conditions, that experimenters too often use college students for subjects, and that it is possible for the prejudices and biases of the experimenter to influence his results. All these criticisms are legitimate, but it is perhaps too easy to be overimpressed by them.

Psychological theories summarize and explain large numbers of observations and potential observations. In doing so, theories typically invoke hypothetical constructs, which are useful intellectual tools that meaningfully link together two or more variables. Hypothetical constructs are inferred, never directly seen. If something inferred is later seen (like the planet Pluto), it loses its status as a hypothetical construct.

Like observations, theories vary widely in their acceptability. The extent to which a theory conforms to the "facts" is certainly important, but there are other considerations as well. F. Allport reminds us that psychological theories should be logical, should be capable of proof or disproof, and should offer something in the way of an explanation. In cases in which two or more theories are equally satisfactory in other respects, preference should be given to the theory that is more general, in the sense that it accounts for a wider range of behavior, or to the theory that is more parsimonious, in that it involves the fewest and simplest concepts.

This chapter has covered the ground rules followed by many psychologists. These rules are based on the assumptions of science. Following these rules provides, perhaps, the most adequate observations and explanations available at any given point in time. However, conscientious application of these rules does not produce hard, unassailable facts or permanent explanations. What is fact today may seem fiction tomorrow, and today's most favored theories will ultimately appear inadequate and obsolete.

3.
Perspectives on Man

Suppose during the first week of school you were to saunter around campus and drop into different classrooms to catch fragments of opening lectures. In the process you might discover something rather puzzling.

8:15 A.M., Main Lecture Room, Harding Hall. "Try as we may, we cannot avoid it: man is a biological organism. Much of his behavior can be understood by looking at his biological origins. At some point in the distant past, man began to emerge as one of the ninety-some different species of primates. That is, he became separate from what you may think of as the other monkeys (polite laughter). As a result of his evolutionary history, he walks erect, is relatively hairless, has no tail to speak of, and has hands that are unusually suited for holding and using tools.

"Of course, we need not look to the dim past to see how biological factors affect man's behavior. We are all aware that much human behavior results from cyclical processes within the body. Respiration is a short cycle; sleeping, eating, and women's menstrual cycles are all longer. We are also all aware of some of the dramatic effects of disturbances in that chemical workshop that constitutes the human body. Intoxication, for example, can produce a loss of coordination and a decrease in the ability to show good judgment. *To understand man and how he behaves, we must never lose sight of the fact that he is a biological organism.*"

10:15 A.M., Booth Memorial Theater. "To some extent, each person is like other people. But to some extent, each person is unique. None of us would be surprised to find classmates of the same height, weight, age, and sex reacting quite differently to the same set of conditions. For example, if three classmates had mud splattered on their clothes by a passing truck, you would not be surprised to hear one cursing the truck driver, the second cursing himself, and the third not cursing at all.

"What accounts for such tremendous differences in behavior among biologically similar organisms? I suspect it is their unique environment, which dictates the kinds of things that have happened to them in the course of their lives.

"Perhaps you have heard of cases of children who, for one reason or another, were raised in isolation by unloving parents. In 1947 Kingsley Davis reported the case of a girl, Anna, who had been raised in an attic room from the age of half a year to the age of 6 years. When found by the authorities, she could not talk, walk, or do anything that Davis felt showed intelligence. Anna's retardation could not be due to an inability to learn, for she later started acquiring these skills. No, Anna presented a picture that could only barely be called human because she was the product of a harsh and unusual setting. *To understand man and how he behaves, we must never lose sight of the fact that he is a unique product of his unique environment.*"

4:15 P.M., Room 6, Avian Sciences. "In 1970 it was estimated that there were more than 200 million people in the United States. With a total area of 3,675,633 square miles, one should find on the average about 54 persons per square mile. If people were distributed evenly and then walked around silently and blindfolded, eventually some would quite literally run into each other. In this way, people would influence one another because of their sheer numbers.

"Population density has important effects on behavior. But, of course, people cannot be likened to randomly moving gas molecules. They actively seek each other out or avoid each other. They form and dissolve attachments and associations. They influence one another through radio, television, the movies, the mails, the printed word, and through intermediaries, as well as on a face-to-face basis.

"Man exists in a social environment. What he does is very much influenced by the presence and actions of others. *To understand man and how he behaves, we must never lose sight of the fact that he is a product of his social setting.*"

Such fictitious introductory lectures are not improbable. Many schools offer courses with these different thrusts. Each course attempts to provide some understanding of man and the things man does, but there are considerable differences in their approaches. The first course traces regularities in behavior to the biological nature of man. Stress is on evolution, heredity, and the intricate workings of the body. The second course traces regularities in behavior to differing environmental conditions. Stress is on the individual's past history and present circumstances. The third course traces regularities in behavior to man's relationships with others. Stress is on social interaction and society. Which approach is right—in that it *really* tells us about man's behavior?

Each approach is at least partly right, for man's biological nature, his past experiences, and his position in the social network all contribute to his behavior. I say "contribute" rather than "cause," for they exert their influences simultaneously.

Each approach is at least partly right, for man's biological nature, his past experiences, and his position in the social network all contribute to his behavior.

To gain a perspective on man, we must impose some organization on the many forces acting on him. A starting point is to note that some of these forces seem to originate *outside* the person, whereas some others seem to come from *within*.

SITUATIONAL AND DISPOSITIONAL VARIABLES

Some of the forces acting on the individual are products of the immediate *situation* in which he finds himself. For this reason, they can be referred to as **situational variables,** or, since they have their origins external to the person, *forces from without.* Situational variables include the general nature of the setting, the objects found in the setting, the spatial arrangement of those objects, the number and type of other people present, and the relationships of those people to the behaving individual.

A good understanding of situational variables can help us to understand why different people often act in similar ways in the same situations. In effect, different people are subjected to the same forces from without. Thus even "cheerful" people may be morose at funerals and "confident" people insecure when criticized by their boss. *Situational variables also help us to understand why the same person acts differently in different situations.* Someone like Ebenezer Scrooge who always seems stingy may not prove so stingy on Christmas Day. Although he remains the "same person," the forces from without change at that time of year.

Other variables contributing to behavior originate within the individual. These **dispositional variables** include such things as biological states, habits, attitudes, and personality. If persistent over time, they operate in many different situations in which the individual finds himself.

Dispositional variables are helpful for understanding why the same person acts in similar ways in different situations. They can describe the individual's core of consistency. *Dispositional variables are also useful for helping us to understand why different people act in different ways in the same situation.* On the inside, each person is unique, and he shows his uniqueness wherever he goes. Situational and dispositional variables thus help explain the consistencies and inconsistencies of a given person and the similarities and differences among different people.

*Relationships between Situational and
Dispositional Variables*

Situational and dispositional variables are related in three ways. First, they operate together to produce behavior. Second, situational variables, which are initially apart from the person, can be translated over time into dispositional variables, which are a part of the person. Third, even though many different situational and dispositional variables jointly contribute to behavior, it is possible to study the effects of one variable at a time.

1. *Situational and dispositional variables both contribute to any given behavior.*
To make reasonably accurate predictions about behavior, both situational and
dispositional variables must be taken into account. Thus, to make the most
effective statements, the psychologist might say that person x in situation y
will behave in fashion z.

Imagine that you are watching a couple, George and Marsha, returning from
a pleasant and friendly first date. Your job is to predict whether George will
make an amorous advance. You may also wish to predict Marsha's reaction, but,
as you'll soon see, predicting George's behavior is difficult enough.

One situational variable George might be affected by is the general setting.
If the couple is parked outside Marsha's house, are the minimal requirements
of privacy (relative darkness, no near passersby) met? Another important
situational variable is the nature of the responses or "cues" emitted by Marsha.
As their eyes meet, does she seem to smile somewhat seductively, or does she
glare? Does she lean a little closer, or does she move away and light up a
cigarette? Does she move her purse from the seat and place it on the floor, or
does she take her purse from the floor and place it between them on the seat?
All these variables, which could encourage or discourage George, originate
outside George's skin.

Yet George is not entirely at the mercy of these factors. His past experiences
and present expectations will also be important. Has George learned to be self-
confident and assured, or is he shy and retiring? Does he fear women, "respect"
them, or view them as slaves? Then there are sheerly biological considerations.
What about George's hormonal activity? And did the beer he had earlier relax
him, or did it mix poorly with the pizza to produce ominous rumbles?

If George (1) is shy and afraid of women, (2) dated Marsha because his mother
told him to, (3) has underactive hormones, and (4) is suffering from an upset
stomach, it would seem that the dispositional variables are working against his
making an advance, no matter how congenial the setting. If (1) there are a
number of spectators in the vicinity, (2) Marsha places her purse on the seat
between them, and (3) she moves away and voluntarily drops a contact lens, it
would seem that the situational variables are working against George's making
an advance, no matter how favorable his internal state. If there were a convergence of all these forces, one could feel quite sure that nothing of an amorous
nature would happen. On the other hand, if George is self-confident, has a high
hormone level, and is in the pink of condition, while Marsha's response is

nothing but smiles and come-hither looks, quite the opposite would be predicted. It would be less clear, though, if circumstances were mixed, such as if George were shy and timid while Marsha assaulted him with unholy eyes, or if George were confident while Marsha desperately pressed against the door on her side of the car.

To understand behavior, then, it is necessary to take a multitude of forces into account. Situational variables providing forces from without and dispositional variables providing forces from within *interact* to determine behavior. This simply means that one type of force alone is unlikely to be entirely responsible for any observed behavior. Yet it is also worthwhile to note that a behavior does not always depend on a miraculous convergence of forces but instead may be **overdetermined.** That is, there are enough forces contributing to it such that, in the absence of any one force, it is still likely to occur.

2. *Changes in situational variables may produce or alter dispositional variables.* Forces from without may give rise to subsequent forces from within. A splendid example of this principle can be found in acquisition of morality, or the ability to tell right from wrong. The young child, attempting to raid the cookie jar, may be physically restrained by his mother, who slaps him and calls him naughty. Later, an ominous glance from Mother will suffice to keep him away from the cookies. His good behavior in these two cases is very much a result of a force from without: Mother's prohibitions. Still later, however, the child will restrain himself even in the absence of his mother. Now he has a conscience. This conscience is very much a force from within. Whereas his good behavior was originally a product of external constraints, it is now a product of internal control.

3. *Single variables may be studied in isolation.* Because it is so difficult to obtain a good grasp of even one or two variables, a researcher rarely, if ever, tries to take into account all the forces acting on an individual at a given point in time. Instead, he is likely to focus on only one or a limited number of variables. The experimental technique allows him to do so. Applied correctly, it enables the researcher to make his observations in such a way that the uncounted other forces that *could* influence the behavior under study are unlikely to operate in a systematic way.

Sometimes selected situational variables are the focus of attention, and dispositional variables are ignored. This technique leads to hypotheses such as "People will respond more vigorously when they are being watched by others" (Zajonc, 1966) and "Conflicts between groups of warring children can be reduced if the groups must work together to solve some problems of importance to both groups" (Sherif & Sherif, 1969). Note that in these hypotheses nothing is said about biology, heredity, personality, or anything else inside the person's skin.

At other times, focus is on the effects of selected dispositional variables, and the contributions of situational variables are studiously ignored. The important consideration, which makes research possible, is that there are methods so that different contributants can be singled out and studied one at a time, even though any specific behavior will be the result of many different contributing forces.

BIOLOGY, THE PERSON, AND SOCIETY: SOME FORCES ACCOUNTING FOR REGULARITIES IN BEHAVIOR

Let us now turn to an overview of some of the forces that account for regularities in behavior.

Biological Bases of Behavior

Each animal is a biological apparatus. This apparatus at once provides the capacities for certain types of behavior and imposes limitations that make other types of behavior impossible. As an animal, each man or woman has such a set of capacities and limitations. Some of these characteristics are attributed to membership in the species *Homo sapiens* (erect stature, highly effective brain, very useful thumb arrangement, and so on), whereas others are more idiosyncratic to race, tribe, or family (good eyesight, long legs, good musculature, and so on). Occasionally, biologically given capacities and limitations are easy to identify. A man with long fingers will find it relatively easy to master the piano; a man with short legs will find it difficult to become a basketball star. More typically, behavioral regularities are not so easily linked to biological structure and function, and biological givens are often much harder to identify than are long fingers or short legs.

Biological bases for regularities in behavior have been sought in (1) *heredity*—that is, the processes by which characteristics are transmitted from the parents to the offspring at the time of conception; (2) *normal physiological processes,* which allow the organism to sustain life in comfort; and (3) *organic pathologies*, or physical abnormalities, which alter or disrupt normal behavior.

Heredity

Heredity is responsible for many of the differences between species, as well as for many individual differences within species. This subject is mentioned only in passing, for in later chapters you will see that heredity has been linked to intelligence and emotionality and, with somewhat less success, to personality.

Normal Physiological Processes

The body, as an intricate chemical workshop, is always active. Much of what happens in this workshop involves cyclical, recurring events necessary for comfort and survival. At present quite a bit is known about the biological bases of behavior necessary for life, such as breathing, sleeping, procreating, and the elimination of waste products.

For example, the reproductive cycle accounts for some interesting regularities in behavior, as most of you probably know from firsthand experience. For both men and women, heightened and decreased sexual interest is associated with hormonal and endocrinal factors. In men, interest may remain high until the hormonal level is reduced. In women, interest varies according to a monthly (28-day) cycle, and different points in the reproductive cycle can be associated with changes in nonsexual behavior as well.

In the woman's monthly cycle, the hormonal level fluctuates regularly. Most of the time a high level is maintained, but it is decreased during the premenstrual and menstrual phases of the cycle. Reviewing numerous studies in this area, Paige (1969, 1971, 1972) has noted some interesting aspects of women's behavior under the influence of the low-hormone phase (popularly thought of as "the curse"). First, women in the low-hormone phase are about twice as likely to have accidents as they are during other points in the cycle. Such increases have been noted in accidents in the home, in the factory, and on the road. Second, admissions to mental hospitals rise during the low-hormone phase. Furthermore, female patients in mental hospitals are more likely to have acute psychiatric outbreaks during this phase. It would seem, then, that the low-hormone phase or "curse" is associated with an exaggeration of unwanted psychiatric symptoms. Finally—and perhaps most impressively—the rates of both suicide attempts and successful suicides rise just before and during menstruation.

Thus it would seem that certain distraught actions on the part of women stem from the lowered level of hormonal activity during the eight-day sequence constituting the premenstrual and menstrual periods. Interestingly, however, Paige argues that much behavior associated with "the curse" is socially produced and not strictly the result of biological factors.

Organic Pathologies and Behavior Change

Certain types of normal behavior are dependent on normal physiological processes. If there is a disturbance in these processes, behavior changes are likely to result. Such disturbances (organic pathologies) may be traced to injuries to the brain or nervous system; changes in hormonal, endocrinal, or blood chemistry; accident, disease, or nutritional deficiencies; or to the ingestion of drugs or stimulants.

Such disturbances may be traced to . . . the ingestion of drugs or stimulants.

To understand the effects of organic pathologies, the physiological psychologist may experiment with stimulation or ablation (removal) of different parts of the nervous system or use surgical or other techniques (such as drug injection) to upset the delicate balance of nature. Often he produces an animal that is in some way worse off than the one he started with—perhaps stripped of earlier capabilities, perhaps fat and grumpy, or perhaps subject to violent seizures. But it is encouraging that this is not always so. In some cases researchers have been able to improve on nature. For example, Bresler and Bitterman (1969) have produced some "supergoldfish" with a learning capacity surpassing that of normal fish. They accomplished this feat by grafting extra brain material onto the fish.

Psychological Antecedents of Biological Changes

Thus far our discussion has centered on biological changes as antecedents of behavior changes. However, it is also true that there are psychological antecedents of biological changes. A man confronted by a frightening situation may tremble, perspire, and report a tightness in the stomach and a dryness in the mouth. A woman plagued by worries may break out in a fiery skin rash. A harassed executive may develop an ulcer or a propensity for a heart attack.

Brady (1958) gave two monkeys electric shocks every few seconds. Both monkeys had a lever to push. One monkey's lever was a dummy, which did nothing. The other monkey's lever, if depressed, prevented both monkeys from receiving the shock. This latter monkey was described as in an "executive position," for it was incumbent on him to protect them both. About three weeks after the experiment began, the executive monkey died as the result of a large, perforated ulcer. The other monkey was in good health. Since both monkeys received the same number of shocks, it appeared that the responsibilities and pressures of the "executive position" were responsible for the fatal ulceration.

The Place of Biology in "Psychology as a Social Science"

There is a tremendous mass of literature describing the biological antecedents of behavior. Man *is*, after all, a biological organism. Yet it is still possible for the psychologist to make useful statements about behavior without drawing on biological concepts. In much, if not most, of psychology, inferred psycho-

logical processes are used to link behavior to its antecedents. In effect, hypothetical constructs serve in the place of blood-and-guts structures.

It is not possible to flatly state that it is better or more scientific to approach
behavior in terms of hypothetical constructs or in terms of blood-and-guts
structures. The relative worth of each approach in a given case depends on the
extent to which it is logical, succinct, capable of proof or disproof, and,
eventually, proven or disproven. The extent to which an approach satisfies
these stringent criteria may depend, in turn, on the type of behavior in question.

Many intriguing forms of behavior have not been related to the intricate
chemical workings of the body but have been linked to such factors as past
experiences and the demands of the immediate situation. In these cases the
behavior either is understood in terms of inferred psychological processes or is
not understood at all. Much of the behavior studied by psychologists interested
in motivation, perception, learning, and child development falls into this
category, as does most of the behavior commanding the attention of the
psychologist interested in personality and social psychology. Since this text
stresses an understanding of personality and social psychology, you will read
more about the valiant attempts to infer psychological processes than about
the equally valiant attempts to identify and understand behaviorally relevant
biological structure and functioning.

Individual Bases of Behavior

Many persons agree with Gordon Allport's contention that the main concern
of psychology is the individual. Although psychology often involves examining
selected aspects of people's behavior, the ultimate goal is a full understanding
of the individual in all his complex glory. This understanding requires a full
consideration of the person's past and present. Emphasis is likely to be on his
environment and on how things that have happened to him throughout his
life have molded him into a person who is in many ways unique.

Psychologists who concentrate on linking regularities in behavior to the individual frequently seek to discover, describe, and explain personal characteristics
referred to variously as **genotypic traits,** or simply **traits.** These relatively
enduring characteristics, attributes, or properties of the individual are dispositional variables—but of a very special kind. A given trait must show itself in

a variety of situations and under many different circumstances. Traits thus help to account for why a person seems to behave rather consistently as he or she moves from place to place.

Traits are inferred and, once inferred, serve to describe and summarize a great deal of the person's behavior and to allow predictions to be made about his or her subsequent behavior. For example, if you know a rather independent and self-sufficient woman who does her own plumbing and electrical repairs, sends attacking men and/or large dogs fleeing with an exhibition of judo, and has numerous loud arguments with local merchants, schoolteachers, and the mayor, you might decide that each of these activities reflects an underlying quality you choose to label "ascendance." Once you have inferred this trait, you might predict a near-violent reaction if a rather pushy solicitor calls at her home at an inconvenient hour to ask her to vote for a political candidate not for her choosing. On the other hand, if you know a meek, ingratiating woman who is a den mother for the Cub Scouts, works for the PTA and two church organizations, likes to cook elaborate meals for sick neighbors, and makes a point of telling everybody what she thinks they would like to hear, you might infer a different underlying quality that could be labeled "submissiveness." This inference would lead to the prediction of a more hospitable reception for the unwelcome political solicitor.

How broad or pervasive are traits? In the case of the two women, for example, in how many situations will their respective "ascendant" and "submissive" qualities appear? Traits are defined by their apparent operation in a variety of situations. Yet there might be some conditions under which the self-sufficient woman would act weak and feminine and some conditions under which the mild-mannered and ingratiating woman would stand up for herself.

How enduring are people's traits? By definition, traits are persistent. But they must also be subject to change. Otherwise, penologists, educators, and psychotherapists who try to change people would be put out of business. Opinion seems to be that, although traits are basically persistent, they can be changed if the appropriate circumstances are created.

D. R. Miller (1963) has observed that most people exhibit certain personality inconsistencies. In support of this statement, he cites a study by Cottrell (1942), who presented students with two case histories and asked them to rate the personalities of the children involved. One case history described a child who was uncooperative at home, where he sulked and bullied younger children. The other case history described a child who spent a great deal of time daydreaming at school and, being quite timid, was bullied by his classmates. As you might expect, the students described children with two rather strikingly different personalities. But the two case histories were of the same child, who acted quite differently at home and at school. This study reminds us that an individual's "personality" sometimes varies greatly according to the situations in which it is observed. Thus we should be a bit cautious in our search for underlying, genotypic traits.

In conclusion, antecedents of behavior can be sought in the person and in his past history. The individual as a contributor to his own behavior will be examined repeatedly in subsequent chapters.

Social Bases of Behavior

People influence one another in systematic ways that thereby contribute to individual behavior. Psychologists with many different interests place a strong emphasis on the effects of social variables on behavior.

Why is the psychologist, who typically concentrates on the *individual*, so concerned about social relations? First, a large part of any individual's behavior is social, in that it involves responding to other people. Painting a picture of the whole person without including his reactions to others would be similar to trying to play a Bach fugue using only the middle ten keys of a piano. Each performance would be lacking. Second, the search for the formation of genotypic traits has typically led to a consideration of the individual's past experiences. A very important set of experiences for molding the person are those that he has had dealing with others. Third, when people are asked to describe their lives, social relations are seen to play an important role. People often consult psychologists because of difficulties with parents, teachers, employers, sweethearts, or friends. Even when their problems do not on the surface appear to center around interpersonal relations, a more careful examination may suggest the contrary. Fourth, the framework within which individual behavior is evaluated is socially imposed. For example, consider "abnormality." I doubt that a lone individual could be considered abnormal. It takes at least three people: two to act one way and define what is normal and a third to act another way and be branded abnormal. Fifth, when some very identifiable, physical handicaps are stripped of their social ramifications, they become unimportant or uninteresting. If you were born with one ear twice the size of the other, there would be no necessary hazard to your biological survival. (You might even hear better from that side of your head.) However, the way other people react to you could make you quite miserable. Sixth, even when it appears that there is a simple biological explanation of some form of behavior, important social variables may also be found. You might think that when marijuana is smoked, the active ingredients simply take effect, produce a favorable "high," and thereby encourage a repeat performance. Becker (1953), however, suggests that learning from others is also required. Repeated marijuana users have learned from others how to smoke marijuana in such a way that it produces real effects, how to recognize these effects, how to connect them with the consumption of marijuana, and how to view these effects as pleasurable rather than as bizarre and frightening.

Each person is influenced by social units of many different sizes. At one extreme he is affected by the two-person group, which involves himself and one other. At the other extreme, he is affected by society, which involves himself and perhaps hundreds of millions of others. All social units provide pressures to conform, the opportunity to learn from others, and a set of *social standards* for evaluating one's own and others' behavior. But there are considerable differences in social units as one moves up the scale from the family to General Motors to the United States of America.

The Group as a Contributor to Individual Behavior

For now, **groups** may be defined as collections of people who have some sort of relationship to one another. By convention, **small groups** are defined as those in which each individual has the opportunity for face-to-face contact with every other person in the group. Large groups are more impersonal: each member has the opportunity for face-to-face contacts with only some of the other group members.

Everyone has contacts with a large number of people. These contacts can be described in a number of ways. One way is according to whether the relationship seems to be deep and personal or superficial and impersonal.

Deep, Personal Contacts. Perhaps most important to each individual are those social contacts that are intensive and sustained and that involve a continuing recognition of each person's separateness, distinct personality, and unique strengths, weaknesses, and needs. When two or more people relate on this intimate basis, they are said to constitute a **primary group**. In most societies,

Social contacts may be intensive and sustained and may involve a continuing awareness of each person's unique personality . . .

. . . or they may be fleeting and lack intimacy.

pairs of sweethearts, groups of personal good friends, and most families constitute primary groups. Many other collections of people (such as Miss Mawkins' third-grade class, college roommates, or the 11-man army of Andorra) *could* constitute primary groups, but this may not be taken for granted.

Many psychologists consider the primary group the most important influence in shaping the individual. As you will later see, the primary group is extremely important in the formation of the person's self-concept. For example, a continual nagging or berating by parents can make a child feel incompetent and unworthy, no matter how well his "objective" record speaks.

Superficial, Impersonal Contacts.   At other times, social contacts are fleeting and lack intimacy. People who relate to one another without recognizing each individual's distinct strengths, weaknesses, and needs are said to constitute a secondary group. Secondary-group contacts are characterized by an impersonal, businesslike quality. In our society these contacts include those between ticket collector and passenger, teacher and student (in a large class), and merchant and customer.

Although they are impersonal, secondary-group contacts can have profound individual consequences. It is not difficult to understand why a subway token collector may develop a view of the world as cold, callous, and indifferent; why psychiatrists may become very cynical; and why policemen may become depressed and prone to suicide. These persons' social contacts can provide a one-sided view of man that might not be maintained if they were exposed to other facets of the people they deal with. In one way or another, everyone can suffer from secondary-group contacts; they are a constant source of dissatisfaction if one's unique problems are never taken into account.

There are, however, good reasons why people do not try to establish primary-group relationships with everyone they encounter. First, it is unlikely that most people have the time, energy, or inclination to get to know personally everybody they contact in the course of their daily lives. Second, businesslike relationships are often very efficient because the two or more participants' unique personalities and circumstances do not provide an extra source of variability in their behavior. Try to buy a postage stamp from your good friend and neighbor. You may find that he is not at home, does not have a stamp, is unwilling to part with his last stamp, cannot make change, or wants you to help him move his water bed while you are there. Try to buy a postage stamp from a very impersonal clerk at the post office during business hours, and you are assured of speedy success. Finally, since people engaging in secondary-group contacts do not relate to each other as unique individuals, one or both of them could be replaced without making much of a difference. Whichever postal clerk sells you a stamp will make little difference to you. Similarly, whichever customer the clerk sells the stamp to makes little difference to him. This substitutibility is quite handy for the smooth operation of a society.

Organizations as Contributors to Individual Behavior

Large social units that are predominantly oriented toward the attainment of specific goals are called **organizations.** These include such social units as the Franciscan Monks, General Mills, the United States Coast Guard, the Women's Christian Temperance Union, and Sam Quentin Prison. Within these social units there are accepted rules for regulating the behavior of the participants. Individuals within organizations often have carefully prescribed relationships with one another (for example, admiral-commander-chief-seaman), and, as you will see, a knowledge of these prescriptions can take us a long way toward understanding behavior. If, for example, an admiral and a seaman meet, it is easy to predict who will salute first.

Many of the contacts among people within an organization are of the impersonal type characteristic of secondary groups. However, organizations also provide a framework for the emergence of primary groups. People within small military contingents and within small departments of large industries often form close, intimate groupings.

The personal effects of membership in organizations are as varied as the organizations themselves. Fraternal organizations or lodges often contribute to unusual or even bizarre behavior in adults. Membership in the military is known to have a tremendous impact. Studies of the American soldier during World War II suggested that men changed many of their attitudes and views when they entered the army but then returned to their "real selves" when they were discharged. Prisons have clearly demonstrable effects on their inmates. Indeed, contemporary American prisons often serve as schools for crime, rather than as rehabilitation centers, as planned. Very harsh internment camps produce apathy and withdrawal.

Considerable attention has been paid to the effects of membership in large industrial organizations. Many of these organizations exert a pervasive influence on their employees, regulating their behavior not only on the job but elsewhere as well. Thus the junior executive may live in a prescribed neighborhood, drive a certain brand of automobile, send his children to a designated school, campaign for a certain political party, and vacation in prescribed locales. This type of life has been well described. The keynote seems to be a certain type of conformity, and the way of life involved is a popular target for criticism. The fact that this life-style helps people to achieve common goals and often proves satisfying to them is often ignored.

Societies as Contributors to Individual Behavior

A **society** is a special kind of large, complex social unit. It serves to coordinate and articulate all the individuals, groups, and organizations that it comprises. To do so, societies maintain special rules or standards for behavior. Since many of these standards are so widespread and time honored, they are, for the most part, unquestioningly accepted by the society's members. I doubt that you think twice about wearing clothes in public, driving on the right-hand side of the street, or using money to pay for goods and services. However, because the people and groups coordinated have many different needs and interests, there is a certain amount of give or play in many of the rules of a society. For example, in our society there are people and groups that are clearly at cross purposes. There are Republicans and Democrats, religious fanatics and hard-core atheists, people who manufacture cigarettes and people who propose legislation forbidding cigarettes, peaceniks and the Joint Chiefs of Staff. To satisfy all these different people and groups, a society's rules must be flexible enough to allow for variations but tight enough to ensure that the society will not disintegrate.

When we compare people from various societies, we typically find that they are different—the extent of these differences depending in part on the degree of dissimilarity of the societies. The most prominent disparities, such as language, dress, and customs, reflect societally caused regularities in behavior. But what about less superficial differences, such as in personality? Suppose we compared two Americans with two Chinese. Would there be striking similarities when we compared the personalities of American$_1$ and American$_2$ and when we compared Chinese$_1$ with Chinese$_2$? Would there be equally striking differences if we compared the personalities of American$_1$ and American$_2$ with those of Chinese$_1$ and Chinese$_2$?

Although there is some suspicion that people from different societies have somewhat different personalities, convincing proof is hard to obtain (Inkeles & Levinson, 1954, 1969). First, it is necessary to solve the problem of defining the societies, which may or may not be distinguishable on the basis of national boundaries. For example, politically speaking, Alaska and Hawaii are parts of the United States. But Alaska, Hawaii, and the mainland are different in so many ways that it is not a foregone conclusion that they can be considered different parts of one society. Second, there is the problem of devising personality measures that give comparable evaluations of people from different lands. Certain personality tests approach adequacy when applied within a society, but they may lose reliability or validity when administered to people who have different customs and who speak different languages. Third, since it is impossible to evaluate everyone from a given society, there is the problem of choosing whom to assess. If you compare sailors from the United States with old maids from China, you would probably find considerable differences in personality. But it would not be clear that nationality alone accounted for these differences. Finally, it is likely that there are such tremendous personality differences *within* a society that the differences *between* societies seem unimpressive. For example, our society includes the Boston fisherman, the Chicago mortician, the San Francisco spinster, and the New Orleans sheriff. Does it seem plausible to claim that they are basically similar because they are all Americans?

Position, Role, and Status: Attempts to Understand
Individual Behavior without Considering the Individual

Primary groups, secondary groups, organizations, and societies are **social networks**—grids of people bound together by communication, influence, rights, and obligations. Each person within a network has some specifiable relationship to the other members. He has, in effect, a particular **position** within each social unit. Thousands of very common words describe these different positions. In the family, one can have the position of father, mother, or child. In the industrial firm, one can have the position of secretary, salesman, or chairman of the board. In society, one can have the position of doctor, lawyer, or Indian chief.

Associated with these different positions are specified ways of behaving. For example, among other things, the father is supposed to provide for and protect his family; the secretary is expected to take shorthand, type, and file papers; and the doctor must take care of the health needs of others.

Role theorists suggest that a person's position within a social network accounts for his or her behavior. When someone assumes a given position, such as father, secretary, or doctor, other people apply pressures for him to engage in the behavior specified for that position. The term **role** is used to refer to a set of expectations concerning what someone in a given position is supposed to do and to the actual behavior of the person occupying the position. Role theorists maintain that anyone in a given position and assuming the associated role behaves similarly to anyone else who *could* be in that position and assuming that role.

Role theory thus suggests that knowing where a person is located within a group, organization, or society leads to some understanding of his behavior. In support of this contention, they point out that there is great variability in individual behavior as the person moves from position to position within a social network and that there are great similarities in the behavior of different individuals who occupy any given position. Any apparent consistencies in a person's behavior could be attributed to the similarities of the various positions he occupies.

Some role enthusiasts imply that *all* regularities in significant human behavior can be accounted for in terms of position and role. The implication is that it is not necessary to consider personality or any other property of the individual in an attempt to understand his behavior!

Although roles may establish certain minimal requirements for behavior, there are tremendous individual differences in how people *interpret* and *fulfill* these requirements (Miller, 1963). All waiters deliver food. But in the same restaurant it is possible to find some waiters who are slow, grumpy, and prone to make mistakes; some waiters who are crisp and efficient; and some waiters who are unnervingly folksy or chummy. Pastors are supposed to preach on Sunday. But it is possible to find, within the same denomination, pastors who dress conservatively and deliver stiff, boring sermons and long-haired pastors in mod clothes who deliver stirring, relevant sermons in between rock selections. Then, too, why should one person become a waiter and the next person a minister? Most psychologists, then, believe that we cannot fully understand individual behavior without considering the individual.

But in the same restaurant it is possible to find some waiters who are slow, grumpy, and prone to make mistakes; some waiters who are crisp and efficient; and some waiters who are unnervingly folksy or chummy.

Associated with each position and role is a certain social status. **Status** is a rough synonym for social value or social worth and is something that is conferred by the reactions of others. The person who is looked up to or admired because of his position enjoys high status. The person who is avoided, ridiculed, or scorned because of his position has low status. In most of Western civilization, positions of high status are associated with power, money, and luxurious living. Yet status assessment is a complicated enterprise, and in some cases positions of poverty and humility (such as university professorships) are accorded very high status.

Man in the Social Network

In seeking to understand people and the things they do, many psychologists stress the small group as a factor in behavior. People have a real and dramatic impact on each other when they come together in face-to-face situations. In addition, small groups serve as *intermediaries* between the individual and larger social units such as organizations and societies. For example, the family regulates the child's exposure to society and very willingly provides him with its own special perspective—a perspective that is not necessarily adopted by others. Parents may ensure that the child meets only white, middle-class people. Then the child will not appreciate that there are large proportions of society that are neither white nor middle class. The parent may tell the child that policemen are exemplary heroes who work only to protect decent citizens against vicious troublemakers. Then the child will conclude that anyone who is in trouble with the law is a very bad person. Or, the parents may tell the child that policemen are evil tools of a wicked Establishment, which will leave the child unaware that policemen routinely risk their lives dealing with some pretty ugly customers. Parents may tell the child that one political party is responsible for all truth, joy, and beauty in this land, whereas the other is to blame for all national ills. Later, when the child forms close associations outside his family, he will acquire new information that will either strengthen or change his views.

It is unlikely that a person will ever have a complete and undistorted picture of the large social units that affect his life and the lives of people important to him. He must develop his views of organizations and society on the basis of face-to-face contact with only a small percentage of the people who belong to them or claim to know something about them. In effect, small groups provide a lens, and the impact of an organization or society is distorted as it passes through the small group to reach the individual.

PSYCHOLOGY, BIOLOGY, SOCIOLOGY, AND ANTHROPOLOGY

Psychology asks questions about man. Biology, sociology, and anthropology also ask questions about man. In the process, representatives of the different fields may address the same problem, such as aggression. However, their respective approaches to the problem differ drastically. Given a form of behavior such as aggression, representatives of each field typically seek different antecedents of the behavior. The biologist may seek the causes in cells and organs, which are a part of the individual. The psychologist may seek the causes in the individual as a whole. The sociologist and the anthropologist look beyond the individual and seek the causes in collectivities or groups. The sociologist might seek the causes of aggression in abstract networks of interpersonal relations. Position, role, and status might enter heavily into his search. The social anthropologist might seek the causes of aggressiveness in culture. Culture has been defined as the sum of all the ideas, acts, tools, and social relationships that tie a society together. Despite the great differences in perspectives and approaches, all these persons are seeking to explain behavior. They are all behavioral scientists.

Levels of Analysis and the Explanation of Behavior

When a behavioral scientist attempts to understand behavior by referring to biological, individual, or social antecedents, he is operating within the framework of a specific **level of analysis.** As he moves up the scale from smaller to larger suspected antecedents, he is, by convention, analyzing the problem from an increasingly higher level of analysis. The individual level is higher than the biological level because the individual encompasses a number of biological parts. The social level is higher than the individual level because it includes both individuals and their protoplasm.

Biologists, psychologists, sociologists, and anthropologists thus approach a problem from different levels of analysis. These varied analyses have resulted in a number of explanations of the same behavior. Each explanation has different implications if one is interested in modifying or changing the behavior in question. Furthermore, since knowledge is incomplete, it is difficult to appraise the relative value of the different explanations based on the various levels of analysis.

An Application

A few teen-agers are really tough customers. I am referring to the violent types who love to fight, will resort to almost any means to obtain what they want, and seem proud of their violent outbursts. What causes this type of juvenile delinquency?

An explanation at the biological level of analysis might point to constitutional factors. In earlier days, some psychologists spoke of a state known as "constitutional psychopathic inferiority." According to this view, the violently delinquent person was born without a full capacity for understanding and abiding by the rules of society, just as other people might be born without arms or legs. The concept of constitutional psychopathic inferiority proved to be unpopular. But the idea that constitutional factors may contribute to violent outbursts and delinquent acts should not be entirely discarded. First, there is some evidence that adolescents with a certain type of physique (which psychologists call mesomorphic and you think of as athletic) are more likely to end up in trouble than are those with a different type of physique (Glueck & Glueck, 1950). Since the Gluecks' study was necessarily correlational, it is unclear whether the athletic physique predisposes people to criminal activity or whether it is a result of the strenuous exercise obtained by running away from the police. Second, more recent studies (cited in Chapter Six) provide evidence of a hereditary basis for violent activity. Although the exact mechanisms are not fully understood, it appears that a certain genetic composition is associated with a tendency to be easily provoked into violent, antisocial displays. If, indeed, violent delinquent activity can be traced to constitutional factors, there is not much that we can hope to do to change the individual delinquent.

An explanation of the same behavior couched in terms of personality factors would take an entirely different form. The delinquent and violent behavior could be described as a hostile reaction to **authority figures** (people in power) that stems from early childhood. For example, psychoanalytically oriented psychologists might suggest that, in childhood, the delinquent considered himself hindered from obtaining important gratifications by the meddlesome activities of his father (a powerful authority figure). At the time he would have liked to punish the father. But, since he was small and powerless while his father was big and strong, it was not possible, and he could not vent his aggression. His resentment and aggressive feelings had no outlet and persisted over time. As a relatively big and strong adolescent, he gained the ability to inflict harm and is proceeding to attack any authority figures who remind him in some way of his father. Harassing teachers and sassing policemen relieve him of some of his long-smoldering hatred. But, alas, these father substitutes whom he hurts are not the real thing, and the pent-up tensions are never fully discharged. This type of explanation implies that, if the delinquent were properly counseled to understand his feelings about his father and to adopt a new view of authority figures, he would no longer be driven to violent delinquent activity.

Proceeding to the social level of analysis, we might find a plausible explanation couched in terms of small-group pressures. Much delinquent activity can be understood by examining the company the juvenile delinquent keeps. Delinquents often associate with other delinquents. Conformity and learning from others thus encourage delinquent behavior. An implication of this explanation is that a change in the delinquent's associates would reduce his delinquent activity. In actuality, he is more likely to be thrown into jail, where he finds new associates who encourage further transgressions.

Sociologist Robert Merton (1957) has offered an interesting theory of delinquency that seeks the antecedents of antisocial behavior in society. Our society places high premiums on certain commodities such as money, power, fancy cars, and pretty women. People who have these luxuries command respect and praise from others. Through the mass media (radio, television, magazines, and so on) people are made aware of these luxuries and the high values attached to them. The myth is that hard work and sheer determination alone will produce the good things in life; if people do not make it in this world, it is obviously because of their own incompetence.

There are two ways of acquiring luxuries. One is the legitimate way—that is, the way that does not violate the laws of society. People can become lawyers, doctors, corporation presidents, or governors and enjoy good things galore. The second way is illegitimate, since it involves breaking society's rules. In other words, what can't be earned can be stolen.

Many people do not have the intellectual, emotional, or social equipment necessary to obtain luxuries through socially approved channels. Some of them resort to armed robbery, muggings, and other forms of violent behavior as ways to "get ahead." The implication of this theory is that delinquency can be reduced if society stops touting expensive, hard-to-obtain items or if provisions are made so that anyone can obtain them through legitimate channels.

These explanations are only some of those that may be used to account for one form of behavior: violent delinquent acts. It is difficult to appraise these various explanations, because no one has devised an experiment to see which one is best. Certainly each explanation has weaknesses. Attributing delinquency to constitutional factors will be unpopular until someone can state more explicitly how these constitutional factors operate. The individual-psychological explanation is not entirely satisfactory, for many people find themselves disappointed or frustrated as children yet remain law-abiding. If the explanation is based on a consideration of the delinquent's friends, there remains the problem of how he became associated with them in the first place and why they encourage lawlessness. The explanation based on society also has flaws. Although it may

Many people do not have the intellectual, emotional, or social equipment necessary to obtain luxuries through socially approved channels.

be true that lower-class people, who do not have so many legitimate channels for obtaining luxuries, get into more trouble than do people whose road is easier, many poor people get by year after year without running afoul of the law.

None of the explanations cited above provides the whole truth about violently antisocial behavior; but each has some merits. They are by no means mutually exclusive. If certain types of constitutions, certain child-rearing practices, membership in particular groups, or incapacity to reach the good life can be shown to increase the chances of delinquency, we are on our way toward some degree of understanding.

Open Systems Theory

During the late 1950s an attempt was made to integrate all the behavioral sciences from cellular biology to sociology. This integration is known as open systems theory (Miller, 1955, 1960). According to open systems theory, there are certain principles of operation that hold true for cells, organs, individuals, small groups, organizations, societies, and organizations of societies—each of which is a system.

In what ways could such vastly different things as cells and societies be alike? A main feature is that all systems *process information*, much like a computer. Something is fed in at one end, something happens to it inside the system, and a finished or at least partly processed product emerges. The unprocessed information or material brought into the system is called **input**, and the processed or transmitted information or material is called **output**. An example of this information processing at the cellular level is the transmission of the nerve impulse. An example at the individual level is the memorization of vocabulary material in preparation for a foreign-language test. At the organizational level, information processing is found in the collection, sorting, and delivery of mail.

Miller suggests that, for the most part, the quantity of input and output closely corresponds. Thus the more often the neuron receives an impulse, the more often it will transmit. The more vocabulary items the student memorizes, the more he can regurgitate for the benefit of his instructor. The more mail collected, the more mail delivered. However, the information awaiting processing can increase beyond the system's capacity. This situation is called **information overload**, and under conditions of overload the system's performance efficiency decreases and wear and tear increases. The neuron that has just fired cannot transmit again without a brief rest period. The student with too much material to learn cannot learn effectively. The post office may become inefficient during seasonal rushes. But open systems are also highly adaptive: when the information awaiting processing approaches the overload level, mechanisms of adjustment come into play. Miller suggests that systems at all levels have analogous ways of adapting to overload. For example, the student preparing for final examinations and the post office processing Christmas mail might react similarly.

One mechanism of adjustment is to allow a decrease in the standards of performance and be more accepting of **error**. In the press of finals, term papers might not be proofread. During Christmas rush, un-Zip-coded mail for "Boston, Mass." might be sent to "Biloxi, Miss." A second mechanism is the process of delaying, or **queuing**. In this case the system eventually gets everything done, but new information is not dealt with so quickly as it would be otherwise. It must wait its turn. The student may fail to meet due dates or may wrangle an Incomplete in a course to allow more time to prepare for the final. In the post office, patrons may have to wait in line longer to send mail, and it may take the mail a little longer to reach its destination than it would under normal circumstances. Filtering is a mechanism similar to queuing. But whereas queuing involves a general slowing down of all processing, filtering involves selectively processing some, but not all, of the awaiting input. The student could concentrate on certain readings he felt were likely to be included on the final, ignoring others that he would have read had time permitted. The post office might assign priorities to certain classes of mail, neglecting bulk or so-called junk mail until all first-class mail and packages had been delivered. The fourth technique is one of simple omission, or the nonprocessing of information. The student could decide not to bother studying for one final, accept an *F* in that course, and thereby save his neck in other courses. The Postal Service, of course, is not allowed the luxury of omission but can rely heavily on filtering and queuing instead. Finally, systems can attempt to open new channels to increase their efficiency. The student might hire someone to type his term paper, and the post office can hire temporary employees to help with the Christmas rush.

What if these mechanisms of adjustment are not sufficient to handle the information overload? Under extreme conditions the system can no longer perform. The system may then react by escaping the task or by simply breaking down. During finals a student could drop out of school or suffer what is thought of as a nervous breakdown. If organizations are truly swamped, they are forced to close their doors. This has, in fact, happened to post offices in other countries.

The mechanisms for dealing with information overload result in inefficiencies and in a decline in the quality of the output. But these same mechanisms prevent the temporary breakdown or even death of the system.

Open systems theory is approaching its second decade. It certainly has not captured the fancy of all biologists, psychologists, and sociologists. Yet it has made important contributions within certain fields, such as organizational psychology.

CONCLUSIONS

Many variables contribute to human behavior. In this chapter a distinction was made between situational variables, which are external to the person, and dispositional variables, which are a part of the person. Situational variables are useful for explaining why different people often act in similar ways when they are in similar settings, and why the same person often acts in different ways as he moves from setting to setting. Dispositional variables are useful for explaining why different people act differently in similar settings, and why a given person exhibits consistencies in behavior as he moves from place to place. Any form of behavior, however, will reflect the joint operation of both types of variables.

Antecedents of human behavior have been sought in biology, in the individual, and in the social environment. At the biological level, heredity, normal physiological processes, and organic pathologies contribute to behavior. At the individual level, the person's unique personality, which has developed largely as a result of past experiences, contributes to his behavior. At the social level, contact with other individuals and with social units of varying sizes, such as groups, organizations, and societies, contributes to human behavior.

As the behavioral scientist moves from the cell and organ to the individual and to groups of progressively larger sizes in his attempts to explain behavior, he is said to be operating at increasingly higher levels of analysis. Psychologists, biologists, sociologists, and anthropologists use different levels of analysis but may each ultimately try to explain the same behavior. Violent delinquent activity was a case in point. Causes of this behavior have been sought by looking at biological factors, individual-psychological factors, small-group processes, and society. Each explanation alone has serious drawbacks, but each also makes some contribution to an understanding of the problem.

Open systems theory represents an attempt to unite the behavioral sciences. According to this theory, cells, organs, individuals, and social units of varying sizes are all systems. Principles of operation can be identified that supposedly hold true for all the different systems. Thus it is expected that, under analogous conditions, the cell, the organ, the individual, and the group will operate or behave in similar ways. The example given in this chapter pointed to how different systems such as an individual and an organization might react similarly when there is simply too much for them to do.

2

Basic Processes

The next three chapters will introduce you to some basic psychological processes, which are not to be confused with principles of behavior. **Principles of behavior** are statements about cause-effect relationships. They are assertions that under specified conditions certain types of behavior are likely to result. They describe *what* happens. **Psychological processes** are mechanisms that serve as intermediaries between the specified antecedent conditions, on the one hand, and behavior, on the other. Psychological processes describe not only *what* happens but *why* it happens as well.

The distinction can be clarified by the following example. One psychologist I know was plagued by the presence of a lovesick and noisy basset hound on his property. Each time he saw the hound, he chased it away, occasionally giving it a thump or two with a stick. Later the psychologist's presence alone was sufficient to scare away the dog.

The principle of behavior in this case was simple. The antecedent condition was a thumping and the behavioral result an avoidance of the psychologist. Yet a psychological process within the dog must have intervened between the

75

earlier beating and the later avoidance. The inferred psychological process in this case would be called learning.

Anyone who is interested in controlling or changing behavior can get by with a knowledge of principles of behavior. But if the interest turns to *understanding* and *explaining* behavior, there must be some knowledge of psychological processes as well.

Understanding psychological processes is the more challenging task. Knowing principles of behavior does not imply an understanding of psychological processes, but understanding psychological processes makes it possible to derive many useful principles of behavior.

Singling out some psychological processes as more basic than others is a tricky business. The processes covered in the next three chapters are ones that I consider to be basic in one or more of the following ways:

1. The process accounts for some of the simpler or more basic forms of behavior, such as that displayed by the basset hound.

2. The process operates in many different contexts and situations. It affects the behavior of all humans and perhaps that of a number of different animals as well. Thus the same basic processes that account for the basset hound's behavior may also account for a small child's fear of fuzzy objects, an adolescent's reluctance to spend much time at home, or a national leader's refusal to attempt serious negotiations with a real or imagined enemy.

3. The process may be extended, elaborated on, or considered in combination with other processes to account for very complex and seemingly mysterious behavior. Thus an understanding of the same processes that account for the basset hound's behavior may contribute to an understanding of what is commonly thought of as mental illness and its treatment.

Chapter Four describes how the individual receives and interprets information, how conditions inside and outside the skin provide instigators for behavior, and how semipermanent modifications of behavior can result from changing environmental conditions. The chapter thus presents some rudiments of perception, motivation, and learning.

Chapter Five describes some of the ways in which the presence and actions of other people influence individual behavior. By tradition, these topics are not usually thought of as quite so basic as perception, motivation, and learning; but they do fulfill the three criteria I have outlined.

Chapter Six describes some of the processes that may account for the common observation that people of different ages are likely to act in different ways.

4.
Some Individual Psychological Processes

In late 1970 *Life* magazine ran a heavily illustrated serial entitled *Krushchev Remembers.* This feature, attributed to the once-powerful Russian Communist premier, elicited lively comments from the readers. In one letter to the editor, the writer expressed little interest in Krushchev's statements but great interest in the accompanying photographs. He was impressed that *all* the Russian leaders from the 1930s to the 1950s (such as Stalin, Malenkov, and Beria) looked like thugs, hoodlums, and gangsters. Why should this be the case?

One possibility is that thugs were very likely to come into power in post-revolutionary Russia. It is also possible that thugs have certain prominent identifying facial characteristics (such as coarse noses, cauliflowered ears, and sinister eyes). Indeed, in the nineteenth century, before fingerprinting was common, identification of individual criminals was made by means of a complex set of facial measurements. From a large set of such measurements, attempts were made to identify criminal faces, such as Stalin, Malenkov, and Beria could have possessed. The idea at that time was that crime could be reduced by keeping people with tattletale faces off the streets. But this ingenious possibility didn't work, for the faces of thugs and hoodlums are indistinguishable from those of decent citizens, as any perusal of portraits of the notorious American gangsters of the 1930s may suggest. It is doubtful, then, that all postrevolutionary Russian leaders had special "tattletale" faces.

A second possibility is that the sinister appearance of these men resided only in the eyes of the beholder. Most likely, the viewer's attitudes about the Russians' behavior, knowledge of the context in which the pictures were taken, Western social values, and American tastes all combined to produce pictures of gangsters. If the same men had been Joe Stalin, American sea captain, George Malenkov, restaurateur, and Larry Beria, bank teller, I doubt that they would have looked evil at all.

Let's turn now to the basic individual psychological processes that help account for such phenomena as the *Life* reader's impressions. The questions raised in this chapter are: (1) How does the individual receive and process information? (2) What are the instigators of behavior? (3) How is behavior modified as a result of past experiences? These are questions about perception, motivation, and learning, respectively. Although each topic will be dealt with in turn, the various processes are very much intertwined.

RECEIVING INFORMATION

Among philosophers, a **solipsist** believes that the only verifiable reality is that which he personally experiences. There is nothing else. When he dies, the universe is destroyed, and reality no longer exists. Most psychologists assume

Each person is capable of knowing something about the world-out-there because it bombards him with physical energy, which we think of as sights, sounds, and smells.

that a real world and universe exist in physical form independent of any individual. Each person is capable of knowing something about the world-out-there because it bombards him with physical energy, which we think of as sights, sounds, and smells.

A change in physical energy that impinges on the individual, typically eliciting some sort of **response,** is called a **stimulus.** A passing bus, for example, reflects light rays (an energy change), creates sound waves (an energy change), and throws off a number of very small chemical particles (an energy change) that its engine has produced. For convenience in describing stimuli, it is sufficient to refer to the object that causes the changes—in this case, the bus.

There could be any one or a combination of countless stimuli in the person's presence at any point in time: Abraham Lincoln, an alligator, a totem pole, a large steamship, three plum trees, or a crowd of commuters. If a person had no way of knowing what was there, he would live in a state of complete uncertainty. Anything that helps to reduce uncertainty is called **information.**

Stimuli provide information, but, to do so, the energy changes must first be detected or received and then coordinated and organized to allow a proper identification. To know there is a big, red, speeding, smelly bus out there, then, it is necessary to *receive* and *process* the energy changes, thereby converting them into useful information.

Reception

A tremendous number of highly sensitive nerve endings called **receptors** are located throughout our bodies. Some receptors are found within the body and respond to such stimuli as movement or a lack of the substances necessary for life or comfort. Others are on or toward the surface of the body and respond to the external energy changes produced by such stimuli as a passing bus. In some areas of the body (such as the eyes, ears, and nose) receptors are bunched closely together; in other areas (such as on the surface of the back) they are spaced far apart.

Each receptor is believed to react only to very specific stimulus qualities. Of the receptors in the mouth and on the tongue, for example, some will respond only to sweetness, some only to saltiness, some only to bitterness, and some only to sourness.

When there is sufficient stimulation to activate a receptor, an impulse is transmitted. Something like a moving bus would activate thousands of receptors, and the impulses from these receptors would be entered or **encoded** into the nervous system. In raw form these impulses are called **sensations.** The next step for reducing uncertainty is to somehow make sense of sensations.

Perception

Perception refers to the inferred psychological processes that organize, structure, and interpret incoming information. Perception involves much more than sensation.

A chocolate-covered grasshopper illustrates the difference between sensation and perception. Looking at the morsel would activate thousands of individual visual receptors and provide information concerning size, shape, and color. Touching the delicacy would activate tactile (touch) receptors and impart information concerning weight and texture. Eating the grasshopper would activate even more receptors and would provide some evidence that the substance is predominantly sweet and salty but just a trifle bitter. Additional receptors in the oral region would indicate that the item is soft but has a crunchy center. Somehow, by means of psychological processes, all these little pieces of information combine to produce a chocolate-covered grasshopper. There is some kind of *patterning* or *organization* of the thousands of different sensations and of the raw information they provide.

Internal Stimuli

Suppose that, unlike me, you have rather conventional tastes. If I give you a candied grasshopper to eat and tell you nothing, you might enjoy it. On the other hand, if I let you in on the secret when it is half consumed, you might gag and spit it out. Before I tell you, the candy would be pleasant; afterward it would be unpleasant. The candy remains the same, but your perception of it changes. This is because the energy changes produced by the grasshopper combine with energy changes from within you.

Internal stimuli are sources of stimulation located within the skin. They may be produced by states within the body (such as hunger, thirst, or sleepiness) or by an external stimulus such as the comment "How do you like that grasshopper?" Eating the grasshopper, you cannot see it, and I doubt that you would know it by taste. But once you have been told it is a grasshopper, you know only too well what it is, and what you remember about grasshoppers will suddenly enter into your perception of the candy. The internal stimulation in this case is related to your past experience with grasshoppers. If you had never heard of a grasshopper before, the comment should have little effect on your perception of the candy.

Internal stimuli are private, in the sense that they contribute to one person's perception. External stimuli are public, in the sense that they contribute to the perceptions of all people present. Yet different people's perceptions of the same external stimuli are not likely to be identical, for all perceptions involve private, internal stimuli as well.

Some perceptions, such as dreams, illusions, and hallucinations, seem to be predominantly the product of internal stimuli. Other perceptions seem to be heavily based on external stimuli, as is the case when different people present indicate that they are perceiving things in the same way. When perception corresponds to what is really there, it is called **veridical**.

Gestalt Laws of Perceptual Organization

Where does an organism get the ability to organize and structure thousands of sensations into a coherent whole? One view is that much of this ability represents a gift from nature that comes with the highly complex nervous system. A group of psychologists known as the Gestalt psychologists have identified several easily demonstrated principles or "laws" of perceptual organization that they believe reflect unlearned abilities.

Praegnanz. The law of **Praegnanz** suggests that people have a tendency to perceive things in such a way that the things seem as *simple* and *orderly* as possible. This tendency appears at psychedelic light shows, which present highly irregular, nonsensical light patterns. People impose order on these patterns by searching for simple geometrical figures such as triangles, squares, and circles; they falsely see the patterns as symmetrical or balanced or as changing in time to totally unrelated music.

Closure. The law of **closure** suggests that people have the gift of perceiving things as whole, continuous figures. Within limits, when stimuli are not whole and continuous, the perceiver will fill in the gaps. Very carefully examine any photograph in this book, and you will discover that it is nothing more than a series of unconnected dots.

Grouping. **Laws of grouping** suggest that there is a tendency to see separate elements as forming into coherent groups. For example, you would probably see

38   24   38

either as the measurements of a shapely woman or as three two-digit numbers, not as three hundred eighty-two thousand, four hundred thirty-eight. This is because there is a tendency to see elements that are spatially (or temporally) close as belonging together. There are also tendencies to see as belonging together elements that are similar; that permit the smooth continuation of a line, curve, or contour; or that are moving in the same direction.

Elements that are similar or close in space are seen as belonging together.

Gestalt psychologists suggest that the forms and shapes in this world are the natural units in perception and that they register in the nervous system in such a way as to correspond in a one-to-one fashion with the external stimulus. Perception is immediate, and stimuli are perceived as wholes, not as a bunch of disconnected parts. Perceptual processes reflect the innate, unlearned abilities that come with the complex nervous system.

The Gestalt laws of perceptual organization are so compelling and easy to demonstrate that they are hard to refute. But the Gestaltists' claim that much of our ability to perceive is a gift to the organism is not so invulnerable. Several lines of evidence suggest that inborn perceptual ability is rather meager.

Von Senden (1932) described cases of humans who were born with severely limited vision but were later given sight surgically. When the bandages were removed, they seemed able to detect only gray masses of shifting intensity. They could not immediately identify visual patterns, objects, or faces, even though they had long been able to identify them by touch. Moreover, feeling an object on one visual presentation did not result in an immediate visual recognition of it on subsequent presentations. At best, these people seemed gifted with only the crudest perceptual skills.

Evidence from cases of people who are given sight, although suggestive, is hard to assess, for many factors could contribute to the apparent inabilities. If, for example, the subjects' eyes had always been bandaged, degeneration of the optic system could result. Furthermore, it is difficult to devise satisfactory tests of perceptual skills.

Some of these difficulties were overcome in experiments reported by Riesen (1961), who raised chimpanzees predominantly in the dark. To prevent physical degeneration of the nervous system, Riesen placed a frosted plastic dome over their heads, which allowed them to see unpatterned light. When they were later allowed full vision, they were unable to fixate their eyes on an object and were slow in solving problems requiring the ability to tell one thing from another. Their behavior suggested that the necessary perceptual skills were not free but had to be learned.

In an **illusion,** a stimulus appears to be something that it is not. In the rotating-trapezoid illusion, a trapezoid that looks like a distorted window frame appears to be a rectangle (Allport & Pettigrew, 1957). The ability to see this trapezoid as a rectangle, though, depends on the ability to perceive straight lines and sharp angles. If many perceptual abilities are a gift to the organism, certainly the ability to perceive simple geometric shapes and their components should not have to be learned.

The rotating trapezoid was presented to two groups of Zulu subjects. One group, from a rural environment, had lived in a setting where straight lines and harsh angles were curiously lacking. The other group came from an urban setting in which architectural design featured straight lines and angular shapes. Rural subjects had difficulty seeing the illusion; urban subjects were able to see the illusion more easily. Thus the relatively simple ability to distinguish the components of regular geometric shapes seemed to depend on learning.

Although it is difficult to show that a perceptual skill is innate, it is easy to show that perception is affected by learning. Stratton (1897) and Kohler (1962) had subjects wear prismatic lenses, which give a distorted view of the world. Such prisms may make the world appear upside down, may reverse left and right, may make straight lines look curved, may straighten curved lines, or may surround objects with weird color fringes. (Why these goggles are not featured at psychedelic "head" shops I do not know.) Initially, looking through these glasses, everything appears different and confusing. But over the course of time things appear right and natural. After this adaptation has taken place, *removal* of the prisms may make the world seem chaotic and confusing, but by the same adaptive learning processes the correct way of perceiving is eventually restored.

Psychologists who contend that abilities to perceive are inborn can correctly point out that many such abilities appear early in life. Moreover, demonstrations that organisms *can* learn to perceive do not tell much about initial perceptual abilities prior to learning. The question then becomes *how much* perceptual ability comes with the organism and how much is acquired. A popular compromise position is that certain inherent skills serve as a basis for the acquisition of more sophisticated ways of structuring incoming information.

Learning and Perception

There are three broad ways that past experiences or learning enters into perception. First, in the individual's past, associations have been formed that will affect his present perceptions. Second, the ability to distinguish among stimuli is largely learned. Third, people learn how to recognize important tip-offs or *cues*, which contribute heavily to what is perceived.

Learning Associations

When two things occur at about the same time, a person is likely to form some sort of association or connection between them. Stimulus-response connections are very common. For example, if an adolescent unwisely swills an enormous quantity of beer and then becomes violently ill, later the appearance of the golden brew may make him feel queasy. The stimulus beer has been associated with the response feeling ill.

Associations can also be formed between different stimuli. The word *beer* (a stimulus) can become associated with the thing beer (also a stimulus) and hence indirectly associated with the response to the thing. As a result, the word *beer* could prove sufficient to make the adolescent feel uneasy. The classical-conditioning process, described later in this chapter, accounts for how certain words or typically neutral stimuli can come to elicit emotional responses.

An implication of this ability to form associations is that the perception of a stimulus is partly dependent on what it was associated with in the past. Perlman and Oskamp (1970) presented pictures of men's faces to three groups of subjects. One group saw the faces paired with favorable associated stimuli, the second group saw the faces paired with neutral stimuli, and the third group saw the faces paired with unfavorable associated stimuli. The associated stimuli were the social settings in which the men had been photographed. In the first case the settings were highly acceptable and socially desirable, in the second case neutral, and in the third case unsavory and undesirable. When faces were later presented without the associated stimuli, those that had been earlier presented with favorable associated stimuli were rated the most favorably and faces earlier presented with unfavorable associated stimuli the least favorably. The face alone was sufficient to elicit positive or negative feelings initially evoked by the associated setting.

Since different people form different associations, their perceptions of the same stimulus are likely to differ. The middle-class person who sees policemen helping children, selling tickets to a ball, or directing traffic is likely to view a policeman who comes to his door on a harmless mission in a favorable light and may later describe him as a nice-looking young man. The resident of the ghetto, who has seen policemen only when there was trouble afoot, may see the same policeman on the same innocuous mission as an ugly pig.

Learning to Discriminate

Discrimination refers to the process of distinguishing one stimulus from another. When stimuli are as thoroughly different as an elephant and a Ping-

Pong ball, discrimination is an easy task. When stimuli are quite similar (such as two bottles of the same type of wine produced in different years), it is harder to distinguish between them. Experience with different stimuli makes discrimination easier.

After a stimulus elicits a response, the response itself will have an observable effect on the person who responded. This effect is called **feedback.** In loose terms, feedback tells the respondent if he was correct. At military bases, for example, sentries must salute incoming officers and wave incoming enlisted men through with a sweeping motion of the arm. All sentries know this, but let us suppose that one sentry has trouble distinguishing officers' and enlisted men's uniforms in the dark. If he sees someone in uniform approaching and waves him through with his arm, one of two things may happen. The incoming person may be an enlisted man, who will respond with a smile and a nod. This reaction provides feedback that the sentry's identification of the stimulus was correct. But if the man is an officer and asks "What's wrong with *you*, Private?" feedback indicates that his identification of the shadowy figure was wrong. It does not take many smiles and nods from enlisted men as they are waved through, snickers and sneers from enlisted men when they are saluted, snappy salutes from officers when they are saluted, and even snappier comments from officers when they are waved through for the sentry to learn to discriminate among them. Feedback that suggests a response is correct corresponds to a *positive reinforcer,* and feedback that suggests a response is incorrect corresponds to a *negative reinforcer.* Much more will be said about reinforcers later.

It is sometimes said that all Orientals (or Africans, Indians, Caucasians, and so on) look alike. This statement may simply reflect a lack of experience with Orientals. Since an individual is most likely to associate with his own people and receive feedback from them, he will learn to discriminate best among them.

Malpass and Kravitz (1969) studied the abilities of black and white subjects to discriminate among photos of black and white males. As expected, subjects did a better job discriminating among members of their own race, which probably reflected greater experience with these people. Very intriguing was the additional finding that blacks did a better job discriminating among white faces than whites did discriminating among black faces. The investigators did not see this result as inconsistent with the hypothesis that increased contact with stimuli leads to better ability to discriminate among them. In our society blacks are forced at many points into contact with whites who provide them with very definite feedback. They are likely to have white teachers and employers, to buy from white merchants, and to confront white bureaucrats and officials. Whites, on the other hand, can go through life without such intensive contacts with blacks.

Learning Cues

Not all stimulus elements that contribute to perception are equally important. Some, such as the badge of a policeman, the Reverend in a minister's title, and the rattles on a snake, are especially important. Stimulus elements that impart a great deal of information are called **cues**. Cues enable the perceiver to go beyond the limited information available or to organize a complete perception given limited evidence.

Information imparted by cues is often informative. The unpleasant aroma from some hamburger stored too long is a case in point. But cues can also be misleading. A man with a high, squeaky voice on the telephone may turn out to have the appearance of a professional football quarterback.

Cues are learned as a result of the associational and feedback processes just described. An illustration comes from the learning of depth cues. If you carefully focus your eyes on some distant spot and, without moving your head, look first through one eye and then through the other, you will find the two images quite discrepant. Blended together, the two images permit true 3-D vision without the use of a stereopticon or red-and-green glasses. But it is also possible to gain an impression of depth without using both eyes, as a one-eyed friend of mine has proven. He learned cues that indicate depth. Interpositioning is one such cue. If one object is interposed in front of another, the partially obscured object is seen as farther away. Size and clarity are other cues. When a stimulus appears clear and big, it is seen as closer than when it appears hazy or small.

In the case of my friend, who had binocular vision until he was 12 or so, his first years allowed him to associate monocular (one-eye) cues with binocular (two-eye) depth perception hundreds of thousands of times. When he lost the sight in one eye, the monocular cues had already been well learned. But if he had been born with monocular vision, he would still have learned to gauge depth through the stimulus-response-feedback process. He would not have been sentenced to a lifetime of reaching for things and missing or hitting himself in the mouth with a glass or a cup.

True 3-D vision is not always necessary for gaining an impression of depth.

Cues can provide information around which an entire perception is structured. They are particularly important when there is little other information available. This situation is highlighted by studies of person perception—that is, how one person seems to see another. For example, in the days when instant coffee first appeared, Haire (1950) presented subjects with one of two shopping lists and asked them to describe the female shopper who supposedly had made it. The lists were identical, except that one included a jar of instant coffee and the other included a can of regular coffee. The woman responsible for the list including instant coffee was described as relatively lazy, a poor planner, a spendthrift, and a less satisfactory wife. Haire suggested that at the time a reluctance to brew coffee "right" served as a cue to other undesirable attributes.

Cues and Stereotypes.   McKeachie (1952) had six male college students interview each of six girls. Each girl wore lipstick for some of her interviews and not for others. The men then rated the girls. Girls with lipstick were seen as frivolous, less conscientious, and more interested in the opposite sex; girls not wearing lipstick were rated as serious, talkative, more conscientious, and less interested in men. Since the same girls wore lipstick for some interviews and not for others, we would not expect the different ratings to be due to underlying differences among them. Apparently, the men were responding to then-prevalent *preformed ideas* about women who wear lipstick.

When cues activate such preformed ideas, the perceiver is responding to a **stereotype.** Thus, on the basis of skin color or other physical qualities, a perceiver may automatically attribute a person with a number of other characteristics, many of which do not rightfully apply. Orientals may be seen as stoic and impassive, blacks as possessing a natural sense of rhythm, and fat people as jolly. Stereotypes are not necessarily incorrect. For example, Kleinmuntz (1967) notes that older women may be perceived as motherly because most older women happen to be mothers. But stereotypes are usually false, and even when they have some factual basis, it is not difficult to find many exceptions.

Other Perceiver Variables

Since different people form different associations, learn different discriminations, and respond to different cues, they often perceive the same physical stimulus in different ways. Each perceiver has his own set of contributants to perception (such as the results of his prior learning). These contributants that the perceiver himself provides may be called **perceiver variables.** In addition to the factors just mentioned, they include *expectancy, familiarity, personality,* and *needs.*

Expectancy

People often see what they expect to see. Expectancies may be formed by a long learning history or by immediately preceding experiences. Leeper (1935) showed subjects one of two sets of pictures. One set included a picture of a young woman; the other, a picture of an old hag. Then the subjects were shown a picture that could be seen either as a young woman or as an old hag. All the subjects earlier shown the young woman reported seeing a young woman, and almost all subjects earlier shown the old hag reported seeing an old hag.

Expectancies are also formed by the reports of others. Perhaps you, too, have seen the planet Venus as a spacecraft after having it pointed out as such by others. Luchins (1945) presented 12 vague drawings to children and asked them to tell what they saw. Under experimental conditions someone preceded the child with an announcement concerning what was in the picture. Under control conditions the children simply gave their reports. Children in the experimental condition tended to examine the drawings until they could "see" what the other person saw. Much more will be said about the effects of social influence on perception in the next chapter.

Familiarity

Familiarity affects perception in several ways. First, familiar stimuli are easier to detect than are unfamiliar stimuli. Thorndike and Lorge (1944) made estimates of the relative frequency with which words appear in print in the English language. Howes and Solomon (1951) selected 60 words of different frequency and then presented them for very brief periods of time to see how much exposure was necessary for the words to be identified. They found that, under conditions of very low levels of stimulation, it was easier to see the more familiar words. A study by Zajonc and Sales (1966) corroborated this result. Second, if subjects are shown relatively unfamiliar figures and are later asked to draw

Which organism is attending to the novel stimulus—photographer, ram, or both?

them, their reproductions tend to look like familiar figures, rather than like
the unfamiliar figures originally presented. This finding suggests a tendency to
perceive unfamiliar things as similar to familiar things (Weintraub & Walker,
1968). Third, as noted earlier, the work of Berlyne (1966) and others suggests
that people are more likely to look at *unfamiliar* stimuli. Finally, more familiar
stimuli seem to elicit more favorable reactions (a finding that will be pursued
in Chapter Eleven).

Personality

Some psychologists believe that they have detected reliable differences in the
ways people perceive stimuli such as inkblots, which are so vague and ambiguous that the perceiver is forced to rely heavily on internal sources of information to make sense of them. Some of these variations in perception are thought
to reflect personality differences. Specially devised pictures of unstructured
ambiguous stimuli used to assess these individual differences are called **projective tests.** The respondent is said to project his personality onto the stimulus
materials when he describes them. This will be discussed at length in Chapter
Nine.

Needs

The immediate needs of the perceiver also influence what he sees or hears.
This finding is suggested in two studies that involved depriving subjects of
food for periods of 1, 4, or 16 hours. In one study (McClelland & Atkinson,
1948), after deprivation, subjects were asked to report on very vague pictures.
Subjects who had gone without food for 16 hours reported more food-related
objects. In the other study (Atkinson & McClelland, 1948), following deprivation, the subjects were asked to make up stories about pictures of people
engaging in unspecified activities. Longer deprivation was associated with more
stories involving hunger and the need for food.

Why should needs affect perception? One possibility is that it happens through
expectancies. In the past a need (such as hunger) has repeatedly been associated with the need satisfier (such as food and eating utensils). Later, in the
presence of hunger, people will anticipate seeing food or food-related objects.
Another possibility is that perceiving a satisfier reflects the *primary process*
(discussed in Chapter Eight), a very early ability to fantasize or imagine some-

thing that is desired. The imagination could be prompted by whatever stimulus is handy.

Development of a Frame of Reference

Each person seems to have his own characteristic way of structuring, organizing, and interpreting new stimuli. That is, he has a unique **frame of reference**, which is based on learning, expectancy, familiarity, personality, needs, and social pressures.

A frame of reference may help explain why Russian leaders such as Stalin, Malenkov, and Beria look like hoodlums as they stand by the Kremlin wall watching the May Day military parade. Their sinister quality is imposed by the Western viewer, who *associates* them with evil, who *discriminates* them from the good guys, and who *expects* little good from them. The leaders are surrounded by *cues* of ill omen: the hammer and sickle of their army, the tomblike stone wall of the mysterious Kremlin, and the coarse, outdated clothing now worn only by heavies in grade-B movies. Just knowing that they are Russian may elicit a number of unfavorable *stereotypes*. Their Eurasian origin makes them look rather *unfamiliar*, which may attract attention but provides little comfort. The Western viewer may also have *needs* to stress his own perfection at their expense. Finally, there are strong *social pressures* to view the Russians in an unfavorable light, as survivors of the Senator Joseph McCarthy anti-Communist crusade can attest.

For many of us, pictures of Stalin, Malenkov, and Beria do look sinister. You might call it a case of perceiver overkill.

INSTIGATORS OF BEHAVIOR

At least two men have gained notice for seeming to do nothing. One managed to remain seated on an unmoving bicycle for 5 hours and 25 minutes; the other managed to "freeze" and remain motionless in a standing position for four and a half hours (McWhirter & McWhirter, 1971). These stunts attract attention, because such strenuous inactivity is difficult.

People have many different capacities for behavior, and they are usually exercising at least one of them. Most psychologists assume that there are instigators that prompt the use of these capacities and that these instigators somehow work in a selective fashion. Right now, for example, you could be fetching a glass of water, tying your shoes, or having fun with your friends. But instead you are prompted to do something else: to read this book.

The study of the forces that instigate behavior and lend it direction is the study of motivation. Two major theoretical approaches have evolved. One, **drive-habit theory,** is based heavily on the biological requirements of the organism. The other, **expectancy-incentive theory,** stresses cognitive processes —that is, thinking. Although primarily derived from research with animals, drive-habit theory can very neatly account for certain aspects of personality and human social behavior. Similarly, the expectancy-incentive approach, which stresses the organism's ability to anticipate, offers some predictions that have been confirmed by the behavior of supposedly witless animals.

The Drive-Habit Approach

To survive in comfort, we require the *presence* of such things as air, water, a good diet, and sleep and the *absence* of painful stimuli such as a splinter in the foot. The absence of necessities (deprivation) or the presence of painful stimuli has two well-documented effects. First, people will claim that either of these two conditions is unpleasant. Second, under either of these two conditions, people and animals will show an increase in their level of activity. It is the second of these effects that has attracted the eye of drive-habit theorists.

The broad motivational state that underlies an increase in activity is called **drive.** The greater the deprivation or the more painful the external stimuli, the stronger the drive and the higher the level of activity. Behavior instigated by drive (which, because of people's reports, is often characterized as an unpleasant tension state) reflects attempts to evade or reduce that drive and its associated unpleasant tensions. If drive had been increased by thirst, water would be a drive reducer; if it had been increased by the presence of a noxious stimulus such as a freezing blizzard, shelter would be a drive reducer. Water, shelter, and other drive-reducing consequences of behavior are referred to by drive-habit theorists as reinforcers and by other theorists as rewards, feedback, and incentives.

Drive serves only to *energize* behavior. The direction taken by behavior is determined by **habit,** which represents some form of stimulus-response connection—for example, a connection between seeing a red light (stimulus) and applying the brakes of an automobile (response). Thus habits dictate that under such and such stimulus conditions such and such a response will be made—providing, of course, that the organism is impelled to action. For all practical purposes, habits are acquired through the processes of learning.

Drive serves to energize behavior.

Drive will energize any habit. If the organism has learned to make a response that will extricate it from a painful situation or produce an appropriate drive reducer such as food, water, or sleep, this response will be energized. If the organism has not learned how to make a response that leads to drive reduction, other responses will be energized. A raccoon, for example, pelted with hot rain that it does not know how to avoid, will engage in frenzied, repetitive behavior; a rat, hearing a painfully loud noise it cannot escape, will run around in a circle; and a college man, isolated at an all-male school far from any coeds, may be a very vigorous tennis player.

In tests of drive-habit theory, drive is experimentally manipulated by depriving the subject or by applying noxious stimuli. Activity level is assessed by measures of the speed with which a response is started, the speed or strength with which it is executed, and the amount of time that it persists.

According to drive-habit theory, greater deprivations or more severe noxious stimulation should lead to greater activity. Representative of studies relating deprivation to activity are those of Siegal (1947) and Broadhurst (1957). Siegal deprived rats of water for 0, 6, 12, 24, or 48 hours. He then measured the number of milliliters (ml) of water each rat drank in a five-minute period, using amount consumed as the indicator of activity. Undeprived rats drank practically nothing. Rats deprived for 6 hours consumed about 2.5 ml, rats deprived 12 hours consumed about 5.5 ml, rats deprived 24 hours drank about 7 ml, and rats deprived for 48 hours drank slightly more than 7 ml. Broadhurst deprived rats of air for 0, 5, 10, 15, or 25 seconds. They were then allowed to swim through a short underwater alley to receive air. Longer deprivation resulted in much peppier swimming. A similar effect is suggested by W. L. Brown (1961), who describes how he wolfed down unappetizing meals when he was an involuntary guest of a foreign government. The chef's secret? The meals were scanty and often few and far between.

Amsel (1950) and Campbell and Kraeling (1953) have found activity increases resulting from the presence of noxious stimuli. In these experiments, rats received shocks of varying intensity, and the speed with which they ran was assessed. In both studies activity level, as measured by running speed, increased as the shock was intensified. Similarly, soldiers under enemy attack discover they can run faster than they ever believed possible. However, since no one has ever bothered timing them under panic and relaxed conditions, these *apparent* performance increases could reflect inaccurate perception rather than actual increases in performance.

In all the situations just described, drive was produced by survival-oriented, biologically based variables. But drive can also be learned. For example, fear is learned, and fear has drivelike consequences (Brown, Kalish, & Farber, 1951).

J. S. Brown (1961) has suggested that, through learning, the absence of certain substances increases drive. Money is an example. Brown points out that an empty wallet or an overdrawn notice from a bank may produce feelings of insecurity, uneasiness, or anxiety. These learned unpleasant tensions have drive-producing qualities not unlike those of hunger, thirst, and shock.

The Relationship between Drive and Habit

Stimulus-response connections or habits can be strong (well learned) or weak (not well learned). They can also be "right" (that is, reduce drive and produce a better state for the organism) or "wrong" (that is, increase or not reduce drive).

Drive will energize any habit, whether it is right or wrong. In effect, if the "right" response is made, it will be strengthened by drive, giving the appearance of improved performance (as when Siegal's rats drank more water under conditions of greater water deprivation). On the other hand, if a "wrong" response is made, it, too, will be strengthened (as when the animals responding to painful, drive-inducing stimuli ran in circles: they did have the habit of running, but they had not learned how to make a response that would successfully extricate them from the painful situation).

According to drive-habit theory, drive and habit *multiply together* to produce a response of a given strength. If it were possible to make definite numerical estimates of each variable, drive-habit theory would offer very clear predictions. With a habit strength of 2.0 and a drive level of 4.0, there should be a response of strength 8.0. Although such precise numerical estimates are not possible, there are three important implications of the multiplicative relationship, and each has at least some support from data.

First, both drive and habit must be present for a particular response to occur. Without drive, a response simply will not be performed; without some sort of habit or stimulus-response connection, it cannot be performed.

Second, an increase in either drive or habit will strengthen a response. The response-strengthening effects of increasing drive are shown in the deprivation and painful stimulation studies described above; the response-strengthening effects of increasing habit strength are discussed later in this chapter.

Third, within limits, a decrease in drive strength can be compensated for by an increase in habit strength, and vice versa. This point has been illustrated in a study by Fredenburg (1956), who varied both drive and habit.

Drive Reduction?

The face of El Capitan peak in Yosemite National Park is a 3000-foot vertical wall of rock. It may provide a natural resting place for flies, but not much else.

In the fall of 1970, two men climbed this staggering cliff. For almost a month they inched their way toward the top, using spikes and ropes for their ascent.

They slept suspended in slings. An unexpected and unfavorable change in the weather slowed them, with the result that their food ran out. Each suffered from falls but was saved by the rope. They reported all this and described themselves as cold, wet, hungry, and tired in messages they dropped to the ground. But rangers, attempting to rescue them by helicopter, were told in no uncertain terms to leave. Finally, after a month of misery, they made it to the top, there to be welcomed by relatives, newsmen, and assorted well-wishers who had ambled up a path from the back.

Tension reduction? Behavior motivated by needs for necessities, comforts, and pain avoidance? Certainly, the climbers' behavior did not seem to reflect attempts to reduce unpleasant tensions.

Behavior such as this has prompted some psychologists to suggest that organisms may find a certain amount of tension pleasurable. In support of this theory, they point out many cases in which organisms seek stimulation, rather than try to avoid it, and engage in activities for their own sake, not because the activities are necessary for comfort or survival.

Tension reduction?

The importance of stimulation is suggested in the studies of Olds (Olds, 1961, 1969; Olds & Milner, 1954), who placed an electrode at a certain location in the rat's brain. When rats learned how to stimulate themselves by sending a mild electric current through the electrode, they did so at a very high rate. Monkeys, rats, and humans alike will expend effort to look at unusual, novel, and atypical stimuli. People play golf, paint pictures, fly in gliders, and sit on flagpoles: none of these activities seem to be necessary to reduce unpleasant tensions.

In **stimulus deprivation** studies, subjects are kept under conditions that minimize the quality and quantity of sensory input (Bexton, Heron, & Scott, 1954; Heron, 1957; Heron, Doane, & Scott, 1956). Although some experimenters have gone as far as to submerge their subjects in lukewarm water, such studies mainly involve first making the subjects comfortable on a bed and then outfitting them with heavy gloves and slippers, cardboard cuffs, earplugs, and translucent goggles that permit only diffuse light to be admitted. Even when they are handsomely paid, subjects do not find these restful, *low-drive* conditions pleasurable. In studies at McGill University, for instance, subjects paid $20 a day for a life of true ease generally quit after two or three days, and none lasted more than five or six days.

Reduced stimulation is not only unpleasant but has other adverse effects as well. Under low stimulation, thinking becomes disorganized and the ability to concentrate diminished. Under severe and prolonged stimulus deprivation, subjects sometimes report bizarre thoughts or hallucinations. Similar effects have been reported by drivers on tedious hauls and by air crews on long-distance flights.

In short, it would appear that stimulation is often sought and activities engaged in for their own sake. These findings are not easily and elegantly accounted for by drive-habit theory. Thus, at the present time, this theory explains only a part of the picture. Nevertheless, it is a very large part of the picture, and opposing theories must somehow take all this tension-reduction data into account.

The Expectancy-Incentive Approach

The expectancy-incentive approach to motivation suggests that organisms have the ability to anticipate, weigh, and evaluate the consequences of their actions. Before you approach someone to ask for a first date, for example, you may have anticipated the consequences of your action by asking yourself "What are the chances of my being accepted?" and weighed and evaluated these consequences by asking "What is this date worth to me?" and "How badly will I feel if I am turned down?" The person's estimate of the chances that a certain action will yield a certain result or outcome is called an **expectancy.** The value of the outcome to the individual is called an **incentive.** Both expectancies and incentives are highly personal and subjective.

The expectancy-incentive approach to motivation suggests that organisms have the ability to anticipate, weigh, and evaluate the consequences of their actions.

The subjective nature of expectancies is shown in the soldier's belief that he, personally, will not be injured in a bloody battle and in the gambler's belief that he will come out a winner. In fact, the objective odds of the soldier's getting hurt could be quite high, and casinos are not run to make patrons rich. Subjective value of incentives is best illustrated by pointing out that the same thing is not of equal worth to different people or even to the same person at different points in time. Finding $5 is always nice, but I would venture that an occupant of Skid Row would place greater value in it than would Aristotle Onassis. Similarly, to someone sitting down to a steak dinner, a liverwurst sandwich may sound unappealing, but it would be highly prized by a person who had gone without eating for two days.

The strength of motivation to behave in a certain way can be computed by multiplying expectancy by incentive—that is, the subjective estimate that the behavior will produce a certain outcome by the subjective value of that outcome. The higher the product, the stronger the force for that behavior. For example, suppose you had a dime that you were willing to risk in one of three games of chance. In the first game you believed that there was a one in a thousand chance of winning $1. The product of expectancy (.001) and incentive (1.00) would be .001. In the second game there was a one in a hundred chance of winning $10. The product of expectancy (.01) and incentive (10.00) would be .10. In the third game there was a one in ten chance of winning $100. The product of expectancy (.1) and incentive (100.00) would be 10.00. You would probably choose the third game, since both the expectancy of winning and the prize or incentive are higher than in either of the other games. If expectancy did not vary, you would probably choose the game with the biggest prize; if the prize did not vary, you would probably choose the game that you thought you were most likely to win.

Expectancies are formed through learning. We learn that if we go to the refrigerator, we get ice cubes; if we drive on the left, we get into accidents; if we ask a certain friend for a favor, it is (or is not) likely to be granted. Incentive values depend on learning and on our present biological needs. For example, we learn that money is valuable, but whether or not a glass of water is valuable depends on how thirsty we are.

The expectancy-incentive approach to behavior has been popular for about 30 years. Atkinson and his associates (Atkinson, 1958a, 1964; Birch & Veroff, 1966) maintain that it is a useful one but that it must be extended to account for the variety and complexity of behavior. They propose that there are four classes of variables contributing to the strength and direction of behavior: *availability*, *expectancy*, *incentive*, and *motive*. These variables multiply together to produce a *tendency* to respond. However, how the individual does in fact respond depends on the relative strength of all his tendencies in that situation: the strongest tendency is the one that emerges as behavior.

Availability, incentive, and motive (like drive and habit) combine together in a multiplicative fashion. Thus (1) all the variables must be available in some quantity for the behavior to occur; (2) an increase or decrease in any of the variables affects the response likelihood and strength; and (3) within limits, a decrease in the strength of one of the variables can be compensated for by an increase in strength in another.

Typically, scientific tests of this theory of motivation involve varying one or possibly two of the four independent variables, holding the remainder constant, and then assessing behavior (Atkinson, 1964; Birch & Veroff, 1966). Availability, expectancy, and incentive can be manipulated; motives cannot, because they are enduring characteristics of the individual. But motives can be assessed.

Availability

Availability refers to the accessibility of a response to the behaving organism. First, the organism must have the physical capabilities of performing the response. Snakes, for example, will never use scissors. Second, given a physical ability to respond, the organism must also *know how* to make the response. Here is one place where learning enters into this theory. Habit strength and availability are roughly synonymous. Better-learned responses are more accessible or available.

Expectancy

Organisms have the ability to anticipate, and thereby assess, the likelihood that a given action will result in a given outcome. The outcome may be seen as one worth pursuing (*positive incentive value*) or as one to avoid (*negative incentive value*).

This ability to anticipate the consequences of behavior imparts direction to behavior. Simply put, the organism will behave in the way that it expects will produce the best results given the circumstances. When thirsty, people fetch glasses of water, and when tripping over their shoelaces, they tie their shoes, because they *expect* these behaviors to produce results that are, under the circumstances, satisfying. Expectancies can be formed through firsthand learning, through learning from others, or through complex reasoning processes.

Incentive

Incentives are the specific instigators that impel behavior. Incentive value refers to the subjective attractiveness of the anticipated results of the behavior. Positive incentives are such things as food, drink, shelter, and money, which are the goals or rewards that lure behavior. Negative incentives are the deprivations and punishments that deter behavior. In the approach taken by Atkinson and his colleagues, incentive value is attached to the *particular* consequences of an action. If you are extremely tired, catching a catnap in the back of a moving, subcompact car would have one incentive value; a good night's sleep in a luxury motel would have another. Or, if you are familiar with Melville's *Moby Dick*, you might note that, for Ahab, conquering Moby Dick had strong incentive value, whereas capturing run-of-the-mill whales was not nearly so important. Incentive values, then, are the *very specific* values that make one particular activity attractive or unattractive.

Motive

The attractiveness or unattractiveness of a course of action is also affected by motive. **Motive** refers to a preference for a *class of activities* or for reaching a goal of a *general type*. Motives include such classes of activities as exploration and adventure, learning, and contact with other people and, through these activities, such general goals as fame, knowledge, and popularity. Thus, although incentives are very *specific*, motives are very *general*.

Behavior directed toward attaining a specific goal may satisfy several different motives. For example, when someone goes to a great deal of trouble and expense to earn a college degree, the *incentive* might be the degree itself, which allows the possessor to start as a second lieutenant in a branch of industry, rather than as a private. But attaining this specific award would not be the only attraction of the college venture. Learning, scholarship, and achievement might prove enjoyable, and the rich social life found on most college campuses might produce further pleasure. These satisfactions are derived from engaging in general *classes of activities* and are said to satisfy personal motives.

An understanding of people's preferences for classes of activities may help us to understand why individuals engage in activity for its own sake. We will return to this concept of motive throughout the text.

LEARNING

Behaving organisms have the ability to alter their behavior as a result of past experiences. That is, they can learn. In this section we will consider two basic learning procedures: classical conditioning and operant conditioning.

Learning through Classical Conditioning

Some children feel very much at ease around animals. Others may flee in terror when even the friendliest pet approaches. One way this latter behavior may be acquired was long ago demonstrated by Watson and Rayner (1920).

Loud noises produce fear in infants. Watson and Rayner showed a pet rabbit to an infant. This presentation was followed by a loud noise, which reliably elicited fear. After this series of events had been completed a number of times, the child became fearful when the animal was presented alone; it was no longer necessary for Watson and Rayner to present the loud noise. This study illustrates **classical conditioning.** The child was conditioned to respond to the rat with fear.

There are four major terms in classical conditioning: *unconditioned stimulus, unconditioned response, conditioned stimulus* and *conditioned response.*

The **unconditioned stimulus** is a stimulus that reliably elicits a particular response, called the **unconditioned response,** at the beginning of the learning sequence. In the Watson and Rayner study, the loud noise was the unconditioned stimulus; before Watson and Rayner did anything, this stimulus reliably elicited the unconditioned response, fear.

The **conditioned stimulus** is one that, at the beginning of the learning sequence, does *not* elicit a response comparable to the unconditioned response. In the Watson and Rayner study, the conditioned stimulus was an initially neutral furry object. Because the conditioned stimulus does not typically elicit much of a response at the beginning of the learning sequence, it is often referred to as a *neutral stimulus.* But it soon loses its neutrality, because during classical conditioning the subject begins to respond to this stimulus with a **conditioned response,** which is, for all intents and purposes, very similar to the unconditioned response. The conditioned response in the Watson and Rayner study was fear.

The conditioned response differs from the unconditioned response in rather subtle ways. It is called the conditioned response simply because it is elicited by the conditioned stimulus, not by the unconditioned stimulus. In classical conditioning, as the result of a number of paired stimulus presentations in which the conditioned stimulus is followed by the unconditioned stimulus, the subject learns to respond to the originally neutral conditioned stimulus by making the conditioned response. In a sense, the subject comes to respond to the conditioned stimulus *as if* it were the unconditioned stimulus. Thus we salivate when we hear the cry "Soup's on!" (as if food were actually present) or begin feeling edgy when we hear the distant wail of a siren (as if danger were actually present). In the past, "Soup's on!" has preceded food, and a siren has preceded trouble.

Extinction

Are responses learned through classical conditioning ever forgotten? Forgetting refers to a simple reduction or disappearance of a conditioned response in the absence of the conditioned stimulus. If, after conditioning, the conditioned stimulus is not presented for a period of time but is then suddenly introduced, one of two things may happen. First, the subject may make the conditioned response, which suggests no forgetting. Second, the subject may not make the conditioned response, which suggests that forgetting of conditioned responses does occur. Almost all the evidence indicates that the forgetting of conditioned responses does *not* occur. For example, Walker (1967) once conditioned a dog to flex its leg and then gave the dog to a farmer. After two years' service as a hunting dog, the animal was returned to the laboratory and tested. It showed no forgetting of the conditioned leg-flexion response.

However, for the most part learned responses can be weakened or eliminated through a process called **extinction.** In classical conditioning this process consists of repeated presentation of the conditioned stimulus alone—that is, not followed by the unconditioned stimulus. For example, in the case of little Albert (Watson and Rayner's subject), after the conditioning process had been complete, repeated presentation of the rabbit alone should have resulted in the rabbit's no longer eliciting the fear response. It is quite likely that Walker's dog did not encounter the conditioned stimulus during its two years in the field, for, if it had, extinction of the leg-flexion response would have been likely.

One-Trial Conditioning

Each opportunity to learn, perform, or extinguish is called a **trial.** In classical conditioning, for example, each pairing of the conditioned and unconditioned stimuli would constitute a learning trial. For decades psychologists have wondered whether learning takes place bit by bit or suddenly, during one trial. Under many conditions learning appears to be of the incremental or bit-by-bit variety, and the response being learned appears in rough form before it is per-fected. But under certain other conditions learning appears to be very sudden indeed.

Scoline is a drug that produces a feeling of utter horror and dread. It was used as an unconditioned stimulus by Campbell, Sanderson, and Laverty (1964), who first presented a tone and then administered the fast-acting drug. They did this only once. Afterward the tone alone was sufficient to induce feelings of dread. This new response to the tone was very well learned. After a hundred or so extinction trials (that is, successive presentations of the tone alone), many subjects still showed adverse emotional reactions. The conditioned response was neither forgotten nor easily extinguished.

Classical Conditioning and Psychotherapy

Were the investigators conducting the Scoline study unusually cruel? Before you make a judgment, consider that the subjects were chronic alcoholics whose lives had been reduced to shambles. They volunteered for the experiment, rec-ognizing that it might eventually help people reduce their drinking. For exam-ple, the tone could later serve as an *unconditioned stimulus* (since it now reliably elicited horror) that could be preceded by the presentation of alcohol. Through this latter conditioning procedure, drinks could be made to seem unappetizing.

In the past decade or so, relatively simple learning procedures have been applied to help people change behavior that they have found unacceptable. These pro-cedures seem to have been quite successful in certain types of cases, even when intensive individual counseling had failed.

Lavin, Thorpe, Barker, Blakemore, and Conway (1961) applied classical-conditioning procedures to help a man who could not resist dressing in ladies' undergarments. The unconditioned stimulus was apomorphine, an unpleasant drug that produces nausea. The conditioned stimuli were pictures of the wom-en's clothing and a recording of the man describing himself dressing in these garments. The drug was administered, and just before the man became nau-seous, the conditioned stimuli were presented. After very intensive conditioning, the sight of the garments became unpleasant. Through classical conditioning he formed an apparently long-lasting aversion to female clothing.

Learning through Operant Conditioning

The second important learning process, **operant conditioning**, begins with an identifiable stimulus and an organism motivated to respond. Remaining motivated in the presence of the stimulus, the organism will try one response after another until it makes one that appears to be followed by a more satisfying state of affairs. This response will be learned. Later, again motivated and presented with the stimulus, the organism will first try the response that had earlier been successful. For example, if someone is motivated to continue watching a television program and all of a sudden the picture becomes distorted (stimulus), he is likely to race to the set and begin fiddling with the knobs (responses). First he tries one, then another and another, perhaps eventually restoring the picture by manipulating the knob labeled "vertical hold." Later in the evening, if the picture again shows the same type of distortion, he will immediately adjust the "vertical hold" control and not waste time pulling, pushing, and twisting the other knobs.

Remaining motivated in the presence of the stimulus, the organism will try one response after another until it makes one that appears to be followed by a more satisfying state of affairs.

Much learning is of this trial-and-error variety. People commonly try again and again until they reach a solution. If the first attempt fails, they try something else; if that fails, they move on to another possibility. They stop trying different responses when they finally make a *right* response, or one that *gets results* because it secures rewards or spares the person from punishment. In psychology the rewards and punishments that follow responses and encourage or discourage their further performance are typically described as reinforcers.

Reinforcers

A thing or event is defined as a **reinforcer** if it alters the probability or strength of the response that it follows. If the reinforcer increases the likelihood or strength of that response, it is called a **positive reinforcer.** If, on the other hand, it decreases the likelihood or strength of the response preceding it, it is called a **negative reinforcer.** In simple language, positive reinforcers are roughly synonymous with rewards and negative reinforcers with punishments.

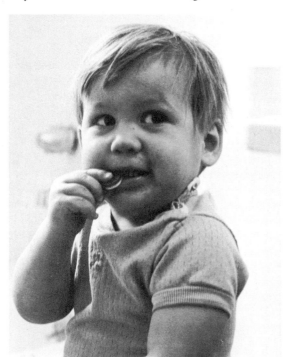

In simple language, positive reinforcers are roughly synonymous with rewards and negative reinforcers with punishments.

Many things can strengthen or weaken a preceding response. Positive reinforcers may be as tangible as a warm, clean, dry diaper or a steak dinner or a new car; they may be as intangible as a nod of appreciation from a close friend or an inner feeling of accomplishment. Negative reinforcers may be as tangible as a spanking or a $25 fine or as intangible as a cold glance from a friend or an inner feeling of failure.

The actual behavior preceding a reinforcer may or may not cause the reinforcement. For example, if you are thirsty and fetch a glass of water, your action is clearly related to the resulting favorable state of affairs. In effect, your action causes you to be reinforced. On the other hand, behavior is sometimes reinforced by unrelated events.

Skinner (1948a) administered positive reinforcers to pigeons without regard to their behavior at the time the reinforcer was given. The pigeons were thus reinforced for whatever they happened to be doing. Eventually, some learned funny little dances, and others learned such activities as bowing to the sides of the box and walking in motions not natural to pigeons. Skinner referred to this learned behavior as superstitious, because there was no causal link between the response and the reinforcement. The fisherman who believes he cannot catch fish unless he is wearing his "lucky" hat is superstitious in the same way: he caught some tremendous fish when he wore this hat in the past, and now he regards it as necessary in making a big haul.

As in the case of responses learned through classical conditioning, responses learned through operant conditioning are not often forgotten—but they can be extinguished. In this case extinction is brought about when the response is no longer followed by a positive reinforcer. After capsizing his boat several times, catching pneumonia twice, and consistently getting poor hauls, the fisherman may no longer insist on wearing his "lucky" hat.

Shaping

To apply operant-conditioning procedures, the teacher simply waits until the learner makes the desired response and then dispenses a known reinforcer. When the child stops his tantrum, he is given his toy; when the dog returns the ball, he is given a scrap of food; when the boyfriend asks for a date, he is given a smile and a nod.

Because a learner can make an almost infinite number of responses, it may take an extremely long time before the teacher can dispense the reinforcer. For example, Isaacs, Thomas, and Goldiamond (1960) wanted to use operant-conditioning procedures to reinstate speech in a man who had been mute for 19 years. All they had to do was reward him after he made a verbalization. But how long would it take before the man happened to say something?

Shaping aids the operant-conditioning process. This procedure involves reinforcing closer and closer approximations of the desired response. At first, any behavior that increases the likelihood of the desired response is reinforced. Later, however, the trainer becomes increasingly demanding about the level of performance shown before the reinforcer is administered.

Isaacs, Thomas, and Goldiamond noticed that the usually withdrawn man had shown some interest in chewing gum, so they decided to try using it as a reinforcer. A therapist met with the man several times a week. During the first two weeks the therapist reinforced the response of simply looking at the gum. During the next week the man had to move his lips before the gum was dispensed. During the fourth week the therapist withheld the gum pending some sort of vocalization. The man, who had already learned to look at the gum and move his lips, began to make raspy, croaking noises when he was shown the gum. During the fifth and sixth weeks, each time the man vocalized a sound, the therapist said "Say *gum, gum.*" At the end of the sixth week the man suddenly said "Gum, please." After this breakthrough he began answering the psychologist's questions. Thus, through shaping procedures, the therapist successfully reinstated speech in a person who had been mute for almost 20 years.

How Do Reinforcers Work?

Whether or not reinforcement is *absolutely necessary* for learning to occur, it is impossible to ignore the finding that certain things or events following a response increase or decrease the subsequent probability or strength of that response. Why should certain conditions following a response result in its being learned?

Drive-habit theorists suggest that reinforcers are effective because they are *drive reducing.* Reinforcers eliminate or diminish drive by reducing its *source.* For example, shelter reduces drive that has been increased by the presence of a painful, stinging hailstorm. It is this drive reduction that strengthens the preceding response.

Consistent with this explanation is the finding that the same reinforcer will not strengthen or weaken behavior at all points in time. Instead, much depends on the state of the organism. For example, food will reinforce the responses of a hungry organism but not of a well-fed one.

Given this explanation, one would expect that improved quantity or quality of reinforcement would improve learning. After all, bigger and better rewards should be more efficient drive reducers. Hutt (1954) produced three different qualities of reinforcers by adding pleasant or unpleasant flavorings to a basic food mixture. Animals were given one of the three types of food in one of three different quantities each time they pressed a bar. Both bigger and better reinforcers stepped up the learning. Later, Bower, Fowler, and Trapold (1959) showed that reinforcers consisting of *greater decreases* in unpleasant external stimulation are more effective than are reinforcers consisting of *lesser* decreases in unpleasant external stimulation.

Expectancy-incentive theorists, however, can easily accommodate all these findings. They would point out that increased deprivation prior to reinforcement and an increase in the quantity or quality of the reinforcement would raise the incentive value of the reinforcer. This increase in incentive value would thus strengthen behavior.

Primary and Secondary Reinforcers

Many reinforcers seem effective because they diminish biological deficits or hardships. Food for the hungry and water for the thirsty are examples. These are called **primary reinforcers.**

Other reinforcers, such as medals, savings stamps, and promotions, do not seem to reduce biological needs in the same sense as do food and water. These **secondary reinforcers** are believed to have acquired their reinforcing properties through classical conditioning. Money and approval from others are good examples of secondary reinforcers. Neither will directly satisfy a biological need. However, each has been repeatedly associated with primary reinforcers (such as food, drink, and shelter) and as a result becomes reinforcing in its own right.

Money and approval from others are good examples of secondary re-inforcers.

Escape and Avoidance Learning

Up to this point I have emphasized conditions in which an appropriate response is followed by a positive reinforcer. It is also common to learn to escape or avoid an unpleasant state of affairs.

An **escape response** is one that extricates the organism from a painful or unpleasant situation. The reinforcement comes from the reduction of externally induced, painful stimulation. An **avoidance response** is one that keeps the organism from experiencing the painful situation in the first place. The reinforcement here may also be the reduction of unpleasant stimulation, which in this case results from a classically conditioned anticipation of what is to come. The distinction between escape and avoidance responding is illustrated by the basset hound example cited earlier. When the dog was chased, he ran away and *escaped* the chasing. Later the dog learned to *avoid* the chasing by leaving whenever the irate psychologist appeared.

In some cases avoidance responses are learned very quickly and are amazingly persistent. Solomon and his associates (Solomon & Wynne, 1953; Solomon,

Kamin, & Wynne, 1953) trained dogs to avoid a severe shock by jumping from one compartment in a cage to another. First a buzzer sounded; a few seconds later the shock was administered. The dogs learned very quickly to avoid this intense shock. Then the shock was disconnected, and the investigators presented the buzzer alone. For hundreds of trials the dogs jumped at the sound of the buzzer, not waiting around long enough to discover that the painful shock no longer followed.

Maintaining and Strengthening Wanted Behavior

In the case of the Scoline-conditioned alcoholics and the avoidance-conditioned dogs, learning was quick and efficient, and the new response was reliably elicited by the stimulus over long periods of time. In other cases learning appears to be slow and imperfect, and the new response quickly disappears. One way to understand such differences in degree of learning or *habit strength* is to take a closer look at such variables as the nature of the reinforcer and the speed with which it is administered.

There are two sets of techniques for measuring habit strength. One set assesses how *proficiently* the response is executed. **Response latency** is one such measure: the faster the subject executes the response when the stimulus is presented, the stronger the habit. A related measure is error rate. If the response is made smoothly, efficiently, and with few or no mistakes, the response is assumed to be well learned. The second set of measures determines the *permanence of the response* once it is learned. To the extent that the subject continues to perform the response in the absence of further reinforcement (or in the absence of additional conditioned stimulus–unconditioned stimulus pairings), it is **resistant to extinction**; the greater the resistance to extinction, the stronger the habit. Whether you are interested in training a dog, a child, or your great-uncle Nat, variables increasing resistance to extinction are useful if you want their new behavior to be maintained in your absence. Perplexingly, the techniques that strengthen learning as indicated by measures of speed and proficiency are not inevitably the same techniques that strengthen learning as measured by resistance to extinction.

Number of Reinforced Trials.   Most studies show that habit strength increases with the number of reinforced trials. This is almost invariably true using measures of speed and proficiency and, under some conditions, using measures of resistance of extinction as well. Harris and Nygaard (1961) first reinforced rats for pressing a lever and then measured resistance to extinction. Different groups of rats had a total of 45, 90, or 360 trials, and the bar-pressing response of rats undergoing more reinforced trials showed greater resistance to extinction. However, Ison (1962) found conflicting results. After 10, 20, 40, 60, 80, or 100 trials, in which rats learned the simple response of running to obtain food, Ison's data showed that, the *greater* the number of reinforcements, the *faster* the extinction. The difference between these two experiments was that Ison's involved a learning problem so simple that his subjects received training far beyond that required for complete, successful learning. The implication is that increasing the number of reinforced trials may *not* increase resistance to extinction if "overlearning" has occurred.

Percentage of Reinforced Trials. The *percentage* of reinforced trials has its most prominent effects on resistance to extinction. Generally, a *decreased* percentage of reinforced trials raises resistance. If you want to keep your dog, child, or uncle on good behavior in your absence, reinforcements should be administered only after *some* of the appropriate responses.

Cowan and Walters (1963) used marbles to reinforce children's aggressive responses to a large doll. Some were given a marble after *each* aggressive act, others after every *third* aggressive act, and still others only after every *sixth* aggressive act. Later, when marbles were no longer dispensed, the children who had received a marble following each aggressive act were the first to stop acting aggressively; the children who received a marble for every third aggressive act gave up their responses less readily; the children who had received a marble following every *sixth* aggressive act maintained their aggressive behavior longest of all.

Reinforcement following some, but not all, performances of a given response is called **intermittent reinforcement.** Behavior so reinforced is highly resistant to extinction, which may account for why some gamblers become addicted to their sport. Lewis and Duncan (1956) had college students pull the handle of a slot machine. During the first eight tries, players won different percentages of the time. Immediately afterward, extinction procedures began (the subjects were not told, of course, that they could no longer win). Players who had been reinforced least frequently were the last to give up playing.

An interesting finding of this particular study was that the subjects who had received *no* reinforcement during the training phase persisted longest during the extinction phase. To understand this, it must be considered that the subjects knew the slot machines *might* pay. Under conditions in which there are

The effects of intermittent reinforcement may account for why some gamblers become addicted to their sport.

no such preconceptions, reinforcement during the learning phase must be sufficent to allow the new behavior to be initially learned (Lewis, 1960).

Why should decreased percentages of reinforced trials lead to increased resistance to extinction? One possibility is that the learning and extinction trials are more similar for the occasionally reinforced subjects. Persons who are reinforced after each trial notice quickly when reinforcement is withdrawn; for them the stimulus situation changes quite drastically. On the other hand, subjects reinforced only occasionally cannot detect this difference. A second possibility is that intermittent reinforcement raises the incentive value of the reinforcement. It is a common observation that the most difficult rewards to achieve are the most highly prized.

Speed of Reinforcement. Prompt knowledge of the results of a response helps one to decide whether to continue making that response or to try a different one. If, after making the response the teacher or trainer wants, the learner is allowed to make a second response before the reinforcement is administered, it will be this second response that is strengthened. Consequently, the balance of evidence suggests that when the reinforcement *immediately* follows the response, learning proceeds more quickly when speed and proficiency are measured. It is not equally clear, however, that speedy reinforcement is the best response-strengthening technique when resistance to extinction is the measure. For example, Crum, Brown, and Bitterman (1951) have shown that, within limits, a delay in reinforcement can increase resistance to extinction. One possibility is that when the organism has learned that reinforcement may be a bit tardy, the interminable "delay" during the extinction trials is not so noticeable as it would be if the organism had learned to anticipate speedy results. On the other hand, if quick results are anticipated, the interminable delay during extinction trials is quickly detected, and it becomes very obvious that conditions have changed.

Eliminating Unwanted Behavior

Except in a very few cases, learned responses can be weakened or lost. According to the **decay theory** of forgetting, when there is no longer motivation to make a response, the habit falls into disuse, weakens, and fades away. However, as you saw in the case of the conditioned dog that showed no signs of forgetting after two years' service as a hunting dog, the process of weakening or losing a response is not quite so simple. It would appear that a response is

. . . learned responses can be weakened or lost.

extinguished when something new is learned that *interferes* with it (**inter-ference theory**). In the absence of new learning, a response is likely to persist for a long period of time. Moreover, when there is *opportunity* to learn a new response, an old response is more likely to be weakened or lost than when there is no such opportunity. For example, after teaching cockroaches to avoid dark-ness, Minani and Dallenbach (1946) allowed some subjects mobility and the opportunity to learn; other subjects were kept wrapped in tissue paper. Later the mobile subjects that had the opportunity to learn did not perform the avoid-ance responses so well as the immobile subjects that did not have the oppor-tunity for new learning.

Three sets of techniques may be applied to weaken unwanted behavior: (1) training new responses to replace the old, (2) withdrawing positive reinforce-ment, and (3) using punishment.

Training New Responses. Some people show strong, unwanted emotional reactions. For example, some students are very fearful of examinations. Clinical psychologists may use special **desensitization** procedures to help such students. First, the psychologist ascertains which of a number of examination-related stimuli elicit the greatest fear. For example, the word *test* may be mildly dis-turbing, a weekly quiz moderately frightening, and final-exam week downright terrorizing. Then, in a neutral setting, the student is taught to relax. Relaxation becomes associated with the least worrisome stimulus and later with more and more threatening stimuli. Over time it is possible for the response of dread to be replaced with a response of relaxation.

The Withdrawal of Positive Reinforcement. Lewis and Duncan's (1956) sub-jects eventually stopped playing their slot machines after they realized they could no longer win. It is quite reliably found that the withholding of positive reinforcement following a response leads to a weakening or elimination of that response. However, this process can take a great deal of time if the response had been earlier reinforced intermittently or if the response in question is an avoidance response.

There are many cases in which psychotherapists have used the technique of withdrawing reinforcement to help rid people of unwanted behavior. For exam-ple, Allyon (1963) used this procedure to train a woman to stop stealing food in the hospital cafeteria. Her food stealing had been reinforced countless times by the consumption of the stolen food. Persuasion, coaxing, and coercion had been tried to no avail. Finally, this woman was made to sit alone during meals. The staff kept a careful watch on her. Whenever she made a move to steal food, they simply removed her from the cafeteria. This technique kept her from having her food stealing reinforced by food consumption. After about two weeks her bad habit disappeared.

Punishment.   Punishment is often used in attempts to eliminate unwanted behavior, but the effects of punishment are more complex than is commonly recognized. Certainly there are studies suggesting that punishment weakens habits (Seligman & Campbell, 1965), but there are other studies suggesting that habits are not always dependably weakened by punishment. Skinner (1938) and Estes (1944) have found that punishment may only temporarily impair the performance of the punished response. Then, too, there are certain problems with punishment. Punishment can produce a rigidity of behavior that makes new learning difficult. Indeed, Walker (1967) notes the **punishment paradox** that punishment sometimes encourages the performance of the response in a manner suggesting greater learning. In animal studies, for instance, shock can elicit running, which is not helpful if running is the response the teacher is trying to extinguish. In human learning, punishment may be seen as an aggressive act by the person who is punished; hence it can elicit *further* aggression in the form of retaliatory behavior.

CONCLUSIONS

Perception refers to receiving and processing information—primarily information about the real world that most of us assume exists outside our skins. Reception begins, appropriately enough, with the receptors, which are highly sensitive nerve endings capable of responding to the energy changes that constitute stimuli. Most stimuli activate thousands of receptors, and the resulting impulses must be combined and organized in some fashion to produce coherent and understandable information. Some psychologists, such as the Gestalt psychologists, suggest that many of these abilities to organize, structure, and pattern incoming stimulation are gifts that come with the organism. Whatever part inborn abilities play, it is clear that learning has important effects on perception. First, through learning, associations are formed, and past associations enter into present perceptions. Second, learning seems to be very important for the ability to distinguish one stimulus from another. Finally, through learning, people come to identify important cues, or parts of the stimulus that contribute disproportionately to how a stimulus is perceived.

Perception involves contributions from external stimuli, which are public and objective, and from internal stimuli, which are private and subjective. Because different people are influenced by different internal stimuli, they often perceive the same "objective" event in quite different ways. The perceiver's expectations, his familiarity with the stimulus, his personality, and his immediate needs all contribute to his perception.

Motivational processes reflect the factors that instigate behavior and give it force and direction. Two major approaches to motivation are the drive-habit and expectancy-incentive approaches. According to drive-habit theory, deprivation of substances necessary for comfort or the presence of stimuli inducing discomfort increases drive. Increased drive provides a push for behavior; it is evidenced in a general rise in the level of activity. The direction behavior takes is determined by habit, or learned stimulus-response connections. Drive-habit theory has clearly demonstrated its usefulness, but it would seem hard pressed to account for the common observation that people sometimes willingly undergo hardships or deprivations and often appear to engage in activities for their own sake.

The expectancy-incentive approach to motivation suggests that organisms have the ability to anticipate, weigh, and evaluate the consequences of their actions. According to one expectancy-incentive approach, four factors combine multiplicatively to determine the strength and direction of behavior: (1) availability, or the accessibility of the behavior; (2) expectancy, or the subjective estimate that the behavior will lead to a given outcome or result; (3) incentive, or the subjective estimate of the value of the result; and (4) motive, or one's personal preference for a class of activities.

Learning can be described as a semipermanent behavior change that results from experience. Two major learning processes are classical conditioning and operant conditioning. In classical conditioning, repeated pairing of an initially neutral stimulus with a stimulus that reliably elicits a certain type of response results in the initially neutral stimulus later eliciting similar responses. In operant conditioning, a motivated organism responds in the presence of a stimulus. After it stumbles upon the "right" response, there is a change in environmental conditions that increases the likelihood that a similar response will again be made under similar stimulus conditions. Environmental changes that affect the likelihood of an immediately preceding response are called reinforcers. The skilled use of reinforcers can encourage the learning of new responses, help strengthen and maintain already learned responses, and help eliminate learned responses that are no longer wanted.

The processes described in this chapter are intra-individual, in the sense that they require only one behaving organism in good operating condition. Other

important basic processes are inter-individual, in that they require the physical
or psychological presence of another person as well. The next chapter emphasizes some of the basic ways in which the presence and actions of one
individual influence the behavior of another.

5.
Some Effects
of Others

Although intriguing and tempting, the old high-wheeled bicycles of the 1860s and 1870s did not achieve much popularity. They were dangerous, difficult to mount and dismount, as well as to ride, and out of the question for women. In the 1890s the introduction of the modern safety bike (those low wheelers so familiar to us today) completely changed the picture. Almost everyone could now ride safely and comfortably. A bicycle craze swept the country. In the United States, the Gay Nineties was the age of the bicycle.

The great bicycle craze has interest in its own right. But it also gave birth to what was perhaps the first experimental investigation of the effects that people have on one another. Triplett (1897) noted that people riding in the company of others seemed to ride faster than when they were riding alone. "Competition" seemed to speed them up. In competitive bicycle races, contestants pedaled faster than they did when simply practicing or racing against the clock.

To scientifically test his hypothesis that competition had an energizing effect, Triplett moved into the laboratory. There he had people wind line around a reel, either alone or in the presence of others who were engaged in the same task. Subjects working in the group setting were faster than subjects working alone. Triplett thus found, as he had expected, that the presence of other persons engaged in identical tasks seems to have a beneficial effect on individual performance.

In this chapter I will discuss some of the ways in which the presence and actions of others influence individual behavior. Cottrell (1972) points out that the *presence* of others is a precondition for all other forms of interpersonal behavior. Let's first examine the effects of the *presence* of others.

121

OTHERS AS ENERGIZERS: A SOURCE OF MOTIVATION

Modern psychologists would describe Triplett's pioneer work as an investigation of the effects of **coaction** on performance. Coaction refers to any case in which two or more individuals of the same species engage in identical tasks independently but in the presence of each other.

Since Triplett's time, many other investigators have probed the effects of coaction on performance (Cottrell, 1972). For example, G. W. Allport (1920, 1924) had subjects perform a number of tasks either alone, sitting in a cubicle, or in a group, sitting around a table. His subjects more speedily crossed out vowels on a printed page, completed more multiplications, thought of more associations to words, and reported more dramatic effects from an illusion when coactors were present than when working alone.

Chen (1937) observed 36 ants excavating nests. He observed them working alone, in groups of two, in groups of three, and then again working alone. Performance was assessed by the speed with which they began excavating and by the amount of work performed by each ant. Under coaction conditions the speed with which they began excavating increased by a factor of six and the amount excavated by a factor of three. The results were probably not due to the ants' learning from each other, for the second time each ant worked in isolation its performance was quite similar to its initial solo performance.

From studies such as Triplett's, Allport's, and Chen's comes fairly consistent evidence that coaction improves or facilitates performance. Indeed, **social facilitation** is a term often applied to this type of situation. Does social facilitation stem from a competitive urge, as Triplett suspected? Competition suggests some form of comparison of one's own performance with the performance of others. As Zajonc, Heingartner, and Herman (1969) point out, it is awkward to attribute a wide range of animals with the abilities and interests necessary for self-other comparisons. But assuming that animals such as ants are capable of the necessary "interpersonal" comparisons, there remains a flaw with the "competition" explanation. Even when the others present are not setting standards with their own rate of performance, they seem to affect individual performance. **Audience studies** examine the behavioral effects of the presence of passive spectators who are merely sitting and watching.

The Effects of an Audience on Performance

Meumann (1904) had subjects working in isolation lift small weights with their fingers. Their level of performance became quite stable. When Meumann looked in on them, however, their performance improved, with no apparent increase of effort on their part. About 60 years later Bergum and Lehr (1963) found similar results. Their subjects, observing a series of lights that generally went on and off in a set sequence, were told to indicate when a light failed to appear in sequence. When a spectator was present, their ability to detect these errors improved.

Travis (1925) examined the effects of passive spectators on performance at a pursuit rotor, which is a device used for testing hand-eye coordination and which is similar to a phonograph turntable. It contains a small spot, or target, perhaps the size of a dime, not far from the rim on the revolving disc. The subject is given a metal pointer, which he attempts to hold on the target. Performance is assessed by the percentage of time that the pointer is kept on the target as the disc revolves. Although the task looks and sounds simple, it is very difficult when the speed of the disc is increased. Travis first let his subjects practice alone until they could perform well. Then he had them perform in the presence of an audience. Once again, performance improved when the spectators were present.

The Effects of Coaction and Audience on Learning
New Responses

Each of the above studies suggests that the presence of spectators has largely beneficial or facilitative effects on behavior. But Zajonc (1966) notes that, in all these studies, the experimenter watched the subjects perform *simple* or *well-learned* responses. Triplett examined the effects of coaction on a very simple task. Meumann, Travis, and Bergum and Lehr trained their subjects until a high level of performance was reached.

But what if the responses studied are not well learned? According to Zajonc, the results will be quite different. Gates and Allee (1933) trained cockroaches to run down the arm of a maze to escape a bright light.[1] Roaches were trained

[1] In conducting cockroach experiments, it is advisable to wear shoes with pointed toes so you can take care of escaped subjects that hide in corners.

alone, in pairs, and in groups of three. The coacting cockroaches learned *less* efficiently than did the roaches learning in isolation. The inhibitory effects of coaction and audience conditions on learning in the cockroach have also been noted by Zajonc et al. (1969). Other studies suggest that coaction impairs learning in Australian parakeets (Allee & Masure, 1936) and in greenfinches (Klopfer, 1958).

Pessin (1933) had 60 subjects memorize lists of nonsense words. Each subject learned one list alone and another in the presence of an audience. The measure of learning was the number of times the subject had to go through the list before all words were memorized. For subjects working alone, this performance required an average of 9.85 trials; for those working in the presence of an audience, the average was 11.27 trials. Thus Pessin's subjects did *worse* when the audience was present. Later, Martens (1969) had subjects learn a complicated hand-eye coordination task involving hitting a moving target. Half the subjects learned this complex motor task alone and the other half in the presence of an audience. Again the presence of the spectators made it more difficult to learn.

On the other hand, once the subjects had learned Martens' task, the presence of the audience improved their performance.

Putting the Pieces Together

On the basis of such studies as those just discussed, Zajonc (1966) has concluded that *the presence of others facilitates the performance of simple or well-learned responses but inhibits the learning of new responses.* To account for this hypothesis, he provides an explanation couched in motivational terms and drawing heavily on the concept of drive.

Drive, as you will recall from the last chapter, is an energizer of behavior. Drive comes from many sources (food deprivation, water deprivation, a hailstorm, electric shocks, and so on), and Zajonc suggests that the presence of other, similar organisms also provides a source of drive. Thus organisms responding in the presence of other, similar organisms should respond more *forcefully* than do organisms responding in isolation.

Drive energizes behavior regardless of the correctness or appropriateness of the behavior. If a task is simple or well learned, the correct or right response will be performed. In this case the presence of passive spectators or coactors would energize this right response, producing an apparently **facilitative** or beneficial effect. But if the task is not well learned, the wrong response will be performed. This response, too, will be strengthened by the presence of spectators or coactors. Strengthening a wrong response produces an apparently detrimental effect on behavior and makes new learning difficult. In either case the response strengthened by the presence of others is referred to as the **dominant** response. Zajonc thus suggests that *the presence of others facilitates the emission of the dominant response.*

A dominant response is defined as the response *most likely to occur* in a given situation. For example, if the odds are 6 out of 10 that a person will drink beer when watching a televised ball game, beer drinking would be a dominant response. Other responses, such as drinking a cup of tea, would be weak or subordinate responses. Zajonc's hypothesis suggests that the presence of co-actors or spectators should strengthen the dominant response, raising the odds of beer consumption from 6 out of 10 to, say, 8 or 9 out of 10.

Although it is very difficult to discover which of a person's many responses to a situation is dominant, it is possible to teach people a number of different responses, one of which will be dominant. This can be accomplished by showing subjects different madeup or nonsense words different numbers of times. The word shown most often will prove to be a more likely or dominant response if the subject is later asked to recite all the words.

Zajonc and Sales (1966) showed subjects nonsense words. Each subject saw different words 1, 2, 4, 8, or 16 times and was asked to pronounce the words as they were presented. Later the subjects were again shown the words, but this time so quickly that it was difficult or impossible to see them. On some alleged presentations, there was just a flash of light; no word was actually presented. During this phase of the experiment, subjects guessed out loud the word they thought had been flashed. Half the subjects made these guesses in isolation and the other half in the presence of a spectator. When the spectator was present, subjects were more likely to make the dominant response—that is, report the word they had been shown most often in the first part of the experiment. In isolation, subjects reported a greater variety of words, which represented subordinate as well as dominant responses. The results thus confirmed the hypothesis that the emission of a dominant response is facilitated by the presence of others.

What are some implications of Zajonc's hypothesis? There is a clear one for weight watchers: eat alone and spare yourself the consequences of having your eating behavior further energized by the presence of others. There is also a message for people who clutch up when taking an exam. When knowledge is shaky, the drive induced by others strengthens wrong answers. Zajonc, with tongue in cheek, has offered a practical solution: study in isolation until the material is well learned, and then take the exam on stage, in front of a large audience.

SPATIAL BEHAVIOR

People occupy space, but not only the space displaced by their physical bodies. Each person's **personal space,** which has been described by psychologist Robert Sommer (1969), is an emotionally charged zone around him (sometimes likened to a soap bubble or aura) that helps to regulate the spacing of other individuals. Let us now consider how the *number of other people present, who they are, and their location with respect to the self* all contribute to regularities in behavior.

The presence and actions of others influence individual behavior.

To begin, let's ask a question about your own behavior. When you enter a large reading room in a library and do not spy an acquaintance, do you just sit down in the nearest empty seat? Or is your choice more complicated than that?

Sommer (1967) observed seating choices in the second-floor reading room of a university library. The room contained 18 large, heavy wood tables. Each table seated 12 people, six on each side. The lighting was uniformly good throughout the room, and the tables were spaced so that it was easy for people to walk by without disturbing others.

Over a three-month period the investigator arrived in the reading room each day when the library opened and for three-quarters of an hour recorded where people sat as they entered the room. The seat selections of the first entrants are particularly interesting, since these persons had the widest choice available. About eight of the first ten people who entered alone sat at a "new," or completely unoccupied, table. Of the *pairs* of people who entered among the first ten people, again, about 80 percent chose an initially empty table. Clearly in both cases the preference was for unoccupied tables. Where will latecomers sit after there is already a person or a couple at each table? They will, of course, sit at an occupied table, but Sommer's results suggest that they will sit *as far as possible* from the table's other occupants so that eye contact is minimized. Thus, if one person is sitting at one end of the table, the newcomer is likely to sit at the other end of the table, leaving many seats (and perhaps the width of the table) in between. Obviously these library users wanted to keep their distance from the other people present.

Territorial Defense

Finding a seat away from others does not guarantee continued personal privacy. As the library fills, a stranger may sit nearby. However, Sommer (1967) and Sommer and Becker (1969) describe special techniques, called techniques of territorial defense, that people use to keep others away. One example involves the use of offensive displays (such as looking studious and busy or perhaps even glaring, snarling, and nose picking). Another involves staking out physical boundaries around the area that is to remain private.

In his observations of arctic wolves, Mowat (1963) observed that a wolf will mark a piece of territory that he seems to consider his by urinating on the boundary. Other wolves, catching the scent, will keep out. The staking-out process used by library visitors may be somewhat less dramatic, but the effects are similar. A table occupant can establish a clearly detectable physical boundary by covering the tabletop with such things as books or the contents of a purse. For extra protection, coats, sweaters, or briefcases can be placed on chairs directly to the right and left. Feet can be propped up on the chair directly across, keeping people away from there too. A library user skilled at territorial defense can effectively keep other potential users away from a four-person table even during rush hour. In these situations people in effect erect "keep out" signs, which others tend to respect.

But what if a newcomer is insensitive to these signs and insists on infringing on someone's personal space? Having one's personal space violated appears to be an aversive stimulus. When others move in close, people often become uncomfortable. Although fairly crowded conditions can be tolerated, people may leave when there is a true squeeze. This result is shown in two experiments by Felipe and Sommer (1966). One was conducted in a mental hospital, the other took place in a library.

In the mental hospital the experimenter chose for a subject a male who was sitting alone and not engaged in any clearly defined activity (such as reading). The experimenter walked over and sat next to this victim. If the victim shifted slightly, so did the experimenter, keeping the distance between them at about 6 inches. Control subjects were patients sitting alone who were not crowded by the experimenter.

A comparison of the length of time subjects remained seated after the experimenter sat down next to them with the length of time uncrowded control subjects remained seated clearly showed the effects of the immediate presence of the experimenter: the experimental subjects got up and moved, whereas the control subjects remained seated. Similar results were found in the library study, in which the experimenter again maintained a distance of only 6 inches from the victim.

This research suggests that, in certain situations, people try to maintain some distance between themselves and strangers. The situations involved were (1) studying in a library and (2) sitting alone with one's thoughts in a mental hospital. But in these two situations interaction with others, especially strangers, is discouraged. Under different conditions in which social interaction is encouraged, people may tend to reduce or minimize the distance and the barriers between themselves and others.

In cafeterias, for example, Sommer (1965) found that people preferred to minimize distance for better communication. At square or rectangular tables, corner seating was popular. When people occupy adjacent seats at a corner, they are physically close, can see each other, and find it easy to communicate. The side-by-side position also indicates closeness. People in friendly, cooperative moods may prefer to sit side-by-side, whereas under less cordial conditions they may prefer to sit across from each other, separated by the barrier of the table. Other variables, such as social status, also play a part. Lott and Sommer (1967) found that college students choosing seats at a table prefer to sit close to equal-status people (such as classmates) but maintain their distance from superiors (such as professors) and inferiors (such as flunking freshmen). Other investigators have suggested that culture, interpersonal relations, emotional states, and personality influence the distance people maintain from each other.

An interesting outgrowth of research on spatial behavior has been a recognition that the man-made environment is not always engineered so that people can arrange themselves vis-à-vis others in the way that they want. In a formal living room, conversation may be curtailed because the seats are too far from each other. According to Sommer, a most notorious example of bad architectural engineering is the arrangement of seats in many airport lobbies. People often show up at airports in small groups. For informal conversations, small clusters of seats are ideal. Within the clusters people can arrange themselves in patterns that promote the kind and amount of communication they desire. But instead of such clusters, seats in airport waiting rooms are more likely to be arranged row upon row, as in a theater. Occupants cannot easily see their partners, and pairs of people may find themselves tightly sandwiched in next to strangers. Although this arrangement certainly does not prohibit casual conversations, it does not exactly encourage them, either.

LEARNING FROM OTHERS

The sheer presence of others influences motivation. The spatial location of others influences where someone will sit or stand. Now let us consider how people are affected by the *observed behavior* of others.

Not too long ago Bandura, Blanchard, and Ritter (1969) advertised in newspapers for snake-phobic people—that is, people with a strong, irrational fear of snakes. A number of persons responded. Some complained that their fear of snakes was so prominent that their activities were highly curtailed and their

People learn from others.

enjoyment of life consequently diminished. For example, they would not hike, camp, hunt, or live or work in the country for fear of encountering a snake.

First the investigators measured the strength of the phobia by means of a behavioral test of snake-avoidance behavior. This test involved several tasks requiring increasing intimacy with a large but harmless king snake. For example, an easy task was approaching the caged snake and looking at it; a somewhat harder task was touching the snake with a gloved hand; the hardest task was allowing the snake to crawl around in the lap while the hands were held still at the sides. Forty-eight people who flunked this initial test miserably were used in the experiment and assigned to various experimental and control conditions.

One group of experimental subjects watched a half-hour color film showing young children, teen-agers, and adults having progressively more intimate contacts with snakes. The film began with individuals handling plastic snakes and ended with them caressing the large king snake, draping it around their necks, and letting it slither over their bodies.

A second group of experimental subjects first watched through a window as an experimenter in an adjoining room played with a snake. Later the subject was invited to join the experimenter and snake. The experimenter, still playing with the snake, encouraged the subject to do the same. They began with relatively easy tasks, such as just touching the snake, and proceeded to more frightening activities.

Afterward subjects were again put through the earlier behavioral test. Subjects in the control group scored as poorly as before. Subjects in the two experimental groups described above performed much more fearlessly and showed a substantial reduction of snake avoidance. They also showed an improved attitude toward reptiles in general.

What happened in this experiment? People with a strong fear of snakes became less fearful after watching other persons engage in friendly activities with a snake. These snake-phobics *learned from others*, and what they learned was to be less afraid of snakes. This study is an intriguing demonstration of **social learning.** Two basic processes that contribute to learning from others are *imitation* and *social reinforcement*.

Imitation

People learn by watching others and by imitating them. **Imitation** occurs when a follower copies the behavior of a **model.** Just about any behavior can be imitated. Mussen and Rutherford (1961) and Hanratty, Liebert, Morris, and Fernandez (1969) have found that children will imitate aggressive acts (Chapter Eleven). Bryan and Test (1967) have found that adults will imitate prosocial, helping behavior (Chapter Fourteen). In the preceding study by Bandura et al. (1969), imitation certainly contributed to the lessening of adults' fears of snakes, and in another experiment (Bandura & Menlove, 1968) children became less fearful of dogs after watching films of models playing with dogs.

Imitative behavior is not limited to humans. Turner (1964) constructed a mechanical hen. Newborn chicks watched this fake hen peck at grains of different colors. Some chicks saw it peck at orange grains; other chicks saw it peck at green grains. Later the chicks showed a tendency to peck at the same color grain that they had seen the mechanical hen choose. Imitation has also been found in studies using rats, cats, goldfish, monkeys, and many other species.

Sometimes, too much behavior is interpreted as an example of imitation. If two people slap themselves in the presence of each other, it may simply mean that each is infested with insects and neither is paying much attention to the activities of the other. Yet some psychological processes that seem complicated and mysterious can be accounted for rather parsimoniously in terms of imitation. Much of what passes for identification may have its basis in imitation. Identification occurs when an individual assumes the characteristics or attributes of someone else. For example, children take on many of the qualities of their parents. As a result, the person identified with and the person doing the identifying may end up with strikingly similar personalities. But this similarity consists of the two acting in similar ways.

Why Do People Imitate?

One theory of imitation suggests that it is learned through operant conditioning. People and many animals imitate because they have been reinforced for doing so in the past. Usually a model is a competent performer whose behavior is rewarded. It is only reasonable that the follower will expect to be rewarded for behaving in the same way. Thus, suppose that the model kicks a stubborn candy machine and makes it dispense purchased candy. The follower deposits a coin and then kicks the machine in the same way. The imitative response of the follower is likely to be strengthened when his own candy bar is dispensed. Of course, reinforcement is not an inevitable consequence of imitation. The model could have dislodged the very last candy bar in the machine or hopelessly fouled up the mechanism with his kick. But imitative responses are often reinforced, and, as you saw in the last chapter, frequent but not inevitable reinforcement can make a form of behavior (such as imitation) highly resistant to extinction.

It is by no means clear that *all* imitative behavior is learned. In Turner's study of newborn chicks, for example, it is difficult to identify a learning process. On the other hand, quite a few studies show that imitation can be taught. Miller and Dollard (1941) had an adult model perform simple tasks, such as going to a certain box and finding a piece of candy. Children were rewarded for imitating the adult by acting in the same way or for *counterimitating* the adult by acting in an opposite way. Later, when new tasks were introduced, children who had earlier been reinforced for imitation again imitated, and children who had been rewarded for counterimitation again counterimitated.

In additional studies, Miller and Dollard found that rats, too, could be taught to imitate. Furthermore, having learned to imitate under one set of conditions, the rats repeated the response under other conditions. For example, rats taught to imitate to get food when they were hungry also imitated to get water when they were thirsty. They also learned to adapt to different models. Rats first learned to imitate *white* rat models. Later, placed in a similar situation but with a *black* rat for a model, they immediately displayed the tendency to imitate. Apparently Miller and Dollard's rats showed a form of intelligent color blindness that seems less common among humans.

When Do People Imitate?

Miller and Dollard have proposed that people imitate when they do not have the skills necessary to "read" or understand environmental conditions and to respond competently on their own. Under such circumstances they turn to successful models who can interpret the situation for them.

Consider the fresh recruit's first day at the front lines. He is a replacement moving with a battle-hardened unit. Artillery shells shriek overhead; each one sounds equally dangerous to him. But at the sound of a certain one, all the veterans jump into a ditch. The recruit, who keeps a close eye on his comrades, does the same. He is thus spared the disastrous effects of a nearby explosion.

As a beginner, a new combatant is unable to distinguish among the various rushes, roars, and whines overhead, whereas the more sophisticated, seasoned veterans can make these complex discriminations. The recruit can, however, easily understand the cues emitted by the other soldiers when they jump into a ditch. In effect, the veterans have read the indecipherable environmental cues for him and provided him with simpler cues that he can understand. Over time the follower will probably learn to interpret the situation directly and to perform successfully in the absence of models. For example, toward the end of his combat tour the former new recruit could be sent out on a solitary mission and have at least some chance of survival.

Who Is Imitated?

According to Miller and Dollard, there are four general classes of people who are imitated. They enjoy their position because they are very good at doing things. In effect, we can trust them to read environmental cues correctly.

First, there are *superiors in the age-grade hierarchy*. People who are older and have had more experience are seen as having a greater ability to understand conditions and respond correctly. Second, there are *superiors in the social-ranking system.* They are seen as competent because they are more successful than are people of equal or lower status. Third, there are *superiors in the intelligence-ranking system.* Their intelligence reflects a better aptitude for effective performance. Fourth, there are the *superior technicians in any field*. By imitating some of the behaviors of doctors, plumbers, lawyers, and television repairmen, we can accomplish some of what they can do without having to undergo their long, rigorous, specialized training.

Yet people are not always discriminating about which aspects of their superiors' behavior they should imitate. A student seeking academic success might imitate the study habits of a proven scholar. But if he were unselective, he might merely ape the scholar's dress and wear whatever type of eyeglasses that happen to be considered intellectual that year.

A consideration of which imitative behavior is likely to be rewarded suggests that people will learn to imitate the successful. The model's competence has been found to be important (Rosenbaum & Tucker, 1962; Zajonc, 1955), but it is not the only consideration. Baron (1970) found that attractiveness of the model was also an important factor in imitation. In his experiment, adult subjects were provided with either of two models. One was made to seem attractive by appearing similar to the subject and by pretending to like the subject; the other model was made unattractive by seeming unlike the subject and by pretending to dislike the subject. Baron's subjects then played a horse-race game with the benefit of seeing the attractive or unattractive models' gambling choices and having some idea about how well these choices worked. Early in the game, successfulness alone was sufficient to increase imitation. However, in the overall pattern of results, attractiveness of the model was also important. If the model was attractive *and* competent, imitation further increased. On the other hand, if the attractive model was incompetent, imitation decreased. This did not happen in the case of the unattractive model. This suggests, perhaps, that potential followers watch attractive models a bit more closely than they do unattractive models.

Others as a Source of Reinforcement

Many reinforcers are administered by an impersonal environment, as when someone must kick a candy machine "just so" to make it dispense goodies. But in our complex and well-populated society, many, if not most, reinforcers are administered by other people. Following Zajonc (1966), reinforcers dispensed by other people may be defined as **social reinforcers.**

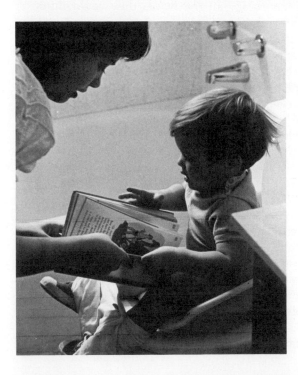

Reinforcers dispensed by other people are social reinforcers.

Social reinforcers fall into two broad categories. The first consists of reinforcers that are not inherently or intrinsically social but happen on a particular occasion to be dispensed by another person. In this category would be included the glass of milk a mother gives her child or the sack of grain a farmer gives his sharecropper. The second category consists of social reinforcers that can come *only* from another person: approval, agreement, love, affection. They are *inherently* social and cannot be procured from an impersonal environment. It is on these latter reinforcers that we will concentrate our attention.

Social reinforcers do not seem to differ from other reinforcers. Some, such as smiles, nods, friendly glances, and verbal approval (Good! Right on! Yes, I see!), serve to strengthen the preceding behavior. Others, such as rejection and statements of disagreement or disapproval (Oh no! Good Grief! @#*$!!!), tend to weaken or eliminate the preceding behavior. Such reinforcers are extremely easy to use, and the person whose behavior is changed may not know the reason why.

Greenspoon (1955) asked subjects to say all the words they could think of. Using "Mmm-Hmmm" as a reinforcer, he reinforced some subjects for emitting plural nouns and others for emitting words that were not plural nouns. When "Mmm-Hmmm" followed plural nouns, there was an increase in the frequency with which plural nouns were emitted. Similarly, when "Mmm-Hmmm" followed words that were not plural nouns, the frequency of this type of response was increased. Greenspoon interviewed his subjects afterward and found that, during the experiment, none of his subjects had been aware of his attempts to manipulate their rate of responding. Centers (1963) has also successfully manipulated the rate with which various utterances are made. Centers' study is particularly intriguing, because his subjects did not even realize that they were participating in an experiment. They thought they were waiting for the experiment to begin in the next room.

Social reinforcement can influence not only the *rate* at which people speak but also *what* they say. Thus statements of attitude or opinion may sometimes be changed as a result of the use of social approval. Singer (1961) influenced subjects' responses to an attitude questionnaire. Krasner, Knowles, and Ullmann (1965) demonstrated that attitudes toward doctors and medical science could be enhanced by social reinforcement. Most usefully of all, Cialdini and Insko (1969) found that, under some conditions, at least, it was possible to use social approval to influence stated opinions about experimental and clinical psychology!

Apparently the person who is administering social approval does not need to be physically present in order to influence stated opinions. Hildum and Brown (1956) conducted a telephone survey and, through social approval, were able to elicit statements for and against a particular philosophy of education. In this study two types of reinforcers were used: "Mmm-Hmmm" and "Good." "Good" had a clear-cut effect on expressed opinion, but "Mmm-Hmmm" did not. The authors suggested that "Mmm-Hmmm" is vague and ambiguous when heard over the telephone, although it may be an effective reinforcer in a face-to-face situation in which it is generally coupled with smiles, nods, and other easily understood forms of approval.

Insko (1965) also tried to manipulate the favorability of expressed opinions during a telephone interview. In addition, his study probed whether the effects of such approval would endure beyond the immediate interview.

Members of Insko's psychology classes at the University of Hawaii were contacted by telephone and asked if they agreed or disagreed with a series of statements concerning the creation of a springtime "Aloha Week." (Aloha Week could best be characterized as a carnival.) Half of Insko's subjects were reinforced with "Good!" for expressing favorable opinions about Aloha Week; the remainder of the subjects were reinforced for voicing unfavorable opinions. Consistent with Hildum and Brown, Insko found an immediate effect of social reinforcement: during the telephone interview, subjects reinforced for "pro" opinions were more likely to give additional "pro" responses.

A week later the subjects received a questionnaire containing a number of propositions about local issues. Included was a key item suggesting that Aloha Week be established. Subjects who had been reinforced a week earlier for "pro" statements were more favorable toward the creation of the Aloha Week. An implication of Insko's study is that the effects of social approval may persevere over time.

So far the evidence has suggested that social reinforcers can influence verbal behavior—that is, what people say. Yet social approval can also influence what people do.

It has long been recognized that social approval may have a great deal to do with such important forms of behavior as aggression (Bandura & Walters, 1963). For example, Davitz (1952) rated the behavior of children playing in groups. Half the groups were given seven brief training sessions during which social approval followed competitive and aggressive responses. The remaining groups underwent sessions in which social approval followed constructive and cooperative behavior. Ratings of the children's subsequent behavior suggested that children who received social approval for aggression tended to be more competitive and destructive in their play; children who had been praised for cooperation were more friendly and constructive. The effects of social reinforcement on overt behavior are examined repeatedly throughout this text, and we shall return to the Davitz study in Chapter Twelve.

Once social approval has encouraged some form of behavior, how can that behavior be weakened or eliminated? All the laws of reinforcement described in the last chapter would seem to apply. For example, one way socially reinforced behavior can be weakened or extinguished is by withholding the reinforcement.

During a series of interviews in which the respondents simply talked without any prodding or specific questioning, Adams and Hoffman (1960) used

"Mmm-Hmmm" to reinforce self-reference statements—that is, statements including such words as *I, me, my,* or *myself.* The experiment was divided into three parts. In the first 10-minute phase the experimenter established the rate with which the subject naturally made self-reference statements. During the second 10-minute phase self-reference statements were followed by "Mmm-Hmmm." During the final or extinction phase, which lasted half an hour, all reinforcement was withdrawn.

During the reinforcement phase Adams and Hoffman found a dramatic increase in the rate of self-reference statements. During the extinction phase the rate of self-reference statements dropped significantly during the first 10 minutes, but there was no appreciable further decrease during the last 20 minutes because the number of *all* verbalizations decreased. Subjects acted as if the withdrawal of reinforcement were quite punishing. Many subjects became upset, and some were quite angry with the interviewer.

*Controlling Behavior through Social Approval:
Some Implications*

Occasionally, when an unwelcome visitor comes to my office, I find myself smiling, nodding, and saying "Mmm-Hmmm," "Yes," and "I see" while I am paying no real attention at all. In this case I am reinforcing verbalizations and prolonging a visit that I'd just as soon terminate. The use of social approval often seems automatic and unconscious, because we have been well conditioned to make reinforcing responses. Adams and Hoffman's study highlights the tensions that arise when reinforcement is withdrawn, and such tensions are unpleasant. When we say "Yes," "I see," and "Good," these tensions are decreased. Thus, when we reinforce others, we are likely to find our own reinforcing behavior reinforced!

It appears that the unconscious use of social approval may control the course of any conversation. This situation poses problems for psychologists who obtain their data through talking to people. Three areas in which this problem becomes particularly salient are psychotherapy, psychological testing, and survey interviewing.

The clinical psychologist or psychiatrist may reinforce verbal behavior or "symptoms" that are consistent with his particular diagnosis and theoretical viewpoint, at the same time extinguishing verbal behavior that might be highly significant for understanding the case. For example, the therapist who believes that people's problems stem from early childhood may reinforce statements consistent with this approach and extinguish statements consistent with alternative interpretations. Moreover, some of the apparent cures that psychotherapists obtain may not reflect a real change in underlying personality but only a superficial change in verbal behavior. Hildum and Brown (1956, p. 108) venture that "... perhaps a patient could even be brought to an appearance of mental health through the encouragement of healthy utterances."

In psychological testing, the problem of the unwitting use of reinforcers arises whenever there are verbal or gestural cues passed between the examiner and his client. Many personality and intelligence tests are administered in a conversational setting. Unless the examiner takes due care not to administer social reinforcement, the results of the tests may be highly inaccurate. For instance, an examiner, charmed by a not-too-bright child, may unwittingly prod him into giving the right answers so that his test scores will not be so low that he will be committed to an institution. Nuthmann (1957) has shown how verbal reinforcement affects performance on personality tests. She administered a paper-and-pencil test to assess "acceptance of self" to 420 students. For some of the items on the test, agreement indicated self-acceptance; for others, disagreement indicated self-acceptance. Subjects who scored very low took the test again, but this time it was administered on an individual basis. Nuthmann reinforced each self-accepting statement with "Good!" In this way she elicited an increasing number of such statements from her subjects, even though they were unaware of the reinforcement at the time.

As suggested by the opinion-shaping studies of Krasner et al. (1965), Hildum and Brown (1956), Singer (1961), Insko (1965), and Cialdini and Insko (1969), the problem of unintentionally reinforcing verbal responses is particularly acute for the public-opinion pollster. It is well known that interviewers often return with information that reflects their own personal biases and prejudices; their unconscious use of reinforcers may partially account for this result. At one time I was interviewed by a representative of a major automobile company who made very clear the answers he wanted to hear. Although the use of social reinforcers may result in an interviewer's obtaining information that makes him *feel good*, it does not provide him with information that is *factually correct*.

GROUP PRESSURES AND STANDARDS

In many situations a person will find himself in the presence of two or more affiliated people, and these other people may simultaneously influence his behavior. In this case it may be said that a group is contributing to his behavior.

In many situations a person will find himself in the presence of two or more affiliated people, and these other people may simultaneously influence his behavior.

There appear to be two major ways in which groups affect individual behavior: through external pressures and through internal pressures. Both have their origins in a set of **standards,** or criteria for behavior. First, these standards will establish how members of the group will evaluate and attempt to influence the individual; hence they result in *external pressures.* In this case groups are believed to apply direct social pressures for the person to act in certain ways: they reward him for living up to established standards and engaging in approved behavior and punish him for failing to do so. Second, group standards are believed to dictate how the person will evaluate his own behavior; hence they result in *internal pressures.* In this case the group's standards are learned or *internalized* by the person. If he knows that he is living up to these standards, he will feel satisfied and maintain his behavior; if he knows that he is not, he will probably feel dissatisfied and a bit guilty and will try to improve his level of performance.

Agreeing with Others

Have you ever stared at a lone star on a very dark night and been surprised when it seemed to move or jiggle? There was nothing wrong with you; it is quite common to perceive a stationary light against a dark backdrop as being in motion. This apparent motion is called the **autokinetic effect.**

Sherif (1936) sat subjects across from a stationary point of light in a darkened room. He asked them to announce when the light began to move and how many inches it moved. Each subject took part in four daily sessions and made 100 judgments per session. Some subjects made judgments alone and then with three other subjects. Other subjects made judgments with three other subjects and then alone. Sherif found that solitary judgments preceding group judgments differed considerably from one another. However, during subsequent judgments within the group setting, the estimates made by different people within a group tended to converge and become quite similar, although the point of convergence was not the same within different groups. Furthermore, the process of making judgments in the group influenced subsequent individual judgments, for these later judgments fell within the range established by the group.

Sherif provided experimental evidence of **conformity, which refers to uniformities in acting and reacting within a group.** Are these similarities somehow caused by the group? To claim this, it is necessary to show (as Sherif did) that there are both similarities *within* a group and differences *between* groups. Differences between groups suggest that the uniformities within groups are due to specific properties of the group.

It is not particularly taxing to locate cases outside the laboratory in which there are similarities within groups and differences between groups. In the military, officers share views and opinions, and enlisted men share different views and opinions. In many other institutions, such as mental hospitals, boarding schools, and prisons, there are uniformities among staff and uniformities among inmates.

Striking evidence of conformity also comes from studies of attitudes. Newcomb (1943) found that college students' political beliefs became more similar the longer they remained in a college that fostered liberalism. Seniors had more uniformly liberal political outlooks than did freshmen, and the political attitudes of freshmen became more uniformly liberal as they progressed through the college years.

A study by Festinger, Schachter, and Back (1950) likewise suggests that people who associate with each other develop uniformities of opinion. These researchers compared two living units at an Eastern college. One unit consisted of small cottages clustered in U-shaped courts; the other consisted of apartments within single two-story structures. Opinions about a university housing council were assessed. Although overall there were differences of opinion concerning this council, there tended to be uniformity of opinion within a given U-shaped court. This was not so true of the people living in the two-story structures. Because of the physical layout of the housing units, people living in the U-shaped courts had considerable social contact with others in the court, but people who lived in the apartments (which did not face each other or were even located back-to-back) had much less contact with their neighbors. In effect, within a cottage cluster there was a group and hence group pressures to conform. In the apartment setting, where physical barriers kept people apart, there was no real group and no pressures to conform.

If certain behavior results largely from pressures to live up to the group's criteria or standards, there should be changes in behavior as a person moves from one group with one set of standards to a new group with a new set of standards. A study by Lieberman (1956) highlights these changes. He appraised the pro-union and pro-management sympathies of workers at a large factory. Some of these workers were then promoted to managerial positions, and others were elected union officials. Those who entered management became more favorably inclined toward management, whereas those who became union stewards became more sympathetic toward the union. Later some of the men who had changed positions were returned to the assembly line. (The union stewards were elected for only one year, and a business recession forced the demotion of some newly appointed foremen.) Back on the assembly line, the stewards became less pro-union and the foremen less pro-management. Thus Lieberman's study suggested that a person's attitudes will change as he moves from one group to another but will revert if he is again placed in his initial group.

Yielding to a False Majority

One of the most startling findings in psychology is that conformity can lead a person to abandon the evidence of his own senses. Asch (1952) presented subjects with a drawn line and asked them to indicate which of three comparison lines was the same length. With the lines Asch presented, this task was easy; when subjects made these judgments alone, they were correct about 93 percent of the time.

Other subjects, however, made their judgments within a group of seven or eight others. Unknown to the subjects, these other participants were **confeder-**

ates—that is, specially trained accomplices of the experimenter. Each person was asked to announce his judgment out loud, and the real subject found himself among the last to report. It had been previously arranged that, on some of the trials, all confederates would unanimously make an incorrect judgment. The subject, coming last, had to weigh the objective evidence before his eyes against the wrong but unanimous judgments of all these other people. About a third of the subjects abandoned the evidence of their senses and conformed with this false majority.

Subsequently Asch simplified the judgmental task by making the differences between the standard line and the incorrect comparisons so great that, when subjects made solitary judgments, they were correct 98 percent of the time. But even under these conditions the false but unanimous reports of the majority led to incorrect judgments by the subjects about 28 percent of the time. This decrease in accuracy is the measure of the extent to which the subjects yielded—that is, abandoned the physical evidence in favor of the reports of the false majority.

Asch also varied the size of the false majority. Subjects were preceded by 0, 1, 2, 3, 4, 8, or 16 confederates. When the subjects made the judgments alone, there was an average of only .08 error. When preceded by 1 confederate, the average number of errors was increased to .33, a very negligible increment. (When there is just one other person, it is easy to believe that he is wrong.) When 2 confederates preceded the subject, the average error increased to 1.53, and when 3 confederates preceded with false reports, the error rate rose sharply to 4.00. When the subject was preceded by 4, 8, or 16 confederates, the error rate did not increase appreciably beyond that figure. Thus, up to a point, an increase in the number of people making false reports increased conformity; but beyond that point, increasing the size of the false majority did not add much to the effect. All of these studies suggest that, when people are preceded by others who unanimously voice false reports, they will be strongly tempted to conform.

In a variation of these experiments, Asch had one confederate serve as a partner for the subject by making correct judgments while all the other confederates made wrong ones. In one condition this partner made a correct judgment on every trial. In another condition the partner began making correct judgments but deserted the subject halfway through. In the third condition the eventual partner initially agreed with the false majority but later made correct judgments. Under all conditions the presence of a partner decreased yielding to the false majority. The full-time partner decreased the yielding throughout the session. When the partner deserted halfway through, the subject began making correct judgments but started conforming when the partner deserted. Finally, when the partner was gained halfway through the session, the subject seemed to gain the courage to defy the majority by giving the correct answer. Apparently, having one person in agreement (at least when there is good evidence that the majority is wrong) provides the necessary support to defy the majority.

Informational and Normative Social Influences

Deutsch and Gerard (1955) distinguish between two kinds of social influences that may contribute to conformity: *informational social influences* and *normative social influences.*

Informational social influences impinge on the individual to accept information from others as evidence of reality. These forces should be greatest when the person is young or unskilled or when the task is ambiguous or difficult. Deutsch and Gerard presented an Asch-type judgmental task but made it difficult by having subjects work on the basis of memory rather than on the basis of visually present lines; in this situation conformity was increased. Tuddenham (1959) found that children tend to be more conforming than adults; similar findings have come from the literature on suggestibility. Kiesler and Kiesler (1969) cite numerous studies suggesting that people are more likely to conform when the task is difficult or when they are relatively unskilled.

Normative social influences impinge on the individual to conform with the anticipations or expectations of others within the group. Pressures are thus applied on him to "go along" with the group and adopt their customs, habits, and accepted ways of behaving. Nonconformists may be subjected to arguments, ridicule, and, ultimately, rejection from the group.

Schachter (1951) explored some of the properties of a group that may contribute to the intensity of its reactions to a nonconformer or **deviant.** First, he hypothesized that, if the members of a group are closely tied together by mutual rewards and satisfactions (a cohesive group[2]), the group will react more unfavorably to the nonconformer than if the group constituted a loose-knit aggre-

[2]Cohesiveness refers to the "groupiness" of a group. A more formal definition is offered in Chapter Thirteen.

gation of people (a noncohesive group). Accordingly, in groups such as the family, bomber crews, bands of trapeze artists, and Siamese twins, who depend highly on each other for satisfactions, there would be greater pressures for conformity than in, say, a group of strangers waiting to be served at a restaurant.

Schachter also noted that, within a group, some rules or criteria are more important than others. For example, in a band of trapeze artists it may be customary to drive red sports cars, but it is more than customary to appear on time for performances and to behave in a rigidly prescribed fashion when climbing a high wire or catching someone who jumps from another trapeze. Schachter thus also hypothesized that the reaction of the group will be intensified if the deviant breaks a rule that is highly *relevant* to its interests, purposes, and goals.

He recruited students to participate in one of four different clubs. They volunteered to join any club that Schachter cared to assign but indicated preferences among the four clubs.

Two *high-cohesive* clubs comprised members who indicated an interest in the club to which they were assigned. The rationale was that within an attractive club the members would be banded together by participation in activities they all found fun and exciting. Two *low-cohesive* clubs consisted of recruits who had been shunted off from their first choices into a club that was, from their perspective, less attractive. In all clubs there was a discussion of the case of a juvenile delinquent, Johnny, who was awaiting sentence for a minor crime. For one high- and one low-cohesive club, this discussion was *relevant* to the avowed purposes of the club (in one case discussing human relations cases; in the other, discussing newsworthy material). For the remaining high- and low-cohesive clubs (which had the avowed purposes of previewing movies and preauditing radio programs), this case was *irrelevant* or incidental to group interests and purposes.

After hearing about Johnny, the discussants were asked to offer opinions as to how the judge should dispose of the case. Should Johnny be put in a warm, supportive environment and given love and understanding? Should he be sent to reform school? Or should the judge's reaction fall between the two extremes?

In each session, club members were able to attain some degree of consensus. But within each club, unknown to the legitimate volunteers, were three confederates who had been given special instructions. One confederate, the *mode,* voiced views that were compatible with the consensus achieved by the legitimate members of the club. The second confederate, or *slider*, initially adopted a position of deviance but let himself be brought into line by the arguments of the legitimate members. The third confederate was an unshakable *deviant* who maintained a position of nonconformity throughout the sessions. Schachter questioned how the rest of the group would react to these confederates.

After the discussion participants completed forms indicating which club members they would like to see assigned to important and unimportant committee positions within the club and which persons they would like to see remain in the club "if it became necessary to reduce the size of the club or assign one of the members to another club." Schachter's results suggested that each club tended to reject the deviant but not the mode or the slider. Furthermore, in the more cohesive clubs the rejection was greater, as shown by a tendency to nominate the deviant for expulsion and for unimportant committee assignments. Finally, by the measure of committee nominations, the intensity of the rejection is greater when the issue on which the deviant nonconforms is relevant. Acceptance and nomination to important committees, of course, are positive reinforcers, whereas rejection and assignment to unimportant positions are tantamount to negative reinforcers.

Reference Groups

When a person looks to group standards for guidelines in evaluating his own attitudes, habits, and level of performance, he is said to be responding to a **reference group**. A **positive reference group** is one whose standards the individual endorses and attempts to meet. A **negative reference group** is one whose standards he disavows. For most people the police may provide a positive reference group, whereas a criminal syndicate provides a negative reference group. For other people the situation might be quite the reverse.

Reference groups, like **membership groups** (the groups to which the person belongs), contribute heavily to conformity (Siegal & Siegal, 1957). Yet it is not necessary for a reference group or its representatives to be physically present to affect the person's behavior. Rather, reference-group standards are *internalized* and referred to in the appropriate situation. Thus there need be no other soldiers present (or even any civilians) for the sentry at Buckingham Palace to conduct himself in a precise military manner. The standards required have been well learned, and it is sufficient for him to know how other guardsmen *would* react *if* they saw him stumble or sneeze.

Reference groups and membership groups may or may not coincide. In the case of the guardsmen at Buckingham Palace, the guards' unit would provide both a membership and a reference group. On the other hand, people may adopt the standards of groups to which they do not belong (the Confederate Army, the Christian Martyrs, the Russian Revolutionaries, the FBI) or find themselves members of groups whose standards they do not accept. This latter case is illustrated by the soldiers who in 1969 mutinied by staging a sit-down strike and singing peace songs. Clearly they were not trying to live up to the standards of their military unit when they undertook this activity.

People refer to the standards of others when evaluating their own behavior.

Multiple Reference Groups

There is no *one* reference group for any individual. Each person probably has as many reference groups as there are distinct parts to his or her life. For example, when I teach or write, I evaluate my performance by comparing it with that of my professional colleagues. When I work on my old car, my reference group is the old-car collectors of America (and particularly a group of local buffs). When I am performing as the manager of my bachelor pad, I evaluate myself by the standards of a still different group. Sometimes standards conflict. Spending half my time on my old car would make the members of my professional reference group wince, but the old-car buffs of America would consider it a wise investment.

Stouffer (1949) examined people's reactions to a situation in which they were forced to choose between the incompatible standards of different groups. Interviewees were asked to imagine what they would do if, working as monitors during an important examination, they caught someone cheating. What would they do if the cheater were a stranger? What would they do if the cheater were a friend? The two sets of standards were those of the authorities and (in the case of catching a friend cheating) those of a small group of friends. In this latter case, if the subject subscribed to the standards of one group, he could not maintain the standards of the other.

The interviewees recognized that under no conditions could the authorities condone cheating. The authorities' standards clearly called for reporting the cheater, which is exactly what the interviewees said they would do—in the case of the stranger. But discovering a friend cheating is a more difficult situation, because it raises conflicting standards that prohibit hurting a friend. In this situation the interviewees said that, if they thought they would not be discovered by the authorities, they would show their friends leniency and not report them. However, this leniency was conditional. If they believed the authorities would discover that they had seen their friends cheat, they might go ahead and turn them in, friendship or not. Stouffer's study does not provide very strong evidence. Yet it does suggest that, if someone is caught in the middle between conflicting standards, he may adopt a *compromise position* designed to minimize the punishments received from either of the two groups.

Such conflicts are rare, however, because the different sets of standards of different groups are unlikely to be equally important to a person at a given time. To the individual out carousing on Saturday night, the standards of a church group are probably not heavily weighted; but when he attends church the next morning, the standards of his fellow hell-raisers may be fervently disavowed. The immediate situation brings one or the other set of standards to the fore.

Charters and Newcomb (1958) influenced responses to a series of attitude statements by varying the salience of the respondent's religious reference group. Thirteen hundred Roman Catholic students at a multidenominational university were randomly assigned to three conditions. In one condition the students attended class at the usual time and place. In the second condition the students met in a different room but were given no explanation for the change. Under the third condition the students also met in a different room but were told that they had been brought together *as Catholics*. Charters and Newcomb hypothesized that, by highlighting subjects' membership in the Catholic Church, they would raise the importance of church standards.

Subjects in all conditions responded anonymously to a number of questionnaire statements, some of which were relevant to membership in the Catholic Church. The statements were worded so that subjects could answer them as Catholics, as students, or as members of other social groupings. It was found that, when they had been reminded of their common heritage as Catholics, subjects were more likely to answer the questions "in the manner prescribed for Catholics." Responses of other Catholic subjects, who had not been sensitized to their Catholic heritage, closely resembled those of non-Catholic controls. Thus, when this particular reference group was made salient by the experimenter's remarks, it became likely to exert an influence on expressed opinions.

Personal Consequences of Reference Groups

If you are interested in problems of personal adjustment, you might note some of the ways that reference groups affect feelings of personal worth and satisfaction. In the army during World War II, advancement was slow through the ranks of the military police. In the Army Air Force, which was characterized by a high fatality rate, promotion was relatively fast. A soldier advancing at an intermediate or normal rate would consider himself successful and like his outfit if the slow-promoting military police served as a reference group. But if the Army Air Force provided the standards, he might consider himself unlucky or a failure. Something similar is noted if a comparison is made of soldiers stationed in the United States and those stationed in the front lines of battle (Jones & Gerard, 1967). At home a soldier given kitchen work might feel miserable because he had received a bad deal; at the front a soldier who stayed behind for K.P. might be happy and consider himself extraordinarily lucky. In civilian life a person's feelings of personal adequacy and satisfaction may depend on whether he compares himself with people in less prestigious or more prestigious occupations; a C student may feel either successful or unsuccessful, depending on whether he compares his own performance with

that of *A* or *D* students. In all these cases feelings of satisfaction or dissatisfaction result from a comparison of what is happening to the self in comparison
with what is happening to others.

CONCLUSIONS

Everyone's behavior is influenced by the presence and actions of others. Other
people have motivational effects on the individual; they enhance the performance of well-learned responses and impair the learning of new responses. In
addition, the presence of others influences the individual's location in physical
space and is an important resource for learning. Other people provide a source
of cues or serve as models for individual behavior. They also dispense rewards
and punishments.

When two or more people simultaneously exert pressure on the individual, he
is subjected to group influences. As a result, he may conform with the expectations of the group and act in ways that make him seem similar to others in the
group. These social influences can be sufficiently strong that the individual
may deny the evidence of his own senses.

Other people need not be physically present to affect individual behavior. People continually compare their own beliefs, standards, and level of performance
with those of members of their reference groups. Each person has a variety
of reference groups, and at different points in time different groups will become
salient. Reference-group phenomena may contribute heavily to an understanding of why one person is unhappy with his situation in life while another person, living under the same objective circumstances, is quite content.

6.
The Life-Span

The next time your mother cracks out the family album in front of strangers, try to keep your embarrassment in tow long enough to appreciate the panorama than can unfold in front of you. There you are: lying helpless in a crib. Playing with a stuffed animal. Enjoying your third birthday party. Off to school. Attempting to ride your first bicycle. Standing with a grinning group of fellow high school graduates. For you, right now, the unfolding story is incomplete, but some of the other pictures in the album, which encompass a greater span of years, should prove quite revealing. Weddings. Reunions. The attractive young woman shown splashing in the ocean is now more interested in the PTA and has daughters of her own who splash in the ocean. The man with the shiny new Model-T Ford is later shown standing proudly in uniform. Later he appears as a paunchy businessman in front of a door to a small shop, and his most recent pictures show him playing checkers. He is now retired.

A family album with good, candid pictures can illustrate how people of different ages act differently. Why should behavior change with age? Certainly, older people have had more experiences and as a result have presumably better learned to discriminate, interpret, and respond. But learning alone cannot account for all the ways people systematically change as they progress through life. Increasing age is also accompanied by biological changes and by changes in the person's position vis-à-vis others in the social network. Any explanation of age-related changes must therefore take these variables into account.

In this chapter our discussion turns to how behavior is affected by the systematic forces that act upon the person as he or she progresses through life. The results of physical and psychological growth are cumulative, and at any point in time the person's behavior will partially reflect what has gone on before. Many age-related changes seem to flow smoothly from earlier ones, rather than appear abruptly and haphazardly, and this process is referred to as **development.** It is the task of the developmental psychologist to identify and understand the influences contributing to this process.

Why should behavior change with age?

Many, if not most, developmental psychologists study children. There are at least two reasons for this—above and beyond the fact that psychologists are not immune to our national pastime of child worship. First, changes during the early years are pronounced and occur relatively rapidly; hence they draw immediate attention. Second, many theories of personality and adjustment stress the importance of early-childhood events and suggest that the adult personality is fairly well formed during these early years. Thus an understanding of the child should lead to an understanding of the adult, and an understanding of the adult should always require some knowledge of the childhood history.

The focus of attention on children seems to have paid enormous dividends. Now, however, there is a growing awareness that there are age-related changes *throughout life* that can be understood by referring to the same concepts that help explain age-related changes in childhood. For example, systematic changes in the biological structure enable the older child to master tasks requiring physical strength; systematic changes in the biological structure later rob the older man of his ability to accomplish such tasks. Or, when the child enters school, his position relative to others in the family, community, and society is redefined, which will exert a profound infuence on his behavior. Later, marriage, parenthood, and retirement will also alter his position relative to his family, community, and society and will also exert a profound influence on his behavior. Thus, although studies of children predominate, developmental psychology now seeks to understand not only changes in childhood but changes in adolescence, maturity, and old age as well.

SETTING THE STAGE: HEREDITY AND MATURATION

Let us now begin at the beginning and consider the origin of the raw materials that will eventually be transformed into a fully functioning adult. *Heredity* and *maturation* set the stage for behavior by producing a biological organism with a range of capacities and limitations. Like all other animals, man is constructed in such a way that some behavior is impossible, some behavior is possible, and some behavior is probable.

Heredity refers to the process by which biological characteristics are transmitted from the parents to their offspring. **Maturation** refers to the normal

Maturation refers to the normal growth processes . . . that result in biological changes over time.

growth processes within a species that result in biological changes over time. Both heredity and maturation have important behavioral consequences.

Heredity and maturation are often described as "nature's" contribution to behavior. Everything else (learning, social influences, and so on) is described as a contribution of "nurture," or environment. At one time there raged a great controversy in psychology concerning the relative importance of nature and nurture. Did Johnny do well in school because he came from superior genetic stock (nature)? Or did he do well because he came from a good home (nurture)? Later it was admitted that the controversy was meaningless, since both nature and nurture contribute to behavior. Without the inherited capacities and the biological maturity to master his lessons, Johnny *could not* become a scholar; without environmental conditions conducive to learning, Johnny *would not* become a scholar. Yet the claim that heredity, maturation, and environment all contribute to development should not obscure the value of examining each factor individually—although, as you shall see, this task is by no means easy.

Heredity

An inherited characteristic is one that is transmitted biologically from the parents to the offspring at the time of conception. Since each parent has many attributes and the two parents may have quite different ones, how can we predict which ones are likely to be shown by the offspring? Although it is not possible to predict with any certainty the characteristics that will be shown by any *individual* offspring, general statements can be made about the probability or likelihood of different characteristics appearing within a family.

At the time of conception each parent contributes to the offspring through complex chemical substances known as genes, which provide a blueprint or code that orders the offspring's attributes. Genes are contained in both the mother's egg and the father's sperm. When the genes of the two parents in effect order two different variations of the same characteristic (such as blue eyes or brown eyes), only one characteristic can appear. The gene that is reflected in an observable characteristic of the offspring is called the dominant gene; the other gene has no apparent effect. Yet this recessive gene is retained in the offspring's own genetic composition for subsequent transmission and will be visible in his offspring if he mates with someone who possesses the same recessive characteristic. As a result of careful studies, it is often possible to make good guesses as to which characteristics are dominant and which are recessive.

It is relatively easy to link physical characteristics to genetic background. But the psychologist, who is interested in behavioral characteristics, faces a much more difficult task, particularly if he is interested in accounting for differences among individuals rather than differences among species. Man's thumb arrangement is such that he can use a hammer; the ape cannot. It is simple for heredity to explain this interspecies difference. Given two men, each with eight fully functioning fingers and two fully functioning thumbs, one may be able to repair or build watches whereas the other has difficulty replacing the cap on a tube of toothpaste. What are the differences in inherited biological structure here? They may exist, but they certainly are not easy to identify.

If offspring have the same physical attributes as their parents, heredity is the only plausible explanation. If offspring behave similarly to their parents, there are many alternative explanations, none of which can be automatically dismissed. For example, if the father and mother of the watchmaker were, respectively, an engraver and an artist specializing in miniature paintings, can it be

When father and son both have blond hair and blue eyes, heredity is the only plausible explanation . . .

However, if the son behaves similarly to his father, there are many alternative explanations, none of which can be automatically dismissed.

said that their manual dexterity was genetically transmitted to the child? It's possible. But it is also possible that the parents served as teachers or models who taught the child to put his hands to good use. In the absence of some sort of clearly identifiable inherited biological structure, the chief problem in demonstrating an effect of heredity on behavior is convincingly showing that an observed heredity-behavior relationship is *not* somehow better accounted for by other factors, such as learning.

Heredity as an explanation of differences in behavior within a species gains plausibility when an experimenter can show that organisms of different genetic composition raised in similar environments behave very differently. This approach has, in fact, proven useful with such organisms as fruit flies, which can be rapidly bred and raised under carefully controlled conditions. The technique is far less feasible for investigations with people. The two most widely accepted methods for studying humans are the method of concordance and the co-twin control.

The **method of concordance** involves showing, through the inspection of family histories, that the closer the blood relationship or presumed genetic composition, the more similar the behavior. Evidence gained by this technique is circumstantial, since many people who are close genetically share similar environments (for example, two brothers living with their parents). The **co-twin control** involves a comparison of two persons of similar or virtually identical genetic composition (such as one-egg twins) who have been reared in different environmental settings. If they behave similarly, the source of their similarity is believed to be heredity, since in different settings the systematic influences of environment should be minimized.

Heredity and Intelligence

Intelligence generally refers to the person's abilities to learn, think, solve problems, and handle himself well in a changing, challenging environment. Inherited capacities are believed to contribute to these abilities.

Skodak and Skeels (1949) conducted a long-range investigation of children who were raised by foster parents. The hypothesis was that, if the children were intellectually similar to their foster parents, intelligence scores would largely reflect environmental factors; if the children were intellectually similar to their true parents, intelligence scores would largely reflect hereditary factors.

The researchers found that, over time, the children's intelligence scores correlated more highly with those of their *real* mothers. However, Skodak and Skeels also noted that the children whose true parents had low scores performed better in the favorable environment provided by the foster home than would have been expected had they been left in the less favorable setting of the natural home. The picture emerging from Skodak and Skeels' study suggests that (1) hereditary factors influence intelligence, but (2) improved environmental conditions may aid intellectual growth.

Why, over time, should the children in this study have seemed increasingly similar intellectually to their true mothers, with whom they did not live? One possible explanation is to be found in the nature of intelligence-assessment devices. Intelligence is difficult to measure at any age, but particularly in the very young. The low correlations between the scores of young children and those of their true mothers could simply reflect the shortcomings of intelligence tests for the very young.

Perhaps the most convincing and eloquent evidence of a relationship between heredity and intelligence-test scores comes from a review article by Erlenmeyer-Kimling and Jarvick (1963). These authors surveyed 52 studies relating the intelligence-test scores of pairs of people to the degree of genetic similarity of the people in the pair. Excluded from the review were studies using poor measures of intelligence (such as subjective estimates), studies using atypical subjects (such as mental defectives), studies involving twins when it was unclear if the twins were identical (one-egg) or fraternal (two-egg), and studies reporting very small numbers of cases. Erlenmeyer-Kimling and Jarvick summarized all the correlations. Their hypothesis—that progressively closer blood ties are associated with more similar intelligence-test scores as indicated by increasingly higher correlations—received strong support. The average correlation for genetically unrelated individuals from different environments was negligibly less than .00. But the average correlation for parent and child was +.50, for fraternal twins +.53, and for identical twins *reared in different homes* +.75. The data also show a clear effect of environment. When persons of close genetic relationship are compared, those who have been reared in the same home show more closely corresponding intelligence-test scores than do those who have been reared apart. Moreover, whereas the average correlation for unrelated people reared in different settings was .00, the correlation for unrelated people reared in similar settings was .20.

The studies reviewed by Erlenmeyer-Kimling and Jarvick encompass a span of 50 years, or two and a half generations. Each individual study probably had its flaws and limitations, but, when they were all combined, the problems associated with each individual one receded into insignificance. For the most part, the average correlations for people of different degrees of genetic similarity were exactly what would be predicted by the laws of genetics discovered by Mendel more than 100 years ago.

Heredity and Other Behavioral Characteristics

On the basis of animal studies it has long been believed that heredity may set the stage for vicious and aggressive behavior. Recent studies suggest that some of the violent temperamental characteristics of men (but not women) might result from certain genetic abnormalities (Bartlett, Hurley, Brand, & Poole, 1968; Forssman & Hambert, 1967; Price & Whatmore, 1967). Persons with a particular type of genetic composition are more likely to commit crimes of violence, such as assault, arson, and murder. It is estimated that the incidence of this genetic abnormality is only 1 in 250.

Hereditary factors have also been linked to various types of mental illness or personality disorders, such as schizophrenia. Whereas only about 1 percent of the general population develops schizophrenia, about 10–12 percent of the people with a schizophrenic parent develop it, about 10–15 percent of the people with a schizophrenic brother or sister develop it, and about 66 percent of the people with a schizophrenic identical twin suffer the same ill fate (Clausen, 1961).

Physique, which is at least partly the result of heredity, has been related to personality (Sheldon and Stevens, 1942). In early studies of this relationship, the same investigators rated both physique and personality. Their procedure was later criticized because it was conducive to experimenter bias (that is, they could have unwittingly made ratings that conformed to their theory). But later studies (Child, 1950; Glueck & Glueck, 1950; Walker, 1962), which excluded or minimized this source of difficulty, nevertheless found a link between physique and personality.

Many studies have examined the contributions of heredity to behavior. These researches have varied widely in terms of their acceptability; yet, taken as a whole, they point to the conclusion that what people inherit certainly contributes to the difference among them. However, the exact extent of this contribution is difficult to determine, because it is almost impossible to parcel out the influences of nonhereditary factors on behavior.

Maturation

The genetic code within each species predetermines characteristic patterns of growth. Growth, of course, implies changes in absolute size, but it also implies changes in shape and function. As a consequence of these biological changes, new potentialities for behavior are gained and others are lost.

Maturation refers to the genetically determined course of growth and development. Within a species maturation proceeds in a very orderly sequence. A typical series of abilities, proclivities, and aversions appears and disappears in fairly fixed order.

Maturation contributes to behavior in three general ways. First (and most commonly noted), maturation can result in the appearance of an ability or a capacity to learn new responses and perform new behaviors. For example, a certain amount of maturation is a prerequisite for all the basic skills such as walking, talking, and forming habits of cleanliness. Second, maturation can produce changes in the motivational state of the organism. Puberty and menopause are examples. Third, the physical changes resulting from maturation can have important social consequences, which in turn contribute to behavior. For example, both the seventh-grade girl who appears to be twice as big as her friends and the ninth-grade boy who appears to be half as big as his friends may be teased or snubbed and hence feel miserable.

Maturation as a Prerequisite for New Behavior

During the early years normal growth processes result in the appearance of new capacities that make possible increasingly sophisticated forms of behavior. There is no way a task can be mastered until there is sufficient biological maturity to produce the necessary musculature and a sufficiently developed nervous system. Evidence that maturation is an important prerequisite comes from a tremendous number of parents' and teachers' reports and from a very few early experimental studies. Gesell and Thompson (1929) studied twins learning how to climb. One twin received intensive training early in life, but he performed no better than his co-twin control. However, when the twins reached a certain age, they both quickly acquired climbing skills. This study suggested that, prior to sufficient maturation, no amount of training will help, but, after maturation, a skill may be easily learned.

Maturation determines the *sequence* in which changes are likely to appear, rather than the *exact age* at which a change is likely. Children, for example, will mature at different rates; some are able to walk and talk before others. It is therefore useful to make a distinction between calendar, or **chronological age,** which is measured with calendars and clocks, and **biological age,** which is measured by events within the person. Two people of the same calendar age can be of different biological ages. Some children are biologically mature enough to acquire skills at an earlier chronological age than are others. Similarly, some oldsters are spry at 80, whereas others seem to be decrepit and out of sorts at 65.

Many parents have strong beliefs about the precise age at which the child should develop skills such as walking and talking. Expectations are usually based on calendar age, which everyone understands. When an expected skill does not appear on time, parents may become anxious and react quite badly. However, an awareness of the tremendous variability in *rates* of maturation should do much to allay their fears.

Detrimental Changes over Time

Maturation is an entirely beneficial process—to young people. But over the life-span there are predictable changes that *impose limitations and result in the loss of previous abilities.* This process is more frequently referred to as **aging.** Detrimental changes over time occur regularly in the older age brackets. Most human capacities reach their peak in the early twenties; then the long, slow downhill run begins.

The extent to which age works to the person's disadvantage depends on the nature of the task he is trying to perform. If it involves speedy reflexes, added years are a hindrance. Miles (1931) explored the effects of age differences on ability to perform simple tasks. He examined the speed with which people of different ages could perform a sequence of operations, such as starting a clock, moving a pencil from one place to another, and then stopping the clock. The best performers were men in their twenties, and they were almost matched by men in the 15–19 bracket. After 30 there was a slow decline with age.

Miles' results are particularly interesting, for one of his tasks was almost identical with that of releasing the gas pedal of an automobile. If, driving at 60 miles an hour, a 20-year-old and an 80-year-old responded to the same stimulus (such as a child dashing out into the street) by releasing the gas pedal, the old man's car would travel about 75 feet farther than the young man's car before the accelerator was released. But as McNeil (1969) points out, as people lose some of their youthful reflexes, they find compensations in terms of "maturity, wisdom, and economic satisfactions." Eighty-year-olds are seldom foolish enough to drive at 60 miles an hour in a residential zone, or they may be rich enough to hire a chauffeur.

As people lose some of their youthful reflexes, they find compensations in terms of maturity and wisdom.

The Joining of Forces

Heredity, maturation, and learning all contribute to behavior, and in practice it is difficult to examine their effects separately. Yet as variables accounting for regularities in behavior, they are conceptually distinct. Hereditary influences are established by the genetic code at the time of conception, and they provide a blueprint for biological organization and development. Maturational influences are evident in the sequential appearance of various capacities and limitations. Learning refers to modifications that also take place over time, but these changes come about as a result of experience.

For the most part, heredity and maturation provide the organism with certain potentials. The extent to which each potential is realized, however, depends on experiential or learning factors. One way of viewing this situation is to think of the person as a computer. Heredity can be likened to providing the diagram or plan for the computer. Maturation can be likened to "wiring up" the computer — adding components that make it possible to handle larger and more complicated problems. Learning can be likened to entering the programs and the data necessary to solve the problems.

LIFE BEFORE BIRTH

After the father's sperm fertilizes the mother's egg, there is a nine-month period of development prior to birth. The original cells multiply and remultiply, and the protoplasm undergoes tremendous, rapid growth. At some point certain cells begin to assume highly specialized functions, and there is a beginning differentiation of the material that will later become various organs and appendages.

The body develops in a fixed sequence, with the head becoming differentiated first. Growth and differentiation then proceed in an orderly way, from head to foot and from the trunk outward. Thus the head is in a relatively final form before the arms develop, and the arms have a definite form before the legs and feet. From a blob, a creature reminiscent of a sea horse emerges, and from this creature, a human emerges. The Museum of Science and Industry in Chicago illustrates these remarkable transformations in an exhibit of humans from conception to delivery.

The prenatal, or prebirth, environment is highly controlled and well regulated; it is geared to provide safety, security, and all life-support functions. The unborn child lives in a fluid-filled sac, which offers all the comforts of a water bed and all the safety of hydraulic bumpers. Through a semipermeable membrane called a *placenta* he is connected with the mother's circulatory system. The placenta provides a supply of oxygen and nutriments and a means for disposing of wastes. (You might note that all this safety and comfort appeared without the aid of NASA engineers.)

Thus the original growth, which sets the stage for later behavior, takes place within an environment that is, by postnatal standards, constant and unchanging. However, this does not mean that nothing much happens there (other than growth itself) that will contribute to later behavior. First, irregularities within the prenatal environment can affect biological development, which can affect behavior. Second, evidence is mounting that *even before birth* learning is likely to occur.

Traumatic Events

Certain conditions within the prenatal environment can have harmful effects on biological development and the subsequent ability to learn and perform. Not all maternal illnesses will hurt the unborn child; there appears to be an effective barrier that prevents this. However, some illnesses, such as rubella (German measles) and syphilis, and some other conditions, such as a high level of X-radiation, can result in a child's being born blind, deformed, or feebleminded. The exact nature of the debility may depend primarily on the *timing* of the upset. Each organ system has an appointed time to develop. If there is a problem, the organ then developing is likely the one to suffer most adversely.

The expectant mother should eat well, take care of herself, and be vaccinated for rubella. It is worth remembering that the kind of trauma that produces birth defects is usually severe (sniffles or a fright at the movie is not sufficient), and even if there is a severe injury or illness, birth defects do not automatically follow. For example, in the days before rubella vaccinations were common, only about 12 percent of the women with rubella during the first three months of pregnancy gave birth to children with noticeable defects.

Learning before Birth

The unborn child will respond to changes in the mother's emotional state. For example, under periods of maternal stress, the unborn child's level of restless activity will increase. When the mother is undergoing stress, her rate of heartbeat will increase. Through classical conditioning, this change in rate of heartbeat could become a conditioned stimulus that elicits restlessness from the unborn child. By the same token, through classical conditioning also, the normal heartbeat rate may become comforting.

In one study (Salk, 1962) newborn infants were exposed for four days to a heartbeat-like noise; babies in a control group were not. Infants exposed to the noise cried less and gained more weight. Furthermore, Salk found that the presence of the heartbeat-like noise allowed the children to relax and go to sleep more easily. These results thus suggest that during the prenatal period the sound of a steady and controlled heartbeat (at 72 beats per minute—the normal heartbeat of a person not undergoing stress) is associated with a state of well-being and relaxation. Apparently, as a result of classical conditioning, the sound still proves comforting after birth.

INFANCY AND CHILDHOOD

At birth the child is thrust into the world, where extraordinary demands are made on him. Immediately he must assume many of the functions formerly handled by his benevolent hostess. For example, oxygen and nutriments no longer arrive through the placenta; if he is to survive, he must breathe, and he must acquire the skills necessary for food ingestion. Of course, early postnatal life is also marked by extreme dependency; the infant requires regular and attentive care from adults.

Must this early care come from other people, or would an automated crib that dispensed food and changed diapers do as well?

Must this early care come from other people, or would an automated crib that dispensed food and changed diapers do as well? It would appear that a lack of close social contacts—even in the presence of good physical care—can produce some surprising adverse effects.

René Spitz (1945, 1946, 1965) has compared children raised in different orphanages and nurseries in which the quantity and quality of social contacts varied widely. In many institutional settings there are few people to provide contacts, and those who do are not likely to have as much interest in each child as would a natural or foster mother.

In one study Spitz compared babies raised in two kinds of institutions. In the first, children were stimulated, had toys, could see other babies, and enjoyed periodic visits from their mothers. These children seemed alert and sensitive. They walked and talked at about the same age as children raised by mothers at home. In the other institution, the children received few or no visits from their mothers and were not even allowed to see other children: sheets hung over the sides of their cribs left them with only a view of the ceiling. These children were not alert, developed slowly, and proved susceptible to illness and infection.

It is not absolutely clear what caused the differences within the two settings. It could be differences in tender loving care. It could simply be a matter of stimulation, for, as you saw in Chapter Four, conditions limiting sensory inputs can produce deleterious effects. It could be the result of a decreased opportunity to learn. Yet close contacts with concerned individuals would seem to remedy all these ills.

Dependency and Socialization

Dependency refers to reliance on others. Jones and Gerard (1967) have made an interesting distinction between two types of dependency. The first is **effect dependency,** which is dependency on others for care and for gratifications. The second type is **information dependency,** which is a dependency on others for information that helps in perceiving, interpreting, and understanding the world. Compared to adults, children and adolescents generally display greater effect and information dependency. This dependency gives the parents and other adults a strong hand for teaching children basic skills and forming them into properly behaving persons. Adults control rewards and punishments. In addition, even adults who are irrational, foolish, or stupid provide the child with a source of knowledge.

Socialization refers to the learning processes that transform people into functioning members of social units, such as families and society. Socialization helps the person to coordinate his behavior with that of others and to adopt values, standards, and attitudes that aid him in understanding and adjusting to a complex world. The family and the society benefit because the socialized person is not disruptive and fulfills his obligations to others.

Although socialization continues throughout life, it is generally conceded that it is the parents who provide the *earliest* and *most intense* socialization. Since the child learns so much about the world from his parents, he comes to view it as they do. Thus he acquires (through the social learning, conformity, and reference-group processes described in the last chapter) the parents' values, standards, and tastes.

Socialization within the family begins when the child learns to differentiate himself from other people and from nonpeople; it continues as he learns to adjust to social standards that call for bigger but fewer meals, sleeping during the night, and cleanliness habits; and it does not end before he leaves the family fold during late adolescence.

When the child enters school, the task of his socialization becomes shared by schoolteachers and others. Older children, and indeed children of the same age, assist. For example, playing with other children aids greatly with the socialization process. First, much play requires the coordination of activity among two or more children. Thus play teaches children to get along with others. Second, play often involves imitation of the perceived behavior of adults. In effect, the child has the opportunity to sample and practice the kinds of behavior required in later life, as is evidenced when children play cowboys, policemen, firemen, nurses, astronauts, and house. Their choices will reflect the attitudes of the social models to whom they have been exposed. For example, following the Detroit riots of 1967 I watched the children in one all-black kindergarten play "riot." Only the "losers" took the roles of National Guardsmen and police.

The view that social learning in early childhood determines adult personality is quite prominent in psychology. Both theoretical expectations and clinical and experimental evidence (some of which is introduced in the next few chapters) suggest that early-childhood experiences may form a core around which later experiences are structured. McNeil and Cutler (McNeil, 1966, 1969) have developed this idea into the concept of **life themes,** which are the major preoccupations and basic expectations of the individual. Each theme serves to organize a large portion of the person's behavior. An example of a life theme is materialism. McNeil suggests that the first step in the development of this theme occurs when the parents provide a model that makes the child feel generally anxious and insecure. This insecurity may be strengthened if the parents restrict and overprotect the child and teach him that the world is full of danger. Then, suggests McNeil, they teach him that money and possessions will provide security, power, and safety. He may also be taught that the whole world is a jungle and that everyone else is just as hostile as he is. He will not forget these principles, and they will exert themselves throughout his life.

McNeil has highlighted certain aspects of life themes. First, they are *dynamic,* since they organize and integrate a number of minor behaviors. Second, they are *developmental,* since they are initially acquired during childhood and manifest themselves throughout life. Third, they tend to *color all relevant experiences* after they have been established. (You will recall from an earlier chapter that people tend to see what they expect to see.) Finally, they can sometimes be *contradictory,* as when the theme of brotherly love contrasts with the desire to annihilate one's national enemies.

Acquiring Specific Abilities

Now let us consider how certain specific abilities are acquired: the ability to *talk,* the ability to *think,* the ability to *live by approved standards,* and the ability to *actively master the environment.*

Complex abilities do not magically appear. Developments during the earliest months provide rudimentary skills that, together and in combination, provide a basis for more sophisticated performance. For example, walking prerequires the abilities to assume an upright position, to maintain balance, and to control the legs. At *about* 2 months the child can lie on his stomach with his head and chest up; at *about* 4 months he can sit with support, at *about* 7 months he can sit alone (Shirley, 1931). During the second half-year of life the typical child gains increasing control over his body: eventually he can stand with help, creep, then walk when led, and finally walk alone. The appearance of a walking, talking, thinking being may be a miracle, but it is certainly not one that occurs overnight.

The Ability to Talk

The ability to speak and to understand spoken communications is one of man's greatest gifts. Language has, of course, the important social consequences for the individual of promoting coordination with others and facilitating learning from others. It also helps people make sense of the universe, since it is a factor in perception, thinking, memory, and personality. In *perception*, for example, people may see what they are told they will see, and language may aid with such processes as discrimination. In our society all snow looks alike. But in a society that has several words for snow (one referring to wet snow, one to medium snow, and one to dry but grainy snow), it is easy to discriminate among the different kinds of snow. In *thinking*, language releases the person from the immediate here-and-now, allowing him to brood about the past and anticipate the future. Regarding *memory*, Schachtel (1959) suggests that it is possible to effectively recall something only if a linguistic tag has been attached to it before it is stored away. (It may be possible to remember experiences that took place before language was learned, but these memories are hard to recall and, once recalled, vague and difficult to describe.) As for *personality*, McNeil (1966) feels that language is closely related to important life themes. He cites the example of the compulsive chatterer, who must issue a continuous stream of conversation to keep from becoming more nervous.

The ability to communicate is not limited to man, although complex vocal or written communications, which liberate the user from the present and allow him to adopt the perspective of others (true language), may be specific to humans. In support of this contention, reference is commonly made to the Hayeses' (1951) attempt to teach a chimpanzee to talk—an attempt that met with, at best, limited success. It was concluded that, since an animal that is very close to man on the evolutionary scale does not appear to have a capacity for language, it is unlikely that any animals do. However, primates such as chimpanzees, which should be the most likely to have the necessary neural circuitry for language, are severely limited in the area of vocal imitation. (Paradoxically, some birds are highly skilled with vocal imitation but are limited in other ways by their bird brains.) Recently Gardner and Gardner (1969) achieved some success at teaching a chimp named Washoe to communicate with humans by using a sign language similar to that used by human mutes. Washoe can name objects, indicate desires, form simple sentences, and, apparently, adopt the perspective of others. Whether or not Washoe shows true language ability will long be debated. For many people language is sacredly human. My hunch is that, the more Washoe learns, the stiffer his critics' definitions of "true" language will become.

The human infant acquiring language is mastering a staggering task. He must learn both to *receive* and to *transmit*. Associating words with their appropriate *referents* (that is, the things, events, and qualities that the words conventionally signify) is only a small part of the process.

To *receive*, the child must learn to discriminate the speech of selected humans from a horrendous cacophony of background noises. The father's voice must not be confused with the exhaust of a passing truck, a vacuum cleaner, or the droning of a television set next door. Once the child can filter out the vocalizations of selected models, he must learn to cut through the variations in pitch, timbre, resonance, and tempo and make fine discriminations among the basic sound units (**phonemes**) of the local spoken language. Finally, he must learn to recognize these phonemes as they are combined into words and strings of words and to associate them with the things, events, and qualities that they signify.

To *transmit* further requires the ability to form phonemes and to emit them in combinations and patterns that will provide information. The complexity of this task is astounding. First, pressures must be built up in the lungs. The air is then released through the larynx, which vibrates and produces sound waves. These waves then pass through the throat, mouth, and nose. Manipulation of the shape of these chambers produces modulation of the voice: vowels are formed by changing the shape of the mouth; consonants are formed by blocking and then suddenly releasing the air supply. Breathing and oral-cavity changes must be coordinated, and some actions must be undertaken in advance because of the time lapse between the initiation of the speech and the emission of the sound. Then, too, there are special problems. For example, in the case of words with numerous consonants, production of the first consonant sound requires pressure to be released. However, if too much pressure is released, the word will end prematurely.

Mastery of these tasks begins with the birth cry and continues as feeding and teething provoke exploration of and control over the vocal apparatus. Amidst bubbling, babbling, and cooing, recognizable phonemes appear during the first half-year of life, and the number of different phonemes rapidly swells. The child will quite competently produce all the sounds found in all the languages of man—sounds that will later be difficult to remaster when, as a college student, he tries to speak a foreign language. The sounds that are not part of the language of his culture will drop out of his repertoire, but other, more relevant sounds will be strengthened by positive reinforcement.

Receiving and transmitting skills develop hand in hand. Generally, though, the child can recognize words before he can use them. The passive vocabulary (words that can be understood) will always be larger than the active vocabulary (words that can be correctly used). For example, the average 20-year-old person can understand 50,000 words but has an active command of only 10,000.

After the formation of the first few words, vocabulary grows at a rapid rate. Whereas the 1-year-old can speak only two or three words, the 2-year-old has in his vocabulary about 200-300, the 3-year-old about 900, the 4-year-old about 1500, the 5-year-old about 2000, and the 6-year-old about 2600. As vocabulary develops, so do the child's skills at combination and usage. At first one word serves as a sentence (although, admittedly, subject-free and predicate-free sentences can be hard for the uninitiated to understand). Surprisingly enough, however, the child often picks a word that conveys his meaning very clearly.

From 2 or 3 years of age on, the story is one of polishing the skills of combining words into increasingly complicated, societally approved sentences. "Johnny no squeeze" eventually becomes "How dare you accuse me of squeezing the toothpaste tube in the middle!" Furthermore, whereas early language deals with concrete matters of direct relevance to the child, greater maturity is associated with an increased ability to discuss abstract issues of little personal relevance.

Several factors are believed to affect the speed at which different levels of language proficiency are attained once sufficient maturation has occurred. First, a *language-rich environment* seems to be beneficial, since it gives the child a good chance to discriminate the phonemes important in his culture, provides more vocalizations to imitate, and suggests that the world is supportive of vocal behavior. Second, the *quality of the model* is also considered important. If a model is dull or inarticulate, a handicap is imposed. On the other hand, Demosthenes and Richard Burton would make great parents in this respect. Many adults seem to know the importance of being a good model. Brown and Bellugi (1964) found that, when adults talk to 18–30-month-old children, they use relatively easy words and short, grammatically correct sentences. A third important factor is *reinforcement variables.* Language acquisition may be speeded when appropriate verbalizations are reinforced. As obvious as this may sound, parents sometimes lose sight of this fact. A father who hears "Gvawa" as "Father" because of his own needs may inadvertently reinforce the child for making a response that is only the merest approximation of the one desired. If this reinforcement marks an early step in shaping the child's speech—fine. But if the father remains satisfied, the child will have little reason to improve his articulation.

The Ability to Think

Information processing ranges from instinctively or reflexively responding to a sharp noise to formulating and testing scientific hypotheses. Thinking refers to information processing that is not instinctive or reflexive. Thinking requires the ability to identify things, to lump them into categories, and then to specify the relationships among the categories.

Concept formation is a term frequently used to designate the lumping of stimuli into categories. In the state of California, for example, a red light, a blinking red light, a stop sign, and an officer holding up one hand are all classified into the same category. As Manis (1966) suggests, the "most basic aspect of concept formation is that it involves a single response" (such as stopping a car) "that is to be associated with a variety of distinguishable stimuli" (such as red lights, blinking red lights, stop signs, and gesturing policemen). Concepts are therefore *constellations of specific instances* that elicit similar reactions. A system of concepts provides a framework for reacting to the world. Greater information-processing capacity, representing maturation, and increased incoming information, representing new experiences, combine to foster the development of this system over time.

As the child develops, the number of available categories grows. People, who were once lumped into one category, which elicited smiles and laughter, are later lumped into two categories: those who are liked and still elicit smiles and laughter and those who are disliked and elicit fear or rage. Later the ability to categorize categories emerges. The child comes to recognize, say, the difference between his mother's and his father's families. And, very importantly, the skill of assigning things to more than one category develops. The older child can appreciate how someone could simultaneously be bad (for stealing medicine) and good (by using the medicine to save a life), whereas the younger child cannot. Throughout these developments the number of correct assignments to categories increases.

The amount of information a person can process in a refined way thus increases with maturity. Moreover, the *characteristic ways* a person thinks will change over time. Careful descriptions of these changes during childhood and early adolescence have been provided by the Swiss psychologist Jean Piaget. For more than 40 years Piaget has studied the development of language, reasoning, and morality. His approach entails in-depth investigations of relatively small numbers of children, rather than more superficial examinations of larger groups. Piaget's writing has been very extensive, and he himself has been reluctant to summarize his findings. Fortunately, detailed English summaries of his work have been prepared by Flavell (1963) and others, and a number of writers have provided good overviews (for example, Brown, 1965; Sigel, 1964).

Piaget is a stage theorist: he suggests that the developing child passes through several identifiable stages called periods, each of which is characterized by a point of view and a set of approaches to solving problems. There are four main stages of intellectual development: the **sensorimotor period,** the **preoperational thought period,** the **concrete operations period,** and the **formal operations period.** Each period comprises a number of phases, and each period and phase are based on the preceding ones. Although the sequence is unvarying it is seldom possible to specify the exact age at which a child "should" enter or leave any period. The ages cited in the following discussion are only rough landmarks.

Sensorimotor Period (Birth–2 years).   The elephant, according to one British adventurer (Clarke, 1969), has a brain the size of a baseball but often acts as if he had no brain at all. The child, on the other hand, has a brain that will prove to be of enormous capacity. But at birth the child, like the elephant, must live on the basis of reflexes—that is, unlearned, automatic stimulus-response connections common to the members of a species.

The infant responds to his environment instinctively. During the first two years of life he will become less reflexive as he organizes his actions to respond in a more discriminating way. The accomplishments of the first two years are many (Sigel, 1964). He distinguishes himself from other objects and locates himself in space. He acquires the ability to identify the permanence and substantiability of objects. These skills give him a beginning awareness of cause and effect, of time and space.

Much of the intellectual development associated with the sensorimotor period involves learning to coordinate muscular activities. But as the child progresses through the period, he becomes able to solve very simple, concrete problems.

There appears an extremely rudimentary ability to *manipulate symbols* and hence to reason new solutions by thinking instead of having to derive them through a tedious process of trial-and-error learning. This ability sets the stage for the next period.

Preoperational Thought Period (2–7 years). In the early phase of this period (2–4 years) the child accepts conditions without reflection and pretty much at face value. His organization and classification methods are based more on physical properties than on reflective thought. As Sigel (1964) suggests, the child will classify on the basis of one dimension (such as good-bad), but is unable to cope simultaneously with a number of different dimensions. Meanwhile, he continues learning to distinguish symbols from objects, relying more heavily on the manipulation of symbols and less heavily on try-it-and-see for obtaining results.

During this early phase of the preoperational thought period, the child is egocentric, or "me-ish," in his orientation. He views the world from a very personal point of view, interprets things almost exclusively in terms of how they affect him, and has great difficulty in adopting others' perspectives. This difficulty is exemplified in the case of 4-year-old Stuart, who was observed by Lucretia Williams (reported in Stone & Church, 1957, p. 124).

> *Stuart:* "Me" is a name, you know. My name.
> *Teacher:* "Me" is my name, too.
> *Stuart:* No, it is *mine.* How can it be yours? I am me.
> *Teacher:* I am, too.
> *Stuart:* No, you are not "me." I am me. You are you. (After a pause for quiet meditation.) I am me. You are not me to me, but you are me to you.

From 4 to 7 the child's skill at using and manipulating symbols further improves. According to Sigel, three important abilities emerge during this age: (1) the ability to handle number concepts, (2) the ability to see relationships, and (3) the ability to think in terms of concepts (although classifications are still made on the basis of a single attribute). The child is said to be *intuitive*, for, although he can form concepts, he cannot necessarily verbalize the rules involved.

Concrete Operations Period (7–11 years). During the concrete operations period the child begins to use reasoning processes that appear logical. He is capable of increasingly sophisticated mental processes, but his logic and reasoning are applied only to tangible or concrete (rather than abstract) situations. For example, show a child of 7 or so three dogs of different sizes, and he may be able to order them according to size. But if you simply tell him "The black dog is bigger than the brown dog and the brown dog is bigger than the white dog" he may not be able to tell you whether the black or white dog is the larger of the pair. His abilities do not include abstract verbal propositions.

As this period progresses, the child becomes capable of performing several new operations or mental acts, such as *reversibility* (removing or canceling out steps to restore the original state of affairs), *transitivity* (if *A* is bigger than *B* and *B* is bigger than *C*, then *A* is bigger than *C*), and *seriation* (arranging items in terms of increasing or decreasing values). There is also an improvement in his classification abilities. Moreover, he learns to consider different attributes or dimensions of a stimulus and to relate them to one another.

During this same period the child becomes able to handle invariance, or *conservation*—that is, the notion that certain qualities (such as weight, mass, or volume) can remain constant even though other dimensions (such as shape and form) are changed. Earlier, if the child were shown a lump of clay that was then squashed, compressed into a ball, or rolled into a long, thin cylinder, he would believe that the amount of the clay was also varying. In the concrete operations period he recognizes that, in the process of changing the clay's shape, nothing is added or taken away.

Formal Operations Period (11–15 years). The final period of intellectual development is reached during preadolescence, when the child acquires the ability to reason in a logical, even scientific fashion. He can now deal not only with concrete situations but with abstract verbal propositions and relationships as well. This capacity allows him to formulate hypotheses and to test them mentally. For example, as Brown (1965) notes, if the child is presented with four similar containers of colorless and odorless liquids, which, when mixed in certain combinations, will produce a mixture of a yellowish hue, the intellectually mature can discover that combination through logic and careful experimentation. The child who has not reached the formal operations period can at best blunder his way through.

In sum, developmental psychologists in the tradition of Piaget have found that, as the child passes through a theoretically invariant sequence of stages, he progresses from a state in which he cannot distinguish himself from other objects to a state in which he can reason scientifically. In effect, he moves from the naïve, unsophisticated, and concrete to the practiced, sophisticated, and abstract.

In this discussion, which was based heavily on Sigel (1964), I have described general trends, rather than the mastery of specific concepts. The child must learn what is impermanent, fleeting, and fantasy and what is real and stable; he must learn to correctly distinguish between cause and effect; he must develop some idea of time; he must develop a sense of right and wrong. Piaget and his followers have explored the attainment of such concepts in great detail.

The Ability to Live by Approved Standards

Why do people so often engage in "good" behavior and refrain from "bad" behavior? There are two major explanations: social control and internalization. **Social control** theorists suggest that people are good because they are usually under surveillance from other people. Maintaining good conduct is simply a way of avoiding arrest or other adverse reactions. Furthermore, these proponents speculate that, in the absence of surveillance, people will not maintain good conduct. To support this contention, they point to high crime rates and to some experimental studies suggesting that even decent citizens may commit petty crimes if they think they will not be discovered.

Social control theorists speculate that, in the absence of surveillance, people will not maintain good conduct.

Internalization theorists suggest that people develop internalized standards for conduct, and these standards, not policing by others, maintain good conduct. Most of us can think of things we would not do, no matter how slim the chances that we would get caught. In experiments in which cheating and stealing were made possible, not every subject engaged in these behaviors. Moreover, subjects who do misbehave in these experiments would not necessarily seize the opportunity to commit serious crimes such as grand theft, arson, or murder.

Some theorists have stressed social control and ignored internalization; others have done quite the opposite. In point of fact, however, social control and internalization are highly interrelated.

Social control is a part of the socialization process. Older people monitor the child's behavior and provide him with clear feedback. The parents are the leading models, and they dispense rewards and punishments to shape the child's behavior in accordance with their moral standards. Over time, however, the standards are internalized.

It is often suggested that the standards children internalize are those of society. Yet these standards merely *reflect* those of society; they *are*, most likely, the standards of the parents. Such standards tend to be ideal as opposed to real, since parents teach the standards they want the child to observe, not necessarily those they live up to themselves.

Keeping out of trouble is one thing; making moral judgments is another. The former can be brought about by simple reinforcement, but the latter requires thinking abilities. Moral judgments involve a knowledge and application of moral rules. Complicated judgments (Should a man steal some money to save the life of his wife?) require complex, abstract rules. Older children, who can deal with abstractions, will make more adultlike moral judgments than will younger children. Even Solomon, during his concrete operations period, was not wise.

The Ability to Master the Environment

As the child learns to walk, talk, think, and behave in socially approved ways, he is acquiring more than a set of specific skills: he is acquiring general mastery of the environment. His new skills make him less effect dependent and less information dependent, since he is increasingly able to satisfy his own needs and to derive solutions by himself. It may be that each child comes equipped with a motive (Chapter Four) for mastery—a motive that contributes to virtually all his behavior. Or perhaps, although activities contributing to mastery of the environment are at first necessary to satisfy immediate needs, over time they may become satisfying in their own right. Whatever its origin, many young children seem to show a zest for independence and accomplishment.

Competence behaviors are those that suggest independence and self-reliance. They include trying things on one's own before seeking help from others, facing up to present circumstances, and deliberately seeking new and challenging conditions. Competence behaviors, in turn, are believed to be associated with personality. The person who frequently engages in competence behavior may feel successful, self-confident, liked by others, and very worthwhile. The person who almost never seeks to meet challenges may feel unsuccessful, inferior, disliked by others, and not at all worthwhile. In short, he feels like the psychological equivalent of a 98-pound weakling.

Competence behaviors are those that suggest independence and self-reliance.

Several studies have sought the antecedents of competence behavior in child-rearing practices. Hatfield, Ferguson, and Alpert (1967) observed mothers interacting with their children. They found that a permissive attitude that allowed the opportunity for assertive actions was an important requirement. Baumrind (1967) interviewed the mothers of assertive, self-reliant children and compared them with the mothers of withdrawn, less self-reliant children. She found that the mothers of the assertive children were loving and communicative and demanded independent actions. Baumrind and Black (1967) also found that demands for independence and good performance were associated with self-reliance. The picture emerging from such studies is that the assertive, self-reliant, competent child has been given the *opportunity* to try things for himself and has been *encouraged* and *rewarded* for efforts in this direction. An anxious, worried, overprotective mother is likely to keep competence behaviors from developing.

BEYOND CHILDHOOD

By the end of childhood, as a result of learning and socialization, the person is a far cry from the product that emerged from the womb about a decade earlier. The walking, talking, and thinking being that is the preadolescent, however, still has a long way to go to become a fully accredited, fully enfranchised young adult. Hopefully he will eventually become an adult whom others refer to as "mature" and "wise." Yet he will never become a *finished product*, because age-related behavior changes continue as long as life itself.

Adolescence

Perhaps few stages of life are surrounded by as much confusion as is **adolescence;** that is, the transition from childhood to adulthood. This confusion stems in part from the seemingly inconsistent behavior of the adolescent and in part from myth, prejudice, and a lack of agreement among observers.

Although most people agree that adolescence encompasses the "teen years" and marks the period of transition from childhood to adulthood, there is little consensus concerning the boundaries of adolescence or, indeed, how these boundaries should be determined. Our cultural definition of the limits is vague and nebulous, with adolescents including all those people who are too big to be called children but not sufficiently socialized to be called adults. (However, most people agree that adolescence is really over when the person reaches age 30!)

Certain behavior seems "typically adolescent," but it is difficult to establish rigid behavioral definitions of the boundaries, since much of the adolescent's behavior is *continuous* with earlier behavior and does not represent an abrupt transition. For example, adolescence is a time for seriously considering various vocational and occupational alternatives. Yet the way is paved during childhood and the preteen years as the 5–10-year-old discovers that work is both necessary and rewarding and subsequently starts learning to organize his time and energy (Havighurst, 1964).

It *is* possible to arbitrarily establish boundaries on the basis of physiological indicators (the ability to reproduce, the appearance of pubic hair, the development of breasts, and so on), but there is not always agreement as to which indicators should be chosen. Furthermore, although this approach is perfectly legitimate and scientific, the tremendous variations in rate of maturation can produce some surprises that do injustices to other conceptions of adolescence. For example, using physiological indicators, Reynolds and Wines' (1948) study reported an adolescent female who was only 8½ years old and an adolescent male who was only 9½; their oldest nonadolescent male and female subjects were both a little over 13. By all other definitions (including those most likely maintained by such important people as parents and teachers) the 8- and 9-year-olds would probably be considered children and the early teen-agers adolescents.

Despite this lack of agreement about the exact boundaries of adolescence, at some point in the person's life there will be a *rapid growth spurt* and a *detectable shift of roles*, after which the person's adolescence has undeniably begun. Both the rapid growth spurt, which is a result of maturation, and the slow and gradual shifting from the role of dependent child to that of autonomous adult have important behavioral consequences.

The Rapid Growth Spurt

At about the same time that reasoning abilities reach maturity during the period of formal operations, there is a sudden spurt toward biological maturity. With the attainment of **puberty,** which is defined in terms of the capacity to bear offspring, come changes in the internal chemistry of the body, rapid growth, and the development of secondary sex characteristics. Boys develop facial and body hair and, following an uncomfortable transitional period, a permanent deepening of the voice. Girls begin to menstruate, develop breasts, and undergo a general softening of the contours. The capacity for adult sexual behavior and an increased interest in sex are reflected in a dramatic increase in sexual activity of many types (masturbation, erotic dreams, homosexual acts, heterosexual petting, coitus). However, as Douvan and Gold (1966) point out, the girl's level of sexual activity is likely to be lower, presumably because of the dual social standards that allow males greater freedom.

The increased interest in sex is also shown by greater sex consciousness or sex awareness. For example, Lessler (1962) prepared masculine and feminine stimulus cards. The masculine cards contained harsh, angular shapes or coarse, rough textures; the feminine materials contained smooth, rounded shapes and soft, fine textures. Lessler asked preadolescents, adolescents, and college students to sort these cards into masculine and feminine piles. Although all subjects were able to do so, those who had reached adolescence did a superior job.

Not surprisingly, with a rapidly growing body and a keen interest in sex, adolescents often experience a new self-awareness. Standards of beauty and ugliness become very important. All of a sudden the adolescent may decide that he is too big, not big enough, or horribly out of proportion compared with what he would like to be. Worse still, the same chemical changes that led to an increased interest in the opposite sex may also be related to a severe case of battlefield face. Any or all of these factors could lead to a fear of rejection by others.

I would like to report that such fears are not based in reality, but I cannot. Bigger and stronger people with better looks often seem to have a better go of it, just as advertisements seem to suggest. For example, the importance of physical characteristics in late adolescence is shown in a study by Walster, Aronson, Abrahams, and Rottmann (1966), who set out to explore some of the factors related to dating. Dates were arranged for a large number of college freshmen. In return, these freshmen completed several personality and attitude scales and were questioned by a panel of interviewers. Walster and her associates investigated the reasons for continuing or discontinuing the dating relationships. Although a wide range of measures had been used, the personality variables examined failed to account for dating. Wanting to date a particular person, actually asking for a date, and accepting an offer for a date related only to the physical attractiveness of the person.

In addition to a heightened interest in sex, many new forms of behavior result from the adolescent growth spurt. Both males and females must learn new personal-hygiene procedures, and in our society, women must learn to adapt to a number of new garments as well. The rapid growth spurt may produce fatigue. In addition, some individuals require a little time before they can gain control over their suddenly long and gangling arms and legs. The seemingly new body is a source of continual concern during adolescence.

The Shifting of Roles

Adolescence is seen as the period in which the person becomes transformed from a child to an adult. Douvan and Gold (1966) describe this transition as one of the most difficult a person is ever called upon to make. While remaining a son or daughter and meeting up to required obligations, the adolescent must abandon the role of *dependent child* and gradually assume the position of *independent, autonomous adult.*

How does this process of emancipation take place? Through fits, outbursts, and rebellion? You will not be alone if you immediately picture a raging, screaming father pounding on a table, a quivering, weeping mother, and an adolescent refusing to comply. Adolescence is traditionally described as a period of rebellion, conflict, and inner storm and stress. Certainly such scenes are sufficiently common that they seem "obvious," not only to you but to many psychologists as well. What is less obvious is that analogous scenes take place at every stage of life.

Douvan and Gold maintain that the image of adolescent conflict and stress is not necessarily accurate. It has been fostered by studies of delinquent sub-groups and by case histories of adolescents who have been sufficiently disturbed to seek psychiatric help. Yet large-scale studies of *typical* adolescents (for example, Douvan & Adelson, 1966) suggest a *gradual* transition to autonomy, with conflict and rebellion being comparatively minor themes.

Many events during adolescence aid in the transition. Dating allows heterosexual contacts that pave the way for more binding commitments. Holding a part-time job provides pocket money (which also contributes to autonomy), teaches work habits, and forms some basis for a realistic occupational choice later. Peer groups serve as a resource for trying new activities and encourage autonomy by setting standards of independence. Eisenstadt (1956; reported in Clausen, 1968) suggests that these standards are particularly strong in societies in which the family is unable to finish the job of preparing the individual for the transition to the adult world. As the result of many factors, the adolescent is gradually molded into a fully functioning, autonomous adult.

Relative to childhood and adolescence, the adult years may appear basically unchanging. It is true that many exciting maturational events are completed. Yet the adult is by no means immune from age-related changes. Vocational selection, marriage, parenthood, grandparenthood, and retirement are age-related events encountered during the adult years, and all have enormous behavioral consequences. For example, consider the effects of full-time employment. A person's occupation will help determine where he lives, how well he

The adult is by no means immune to age-related changes.

lives, how much leisure he has, and how much money he has to spend. Socialization into his vocational role will contribute to new customs, standards, habits, and attitudes. His occupation will also affect the social status accorded him by others and, most likely, his personal feelings of self-worth.

The influence of such adult life events on personality has been emphasized by Strauss (1962). He has suggested that certain occurrences—many of which are common to almost all of us—produce a **transformation of identity.** According to Strauss, such events as entering or graduating from college, getting a job, marrying, and becoming a parent have more profound effects than is generally recognized by the personality theorists who focus on childhood events as determinants of later personality. Each of these major events of adulthood provides a turning point in the individual's life. At these times he must stop, take stock, and say to himself "I am not the same person I used to be." From Strauss' point of view, development throughout life may be seen largely as a series of related transformations, produced by major changes in the person's position within the social network.

Old Age

Employment, marriage, and parenthood are usually events of early adulthood. For the next 30 or 40 years age-related changes also occur but, for the most part, only on a haphazard basis. Repeated parenthood, separation, divorce, premature death of a spouse, a radical change in employment—all pose challenges for some people but not for others. In later adulthood, however, conditions begin systematically changing again. As children grow up and leave home and as retirement is enforced, the roles of parent and worker are abandoned. Health declines. Friends and acquaintances begin dying off and are not easily replaced, since there are fewer age mates to meet, mobility is limited, and younger people seem reluctant to become involved with older people. The gradual loss of abilities may suddenly become very visible. As aging continues, some persons may exhibit disoriented, bizarre, or childish behavior.

Calendar age per se is not sufficient to produce all these difficulties. At the time of this writing there was a hotel waiter in San Francisco still on the job at 102 years of age. Admittedly his biological aging must have been kind to him, because people have only the most limited control over the loss of their abilities. But there may be certain psychological resources that people draw upon to adjust to old age.

Kutner, Fanshel, Togo, and Langner (1956) interviewed 500 residents of a large city, all of whom were over 60 years of age. With the exception that the respondents included virtually no blacks or Orientals, they represented a variety of backgrounds and social classes and were both native-born and immigrants. First the investigators devised a scale to measure adjustment to old age. Adjustment was defined in terms of optimism or *morale*, which was in turn assessed by responses to such questions as "How often do you feel there is no point in living?" "All in all, how much unhappiness would you say that you had in life today?" "As you get older, would you say things seem to be better or worse than you thought they'd be?"

Responses to this measure were then related to such variables as standard of living, interests, interpersonal relations, attitudes toward leisure, participation in community events, and general attitudes about aging. Two of the broadest conclusions drawn by Kutner et al. were that (1) people can develop inner resources (such as special interests) that help them to enjoy their old age, and (2) no *one* particular pattern of successful adjustment can be identified. Nevertheless the investigators were able to pinpoint several specific factors related to adjustment: age, health, self-perception, and social activity.

People can develop inner resources that help them to enjoy their old age.

Age

Since the ravages of time worsen with age, it seems reasonable to expect morale to decrease with age. The survey suggested, though, that matters are not quite that simple. For women there was a *very gradual* decline of morale with age, but some fairly old women had very high morale. Such diversions as home-making, housekeeping, part-time jobs, and grandchildren could carry them into the seventh and eighth decades. For men the relationship between age and morale was not linear. Compared with men in the 60- to 64-year-old group, those in the 65–69 group showed lower morale. But there was an *increase* in morale in the 70–74 age group. The authors believed that for men age 65 is a critical point, for it is then that they are forced to retire. Later, how-ever, they can develop new interests and resources that improve their outlook.

Health

One of the discouraging features about aging is a decline in health. Poor health leads to feelings of futility and despair. One old person, commenting on the death of a brother, told me: "His hearing went about ten years ago, his sight about five years ago, and his mind at least two years ago. What happened yesterday merely finished the job."

We would therefore expect morale to decrease with failing health. Interestingly enough, in general, this expectation was found to be true for people of low social status but not for people of higher status. Given that the respondents were interviewed at home (and hence weren't sick enough to be hospitalized), two possibilities arise to account for this surprising finding. One is that the better resources of the higher-status respondents provided compensations for failing health. The second is that their relative affluence provided greater assurances for the future: they could expect better health care, especially in the event of hospitalization.

Self-Perception

What we *are* is important, but *how we see ourselves* is crucial. When people are forced to retire even though they consider themselves young, they may respond with bitterness; if they accept society's verdict on their age, they may be able to retire with grace.

How people see themselves is partly determined by what they are, but it is also controlled by the actions of others around them. If, for example, an 80-year-old wants to go swimming under ideal conditions but is persuaded by his family that he is "too old," he may accept this opinion and needlessly deny his inclinations. Indeed, it seems as if contemporary society has provided a number of standards and institutions (retirement communities, old folks' homes, and so on) that may help to strengthen a person's conception of himself as aged, somewhat incompetent, and not quite so valuable as society's younger members.

Kutner et al. devised a method of assessing positive and negative self-images. Those with negative self-images—who saw themselves as just "too old"—had lower morale.

Social Activity

One of the challenges of age comes from the severing of social relationships. Kutner et al. found that respondents who maintained a higher level of social activity had higher morale. Both participants in community social activities and those who retained some form of employment had higher morale than the less active persons. Indeed, the still-employed had the highest morale of all the respondents (even when the added income from employment is not taken into consideration). Kutner et al. concluded: "The social role that provides the greatest degree of satisfaction for most people is the employed role; less desirable is the retiree, and morale responds accordingly."

Given the importance of social contacts, one might expect that old people who maintained closer contacts with their offspring would show higher morale. Intriguingly, this was not the case. In some persons morale *decreased* as a result of greater contact with the offspring. The authors suggest that this situation might be the result of intergeneration conflict.

The developmental processes of aging and socialization continue as long as life itself. For example, Glaser and Strauss (1968) and Kalish (1965) have drawn attention to socialization practices in the death room. Moreover, although dead people are certainly no longer of interest to the behaviorist, it would appear that their commitments to the living are not discharged until they have been the center of attraction in a ritualistic and perhaps even gaudy funeral.

CONCLUSIONS

At birth the person is endowed with a genetic composition that provides a blueprint for biological development. Development that occurs over time and in the absence of learning is called maturation. ~~Heredity~~ and ~~maturation~~ provide limitations and capabilities. The extent to which capabilities are utilized depends on experiential ~~or learning factor~~s. There is thus an interplay of three sets of variables, each of which contributes heavily to human behavior.

In this chapter I have discussed some of the regularities in behavior that can be related to position within the life cycle. Maturation and aging occur over time, and they contribute to behavioral regularities. But, over time too, there are changes in the person's position vis-à-vis others in the social network. Such changes result in new challenges that must be faced, and people learn to face them in sequence. The developmental process is continuous, and the mastery of one challenge provides tools for dealing with the next.

Let me part with a word of extreme caution. You can be a personality psychologist and say cynical things about personality. You can be a social psychologist and make dire predictions about society. But don't try to be a developmental psychologist and say bad things about children. Parents won't let you get away with it.

3

Personal
Consequences

The next five chapters discuss personality and attitudes. Both concepts are used to account for a person's internal predispositions to feel, think, and act in characteristic ways. Both are **personal consequences** of the systematic forces that cast, shape, and temper each of us into a unique individual who, as Murray noted, appears in some ways like all other people, in some ways like some other people, and in some ways like no other person. Much about personality and attitudes can be understood by referring to the basic processes described in the last three chapters. However, in the next few chapters many additional contributing processes are introduced.

Although it is not easy to draw a sharp line between personality and attitudes, personality is generally considered the broader concept. Personality seems to leave its mark on a person's every thought, feeling, and action. An attitude, however, is more specific. Attitudes refer to ways of feeling, thinking, and acting that are elicited by a specific stimulus or a relatively narrow class of

189

stimuli, such as wars, psychedelic drugs, law and order, or racial confrontation. The distinction is thus one of scope: whereas personality appears in every situation, an attitude appears in only a few.

Chapter Seven provides an orientation to personality. After going into some detail about the concept of personality, I will discuss some of the advantages and disadvantages of trying to understand personality solely as a collection of socially learned habits. This is followed by a consideration of the concept of self.

There are many approaches to personality, and Chapter Eight introduces two of them in some detail. You have already heard about behaviorism, which has strongly flavored this text. But these two other approaches—psychoanalysis and humanistic psychology—have also been highly influential, especially in their attempts to explain personality.

Perhaps the major problem in studying personality scientifically is how to measure or assess it. Chapter Nine deals with psychological tests, and the emphasis is on personality tests. Satisfactory psychological tests are very hard to construct, and they all have important limitations. Hopefully I will convince you that, although they are useful, psychological tests are not magical, and their results must be taken with a grain of salt.

Chapter Ten discusses abnormal behavior—that is, behavior that is offensive to personal tastes or social rules. Popular opinion not withstanding, we will discover that this behavior is not always the result of some kind of illness.

In Chapter Eleven the focus shifts to attitudes. This chapter is the last in this section because it provides a bridge between personal consequences, which is the subject of Part Three, and social interaction, which is the subject of Part Four.

7.
Introduction to Personality

A 100-percent American, he always seemed to regret that he was born on July 5, not July 4. Although he was to become very successful, he was of humble origin, and his memories of his childhood were not all pleasant. He remembers, for example being teased by his family and being laughed at by the other people in the small New England community in which he was raised. Forced to work at an early age, he soon discovered that he was a natural salesman, but he found the life of a merchant unexciting and turned to show business.

He was a bright man with boundless energy, which comes through clearly in his report of his life. The picture he presents is one of a friendly, sociable, and likable man who is morally above reproach. Yet careful attention to his report reveals some contradictions to this wonderful picture. First, nowhere in the course of his self-description does he mention forming a close attachment to another person. He does describe his courtship in some detail but rarely refers to his wife when discussing the next several decades of his life. Second, although he could certainly be considered "fun" and "jolly," he appeared to have a cruel streak, which appeared in the form of very rough humor or of self-righteous retaliatory acts. Third, although he clearly loved a joke, he certainly resented one played on him. Fourth, although he was undoubtedly very clever, he repeatedly lost fortunes. Finally, it was not clear to many of his contemporaries that he really was above reproach. In fact, some people considered him the greatest liar and fraud who ever lived.

This man, Phineas T. Barnum, was famous for founding the circus that still bears his name. If you ever come across his mammoth autobiography (1872) and decide to read it, you will probably gain an impression of him—as you would of anybody else whose autobiography you read. After reading Barnum's autobiography, I came to think of him as *bright, energetic, striving,* and *successful* but also as *hostile, gullible,* and *sensitive to rebuff.*

The study of such characteristics—their interrelationships and their underlying causes—is the study of personality. The topic is extremely broad. Most psychologists agree that "personality" refers to the whole psychological makeup of the person and is reflected in everything from his most specific to his most general ways of thinking, feeling, and behaving. *Personality theories are thus very general theories about man and his behavior.*

Personality theories are thus very general theories about man and his behavior.

Since personality appears in all human behavior, a knowledge of any of the forces contributing to human behavior sheds light on the topic. Some aspects of personality may thus be understood in terms of simple learning or motivation concepts or in terms of the social-influence processes discussed in earlier chapters. But attempts to understand personality have led to the development of additional concepts and principles, many of which will be introduced in the next few chapters.

The study of personality is an area in psychology that is particularly rich in theorizing. In a discussion of social psychology, Daniel Katz (1967) suggested that one of its major shortcomings was the lack of sufficient theory to unite a great wealth of research findings. In the field of personality there seems to be no such problem. The theorizing, however, often runs well ahead of the collection of scientific observations that could support or deny it.

Much of the evidence supporting theories of personality comes from clinical psychologists, psychiatrists, and psychoanalysts, who report that things seem to work as would be expected if the theory were true. Such clinical evidence is often presented in a very convincing fashion. People who offer it suggest that it is the only worthwhile evidence, since it comes from a careful and in-depth study of the individual and his life's circumstances. Moreover, they add, attempts to understand personality through the experimental approach are bound to fail: the experimenter cannot hope to faithfully reproduce in his laboratory the tremendous variety of complex and often subtle conditions that combine to produce a unique personality. Although he may be able to get some grasp of one or two variables, he can in no case "take everything into account," and he will thus obtain not only an *incomplete* but a *distorted* understanding of personality.

At the other extreme are psychologists who suggest that case-history evidence is worthless. Under uncontrolled conditions such as those found in the clinic, people tend to be poor observers. Many clinical workers have very particular orientations, and their cases sometimes seem to fit all too nicely within their theories. Could it be that, as a result of their own expectations and needs, clinical observers see their cases in exactly the ways that they *want* to see them?

Between these two extremes are positions of moderation suggesting that neither the experimentalist nor the clinician is a bumbling incompetent. My favorite middle-of-the-road position is that, although case histories are interesting and useful, greater impact is given a personality theory if at some point it is supported by evidence from careful experimentation.

PERSONALITY AS A SET OF SOCIALLY LEARNED RESPONSES

Perhaps personality is nothing more than a set of learned responses. If so, each person could best be understood by examining his learning history. What models were available to him, and what responses were reinforced?

This orientation is reflected in the social-learning approaches of Miller and Dollard (1941) and, later, Bandura and his associates (Bandura, 1969; Bandura

What models are available to him, and what responses will be reinforced?

& Walters, 1963). Many of these theorists' basic ideas have already been presented (Chapters Four and Five). Miller and Dollard, you will recall, applied principles of learning devised by experimental psychologists to topics of concern to the psychologist interested in personality and social psychology. They demonstrated, for example, how principles of reinforcement can be applied to train people to follow the lead of others.

Miller and Dollard subscribed to the drive-stimulus-response-reinforcement approach (Chapter Four). To recapitulate, the initial impetus or motivation for behavior comes from drive, which is produced by deprivation or by the presence of noxious stimulation. As drive increases, so does the activity level of the person. Different responses are made until one changes the environmental conditions in such a way that there is a reduction of drive. Drive reduction is the reinforcer that results in the response being learned. Later, if the organism is presented with a pattern of stimulation similar to that present during the learning, the earlier reinforced response will be emitted.

If personality is nothing more than a collection of habits that were learned in this fashion, it might be possible to get at the "essence" of a person by conducting an inventory of all his habits. Fortunately, the process is facilitated somewhat by the inclusion of additional concepts from the field of learning. For example, the process of **generalization** is useful for piecing together a personality. To amplify, a personality characteristic generally refers to something that underlies two or more of the person's activities. If the psychologist says a man is aggressive when dealing with "authority figures" (perceived superiors, such as parents, police, and teachers, who wield some power over the person), he is reporting how the man will act in more than one situation. Perhaps in all his dealings with authority figures, the man has had aggressive responses rewarded, whereas friendly overtures have gone unrewarded. This seems rather unlikely. Moreover, when a new authority figure (such as a new boss) is introduced, it is quite possible that there will be instant trouble, even though this particular authority figure had never before been encountered. Learning theorists can accommodate such behavior by pointing to the long-known process of generalization, which is the opposite of discrimination (discussed in Chapter Four). After Pavlov (1927) used classical-conditioning procedures to train dogs to salivate at the sound of a certain tone, he discovered that they would also salivate at the sound of somewhat different tones. Just as Pavlov's dogs slobbered in response to one tone after learning to slobber in response to another, our hypothetical man could act with hostility toward one authority figure after learning to be hostile toward another. The dogs have not learned to discriminate among different tones, and the man has not learned to discriminate friendly from frustrating and irritating superiors.

Although the process of learning and social learning described in Chapters Four and Five provide the basis for the social-learning approach to personality, relevant theorizing by Miller and Dollard and their followers goes beyond that described in those chapters. Now let us consider what Miller and Dollard—who based much of their theory on studies of how animals learn—had to say about thinking. Then we will consider the concept of conflict. Other personality-relevant ideas of these early social-learning theorists (suggesting that frustration leads to aggression) are discussed in Chapter Twelve.

Higher Mental Processes

Personality was defined as the whole psychological composition of the individual, reflected in everything from his most specific to his most general ways of thinking, feeling, and acting. Much seems to go on inside our heads, and an approach to personality that fails to deal with this *inferred* mental life is inadequate. Any explanation of personality must have something to say about language, thought, and fantasy.

To theorists in the Miller-Dollard tradition, the mental images, words, or sentences that make up our thoughts can be considered responses. Just like overt behavior, thoughts followed by reinforcement will later be elicited by similar stimuli. Different people may have been reinforced for thinking in different ways.

Perhaps some of people's sex fantasies can be understood in this way. Recurring sexual thoughts may be those that were reinforced by masturbation or by some other pleasurable activity. Similarly, when rising hormone levels contribute to men's sexual dreams and culminate in release or tension reduction (that is, wet dreams), the dreams may be reinforced and hence likely to reappear.

Thoughts are not only responses; they are stimuli that elicit additional responses. Thoughts thus string themselves together into chains. Each thought is a response to the preceding one and a stimulus for the next. In turn, thoughts are tied to overt behavior. A stimulus such as a Salvation Army kettle may elicit the mental response "The Salvation Army is good." This thought may serve as a stimulus to the response "I would like to donate to the Salvation Army." In turn, a series of questions is triggered (for example, "How much loose change do I have?") that will contribute either to walking by rapidly with averted eyes or to stopping, smiling, and depositing some change. In this way thought mediates between one activity (staring at the kettle) and another (walking by with averted eyes).

Conflict

An important contribution of the early social-learning theorists was their development of some of Kurt Lewin's ideas about conflict. These ideas have gained considerable acceptance among many personality psychologists, including some who for the most part may not subscribe to the social-learning approach.

Conflict, in this connection, is something within the individual. Conflict refers to a competition between incompatible responses. Two responses, both of which are mutually exclusive, fight for emission. Torn between the two responses, the person may be left immobilized. The former British prime minister Balfour once spent 20 minutes at the foot of two sets of stairs (both of which joined at a higher level) torn between ascending via the left flight and ascending via the right one (Tuchman, 1966).

Two major classes of responses are approach responses and avoidance responses. **Approach responses** entail moving toward something, and **avoidance responses** entail moving away. For example, restaurants, theaters, nightclubs, and friends' houses elicit approach responses from me, whereas dentists, hospitals, funeral parlors, and courts elicit avoidance responses. My predispositions to behave in these ways can be referred to as **approach tendencies** and **avoidance tendencies,** respectively.

The strength of the tendency to approach or avoid is a function of the nearness of the approached or avoided stimulus. The nearer one is, the stronger the attraction or repulsion. An illustration of the principle that proximity to a desired goal contributes to more vigorous approach activity is sometimes eloquently portrayed in movies when the hero returns from a long journey. Spotting his love as he deplanes, he begins walking faster and faster and, as he gets close, breaks into a full run. Similarly, when forced closer to a stimulus he is trying to avoid, his avoidance activity would become more vigorous. The same hero, finding himself in the river just a few feet from Niagara Falls, would paddle more vigorously than if he were still two miles upstream. The increase of approach motivation as a function of nearness to something desirable is called an **approach gradient**; the increase of avoidance motivation as a function of closeness to something unpleasant is called an **avoidance gradient.** An interesting feature of these gradients is that, although the approach motivation is initially stronger, as the thing or event gets closer, the motivation for avoidance increases more rapidly than the motivation for approach (Brown, 1948). That is, if a stimulus elicits both approach and avoidance tendencies, it will be relatively attractive when still distant in time or space but relatively unattractive when near in time or space. Thus, after months of looking forward to something, people may get cold feet and try to back out.

The simpler forms of conflict are approach/approach, avoidance/avoidance, and approach/avoidance conflicts.

In the **approach/approach conflict,** the person is torn between two attractive alternatives, both of which cannot be realized simultaneously. That is, a choice must be made between two generally happy but mutually exclusive courses of action. At various times television shows have used the gimmick of letting a contestant open one of two mystery doors. He then gets the prize hidden behind the door he selects. This situation should produce an approach/approach conflict. This kind of conflict is not always so "happy" as you might think. A classic example of an approach/approach conflict is that of the logical ass that starved to death between two equidistant bales of hay.

In **avoidance/avoidance** conflicts, a choice must be made between two unattractive alternatives, one of which must be accepted. At one time in the state of Utah, for example, persons convicted and sentenced to death had a choice of facing a firing squad or being hanged. This kind of conflict isn't happy either.

In approach/avoidance conflicts, the person is at once attracted and repelled.

In **approach/avoidance** conflicts, the person is at once attracted and repelled. That is, the positive or favorable features of the object or event elicit approach tendencies, but the negative or unpleasant features elicit avoidance tendencies. Since conditions are rarely all good or all bad, approach/avoidance conflicts are probably the most common. Marriage, for example, can elicit approach/avoidance conflicts. Marriage hypothetically offers a number of inducements. Each potential partner expects to receive a continual flow of love and affection and to enjoy feelings of security, respectability, and social approval. Marriage is, for these reasons, desirable and to be approached. On the other hand, marriage is a rather large obligation and impairs personal freedom in many ways. The prospective groom will have to be cautious about staying out late with the boys and knows that he will have less spending money. The prospective bride may envision herself as soon to be chained to her new home and forced to abandon her career. For these reasons, marriage is something to be avoided. In short, the favorable and unfavorable features of the impending marriage will induce approach/avoidance conflicts within each participant. But, for the sake of an MCP[1] illustration, let's say that the prospective groom is more ambivalent than the prospective bride.

Now recall the earlier statement that, as distance from the goal (in this case, marriage) decreases, both the approach and the avoidance tendencies will continue to increase, but with the avoidance tendency gaining greater momentum. At some point the avoidance tendency might outweigh the approach tendency, and the groom will be tempted to chicken out. Now, in most cases, other forces, such as social pressure, will induce him to go through with it. Yet this is not always the case, and our folklore is rich in stories about women left waiting at the altar.

In a rap session I once heard a proposed solution for the prospective bride. About two weeks before the ceremony the fiance's approach tendency will probably be at its strongest and his avoidance tendency at its weakest. Later the avoidance tendency will gain strength—very fast. So at this point the girl might tell him that her family has decided to forbid the marriage, and as a result the two of them must elope that very night! Since the approach tendency is so strong at that point, he will be likely to go through with it, and the impromptu wedding can be over and done with hopefully before the avoidance tendency catches up. Afterward, the direct gratification of tissue needs and dissonance reduction (which you will read about in Chapter Eleven) will help maintain stability in the relationship.

There are additional forms of conflict, such as the double approach/avoidance conflict in which someone is torn between two alternatives, each of which has attractive and repelling aspects. In all cases conflicts are seen as generally unpleasant and distressing. Conflict notions enter into many theories of personality, particularly those oriented toward the interpretation of "abnormal" or "disturbed" behavior.

The importance of conflict was illustrated in an experiment in which rats were trained to jump from a platform to one of two openings, each of which was hidden by a hinged door (Maier, 1949). On one door was a black circle and on the other a white one. After being prompted by an air blast, the rat jumped. If it made the right choice, the door would swing out of the way and it would land safely inside, there finding food. If the incorrect door was chosen, the door would not yield and the rat would plummet into the net below. During

[1] Male Chauvinist Pig

the first phase of the experiment, safety and food were always associated with one stimulus and a bump and a fall with the other. The rat soon learned which door to choose.

Then Maier introduced the conflict. The still-marked doors were locked randomly, making earlier-learned principles ineffective. The rats began to behave in rigid, repetitive ways. This lack of flexibility can impede any new solutions to a problem, even when such solutions do in fact exist. Some implications of this finding will be traced in Chapter Ten.

The New Look: Human Social-Learning Theorists

Geiwitz (1969) has pointed out that, whereas Miller and Dollard sought to translate studies of animal learning and behavior to produce an understanding of human learning and behavior, the more recent approach of Bandura and his associates has placed greater stress on the *direct study* of human social learning. This trend becomes very apparent when one considers the *content* of the different generations of social-learning studies. Thirty years ago Miller and Dollard conducted studies showing that rats could learn to follow each other in a maze or that children will learn to open the same box that an adult leader opens. Contemporary social-learning theorists teach mutes to speak, snake-phobic people to handle snakes, dog-phobic people to pet dogs, and children throwing tantrums to shut up. *Such recent research has catapulted social learning from something theoretically related to personality to something that is a known antecedent of much intriguing personality phenomena.*

The Social-Learning Approach:
Contributions and Limitations

It does seem possible that personality can be understood through the application of social-learning principles. This approach has several attractive features. First, it flows from theory and research in what might be called the no-nonsense or "hard-nosed" areas of psychology. Many attempts to understand personality do not have such smooth continuity with research and theory in the more "traditional" or "academic" areas. Continuity is advantageous because it enables a researcher to explain seemingly very different forms of behavior (such as an animal turning left in a maze and a man being amiable and sociable at a cocktail party) within one theoretical framework. In addition, the definitions of terms used by the social-learning theorists tend to be rigorous and precise. Since the concepts are so highly workable, the social-learning approach to personality tends to encourage and facilitate research, rather than discourage or retard it. Moreover, as far as I can see, compared with other theories of personality, social-learning theory is perhaps the best supported by the available experimental evidence.

One of the aims of science, you will recall, is to control events. If by various manipulations the theorist can produce predictable results, his ideas about cause and effect gain credibility. One way in which personality theorists try to prove their ideas is by producing personality change. This is attempted within the context of psychotherapy, which represents efforts to change the behavior of people who are not living effectively. Social and other learning theorists use principles of learning for such "therapeutic" treatment. Indeed, the name of this form of psychotherapy—**behavior modification**—splendidly portrays the prejudices and biases of its practitioners, for the therapeutic process is seen as one of weakening and eliminating unwanted responses while eliciting and strengthening wanted responses. Tantrums may be controlled by withdrawing all reinforcement following an episode, smoking may be made aversive by pairing cigarettes with electric shocks, and the hospitalized mental patient may be induced to take care of himself by being rewarded following each self-maintaining act. Compared with most other forms of psychotherapy, the behavior-modification approach yields very clear results.

In some ways the application of learning principles to understand personality is neat, clean, and precise. In other ways it is horrendously awkward. It is difficult, if not impossible, to describe someone's whole personality by tracing out his learning history. Even if this were possible, piecing together a unique personality by tying together hundreds of thousands of learning experiences would be very tedious. It might be compared to trying to build the Taj Mahal out of marbles.

A more serious problem is that there is much behavior that cannot be easily accommodated by the social-learning approach. Certain *variations in response strength,* the *organization of habits into coherent patterns,* and certain *unanticipated directions of behavior* are not elegantly accounted for in terms of the processes thus far discussed. Let us now pause to consider illustrations of each of these mysteries.

Response-Strength Mysteries

Despite social-learning theory, there appear to be a number of cases in which responses maintain, gain, or lose strength independent of (or even contrary to) reinforcement conditions. Thus behavior that is not reinforced (or is even punished) may have surprising strength and durability. For example, some people make characteristic "slips of the tongue," substituting one word for another. Usually an emotionally toned word is substituted for a neutral word: hostile for hospitable, orgasm for organism, lays for weighs, virile for viable, and so forth. Other people's laughter and the resulting embarrassment should be quite punishing, yet the same "slips" can occur again and again. Moreover, why should slips of the tongue almost inevitably have sexual or aggressive overtones even in a society where "nice people" are taught not to express such things?

Mysteries concerning the Organization of Habits

Apparently learning principles alone cannot account for the ways in which various learned habits are fitted together. For example, you may know a soldier who is both very pious and an efficient technician for death. Perhaps the only medal he owns in addition to his "rifleman" badge is one for Sunday School attendance. Certainly it seems odd to picture this student of the Ten Commandments stalking around draped with hand grenades, ammunition bandoliers, and other implements of war. How can people learn and retain such incompatible responses? A psychologist can remain within the framework of learning theory and say that the battlefield provides one type of stimulus triggering one type of response, whereas the church is a clearly different stimulus that triggers another type of response. On the other hand, other psychologists might reply that this rationale does little to explain why one person is really bothered by incompatibilities that another does not even seem to notice. Other theories of personality go to more effort to explain how various types of responses, both compatible and incompatible, are somehow fitted together.

Mysteries concerning the Direction of Behavior

Behavior sometimes seems to take directions that seem unrelated to social-learning principles. For example, Lizzie Borden was a respected spinster in Fall River, Massachusetts. She associated with the best people and went to church regularly. In fact, she taught Sunday School. But all evidence suggests that on August 4, 1892, she dispatched her parents with an axe (Lincoln, 1967). Where did she pick up this evil habit? Who was the model, and where was the reinforcement? Quite a few personality phenomena remain mysterious if we rigidly adhere to a tight social-learning framework.

Conclusions and the Problem of the Self

In evaluating the social-learning approach to personality, its advantages must be weighed against its disadvantages. Balancing the various pros and cons is, to some extent, a personal task. According to my own values, relative to other theories of personality social-learning theory holds up very well. However, there is an additional criticism of the approach—a criticism I have always found difficult to weigh. Some theorists maintain that the social-learning approach is sterile and fails to get at the real *essence of the individual*. The criticism is sometimes voiced in the following form: *Although I may only be patterns of behavior to you, I am more than that to me: I have a self*.

Although I may only be patterns of behavior to you, I am more than that to me: I have a self.

THE SELF IN PSYCHOLOGY

Psychology undertakes the study of people, and each psychologist and student of psychology is a person. As long as the psychologist or psychology student is studying *someone else*, the "patterns of behavior" interpretation of personality may be passively tolerated. But in most cases, no matter how strong the admonitions of the behaviorist, the psychologist or psychology student soon starts ruminating about his own personality. Unless he is unequivocally dedicated to the early behaviorists' position, it is easy to start thinking of his personality as something more than visible patterns of behavior and thoughts that are chains of stimuli and responses. By simple processes of extrapolation, other people become more-than-behavior, too, even though their behavior is the only part of their personality that can ever be seen. The conviction that personality is more than behavior is a painful one; despite the compelling intuitive validity of this claim, it seems impossible to explain to the leering, sneering behaviorist.

Self, identity, ego and *"me"* are roughly synonymous terms that represent this more-than-behavior. Whereas each of us can infer something about another person's self only by looking at his behavior, we think we know our own self through more direct and immediate ways as well. However, in the discussion to follow I must sidestep two controversial issues. First, who is the I who knows the self? For an answer to this, I suggest you contact your family philosopher. Second, I will sidestep the issue of whether or not the self, like the soul, is in fact "more than behavior" and will simply note that concepts such as *identity, me, ego, and self seem useful for understanding personality.*

Characteristics of the Self

Self means different things to different people. D. Miller (1963) suggests that self frequently refers to (1) an object of awareness, (2) a name, (3) a set of bodily feelings, (4) an axis of meaning, (5) a controller of activity, and (6) a product of social relations.

Object of Awareness

The self is something of which one is aware. It identifies the person and provides continuity over time, since everyone considers himself to be pretty much the same person year in and year out.

The self is something of which one is aware.

Name

A person's name is an important characteristic of the self. When you ask people to write an answer to the question "Who are you?" (and have them give as many answers as they can within a specified time limit), the first thing on the list will probably be their name.

As Miller points out, names are much more than labels. They indicate sex. They may give hints about age. For example, all the people I know whose first names are Woodrow and middle names are Wilson are of my parents' generation, not my own. Names can also give clues about race, creed, color, and national origin. People have different expectations about Jacks, Jills, Jacobs, Johanns, and Josés. Moreover, the way a name is used conveys information. You would probably have different impressions of me on the basis of whether I identified myself as Al Harrison, Albert A. Harrison, or A. Alonzo Harrison. So would I.

Bodily Feelings

Self refers also to a collection of bodily feelings. The self is what feels healthy, sick, alert, tired, joyous, sad, comfortable, uncomfortable, quiet, agitated, hungry, sated, or sexually aroused.

The relationship of the body to the self is a rather intriguing issue. Here my point is neither to debate the mind-body problem nor to specify the location of the self within the skin. But I would like to emphasize that different people have different ways of viewing their bodies in relation to their selves.

For some people the body is like a case for the self. For some seedy-looking people, the case is no more than a wrapper, which is considered unimportant. For others, such as models and musclemen, the case is very important indeed.

Some people locate the self in the head, usually right behind the eyeballs. Others take a less limited position but still identify the self with only a part of their body. Hare lips, pimples, and fat are easy to dissociate from the self (perhaps you have heard the claim that inside each fat person is a thin person waiting to get out). Still other people see the body and the self as more of a unity.

Axis of Meaning

The self is a "knower," and everything that is known is known relative to the self. The self is the reference point that gives everything meaning. As Miller notes, for some people (such as the solipsists described in Chapter Four), if it doesn't matter to the self, it doesn't matter at all.

Controller of Activity

The self is also referred to as something that plans, evaluates, intends, and then acts. In this sense some people may consider the self a little man inside the head who pushes the buttons, pulls the levers, and steps on the peddles to keep the machinery operating.

Product of Social Relations

Finally, the self has been taken to refer to the personal consequences of interaction with others. This interpretation has been favored by social self theorists, especially the sociologically oriented ones such as Cooley, Goffman, Mead, and Strauss. The basic thrust of the argument is that each of us, as objects of awareness, perceives other people as being aware of us. Their expectations about us and the way they actually see us are communicated to us. The self develops through a never-ending process of weighing and assimilating these reactions. In the extreme, the object of awareness—the self—exists *only* as a reflection from other people.

The concept of self as a product of social relations is worth pursuing in some detail, since a whole group of theorists have stressed social relations as a contributant to personality. Some of you may find satisfying the implication of social self theory: that man has a self whereas beast does not.

Acquiring a Sense of Self

By now you should be disabused of the notion that man is the only "social animal." Yet there are clear species differences as one moves up the phylogenetic (that is, evolutionary) scale. One important characteristic that may distinguish man from other animals is his ready ability to use language to think and communicate. This capacity frees him from complete reliance on very limited, firsthand experiences.

Although (as you shall see later) postures and gestures communicate a great deal, in their interaction with others people rely very heavily on the use of the spoken and written word. That is, the great bulk of social interaction is abstract or *symbolic*, taking place through the manipulation of symbols. Because of their language abilities, people are able to adopt the perspective of other people and see themselves as they are seen by them. Much of the time they accept as true what the others see. Once accepted, the reactions of others are somehow incorporated into the self. Thus, if others see me as friendly, cheerful, and industrious, I may come to regard myself that way; if others see me as hostile, moody, and lazy, I will probably regard myself as such.

Different people are likely to react to us in different ways. For example, a child's mother could see him as "good," although his teachers see him as "bad." What kind of sense of self would he develop? This depends in part on the relative salience of the different people. Generally, the reactions of people closest to us are more important, and the perceptions communicated by our family and friends carry more weight than the perceptions communicated by casual acquaintances or various functionaries. People whose evaluations seem to carry the most weight for the developing sense of self are called **significant others.**

Others' Reactions and the Sense of Self

Consider yourself dealing with (1) a social inferior, such as a junior high school student who seeks your advice, and (2) a social superior, such as the dean of your college who is hauling you on the carpet. In the first case you may think of yourself as confident and competent; in the latter, insecure and incompetent. This provides a *miniature* illustration of the importance of other people's reactions. I say miniature, because it illustrates fleeting, rather than enduring, consequences.

Maehr, Mensing, and Nafzger (1962) attempted to experimentally manipulate the self by varying the reactions of another person. In this experiment the other person was made "significant" by being cast as an expert evaluator.

Male high school students rated themselves in terms of (1) body coordination and agility, (2) athletic skills, and (3) general physical fitness. Later each student was introduced to the alleged expert in physical education, who had him perform a number of simple tests of coordination and agility. Disregarding the student's actual performance, the expert reacted with approval or disapproval. In this phase the subjects thus discovered how they were seen by someone else who was supposedly highly qualified to make an accurate evaluation.

Next, subjects again rated themselves on the same scales used earlier. Those approved by the expert rated themselves more favorably than they had initially; those disapproved, less favorably. The new ratings thus incorporated the reactions of the so-called expert. The biggest change in self-ratings was found in the area of coordination and agility. The second biggest change was found in the closely related items dealing with athletic skills. The least change in ratings was shown on those items least closely related to evaluated performance—general physical fitness.

Personality, however, implies a sense of continuity over time. If people are continually treated a certain way, the effects may not be transient. A mother who repeatedly points out to her child his faults and inadequacies can bring him to think of himself as someone who is incompetent, inferior, or worthless. Believing him unable to accomplish some task, she does it for him, thus ensuring that he will not learn. In this way she perpetuates his inabilities.

On the other hand, if a mother views her child as competent and worthwhile, there could be a different result. Coopersmith (1967), in a study of sixth-grade children, found that, if people such as parents viewed the child as competent and worthwhile, the child was likely to see himself in a similarly favorable light. This and other studies suggest that acceptance of the child encourages his acceptance of himself. What kinds of parents are likely to be accepting of their children? The answer is parents who accept themselves. Medinnus and Curtis (1963) gave two measures of self-acceptance and one measure of acceptance of child to 56 mothers and found a significant positive relationship between self-acceptance and child acceptance. In general, the evidence seems to suggest that acceptance of the self or of others as worthwhile seems to start in motion a very positive chain of events.

Of course, the extent to which people see themselves in a favorable light will depend on other factors as well. Ruth Wylie has kept a sharp eye on the concept of self and has twice reviewed its use in psychology (1961, 1968). In the more recent paper she reviewed, among other topics, the effects of experimentally induced success and failure on self-concept. Several streams of theorizing have entered into ideas about the effects of success and failure on the degree of favorability with which the person sees himself. One hypothesis is that self-regard is learned through successes and failures. Although success makes the self glow like a thousand suns, failure makes one look bad. Another common hypothesis is that people try to maintain positive self-concepts. A third is that they will tend to resist information that is discrepant with their basic self-concept. These hypotheses, it should be pointed out, are by no means mutually exclusive. For example, people may learn a positive self-concept, strive to maintain it, and resist evidence hinting that they are not so worthwhile as they believe.

In support of the first hypothesis—that success and failure affect self-concept—results of 19 studies reviewed by Wylie suggest that people may change their self-evaluations following experimentally induced success or failure, although this is more likely to happen in some specific area (for example, "I am a bad shuffleboard player") than in a more general sense (for example, "I am a rotten person"). In support of the second hypothesis—that people try to maintain positive self-concepts—some studies found that more favorable self-ratings following success are more common than less favorable ratings following failure. And, in support of the third hypothesis—that people seek to avoid self-damaging information—failure, rather than lower self-ratings, may trigger off defense mechanisms (Chapter Eight) that serve a protective function. For example, instead of saying "I certainly am an incompetent fool," the failing person

might say "Now look what you made me do," thus drawing attention away from his own lack of success.

Stigma

The stigmatized are people who have an unwanted attribute or *stigma*. By itself, it is not necessarily incapacitating; but it serves as a sign to others, who interpret it (often unfairly) as showing that the possessor is inadequate, incompetent, guilty, or in some other way of low social worth. They consequently react to the person with evasion, rejection, hostility, or an air of condescension or patronization. Goffman, who wrote extensively about this process, has identified three main classes of stigma (1963, p. 4):

> First there are abominations of the body—the various physical deformities. Next there are blemishes of individual character perceived as weak will, domineering or unnatural passions, treacherous and rigid beliefs, and dishonesty, these being inferred from a known record of, for example, mental disorder, imprisonment, addiction, alcoholism, homosexuality, unemployment, suicidal attempts and radical political behavior. Finally, there are tribal stigma of race, nation and religion, these being stigma that can be transmitted through lineages and equally contaminate all members of a family.

People such as the physically handicapped can develop a sense of themselves as pitiful or repugnant when they discover that others see them as such. Those with "blemishes of individual character" can have their sense of worthlessness initiated or strengthened by rejection from others. In one case a woman reported that, although she experienced normal sexual desires during high school, she somehow developed a reputation of being a lesbian. Ignored or teased by boys, she turned to women for companionship and, eventually, for sexual gratification. In the case of tribal stigma, members of minority groups occasionally accept some of the rather humiliating attributes that other groups place upon them. Perhaps some "Jewish mothers," "Uncle Toms," and "Tio Tacos" are products of this reaction.

Some of the more flamboyant characteristics of deviants such as homosexuals, drug addicts, delinquents, and criminals appear to be brought about by others' stern responses to them. The possible end effect—disrespect for society—is not so much a result of the initial "crime" as of others' reactions to the person once he has been identified. The "capture and branding" process defines the individual as deviant, and people come to react to him in particular ways, such as by avoidance or rejection. The drug user, after capture, may suddenly find it difficult to find a job or make new friends. He is forced to find acceptance from other drug users. As he associates more closely with them, rejection by "decent citizens" intensifies, forcing him into increasingly closer contact with people who help to reward and strengthen his addiction.

Incidentally, gender (of the female variety) may be a stigma of sorts. According to Wylie (1968), studies of sex differences and the self-concept suggest that, from childhood on, people have strong beliefs about sex stereotypes—that is, society's expectations for men and women. Generally, a cult of male superiority begins in childhood, and the relative favorability of the male stereotype increases at least through college. Furthermore, to some extent people accept the appropriate sex stereotype and let it enter into their self-concept.

The theory that we are what others see us as can be attractive, particularly to sociologically oriented theorists who prefer not to get tied up in such issues as genetics, maturation, bodily needs, and the dynamics of unconscious mental forces. Social self theorists have come up with some interesting stuff, but no amount of selling has convinced me that it has "wrapped up" the problem of personality. First of all, the social factors identified by the social self theorists are not the only antecedents of personality. This becomes embarrassingly clear when people show conceptions of themselves that are not consistent with other people's evaluations. For example, a man who considers himself suave, debonair, and dapper may be considered a pompous ass by his family, friends, and associates. In addition, a very difficult issue is inelegantly sidestepped by the social self approach. Social self theorists basically suggest that we are one thing or another because others see us as being that way. Remaining unresolved is the issue of why in the first place people should see person x as industrious, responsible, and mature and person y as lazy, irresponsible, and immature.

Components of the Self

As you by now know, people act differently at different times. Many people seem inclined to believe that the *more likely* behavior of someone else represents his "true self." When a person who is usually sociable and cheerful becomes withdrawn and grumpy, another person may say "He's not himself today" and anxiously offer some reasons why. The person behaving atypically may concur with this judgment or, indeed, offer it himself. "I'm just not myself right now" seems to be a sufficient apology for many unwarranted acts. But if someone is not himself, who is he?

We may see the more common behavior of someone else as reflecting his real self. But in viewing ourselves, no matter how frequently we act in a certain way, we may not take it as representative of us. For example, it may be very clear from the reactions of others that a woman is acting terribly. She may recognize that "I am *acting like* a weak, snively little gossip right now" but then add "although deep inside I *am* a strong, decent, and worthwhile person." Or, in another case, a man may feel that, even though other people seem to like him, they would be filled with horror and revulsion if they knew what he was "really" like. But which is the real self—the friendly Dr. Jekyll whom everyone almost always sees or the much less probable Mr. Hyde who may exist only in imagination and dreams?

But which is the real self—the friendly Dr. Jekyll whom every-one almost always sees or the much less probable Mr. Hyde who may exist only in imagination and dreams?

One possible answer is that there is more than one self. For example, to account for those cases in which someone is "not what he appears," two selves may be invoked: one publicly shown and the other private. Carl Jung, the Swiss psychoanalyst, made a distinction between the self and the persona. The self refers to the real, inner you, whereas the persona refers to the social facades or masks you adapt to certain social situations.

Core Identity, Subidentities, and Personas

D. R. Miller (1963) has offered an interesting theory of the structure of the self that describes why any "self" may seem different at different points in time. The self (or total identity, to use his term) can be visualized as consisting of three parts: the *core identity,* or real, inner self; the peripheral and rather phony *persona;* and some components known as *subidentities,* which fall between the two extremes.

The **core identity** is the center of personality. Formed first and remaining from cradle to grave, it contributes to every psychological characteristic of the person. The core identity establishes general ground rules for social behavior and sets very general goals in life. It also sets in motion basic mechanisms for psychological self-protection (Chapter Eight) as well as the mechanisms leading toward what Miller calls self-enhancement and what other theorists have called personal growth, self-actualization, or the realization of human potential (Chapter Eight). As the innermost self, the core identity is the main object of appraisal when ruminations begin. It is also the hardest part of personality to change.

Subidentities mediate between the core and the demands of a particular situation. Everyone has a number of subidentities. They are elicited when the person finds himself in one of his typical social roles. Role behavior, as you may recall from Chapter Three, results from the prescriptions associated with a position in a group, an organization, or a society.

Miller agrees that a person's position in a social network is of great importance. But he suggests that, although social roles set *minimal requirements* for behavior, how a person *actually behaves while occupying the role* is something else. Each person who is placed in a given position will fulfill the associated role in a unique way. This uniqueness reflects subidentities. The minimal requirements of a role are the same for all people who play that role (all firemen must answer a call of distress), but a subidentity is unique to the individual (not all firemen cheerfully rescue cats from trees).

Miller suggests that there may be as many subidentities as there are regular parts to the person's life. Let's consider the case of a 35-year-old businessman, Mr. Amazing. Mr. A. has a *masculine subidentity,* which comes to the fore when he deals with women, swaps stories with the men in the locker room, or reads the latest issue of *Playboy*. Generally Mr. A. is a slightly above-average dresser; but when he is preparing for a date, he is very careful to dress to his best advantage. He dates regularly and enjoys being seen with attractive women but will repeatedly date only a woman who shows to him inner worth as a person. On a date he chooses fun and exciting activities, such as attending avant-garde plays, nightclubs, and Go-Go joints, followed by a snack at an expensive, exotic, but out-of-the-way cafe. It is very important to him that his feminine companion for that evening like him and have a good time with him, and he is very careful to make sure that this is the case.

Mr. A. also has an *occupational subidentity*. He is a very energetic salesman, knows his products well, and is willing to work as many hours as are necessary to secure an important contract. He does not mind the fact that his business requires that he travel several months a year, and he generally enjoys the potential customers whom he so lavishly entertains. They, in turn, enjoy his refreshing frankness and candor. Mr. A. prides himself on his ethical standards: he would rather not do business than misrepresent himself or his firm.

Mr. A. also has a *subidentity as an uncle*. This appears whenever he visits or thinks about his brother's and sisters' families. When he is with his nieces and nephews, he attempts to be tolerant, understanding, and an exemplary person. He enjoys amusing his nephews and nieces, gives them expensive Christmas and birthday presents, and will often surprise them with little trinkets or sweets. Unlike a parent, an uncle can leave when he is in a bad mood or when children become edgy. Since his nephews and nieces see Mr. A. only under the best of conditions, they think of him as a wonderful and remarkable man, and he fully enjoys their admiration and affection.

Mr. A. is a man, a salesman, and an uncle. He meets all the minimal requirements for these roles. *But he also fulfills each role in his own unique way.* Other men, as men, might not have such an active dating schedule. They might show less concern for their dates, prefer quieter activities, or choose to go steady. Other men, as salesmen, may not know their business, may be reluctant to work as hard as Mr. A., or may fail to maintain strong ethical standards. Other men, as uncles, may not be quite so tolerant, understanding, and willing to go out of their way. In short, other men would not necessarily show tremendous energy, a zest for accomplishment, and a concern for "doing the right thing" as they moved from situation to situation.

The **persona** is the most peripheral part of the self. It is that part of the personality that is shown to the world. It is modeled after what the person would *like* to be like, what he is *told* to be like, or what he feels he *should* be like, rather than what he feels he really is like. The persona is very responsive to the immediate pressures of a social situation and is hence often described as a facade or mask, the inspiration coming from the accentuated face masks worn by the actors of ancient Greece.

The persona is shown by the newly enlisted soldier when he courteously asks "Would the colonel care to have his shoes shined?" It is also shown by the novice schoolteacher who is cheerful and pleasant even though "inside" she feels bored or sick to her stomach. Eventually both the soldier and the teacher are likely to develop full-blown subidentities—the former, perhaps, as a man of military virtue and the latter as a popular pedagogue.

Even in the phony antics of a persona, something of a subidentity or a core seems to shine through. For example, actors are professional phonies. They adopt personas for money, trying as hard as possible to be like the character they are hired to play. Different actors adopt different personas with different degrees of success. Think how your impression of George Washington might change if you saw him played in turn by Charlton Heston, Vincent Price, Clint Eastwood, and Bob Hope.

The Concept of Self: A Beginning

At the scientific level the self is a hypothetical construct used to account for the continuities in the behavior of different individuals. It is inferred from what people say and do. At a personal level the concept of self has compelling intuitive validity. It is an object of awareness, a name, a set of bodily feelings, an axis of meaning, a controller of activity, and a product of social relations that each of us knows firsthand.

Whether or not "self," like "soul," represents more than behavior, the self is of use scientifically because it is the product of specifiable antecedents and is reflected in observable behavior. Although the self can be studied scientifically, nobody claims that this type of research is easy. Nonetheless, hundreds of studies of virtually all shades of acceptability have been related to the concept of the self (Wylie, 1961, 1968).

As Wylie (1968) notes, although the concept of self has immense potential, it presently is *not* on a particularly solid footing. "Self" is apt to be a sloppy term and one that is thrown about quite loosely. It infuriates the tough-as-nails psychologists, for it is hard for them to discriminate it from "ghost." Although there certainly is research hinting at the usefulness of the concept, it often suffers from serious methodological flaws and does not tie together neatly. The term needs better definitions, so that everyone can understand what it means, and more work is necessary to formulate a series of interlocking research problems. Speculation about the nature of self is fun, but, as Wylie has pointed out, gradualness, drudgery, and patience will be required for realizing the concept's enormous scientific potential.

 CONCLUSIONS

Personality refers to the whole psychological makeup of the individual that makes him in some ways like all other people, in some ways like some other people, and in some ways like no other people. Personality theories tend to be very general theories about man and his behavior.

One way in which personality may be understood is as a collection of learned behaviors that result from social-learning processes. This approach represents an integration of the principles and methodology of the experimental psychologist, on the one hand, and the interests and needs of personality and social psychologists, on the other. The approach tends to be rigorous, precise, and supported by a wealth of experimental evidence. Furthermore, recent research has catapulted social learning from a process theoretically relevant to personality to a process that is demonstrably responsible for many intriguing forms of behavior. Nonetheless, social-learning theory does not seem to adequately explain certain variations in response strength, the organization and integration of habits, and certain unanticipated directions of behavior. Other theorists have introduced additional concepts to deal with these issues.

Some critics of social-learning theory argue with great conviction that personality is more than patterns of behavior. To represent this "something more," the concept of self is often invoked. Whatever else self may be, it is the product of lawful antecedents, and it is tied in with behavior. Some of the antecedents of self have been found in social relations.

Speculation about the nature of the self is fun and may eventually pay huge dividends. However, although there has been research promising some scientific usefulness of the concept of self, Wylie persuasively argues that the concept at present does not have a firm scientific footing. Self is likely to be a vague term that communicates little, since it means different things to different people. Much of the research on the self has been criticized as seriously flawed. But whether or not the psychologist ever completes the task of putting the concept of self on a firmer basis, the idea of self appears to be here to stay.

8.
Psychoanalytic and Humanistic Orientations

Three major intellectual forces have shaped the course of present-day psychology: behaviorism, psychoanalysis, and humanistic psychology. The first two movements date from the beginning of the twentieth century, whereas the third is a more recent development.

The early behaviorists, you may recall, argued that, if psychology was to be scientific, psychologists must deal with observables. Behavior is observable and hence appropriate for study. Thoughts, feelings, and other features of "mental life" were acceptable for study only insofar as they are evidenced in behavior. Although the impact of the behaviorists is most clearly seen in modern experimental psychology, it is also apparent in the learning approach to personality, the behavior-modification approach to psychotherapy, and a considerable portion of personality research. But the picture of man that the early behaviorists presented is basically a rather minimal one. Personality is for the most part a set of behavior patterns.

The psychoanalysts contend that understanding a person requires going beyond behavior and considering "mental life" as well. Dealing with people on a one-to-one basis, their psychological sleuthing resulted in a very intricate picture of man as a being chock full of thoughts, feelings, wishes, and impulses. This picture evolved as a grim one, perhaps because it was pieced together from the study of troubled people in the clinical setting.

218 Psychoanalysis has been around so long that some psychologists now consider it only of historical interest. Others, however, consider it as still relevant, and

a few see it as the most satisfactory approach to personality that is currently available. Whatever one's position, there is no getting around the fact that many of the concepts and principles introduced by psychoanalysts are widely used by psychologists and laymen alike for describing and understanding personality.

Unlike either behaviorists or psychoanalysts, proponents of the Third Force suggest that man has a great deal of control over his own fate.

Humanistic psychology, also called the Third Force, is a relatively modern movement. Unlike the behaviorists, humanistic psychologists present man as a psychologically rich organism. Man thinks, desires, wants, worries, needs, loves, fears, dreads, cares, aspires, and hopes, as well as behaves. Unlike the psychoanalysts, who describe man as the victim of hidden forces, humanistic psychologists stress the positive, striving nature of man. Unlike either behaviorists or psychoanalysts, proponents of the Third Force suggest that man has a great deal of control over his own fate; moreover, they are less concerned about being proclaimed "scientific."

Partly because of its youth and partly because its advocates are not nicely regimented, humanistic psychology is not so well developed or integrated as the other two forces. However, it does have an important underlying philosophy, and many ideas introduced by the humanistic psychologists seem to be currently gaining in favor.

THE PSYCHOANALYTIC THEORY OF PERSONALITY

Psychoanalytic theory was formulated during the early decades of this century by Sigmund Freud, a Viennese physician. A keen observer, Freud was very sensitive to new discoveries and was quite willing to adapt his theories on the basis of them. He kept painstakingly complete records of his changing thoughts. Here I can describe only some of those aspects of psychoanalytic thought that I consider the most useful for describing and understanding personality. If you are interested in tracing Freud's ideas over time, you might want to read Brenner's (1957) *An Elementary Textbook of Psychoanalysis* or Hall's (1954) *A Primer of Freudian Psychology*. Only then should you approach the 24 volumes representing the *Complete Works of Sigmund Freud*!

Two Principles

Let's begin with what Brenner (1957) has described as two of the most fundamental principles of psychoanalytic theory. First, *All behavior is determined—* that is, lawfully caused. Second, *we are not always aware of our behavior and its causes.*

All Behavior Is Determined

Determinism is the fundamental assumption of science that makes plausible attempts to predict and control events. The principle of determinism simply states that there are lawful relationships among causes and effects. If conditions appear whimsical, capricious, or without rhyme or reason, it is because the observer is not clever enough to associate the conditions with their lawful antecedents. Applied to psychology, this principle states that all thoughts, feelings, and actions are the results of previously existing conditions.

The principle of determinism is indeed ancient, but the psychoanalysts were the first to trace some of its intriguing implications. First, if there is no such thing as random or accidental behavior, even the most trivial and seemingly unobtrusive actions must be caused. For example, the choices of a pencil over a pen, Danish modern furniture over Italian provincial furniture, or cooked carrots over raw carrots must all have their antecedents. Psychoanalysts suggested, furthermore, that the causes of much seemingly trivial behavior can be found in important, deep-set facets of personality formed early in life. For example, the choice of cooked carrots over raw carrots might be related to motives stemming from early childhood. A preference for cooked carrots could indicate a longing for the joys of earliest infancy, when all food was warm and mushy. A preference for raw carrots could reflect ways of responding that were learned during the stage of life when teething and biting were important.

Another implication of determinism is that even mistakes and accidents have their causes. The psychoanalysts suggest that these causes, too, may be found in personality. In a classic example, a man made the seemingly harmless mistake of stopping for a green light while driving to his wedding. This action could suggest a strong reluctance to tie the marital knot, and psychoanalysts might seek additional evidence of some force inside the man telling him to *stop*. In a less reknown instance, I once heard a scholar presenting a paper to a group of psychologists. The scholar was trying to describe a make-believe pill composed of red gelatine. Somehow, he said "red genitals." Such a slip of the tongue might lead psychoanalysts to speculate that this man had some special concerns about sex. As for accidents, not too long ago a burglar entered a liquor store in the dead of night, pilfered the cash box, and then, fatigued by his efforts, took a catnap inside the store. He was found there in the morning sound asleep by the store owner, who quietly summoned the police. Psychoanalysts would speculate that this ill-timed sleep, which could lead to nothing but capture, reflected a need on the thief's part to be punished for his transgressions. Indeed, casebooks of psychoanalysts (for example, Menninger, 1938) report many cases in which self-defeating and self-destructive tendencies appear to stem from a desire to be punished.

Psychoanalysts suggest, then, that seemingly innocuous choices, mistakes, and accidents are all caused and that the cause is often found in personality variables such as personal needs and motives. The man who stopped at the green light on the way to his wedding showed motivation to avoid marriage. The convention speaker was apparently more interested in red genitals than in red gelatine. The burglar who took an ill-timed rest may have wanted to be punished. But is not all this activity rather devious? The reluctant groom could have refused to get married. The speaker could have talked about red genitals to his friends in the locker room and spared himself considerable embarrassment. The burglar could have simply turned himself in to the police.

We are not always aware of our behavior and its causes.

Freud suggested that people are not always aware of what they want and hence cannot act to satisfy their motives in simple and direct ways. In effect, their needs, impulses, and sometimes actions are "secret," not only to other people but to themselves as well.

Levels of Awareness

People's wishes, feelings, impulses, perceptions, and memories differ in terms of accessibility to awareness. Freud suggested that there are three levels of awareness: the *conscious*, the *preconscious*, and the *unconscious*.

Material of the **conscious** consists of all that the person is aware of at a given point in time. Right now (hopefully) you are conscious of the words of this text. You are probably also aware of your general surroundings, the presence or absence of other people, and, perhaps, eyelids of lead and a strange throbbing sensation in the back of your head. Everything in awareness in the immediate here-and-now is part of the conscious, and, for the most part, people can give direct reports of it. Freud believed, however, that material in awareness constitutes only the smallest part of the person's psychological makeup. There is also much material stored out of awareness.

The **preconscious** contains material that is not presently in awareness but that can be recollected or brought into awareness in undistorted form. For most of us, the design of the American flag, our telephone number, and our father's first name are readily accessible memories stored in the preconscious. The **unconscious** likewise consists of hidden mental life. But this material *cannot* be summoned into awareness in undisguised form. The existence of this material must be painstakingly inferred.

Material is relegated to the unconscious because it is somehow painful or unpleasant. In this context, though, the words *painful* and *unpleasant* require some explanation. Sheer physical pain (such as that associated with a stubbed toe) and many forms of unpleasant stimulation (such as the odor of a rotten egg) do not really qualify. What does qualify is material that is unpleasant or painful because it reflects poorly on personal ability, adequacy, or moral character. For example, the pain of burns suffered by the driver in a car accident may be recollected, but the driver may have no recollection of how his negligence caused the accident or of the ensuing events during which he left the

Psychoanalysts suggest that much, if not most, mental life resides in the unconscious—out of sight but not quite out of mind.

scene without waiting around to aid any of his injured passengers. The basic process of shoving painful or unpleasant memories, perceptions, impulses, and even actions out of awareness is called **repression.**

Psychoanalysts suggest that much, if not most, mental life resides in the unconscious—stamped down, out of sight but not quite out of mind. The existence of this material is inferred from the careful analysis of mistakes, accidents, and dreams and from the finding that episodes and events that people simply cannot remember at one point in time are sometimes brought into awareness later. In other words, although material from the unconscious cannot be voluntarily summoned into awareness, disguised traces of it repeatedly rise to the surface, making it shown in word and deed.

Experimental Studies of Repression

Much of the evidence supporting the psychoanalytic theory of personality comes from the casebooks of Freud and his followers. Repression, however, is a psychoanalytic concept that has generated some interesting experimental studies (for a review, see MacKinnon & Dukes, 1962). The earliest studies of repression examined, simply enough, people's abilities to recall pleasant and unpleasant experiences, with the expectation that people would be more "forgetful" of the unpleasant. Jersild (1931) asked respondents to list all the pleasant and unpleasant experiences of the preceding three weeks. Asked still later to reproduce these lists from memory, the subjects showed a greater "forgetfulness" of the unpleasant. Stagner (1931) had respondents write one pleasant and one unpleasant event and then list all the objects, events, and sensations associated with each. When they later tried to reproduce these lists, they had better recollections of the circumstances surrounding the pleasant event.

A movement away from the personal interview approach came with the discovery of the *interrupted-task technique.* Bluma Zeigarnik (1927) had found that subjects remember incompleted tasks—that is, tasks they were not allowed to complete because they were interrupted by the experimenter. An explanation of this finding centers around the Gestalt principle of closure (Chapter Four), which suggests that when perceptions or tasks are incomplete, a tendency exists to complete or finish them. In Zeigarnik's research, failure to complete the task did not reflect unfavorably on her subjects' feelings of self-worth. However, Rosenzweig (for example, 1943, 1952) reasoned that, if incompletion signified personal failure and hence reflected poorly on the self, incompleted tasks would tend to be repressed and less easy to remember. Subjects were given a group of picture puzzles to complete, and it was arranged that each subject could finish only half. One group of subjects was presented the puzzles in an informal spirit, so that failure to complete them would not be psychologically painful. The remaining subjects were told that the puzzles represented an intelligence test. Under these latter conditions, incompletion would suggest a lower mentality, which is not particularly comforting. Rosenzweig expected, and found, that, whereas under informal conditions subjects would remember a greater proportion of *incompleted* tasks, under formal conditions repression would result in a better recollection of *completed* tasks, which indicated success on the "intelligence test." In a similar vein, Glixman (1949) gave college students paper-and-pencil tests arranged so that the subjects could complete only half the items. In the *neutral* condition, emphasis was placed on the test itself, rather than on the individual's performance. In the *nonneutral* condition, subjects were led to believe that their performance on the test would indirectly reflect on their personal abilities. In the *stress* condition, subjects were told that their performance was a clear indicator of personal success or failure. In accordance with the principle of repression, Glixman found that increased stress was associated with a decreased ability to recall the items that were not completed.

Psychoanalysis is a form of psychotherapy, as well as a theory of personality. An important aspect of the treatment process is that whatever causes repression can be removed, thus allowing unconscious material to rise into awareness. Experimental proof of what MacKinnon and Dukes (1962) call the "return of the repressed" is of great interest, for it would suggest that material was indeed stored in the unconscious, rather than "never learned" or "erased from the mind." In a rather complicated experiment, Zeller (1950) had subjects memorize material. For half the subjects, this material was made unpleasant by association with personal incompetence and failure. These subjects were less able to recall the material. Later, for the same subjects, the repressive force was removed by associating the same material with personal success. At this point their ability to recollect the material improved. Thus Zeller's findings suggest that repression produces a temporary inability to recall unpleasant material; when the conditions causing the repression are removed, the material may rise into awareness. This certainly implies that, rather than being "erased from the mind," certain memories are locked out of sight somewhere, and that place might as well be called the unconscious.

The Perceptual Defense Controversy.   In some ways the essence of the concept of repression is to be found in the proverb "See no evil, hear no evil, speak no evil," although in repression this good sportsmanship results from unconscious factors rather than from voluntary self-control. In more recent years studies related to repression seem most concerned with "See no evil," or perceptual defense.

Bruner (1948) suggested that people ward off disturbing stimuli by refusing to perceive them. In accordance with this hypothesis, McGinnies (1949) showed *neutral words* (such as *stove*) and emotionally toned *"dirty" words* (such as *whore*) to subjects for very brief periods of time. A measure of emotionality was taken, and subjects were asked to report what they saw. He found that it was more difficult for subjects to recognize and report the dirty words. He also found that subjects sometimes had emotional reactions to the dirty words, even though they could not report them. This suggests that, even though the dirty words could not be reported, their emotional quality had some sort of impact.

Howes and Solomon (1950) countered that McGinnies was not dealing with repression but with the effects of word frequency. Dirty words, they argued, are less likely to appear in print; since people have had less practice reading them, the words are simply more difficult to recognize when presented very briefly. In this connection the researchers later presented evidence that *more frequent* words were easier to recognize (Solomon & Howes, 1951).

Throughout the 1950s, a rather fierce battle raged. Complexity was added to the issue when it was discovered that word frequency and word favorability, or "goodness of meaning," are closely interrelated (Chapter Eleven), so that *less frequent words tend to be unpleasant*. Thus the difficulty in recognizing infrequent words might be because these words are unpleasant! The issues involved in the perceptual defense controversy are very complex. Whereas dirty words seem more difficult to recognize, it is not at all clear that some form of repression is the process responsible.

Defense Mechanisms

Repression is frequently referred to as a **defense mechanism,** since it serves to protect or defend the self from an awareness of unwanted conditions. There are other defense mechanisms that involve perceptual distortion, wishful thinking, and excuse making. Each contains an element of repression, for in one way or another something unpleasant is kept from awareness. The concept of defense mechanisms is one of the more enduring contributions that the psychoanalysts have made to contemporary psychology.

Everyone uses defense mechanisms to some extent, and different people have preferences for different ones (Blum, 1969). Since conditions are rarely all favorable, defense mechanisms are useful. Among other things, they allow us to live in a crowded society in which the expression of certain impulses could spell disaster. However, continual reliance on one or two may prevent more realistic attempts to deal with harsh conditions.

Defense mechanisms operate at the level of the unconscious. As a result, it is much easier to see their operation in others than in the self. It is possible that an understanding of defense mechanisms is a greater aid to understanding personality than is an understanding of some of the major personality theories themselves.

Denial

Denial involves refusing to recognize harsh conditions and imagining happier conditions in their place. Patients told that they have a fatal illness may

Denial involves refusing to recognize harsh conditions and imagining happier conditions in their place.

believe that they are victims of a mistaken diagnosis, that they will be one of the two in 10,000 cases who will miraculously pull through, or that medical research will devise a cure in time to keep them from an early grave.

Isolation and Undoing

Isolation and undoing are highly related defenses. Isolation involves stripping painful impulses and memories of their strong emotional components. For example, the circumstances surrounding a divorce may have access to awareness, but the painful emotions and feelings that should be associated with those circumstances remain out of awareness. Intellectually, the person knows that something bad has happened, but there is a numbing of the associated emotions. Undoing refers to attempts to erase impulses or memories by acting in a way that should produce their opposite. For instance, after participating in a raid that results in the demolition of a village and a near annihilation of its inhabitants, a soldier may volunteer to help reconstruct the village and offer substantial aid to the survivors.

Identification

Identification usually refers to the general process of taking on the attributes of others. This process is an important part of socialization. But when the person assumes someone else's attributes because they are more acceptable to him than his own, we may say that identification is being used as a defense mechanism. In one restaurant I saw a man of 50 employed as a busboy. His demeanor was not the one of hang-loose dissatisfaction I expected from someone whose station late in life was cleaning soiled dishes and slop from the Formica counter of a chrome- and Naugahyde-bedecked hash house. It was, rather, the manner of someone serving the crowned heads of Europe. Psychoanalysts might suggest that, by assuming the qualities of a prestigeful and successful waiter, he could reject the reality of his menial position.

A special case of identification as a defense is identification with the aggressor, in which the person assumes the attributes of someone who is capable of inflicting harm. Perhaps this behavior allows him to imagine that he possesses some of the power of the aggressor and thereby reduces the imbalance of power between the big, strong aggressor and the poor, weak self. Or perhaps it allows the person to believe that, from the aggressor's standpoint, his behavior is now above reproach and hence weakens the grounds for the aggressor to aggress.

Projection

Whereas identification involves incorporating the attributes of others, **projection** involves ascribing one's own unwanted attributes to someone else. Thus, instead of seeing oneself as looking for trouble, the person sees others that way. This process is believed to be common among people who wrongly believe that they are being hounded and persecuted by others. For example, a person may develop hate toward a demanding supervisor and want to see him fired but avoid recognizing his spiteful impulses by saying to himself "My supervisor is out to have me fired."

Rationalization

Aesop (700 B.C.) is credited with a story about a wolf that wanted some luscious grapes but could not quite reach them. The wolf's later claim that "They are probably sour, anyway" would probably be classified as a **rationalization**— that is, an unconsciously concocted excuse for any display of inadequacy, incompetence, or moral failure. By deciding that the grapes were worthless, the wolf did not have to confront the issue of its own inabilities. Rationalizations take many forms. The sour-grapes rationalization of the wolf numbed failure by making it insignificant. On the other hand, the "sweet-lemon" rationalization involves accentuating the positive: the nice thing about losing a job is that it allows you to sleep late in the mornings.

In effect, rationalizations are often justifications. Sykes and Matza (1957) have discussed some of the ways juvenile delinquents try to disavow guilt by justifying their crimes. (1) They can claim that they are not responsible for what they did and picture themselves as more acted upon than acting, saying, perhaps, "I did it because I am mentally ill and the product of a sick society." (2) They may argue that no real harm was done. Adopting a Robin Hood conception, they may see themselves as redistributing the wealth in a more fair and equitable way. (3) They may consider themselves righteous retaliators, punishing the victim for his wrongs. Statements such as "He had it coming" might exemplify this technique. (4) They may excuse themselves by appealing to higher loyalties, thus attempting to nullify the rules that apply to each of us as members of society. "I knew I shouldn't have stolen that money, but it was necessary to help a friend."

Reaction Formation

Sometimes feelings are very mixed. For example, it is possible for us to love someone but simultaneously hate him because of the power he wields over us. One component of this mixed feeling is acceptable (love), but the other is not, because we have been taught that we should not hate. Reaction formation refers to relegating the unacceptable member of the pair to the unconscious and keeping it there by means of heavy emphasis on the other (Brenner, 1957). Reaction formation can be detected by an irrational emphasis on one set of feelings and a denial of the other. For example, a person who wants all potential weapons such as sharpened pencils kept in an inaccessible place "so that nobody will get hurt" may be defending against his own potentially murderous impulses.

Regression

Like identification, regression is a general process that is sometimes used defensively. Regression refers to reverting to a mode of behavior associated

Regression refers to reverting to a mode of behavior associated with an earlier and happier stage of life.

with an earlier and happier stage of life. Financially ruined, the stockbroker may enter into what people call a second childhood; or, under stress, a society matron may act like a giggling schoolgirl. In the extreme, a person may revert to behavior characteristic of earliest infancy or before, perhaps even adopting the passivity and posture of the fetus in the womb. It is as if by reverting to an earlier phase of life all subsequent time is obliterated, hence eliminating the present harsh conditions.

Earlier I noted that, in moderation, defense mechanisms may be useful. This may not be true of regression. As people progress through life, they acquire new skills for coping with the difficulties they encounter. If a person regresses, these skills (which have been acquired since that earlier time) are lost. Thus, at a time when the going gets rough and all skills should be mobilized, many are disavowed. For this reason one may speculate that regression does not serve as much of a defense at all.

Mental Systems

The memories, perceptions, and impulses that reside in the conscious, preconscious, and unconscious are *dynamic*— that is they shift and change, perhaps moving in the process from one level of awareness to another. Psychoanalysts suggest that the interplay of forces that causes this shifting and changing stems from three mental systems: the id, the ego, and the superego. Each system functions in some way to adjust behavior to internal and external conditions. Among other things, the relationships among these systems are responsible for innocuous choices, mistakes, and accidents. They are also responsible for keeping the motives for these activities, and perhaps even the perception of them, out of awareness.

The Id

The principle of hedonism states that organisms seek pleasure. The earliest-developing system of the mind, the **id**, functions along this principle. Technically speaking, the id operates to *reduce tensions*, which arise from deprivations and privations, such as going without mother's milk or being forced to lie in the clammy muck of an unchanged diaper.

The principle of hedonism should not be new to you. But perhaps the idea that there is a whole component of personality that is *totally devoted* to pleasure

The earliest-developing system of the mind, the id, is totally devoted to pleasure seeking.

seeking is a bit more novel. I say "totally devoted" because Freud suggested that this personality system unthinkingly and urgently acts for immediate satisfactions without any consideration of social amenities or the ultimate consequences of the action. This system is so impetuous, impulsive, and directed toward immediate results that it involves little consideration of the conditions imposed by reality.

Freud believed that the operation of the id produces *pleasurable mental images* —that is, fantasies of happier conditions that would to some extent reduce tension. For example, if the young infant goes unfed, resulting unpleasant tensions will motivate him to imagine food. This mental image, derived from memory, supposedly reduces the gnawing hunger and reinstates a feeling of comfort. Reducing tensions by conjuring up or fantasizing a satisfier is referred to as the **primary process.** Its workings are believed to be evident in dreams, hallucinations, imagination, fantasy, wishful thinking, pipe dreams, daydreams, and, most likely, certain types of drug experiences. As Hall (1954) points out, the relationship of mental imagery to needs is commonly recognized in the case of the thirsty traveler who thinks he sees water and in the case of the bachelor who has wet dreams. But it is less often recognized that images such as those accompanying wet dreams may help to reduce the tensions that produced them.

If the primary process were completely effective, you might respond to someone who offered you some lunch, "Oh, no thank you. I just thought of breakfast about an hour ago." This does not happen, because it is quite impossible for the primary process to effectively change the objective conditions that gave rise to the tensions. Think about breakfast all you want, but the physiological or external cues that contributed to the gnawing hunger still remain. Efficient tension reduction requires that the person wait until the conditions in the real world change or that he somehow instigate the changes himself. Real food must be produced or the clammy diaper actually changed. The second system of the mind to develop, the ego, makes this possible.

The Ego

The **ego** is not wishful; it is thoughtful and realistic. Whereas the id deals in fantasies, the ego deals in realities, coordinating personal needs and real-world conditions for better results. The mental process that helps find or produce more satisfactory conditions in the real world is referred to as the **secondary process.** In effect, the ego forces delay of gratification until such a time as the underlying source of tension can be eliminated. Thus, although at a very early age the thought of milk may diminish hunger-induced tensions, as the child acquires the skills for distinguishing between fantasy and reality, he learns that his tensions are more effectively reduced when milk is actually found and consumed.

The operation of the ego is seen as responsible for a tremendous proportion of human behavior. Ego activity is reflected both in simple self-maintenance and self-protective acts, such as fetching a glass of water or stepping out of the way of a speeding cement mixer, and in the planning and execution of complicated, long-range tasks, such as attending college or saving for retirement. A satisfactorily functioning ego is responsible for behavior we consider direct, purposeful, adaptive, realistic, strong, and competent, as opposed to behavior we consider wishful, fanciful, dreamy, or "sick." Since many people seem to spend more time coming to grips with realities at the expense of manufacturing fantasies, a whole contingent of psychologists has devoted its efforts toward a better understanding of the ego and its functions. Appropriately enough, these psychologists are referred to as **ego psychologists.**

The ego is *amoral*, in that it does not involve judgments about the moral correctness of an activity. It is true that criminal behavior might be overruled if it were perceived that the weed of crime bears bitter fruit. Stealing food and then being carted off to jail before it is consumed would be no better, and perhaps worse, than having to settle for the fantasy of a hamburger deluxe. Moral judgments come from the third system of the mind, which Freud referred to as the superego.

The Superego

The **superego** is the last mental system to develop, usually during the third or fourth year of life. It is the moral system of the mind, involving standards of right and wrong. It dispenses built-in rewards and punishments for behaving, respectively, in acceptable and unacceptable ways. The **ego ideal** is the component that rewards people for behaving in a morally correct or exemplary fashion. Attaining standards of excellence thus gives a deep-seated feeling of a job well done. The **conscience** is the component of the superego that prohibits evil activity or administers punishments for doing something wrong. It can punish not only for evil actions but for evil thoughts or wishes as well. Sometimes the workings seem direct, as in the case of a man who "accidentally" shoots himself after rigging a vicious booby trap. At other times the punishment takes the form of a vague, diffuse unpleasantness that we refer to as guilt.

Whether or not one subscribes to the psychoanalytic theory, it certainly does seem useful to think of internalized, self-administered rewards and punishments. We can feel them, and we often refer to them when trying to describe human activity. As I pointed out in Chapter Six, the rules that are internalized probably represent a set of idealized, purified standards that parents contrive to impart to their children.

The processes of the id, ego, and superego may operate in harmony and thereby contribute to effective living. For example, if you were in need of food, the id might produce from memory the thought of a hamburger. The ego would help you find a real hamburger, perhaps at a crowded neighborhood hamburger stand. The superego would dictate that you politely wait your turn and pay for it when served. Unfortunately, sometimes there is a clashing of systems. For example, the pleasure-seeking part of you may want immediate sexual satisfaction. The moral part of you may forbid that you even think of such a thing. To keep the evil need from awareness, one of the defense mechanisms may be brought into play. If the conflict between the lusty impulse and the conscience's stern dictates is so strong that most of your time is spent using the latter to control the former, energy is robbed from more constructive activities. Some such destructive conflicts may stem from early childhood.

Early Childhood and Adult Personality

Psychoanalytic theory is a developmental theory, in that each person is believed to pass through a series of developmental periods called **psychosexual stages**. Each stage is characterized by the emergence of new needs: to attain new forms of gratification, to master new tasks, and to solve new problems in interpersonal relations. Satisfying these needs frees the person to deal with the challenges posed by the next psychosexual stage. However, needs arising during a certain stage may not be satisfied. In this case they will persist, lingering on at the level of the unconscious because due to their infantile nature they reflect poorly on personal ability or moral character. The potentially painful nature of childhood-based needs is apparent when one considers that they include such things as needs to return to mother's breast, to abandon bowel control, or to marry Daddy.

The existence of hidden, childhood-based needs is inferred in part from dreams and fantasies (which represent attempts by the primary process to deal with the needs), in part from slips of the tongue (which indicate a temporary failure of repression), and in part from suggestive or tattletale actions (which represent disguised behavioral attempts to satisfy the needs). Because of their origin, these behaviors are said to be **derivatives** of the psychosexual stage that gave rise to them. They represent a compromise among the need, the reality orientation of the ego, and the moral dictates of the conscience. For example, the very young child has a need for generous suckling and feeding; if unsatisfied, this need may persist into adulthood. Grown people, however, are not supposed to use baby bottles or pacifiers or to spend hours sucking the nipples of others. More practical or realistic and less forbidden are activities such as smoking and drinking, which are analogous to nipple sucking; thus these activities may be sought by the person deprived in early infancy. Unfortunately, they are only temporary, make-do measures and do not completely erase the underlying need. For this reason, both the need and the derivative are likely to persist.

Before further tracing how a failure to satisfy a need during early childhood can result in certain forms of adult behavior, you might note that relating dreams, fantasies, mistakes, accidents, and other derivatives to the events of early life is no simple task. It may require that the psychoanalyst listen to the person three to five times a week for two to five years. The analyst must cut through his patient's defenses, which are working to keep matters disguised. Remember, now, that these defenses include such processes as reaction formation, which results in needs, memories, perceptions, and impulses being palmed off as their opposites; denial, which makes the person seem like a numbskull; and regression, which blots out some of the present.

Although the popular view is that psychoanalysts have almost imaginary powers (a view that they have not always conscientiously striven to overcome), identifying and interpreting derivatives call for a great deal of supporting evidence, even in cases in which the behavior or fantasies in question seem to be "obvious" instances of something. Thus an old maid's dream of a car with a long, pointed hood might elicit knowing winks from self-styled analysts who "know" that such a car is a disguised symbol of a man's penis, perhaps appearing in her dream as a result of unsatisfied sexual longings. But it may turn out on further investigation that the car was like one once owned by her grandmother, who provided for her when she was small. In this case the car could represent not a desire for a man, but a longing for the secure conditions of early childhood. Then, too, the car could simply represent a car, and this possibility cannot be too quickly disregarded.

The Psychosexual Stages

Freud pointed out that on the surface of the body there are a number of zones, called **erogenous zones,** that are very sensitive to touch. Stimulation of these erogenous zones brings special pleasures that are often described as "sexual." Freud believed that, at different stages of childhood, needs seemed to center around the pleasurable stimulation of different erogenous zones. He named each psychosexual stage after the zone that he thought was most sensitized at that time. Simultaneous with the apparent sensitization of a new erogenous zone is the appearance of new tasks, new demands, and new human-relations problems. Psychoanalytic theory has evolved in such a way that each psychosexual stage is thus useful for understanding the concerns, interests, and skills that gain in importance at different points in early life.

The Oral Stage

Freud suggested that the first sensitized erogenous zone is the oral region, which consists of the mouth, lips, and tongue. The first life issues center around ingestion, since the prime need is food and the prime satisfaction is consumption of it. Supposedly, prolonged and generous feeding leads to satisfaction of oral needs, whereas ungenerous feeding does not.

Associated with early feeding is much that gains importance in its own right. During feeding, the infant is loved, touched, and fondled. He is passive and is waited on without demands being made upon him in return. He discovers whether his needs will be satisfied, and a sense of trust (or distrust) is learned. Trust, in this context, is a sense of faith in oneself, in others, and in the world.

Since stimulation of the oral zone, food ingestion, love, passivity, and trust or distrust are all associated with the **oral stage,** a very wide range of behaviors could thus be interpreted as originating in that stage. For example, alcoholism may reflect unsatisfied needs of the oral stage or a regressive response to present frustration or failure. Drinking itself is analogous to the consumption of milk during early infancy, and sufficient alcohol may restore a state of perceptual diffuseness, which may also be characteristic of early infancy. As Wolowitz (1963) once pointed out in a lecture delivered at the University of Michigan, if the drinking takes place in a cocktail lounge, the drinker may be waited on. This, coupled with a lack of pressures and responsibilities, contributes to a passive existence. Furthermore, good bartenders and waitresses are like good mothers. They are tolerant, accepting, and willing to serve on the basis of very minimal cues. Finally, in the cocktail lounge people can say and do what they ordinarily wouldn't, perhaps because they usually utilize the skills of well-civilized, highly socialized adults.

Many of the issues of each psychosexual stage are highly interrelated. As a result, disturbances during a given stage are likely to result in a *number* of later derivatives, rather than one derivative alone. For example, the drinker might also show passivity; a concern for receiving love, affection, and social approval; and, perhaps, a basic distrust of other people. These various attributes should all cluster together, with either most of them or hardly any of them being characteristic of the same individual. If the whole package of attributes is or is not found in the same person, it becomes plausible to view these derivatives as reflecting one underlying factor, which might be called "orality."

In an extensive and intriguing study, Blum and Miller (1952) sought oral-stage derivatives among third-graders. After defining "oral characters" in terms of self-stimulation of the oral zone (nonpurposive mouth movements such as thumb-sucking, lip licking, tongue rolling, and bubbling), they tested a number of psychoanalytically based hypotheses about the nature of the oral character. The first hypothesis, quite reasonably, was that oral characters would show a greater interest in food. Oral characters were rated by teachers as showing a "greater interest to eat at lunchtime, as if eating were particularly important." More intriguing was the actual food consumption. Each day for 15 days, a period of time was set aside when the children could eat as many 1-ounce cups of ice cream as they wanted. As expected, the oral characters consumed the most.

Since love and approval are coupled with feeding, oral characters who have presumably been deprived of love and approval should show more behavior directed toward securing affection. Oral characters were rated by their teachers as more eager to have other children like them. They were also rated as more dependent, seeking more attention from adults and other children. Behaviorally, the oral characters were observed to have a slightly greater tendency to approach the teacher to seek reassurance and approval.

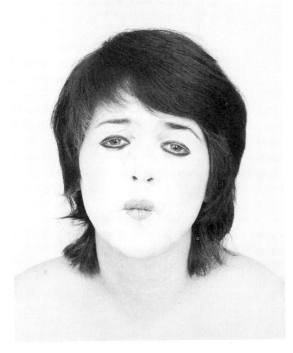

Oral characters are believed to show an excessive concern with love and approval.

A third psychoanalytically based hypothesis was that oral characters should be more concerned about giving and receiving. Both gifts and food signify love, affection, and approval and according to psychoanalytic thought can to some extent substitute for each other in the unconscious workings of the mind. Therefore the receipt of one (such as a gift) should partially reduce interest in another (such as food). On one day during the experiment the children were given gifts of pencils and on another day gifts of crayons. On both days there was a highly significant drop in ice-cream consumption. Apparently the receipt of a gift reduced some of the needs for food, just as Freud might have expected.

The final hypothesis that will concern us here dealt with social skills and was based on the supposition that, as a person successfully advances through a psychosexual stage, he acquires new and more sophisticated ways of dealing with others. The oral character should thus rely more heavily on immature social skills associated with the oral stage. Reliance on these primitive social skills should be reflected in difficulties in interpersonal relations, and oral characters should have fewer friends.

In private interviews, each child was asked which children in his class he (1) liked the least, (2) would most like to invite to a party, and (3) considered a good friend. Popularity scores were then computed, and oral children proved to have fewer friends, which did suggest less sophisticated social skills on their part. This finding was substantiated by Miller and Stine (1951), who found in a study of older children that greater orality was associated with less popularity.

Blum and Miller tested their psychoanalytically based hypotheses using a number of different measures. Not all results were favorable to psychoanalytic theory, but the overall batting average was impressive. By chance alone, Blum and Miller should have found 4.41 statistically significant correlations between nonpurposive mouth movements and the various other measures. In point of fact, they obtained 33.00 significant correlations, which suggests that their results did not reflect chance.

The Anal Stage

The second erogenous zone to gain in importance is the anus. Freud believed that during the **anal stage,** important pleasures came from the retention and elimination of feces.

A central task arising during this stage is toilet training. The child has no inborn disgust reaction to bodily waste products, but his parents certainly do.

When he is about 2 years old, his parents begin insisting on the retention and relinquishing of waste products under a highly specified set of conditions. For the first time in his life, serious demands are placed upon him.

Cleanliness training may involve terrifying aspects, even when the parents' procedures are not harsh, irrational, or stupid. The child is sometimes left alone, perched precariously on a high seat with a hole in it. The seat is in turn on top of a larger seat, which contains an aperture sufficiently large for a small person to fall through. Anything that does fall through comes to rest in a pool of liquid, later to vanish in a whirling vortex. All this takes place in a strange room that is a unique combination of American Baroque and Hospital Asepsis.

The parents teach that cleanliness is right and filth is wrong. The child learns to be "responsible"—that is, to do what the parents demand. The internalization of these standards produces a rudimentary superego. But the lesson can be too well learned, and the child can become oversensitive to all forms of filth and disorder in later life.

Since the standards learned during this stage have to do with filth, one of the chief derivatives of the anal stage is a concern about cleanliness and persistent reactions against all forms of filth and disorder. This derivative can appear in a very obvious form, such as frequent floor scrubbing, car polishing, and hand washing, or in very symbolic and disguised form, such as a harsh condemnation of dirty books. Exaggerated concerns for cleanliness, neatness, and order can make the anal character's life miserable and do little to cheer his associates who do not share these overconcerns with cleanliness. For example, I doubt that most women who scrub their floors repeatedly find this activity highly rewarding, and I doubt that most Americans would have a good time at a party where the hostess demanded that they remove their shoes before entering her home.

Freud believed that cleanliness training provided the arena for a power struggle between the child and the parents. The parents make demands on the child, and he struggles to retain control over the natural, the spontaneous, and the pleasurable. This power struggle can be reflected in a later obstinacy, which reflects a persistent need not to give in to the parents. Couch and Keniston (1960) have traced "negativism" to the anal stage, and more recently Bishop (1967) has presented experimental evidence suggesting that anal characters are more obstinate and less willing to yield to the indirect demands of other people.

The Phallic Stage

Psychoanalysts suggest that in the third psychosexual stage, which typically begins around the third year of life, the genitals become sensitized, as suggested by masturbatory activity. During this phallic stage, boy-girl differences become prominent to the child. The perception of boy-girl differences, coupled with concerns about punishment for an increasing attraction to the opposite sex, produces irrational fears and resentments.

Earlier in life a child could easily assume that all other people possessed the same anatomy. Discriminatory powers were not highly developed, walking was an imperfect skill, and imprisonment in a playpen was likely. At about age 3, however, the child has the perceptual abilities, the motor skills, and the curiosity to discover sex differences. He does not, however, have the adult *explanation* of these differences.

Boys observe that girls seem to be missing something that they themselves possess. To explain this, they may imagine that girls lost their penis as a punishment for a wrongdoing. They may speculate that they, too, have committed some wrong and may suffer the same horrible fate. This feeling can result in later castration anxiety, an exaggerated fear of harm to the genitals or, thanks to partial repression, a fear of harm to other parts of the body. Castration anxiety can take the form of a fear of sharp implements, such as scissors, or it can be manifested in the practice of some World War II flyers who sat on their bulletproof hats and vests, showing callous disregard for heart and brains.

During this stage, also, girls discover that males have something that they do not have. Were they born a partial cripple? At birth did they, too, have male genitals, only to later lose them as punishment? This feeling may appear later as a resentfulness of men because they had no such previous losses. This resentfulness, rather undiplomatically called penis envy, supposedly appears in women's attempts to prove sexual equality or superiority by means of vicious, sarcastic attacks on men.

Disturbing thoughts about impending or occurred mutilation are instigated or strengthened by events associated with the child's interest in the parent of the opposite sex. Freud suspected that the sensitization of the genitals during the phallic stage resulted in a rudimentary desire for a partner of the opposite sex and that the person selected was likely to be the parent, since the parent is the most frequently contacted adult. The son's involvement with his mother is referred to as the **Oedipus complex** and the daughter's involvement with her father the **Electra complex.** Let's follow the pattern of events for the son-father-mother triangle, since the psychoanalysts are most explicit about it.

The son's attraction to the mother is accompanied by hostility toward the father, who is seen as a powerful and frustrating rival. Supposedly, a natural consequence of frustration is aggression (Chapter Twelve); but since aggressive impulses toward the father are unacceptable, they are translated, through projection, into "Daddy hates me." To avoid imagined punishment from the father in the form of castration, the son becomes like the father—that is, identifies with him. This process involves adopting the father's moral values and standards and is hence an important step in the development of the superego.

Social behaviors during this Oedipus or Electra phase can serve as models for patterns of social behavior later in life, since the person caught up in these complexes reenacts the behaviors as an adult. For example, a man may unconsciously seek a marital partner who is similar to the longed-for mother. Or, a woman may attempt to steal the boyfriend or husband of another, not realizing that this behavior reflects a repressed need to steal her father from her mother. If she succeeds in taking a man away from someone else, she may discover that he is no longer of interest and will set out to reenact the scenario once again.

Hall and Van de Castle (1965) examined the hypothesis that in dreams men would express castration anxiety and women would express penis envy and a wish to make themselves equal by symbolically castrating men. Dreams, you will recall, are believed to contain usually repressed material that slips into awareness in disguised or symbolic form.

First the researchers established criteria for evaluating the various symbols and events in dreams that could indicate castration anxiety or a castration desire. For example, if a man dreamed that he was being cut, bitten, or clawed, this content was considered representative of castration anxiety. If a woman dreamed that she had a penis or male secondary sex characteristics such as a beard, this content was considered to reflect penis envy. Dream reports were then read and evaluated by two judges, and there was good agreement between them, which suggested that their scoring procedures were reliable. By the criteria selected, males were more likely to have dreams representing castration anxiety and women dreams representing penis envy.

The Latent and Genital Stages

Freud believed that the oral, anal, and phallic stages were the most eventful. Following the phallic stage, children supposedly enter a period of quiescence (the **latent stage**). From ages 4 to 14 erogenous zones are relatively desensitized, and not much new of significance happens.

The concept of the latent stage is perhaps the most criticized psychoanalytic idea. We now believe that stimulation of the erogenous zones is still sought, and, as I pointed out in Chapter Six, there are many important personality-formative events associated with middle childhood. For example, the child enters school, acquires new models, and develops new working relationships with other people.

At puberty the genitals again become important as mature sexual desires appear. This phase is the **genital stage.** But the onset of adult sexual impulses by no means implies that the person has resolved all the issues of his earlier psychosexual stages. Earlier needs may be reflected in the conditions under which sexual relations become attractive. One person may "love" someone because he satisfies deep-set needs for passivity; another may "love" a person who submits to his orders; a third may "love" someone who is already possessed by another.

I doubt that the transition to mature sexuality is ever an easy one. Our society is curiously lacking in effective, standardized socialization practices that encourage a responsible and healthy outlook on sex. Haphazard socialization techniques, coupled with a strong emphasis on sex, make it easy for people to forget that their dates, lovers, or spouses are unique *persons*, not simply objects to be used. The establishment of a mutually satisfactory relationship with a member of the opposite sex requires more than good luck during each psychosexual stage; it requires hard work during adulthood as well.

Psychoanalysis: Contributions and Limitations

The psychoanalytic theory of personality is a complete theory. It is perhaps the most general of the general theories of behavior. At the time it was introduced, it had a tremendous impact on thinking about man. It was one of the first theories to deal with the *origins* of personality; prior to Freud, the main concern seemed to be one of classification and labeling. Psychoanalytic theory suggested that an understanding of early-childhood events contributed heavily toward understanding later personality. It sensitized people to the possible importance of things such as toilet training and castration fears, which "nice people" didn't discuss. Psychoanalysis made salient the concept of the unconscious and introduced the self-protecting mechanisms of defense. All these contributions have so shaped the course of modern psychology that their origins are often forgotten. Sadly for Freud, who wanted to be remembered as a man who disturbed the sleep of the world, what *are* quickly associated with his name are some of his least fruitful concepts, which have not been blended in with modern psychology. These concepts have not been dwelt upon here.

Psychology has not stood still during the 30-odd years since Freud's death, and developments during this time have certainly highlighted some of the problems with the psychoanalytic orientation. Criticisms of psychoanalysis abound.

First, it has been suggested that, for various technical reasons, psychoanalytically based hypotheses are impossible to test scientifically. I do not believe this. Neither did the authors whose research was reported thus far in this chapter. But, on the whole, given the importance and level of acceptance of psychoanalytic theory, it is true that there is relatively little supporting experimental evidence.

A second criticism has to do with the concept of the unconscious. Freud introduced the concept to help account for behavior that was previously unexplained. But the content of the unconscious can be inferred only when the material erupts to the surface. At this point it is no longer in the unconscious. Would it not be simpler to forget about the distinctions among the conscious, preconscious, and unconscious?

Third, although psychoanalysts sensitized students of man to early-childhood events, they drew attention away from the important events of later life. In the discussion of developmental psychology (Chapter Six) you read how some of the events of middle childhood and later life can produce significant alterations in behavior. To be satisfactory, a complete theory of personality must have some way of dealing convincingly with these later life events.

Fourth, psychoanalysis has been criticized for overplaying the medical model, which, as you may recall, suggests people who show unacceptable behavior are "patients" who suffer from "mental illnesses" and may be interned in a "mental hospital" as a part of their "treatment." This medical model had the

Critics of Freud correctly argue that personality formation does not end here.

wonderful effect of removing the shackles from "mental patients." It led to predominantly tolerant and compassionate reactions to the "mentally ill," as opposed to reactions of hostility, fear, and ridicule. However, the "mental illness" conception implies certain causes of unacceptable behavior and a necessity for certain types of treatment procedures. In Chapter Ten we will explore more fully why the "mental illness" approach may not be the most useful one thus far devised.

Finally, Freud arrived at his theories after dealing with a large number of people who came to him for consultation and help. These people did not visit him for the fun of it; in one way or another, they were living unhappy and ineffective lives. It is therefore not surprising that the picture of man these people presented was a rather discouraging one. Freud understood them by believing that they were driven by tensions and that their personalities were shaped by the clashing of hidden psychological forces. He found them often unaware of the reasons for what they did, and he considered many of their actions infantile because they expressed impulses lingering on from early childhood. Other psychologists have been at least equally impressed by mature, well-rounded people who are living their lives happily and effectively. Their orientation emphasizes the capacities, abilities, and activities that attest to the positive, striving nature of man.

Freud was a product of his time. He lived in a repressive Victorian society and treated particular kinds of cases. We can only speculate what form his theorizing might have taken if he were presently alive and well and practicing in Hong Kong, Paris, or Big Sur, California. Certainly conditions have changed since his time, and psychology *has* advanced. It is fashionable to poke fun at Freud. But perhaps it is now time to simply accept the fact that this man made important contributions to the understanding of all men and to move forward into the future.

HUMANISTIC PSYCHOLOGY

Humanistic psychology represents an *orientation* to psychology (Severin, 1965). Most psychologists with this orientation are rebels: they rebel against the behavioristic approach of academic psychologists and against the pessimistic approach of the psychoanalysts. They question these traditional psychologists' views of man, the value of their questions about man, and the kinds of methods that they typically employ.

Orientations can be adopted to varying degrees. Some humanistic psychologists seem to feel little indebtedness to the offerings of psychoanalysts and traditional academic psychologists. Others subscribe more fully to the *Articles of Association* of the American Association for Humanistic Psychology (reported in Severin, 1965), which avow respect for differences of approach and open-mindedness regarding acceptable methods. However, all humanistic psychologists believe that psychoanalysts and traditional academic psychologists have been shortsighted and have ignored very important aspects of human thoughts, feelings, and actions. Here I will emphasize some of the features of the humanistic orientation that distinguish it from other approaches to understanding people.

An Approach to Man

The early behaviorists saw man as a collection of response patterns, and the psychoanalysts saw him as a mentally active creature. Like the psychoanalysts, humanistic psychologists see man as more than a pattern of behaviors; but unlike the psychoanalysts, they see man as a *conscious, free, whole being who sets goals and then strives to attain them,* rather than as a hapless victim of mysterious conflicts and tensions.

Unlike psychoanalysts, humanistic psychologists see man as a conscious, free, whole being who sets goals and then strives to attain them.

Man as Conscious

To many humanistic psychologists, man's subjective experiences of himself are more important than his objective deeds and actions. That is, *consciousness,* or awareness, is treated as an important psychological variable. Rather than try to eliminate the subjective, the humanistic psychologists suggest that we should study it and try to understand it.

Man as Free

Behaviorists and psychoanalysts followed the lead of all sciences by adopting the strong deterministic position that all behavior is caused by factors not under the conscious control of the behaving person. Humanistic psychologists, on the other hand, present a picture of man as free to make choices and personally responsible for the course of his own life.

Whether or not man is in fact free, he certainly views himself as having a number of options available among which he may choose. Szasz (1967) suggests that man's impression of freedom may have been strengthened in modern times as a result of two outstanding sets of achievements. First, advances in agriculture, industry, and medicine have freed him from spending most of his time and efforts fighting for mere biological survival. In effect, the time once spent hoeing turnips can now be spent contemplating the nature and meaning of existence. Second, increasingly larger proportions of people are becoming literate and educated. Such knowledge opens up new perspectives and detracts from the strength of the rules of conduct formerly prescribed by religion, custom, and etiquette.

Man as a Whole Being

Many humanistic psychologists argue that man can be considered only as a whole, integrated human; any attempts to understand him as an aggregate of loosely related parts is bound to fail. Trying to describe man by breaking up his personality into a number of component parts (reducing him, perhaps, to a collection of socially learned habits) destroys his essential humanness. At their worst these attempts can be likened to describing a symphony as a collection of musical notes or a work of art as 4628 brush strokes.

Man as Striving

Man's consciousness and freedom of choice allow him to go beyond the minimal requirements for existence and develop his capacities as a human. The tendency to develop one's potentials is considered an important source of human satisfactions and is prominent in the personality theorizing of many humanistic psychologists. We will dwell on this concept of man as striving when we consider the theories of Abraham Maslow and Carl Rogers.

Questions about Man

The image of man implicit in a psychological approach dictates the kind of questions that must be asked about man. The humanistic psychologists, who see man as conscious, free, whole, and striving, thus emphasize certain types of questions.

Since man is viewed as unique in his degree of awareness and freedom of choice, humanistic psychologists suggest that it is not just risky but impossible to generalize from insect or animal to man. They ask questions about man directly. Furthermore, since the intent is to understand man in his environment, not man in the psychological laboratory, they maintain that man must be studied in his natural setting.

How does man experience himself and the world about him?

The kinds of questions asked include: (1) What is consciousness, and how may we think about it? (2) How does man experience himself and the world about him? (3) What goals are important to an individual, and how does he go about attaining them? (4) What is the psychologically strong and creative person like? (5) How may we understand such things as affection, love, personal responsibility, autonomy, fair play, and character strength, which are typically ignored in traditional psychological research? The humanistic psychologist seeks to understand the "individual, the exceptional and the unpredicted" as well as the "regular, the universal and the conforming" (Bugental, 1967).

Developing a Methodology

Since humanistic psychologists stress a nontraditional view of man and ask nontraditional questions, they are understandably interested in developing a new methodology. They argue that, although traditional experimental methods may have been useful in physics and chemistry, they are not so effective for seeking answers about modern man as most psychologists give them credit for. In some cases scientists have been more concerned with fancy methods than with significant questions, and the humanistic psychologists' argument that these priorities should be reversed does not seem unreasonable.

An example of nontraditional methodology is found in a study by Moustakas (1961), who abandoned the sacred principle of remaining coldly aloof from the subject under study. After undergoing a period of great loneliness, he decided to study this topic by going to places where he could find lonely people and then letting himself become as lonely as possible. After he had done this to the point at which he felt some patterns emerging, he described his experiences in a book (1961). Following publication of his book, he received some 500 letters that he felt verified his portrayal of loneliness (Moustakas, 1967). These letters, he suggests, validate his study. Of course, we do not know the impressions of people who did not write. Earlier (Chapter One) I pointed out that the reactions of people are so diverse that almost anything may seem obvious or right. Clearly, Moustakas' impressions were "right on" for a large number of people, but whether or not he tapped the dominant reaction to loneliness we do not know.

*Personal Growth Theories: Fulfillment of Human
Potentials as a Motivating Force*

Both the drive-habit theory of motivation (Chapter Four) and the psychoanalytic theory of personality characterize man's behavior as a response to unpleasant tensions. Behavior represents an attempt to move toward a state of quiescence. In the earlier discussion of motivation (Chapter Four), I noted that dissenters from this position suggest that people can also be characterized as *active* organisms that engage in many activities for their own sake. Artists, heroes, great thinkers, explorers, and martyrs, to name a few, do not seem motivated by needs to reduce tensions.

Several psychologists best described as humanistic have organized theories of personality suggesting that people strive to exercise their abilities in such a way as to use their potentials to the utmost. In other words, they strive to grow and develop psychologically. We can call these theories **personal growth theories.**

Several theories of personality suggest that people strive to exercise their abilities in such a way as to use their potentials to the utmost.

The process of personal growth goes by several names, including self-actualization, becoming yourself, self-fulfillment, and, in the vernacular, doing your own thing. Such terms are delightfully imprecise to social philosophers and dreadfully imprecise to traditional psychologists, but, in any event, they are roughly interchangeable. Here I will tend to favor the term **self-actualization,** which was popularized by Maslow.

Personal growth theories suggest that people may undergo a process of unfolding or movement toward some favorable end state. In simplest form, this type of theory suggests that each of us is continually engaging in self-actualizing behavior, because all behavior reflects this sovereign motive. Although a person may appear to be motivated by specific needs for safety, affiliation, and power, each such need is subservient to the all-supreme motive for self-actualization, which provides unity to the person's strivings. When lonely, the person actualizes by seeking others; when insecure, by seeking security; when weak, by seeking power.

Theories suggesting that all human activities reflect progress toward an ultimate end state are **teleological explanations** of behavior. That is, the cause of the behavior is sought in the end state. To give any credence at all to this type of explanation, it is necessary to specify the conditions under which the end state will exert its compelling influence. Simply saying that everything someone says or does reflects self-actualizing tendencies does not provide this careful specification. We might as well say that all behavior is motivated by a desire to become one with God or to return to the sea as amphibians.

In other personal growth theories, some, but not all, behavior represents self-actualization. For one man it may involve leaving a $50,000-a-year job to open a small pottery shop; for another, participating in a soulful rendition of a bassoon concerto; for a third, becoming chairman of the board of a large corporation. But in each case there are rewards from the exercise of the person's unique human potentials.

Maslow's Viewpoint

Abraham Maslow was a personal growth theorist who adopted the moderate position that self-actualization does not account for all behavior. People have a tendency to self-actualize but will not do so unless certain basic *deficit* needs are satisfied. These include needs for nourishment, comfort, and safety. If deficit needs are unsatisfied, the person will remain anxious, apprehensive, and unable to realize his human potential. Simply put, he who is hungry, rejected by his girl, or wearing wet socks will not find fulfillment in a bassoon concerto.

What are self-actualizing people like? Maslow (1956, 1967) identified self-actualizers on the basis of an absence of strong neurotic, psychotic, or anti-social tendencies (Chapter Ten) coupled with evidence suggesting that they were using their capacities and talents to the fullest extent. The people studied were great historical figures, such as Spinoza and Jefferson; great people who were then contemporary, such as Eleanor Roosevelt; and personal acquaintances of Maslow's. The observations took the form of fairly global impressions, and the results (Maslow, 1956) took the form of generalities about self-actualizing people.

1. Self-actualizers quickly and effectively cut through fakery, tomfoolery, and falsehoods to perceive things the way they really are. They are comfortable with the underlying conditions that they find.
2. Self-actualizers are not crippled by shame or guilt or embedded in an impregnable fortress of defense mechanisms. They are accepting of their own shortcomings and tolerant of the faults and foibles of others.
3. Self-actualizers are spontaneous. They have a zest for life and active living. They fully experience and appreciate a wide range of emotions, both joyous and sorrowful.
4. Self-actualizers are problem centered and appear to have a mission in life. This mission reflects something other than self-concern.
5. Compared to the average person, the self-actualizer is detached, in that he shows more need for solitude and personal privacy.
6. Self-actualizers are autonomous. They work effectively and efficiently on tasks without requiring continual support from others.
7. Self-actualizers have a never-decreasing appreciation for life. They continue to react with "awe, pleasure, and even ecstasy" after others have become jaded and indifferent.
8. Self-actualizers are likely to have undergone what Maslow calls "mystical," "peak," or **oceanic experiences.** This feeling involves an impression of opening horizons, a loss of anchoring in time and place, and a subsequent conviction that something very important has happened.
9. Self-actualizers *like* other people. They have sympathy and affection for mankind. Rather than clinging, passive, or possessive social contacts, they have effective relationships that prove rewarding to themselves and to others. Friendships are likely to be selective but deep and enduring. Self-actualizers' acceptance of others is general: their orientation toward people is primarily democratic. This attitude is shown by a lack of bigotry and prejudice and by a lack of aggression in their humor.
10. Self-actualizers are ethical.
11. Self-actualizers have a flair for being creative, original, and innovative. They tend to leave their mark on whatever they touch.
12. Self-actualizers are *not* perfect. They can be "stubborn, irritating, wasteful, and vain." However, Maslow believes that their flaws represent at worst the "lesser human failings."

Maslow's concept of self-actualizers is intriguing, if for no other reason than because he presents a rather encouraging picture of man. Whether the picture he distilled of the psychologically wonderful person is accurate, I do not know. However, I do have some doubts about his claim that there is an ordering of needs such that basic deficit needs must be satisfied as a prerequisite for self-actualization. Against this claim is folklore suggesting that quite a few people who have starved to death in unfurnished attics were creative, individualistic, and spontaneous, whereas some other people who have had every deficit need satisfied have shown few or no indications of self-actualization.

Rogers' Viewpoint

Carl Rogers (for example, 1956, 1961, 1967) is another personal growth theorist who has had a great impact on modern psychology. Whereas Maslow's formulations about personal growth were instigated by an interest in "wonderful people," Rogers' approach evolved from his working with clients in psychotherapy. A self theorist, Rogers suggests that underlying most personal problems is a search for the real self. Each person asks "Who am I *really*? How can I get in touch with this real, underlying self? How can I become myself?" (Rogers, 1956, p. 196).

Rogers believes that personal growth or *becoming yourself* is instigated by a push from within. The push is toward feeling and acting in ways consistent with the real, inner self that is hidden by social roles, the demands of the situation, and a sense of the should. Quite literally, the person who realizes his human potentials is the person who finds himself.

Finding the real, inner self involves dropping the masks or false fronts that have been used to make do in daily situations. These facades are those that other people teach us we *ought* to show. They are probably learned very early in life. "Positive regard" (that is, social approval) from others tends to be *conditional*, in that it is typically received only if the person does the socially right thing or shows the socially accepted facade. This conditional regard can reinforce phony and superficial behavior, which is inconsistent with the real, inner self. *Unconditional regard*, on the other hand, allows a person to be what he wants without risking ridicule or rejection. In a clinical or counseling situation, unconditional regard is very useful for helping the person to discover and express his real, inner self. That is, unconditional regard encourages facades to be dropped, allowing innermost beliefs, feelings, and experiences to be admitted and accepted.

Becoming yourself takes different forms with different people, since everyone is unique. However, Rogers notes certain characteristic trends among people who achieve success in this regard. First, they become *more open to experience*. Second, they tend to have *more trust in their own emotions, beliefs, and actions*. Finally, they tend to view their personality as a *process* or a *stream of becoming*, rather than as a finished product or result.

Focus on the Contemporary

A common theme in psychological theorizing is an emphasis on childhood experiences as contributing to later personality. Learning approaches suggest that personality can best be understood by examining the person's reinforcement history. Psychoanalysts hold that personality is well formed by the time the child enters school. Maslow's theorizing maintains that the basic deficit needs remaining unsatisfied from childhood will impair self-actualization in adult life. In short, many personality theories place a great deal of emphasis on the person's past.

Some humanistic psychologists, unhappy with this emphasis on long-past events, emphasize the immediate, contemporaneous "here-and-now" forces that shape personality. From this **ahistorical perspective,** *earlier experiences are important only insofar as they are represented in the present.* For example, suppose a 35-year-old man incorrectly views his boss as out to get him. Psychoanalysts might seek the cause of his distorted perception in incidents that occurred decades earlier, when, during the phallic stage, the man might have seen his father as out to get him. Psychologists of the ahistorical perspective would counter that the important consideration is not what happened to him many years ago but his present perception of another person as hostile and uncaring. Thus past events assume importance only if they produce present forces; in attempts to understand personality, psychologists might try to deal with these present forces as straightforwardly as possible.

Emphasis on the here-and-now can be traced to the experimentally oriented Gestalt psychologists and to the work of Kurt Lewin (who was himself heavily influenced by Gestalt principles). Lewin made many important contributions to the study of personality and social psychology, not the least of which was his insistence that behavior is invariably a function of both the organism and the environment. Lewin represented people and the forces acting upon them by means of intricate diagrams. His approach drew heavily from topology, a branch of mathematics that is particularly suitable for describing forces. In some ways his system is simple, but it is masked by a rather complex vocabulary. An overview of Lewin's approach can be found in Geiwitz (1969). Here I will emphasize a more contemporary approach that also stresses the here-and-now.

The Gestalt Therapist's View of Personality

Once there was a controversial man named Friedrich ("Fritz") Perls. Fritz was trained in psychoanalysis and was for some time the director of a psychoanalytic institute. But he was also heavily influenced by another European force, Gestalt psychology. What evolved—Gestalt therapy—is more a method of treatment than a theory of personality (Perls, 1969). Nevertheless, the very humanistic Gestalt therapists have much to say about effective and ineffective personalities, and their principles for living provide important guidelines for some people. Of significance here are (1) their very strong emphasis on the here-and-now and (2) the concept of unfinished business.

In Chapter Six I pointed out that an advantage of language is that the user can deal with the abstract. Language frees man from space and time: he can reflect on the past and anticipate the future. However, *he runs the risk of becoming engrossed in these thoughts of other times and other places*. This situation can present serious problems. Thoughts of the past and future are not always pleasant reminiscences and delightful anticipations. Many people spend much time regretting yesterday and worrying about tomorrow. Indeed, since man knows that in endless progression tomorrow will become today and today will become yesterday, he can worry about such complex issues as how he will feel about yesterday's or today's actions tomorrow or tomorrow's actions when tomorrow becomes yesterday. Such brooding takes tremendous time and energy. In the process *the present may pass by*, making little impact on consciousness. Immediate experiences of joy, anger, or sorrow may be continually diluted or lost as life itself slips away.

Language serves in another way to deaden awareness. People are generally well trained to describe themselves verbally, and they use words in such a way as to make themselves seem as knowledgeable and rational as possible. Attempts to deal with personality, both professional and otherwise, often draw on this intellectual ability. For example, getting to know someone often consists mainly of trading information, beginning with rather trivial data such as names, ages, occupations, and places of birth. Later, when more personal information is exchanged, there may be a tendency to *talk about* feelings rather than express them directly (Rogers, 1967). Thus, in at least two senses, language seems to serve as a *shield* that protects the person from full awareness of the present. First, it allows reminiscences and regrets, anticipations and fears to provide a source of distraction. Second, it provides a buffer that impairs the direct expression of feeling when someone is trying to communicate with others. Ironically, since language allows the person to think about the past, he may keep brooding about some dreadful experience; but since language serves as an emotional buffer, it keeps him from expressing these feelings to others.

Many humanistic psychologists suggest that experiencing our feelings and allowing them full expression are forms of self-actualization, leading to a more effective and contented existence. Some even argue that this is true whether or not the feelings are pleasant. Sorrow, as well as joy, is an important part of life. If these feelings are not expressed, a certain part of life is missing. But the failure to express unhappy feelings can have other bad consequences. Gestalt therapists suggest that failing to express a feeling does not mean that the feeling will cease to exist. Suppressed feelings, like repressed impulses, can create tension and conflict and draw energy away from constructive, effective living in the present. It is here that the concept of **unfinished business** enters in.

You will recall that the experimentally oriented Gestalt psychologists offered a principle called closure, which in perception refers to the tendency to perceive incomplete stimuli as if they were finished or complete. Recall, too, Zeigarnik's research (cited in the earlier discussion of repression), which showed that under neutral conditions people tend to remember unfinished tasks—that is, tasks associated with a lack of closure. Such findings as these provided the basis for the concept of unfinished business.

Perhaps you have seen the old movie routine that portrays unfinished business quite exactly. It involves a musician and someone who is trying to sleep. At first, the music itself keeps the victim awake. But the musician, for some reason, leaves the last few notes unplayed. Although it is now quiet, the victim in the adjoining room still cannot sleep. He must first arise, find the instrument, and finish the tune. This scene is funny to most viewers, perhaps because they have experienced similar situations. Such a "lack of closure" proves unpleasant and disruptive and prevents the person from going on to something else.

The kinds of unfinished tasks the Gestalt therapists see as particularly important are those involving expressing feelings toward other people. Perhaps a death in the family has led to grief that has not been fully expressed. Perhaps there are feelings of love and affection that have long been suppressed. Or perhaps there are pent-up feelings of anger and hatred. Although this lingering business may have been initiated in the past, it is important because of its present disruptive effects.

What can be done about unfinished business? It can be finished. To be sure, people can't summon a loved one from the grave to tell him how much they cared. Neither would punching the boss in the nose necessarily be a practical course of action. The Gestalt therapists suggest, however, that it is sufficient for the individual to express his feelings *as if* the other person were present. To encourage this, an empty chair is placed opposite the person, and he is asked to imagine the other's presence. The therapist assists him in seeking out and releasing his unexpressed feelings. A genuine and full expression of the emotions marks the completion of unfinished business. If the process is successful, the person is freed for more effective living in the present.

. . . it is sufficient for the individual to express his feelings as if *the other person were present.*

The Encounter Group Movement

Very much a part of the humanistic orientation to psychology is the encounter group movement. A wide array of powerful interpersonal forces are found in the small group. The possibility that small groups could become training grounds for effective living was recognized in the early 1940s by the group dynamicists, who had an academic interest, the group psychotherapists, who wanted to use groups for the treatment of the mentally ill, and a few daring and innovative persons (primarily industrial managers) who tried to use principles of group dynamics and group psychotherapy to train people in human relations. However, it has been recent, humanistically oriented psychologists such as Carl Rogers who have spurred the development and tremendous growth of this movement during the last five or ten years.

There are several names for small groups that are used as vehicles for understanding one's own personality and ways of relating to others: T groups, encounter groups, sensitivity groups and so on. Here, for simplicity, I will refer to them as **encounter groups.** This label is likely to upset the connoisseur, but suffice it to say that encounter, sensitivity, and T groups all seem to have certain elements in common.

Objectives of Encounter Groups

The main assumption of encounter groups is that participation leads to self-understanding, understanding of others, more effective social relations, and a generally beneficial (but not necessarily comfortable) set of experiences. The general techniques by which these ends are sought include (1) increasing participants' awareness of the environment, (2) increasing participants' communication skills, (3) encouraging people to drop their personas and become themselves, and (4) encouraging trust in oneself and others.

Increasing Awareness. Contemporary life proceeds at such a frantic pace that it is easy to lose contact with the rich wealth of experiences available to consciousness. This happens because people tend to neglect some of their capabilities for perceiving the world. In essence, there is such emphasis on the quickest and most efficient modes of perceiving (such as visually) that other perceptual abilities fall into disuse. Many encounter groups use specific exercises designed to increase awareness by reopening these neglected channels. Most people find that recontacting the world through ignored sensory channels is very pleasant.

Awareness seems to be increased by almost anything that encourages the person to slow down and attend to a broader band of sensory input. Silent meditation is believed to increase sensitivity to sights, sounds, and fragrances. Massaging, tickling, and brisk backslapping are used to reawaken the sense of touch. Some such exercises, particularly those such as massage, which require participants to touch each other, are high risk, in that they raise the participants' fears. An interesting low-risk exercise is the **blind walk,** which only rarely fails to prove intriguing. People form pairs. One person becomes "blind" by closing his eyes and he is led around by the second person, or guide.

Without talking, the guide leads him to stimuli that can be appreciated without the use of sight, such as the rough texture of a tree stump, the smooth texture of a weathered rock, the sound of crashing waves, or the fragrance of a bed of clover. For the "blind" these simple stimuli assume new dimensions that the normal attentional processes ignore. The guide, on the other hand, finds the blind walk a challenge to his creativity and his sense of responsibility. Later the blind man and the guide switch roles so that each can share the different experiences.

A low-risk exercise is the blind walk, which only rarely fails to be intriguing.

Increasing Communication Skills. Many people have difficulties in communicating with others. Despite the best of intentions, in some cases people cannot cut through irrelevancies and get to the heart of the matter when they are trying to speak. Neither can they *really listen* when others are speaking. Although they may say or hear the words, they do not genuinely appreciate the meanings behind them. In extreme cases we find people telling elaborate stories only to prove that they can be more entertaining or more tear-jerking than the others present and deliberately shutting out what others say in order to secretly rehearse for their next verbal performance. In the encounter group attempts are made to break down such communication barriers.

Group participants are encouraged to be open, honest, frank, and explicit, paying close attention to what they themselves and others say. It turns out that one way to enhance communication skills is to consciously strive to do so. Another way is to talk in very simple terms, using subject-predicate sentences and not continuing to the next sentence until it is crystal clear that the message in the first sentence has registered. Keeping communications simple and in the present (in the here-and-now as opposed to the there-and-then) minimizes the problem that such a large number of different thoughts will be expressed in one breath that it will be impossible for the listener to discern the central message.

Not just *what* is said, but *how* it is said, is also considered important. If someone says "I am really angry" in a nice, calm, collected voice, it suggests that he is *thinking about* being angry; if he shouts "I am really angry" while pounding the floor, it suggests that he *is* really angry. A genuine expression of emotion suggests to many psychologists spontaneity, a baring of the inner self, and, perhaps, the completion of unfinished business. For these reasons howling, yowling, and caterwauling are seen as psychologically healthier than an abstract discussion of one's inferred emotions.

Many groups also provide exercises for sharpening nonverbal communication skills (see Chapter Thirteen). For example, members are encouraged to learn about one another without talking. Forming acquaintanceships in this manner can be accomplished through gesturing, facial expressions, and physical contact. In the latter case participants may mill about, staring at one another and stopping to touch hands as they pass. Many people are surprised to discover that hands are expressive and that different people's hands are strikingly unalike.

Dropping Masks and Games.   One thing very clear in all encounter groups is the premium placed on the real, inner self. Any verbal or nonverbal behavior suggesting a facade or social roles is to be abandoned. Participants are strongly encouraged to be open and honest, and encounter group standards allow much greater latitude for self-expression than is found elsewhere in society. To some it may appear that the encounter group is a finishing school or charm school thrown into reverse gear.

Since people in the group expect frankness, they react strongly to someone who comes across as superficial. One problem is that their application and withdrawal of social approval can encourage a new kind of superficiality. It is very quickly apparent that openness and honesty are rewarded whereas guarded secrecy is punished. But for many reasons it may be difficult for a participant to produce the inner self on demand. A handy solution is to come on *as if* open and honest, meanwhile artfully hiding *real* feelings, which may include reticence, blandness, courtesy, or disinterest! Thus, in some cases, attempts to comply with the demands of the encounter situation result in the adoption of a new social mask—the mask of an open, honest, sincere, and sensitive individual.

Close cousins to social masks are the little tricks people acquire to ease getting along with others. They are shown by the flirting woman who promises much but delivers nothing, the clown who never can settle down to business, and the person who is caught up in a never-ending cycle of semideliberately fouling up followed by offering profuse apologies to all injured parties. Since other people are required for the performance of these rituals, they are considered **social games.** Although they may serve some important function for the players, such as keeping important but unpleasant issues in the background, they are believed to block the flow of communication. One function of encounter groups is to identify these social games, point them out to the players, and encourage them to stop.

With the great emphasis on openness in encounter groups, sessions sometimes get uncomfortable. But in groups conducted by capable professionals, enough sensitivity and concern develop for each person's welfare that all usually ends well enough.

Learning to Trust and Accept. The encounter group also promotes understanding by providing members with realistic perceptions and expectations about other people. Members discover previously undisclosed facets of others that they can then compare with undisclosed facets of themselves. Typically, the stripping off of social masks does not bare a rotten core. On the contrary, strength and character are likely to appear. The result is a development of understanding and trust.

Some people seem to develop a basic trust in humanity at an early age. For other people this faith either is never developed or is repeatedly proven false. In the encounter group attempts are made to show participants that they can count on one another. Members may be asked to relinquish some autonomy and place themselves in the hands of others. One effort in this direction is the previously described blind walk. At first the blind man's movements are likely to be awkward and hesitant. But later, when he sees that his guide will not let him be hurt, he may find himself running with him.

The Encounter Group: One Man's Appraisal

Does participating in an encounter group promote a better understanding of self and others and more effective human relations? That is hard to say, because evaluating groups is very difficult. Since 1946 interest in encounter groups has swollen. But there does not seem to be much evidence from carefully controlled studies suggesting that they reliably meet their objectives.

On the other hand, encounter groups do seem to offer something—otherwise they wouldn't be so popular and loudly praised by satisfied users. Very simply put, a great many people who have participated in encounter groups claim that they have gotten something out of them (Rogers, 1967; Greening, 1971). They do not say that encounter groups are always easy or fun, but they do come away feeling that they are somehow better off. Not surprisingly, such people turn a deaf ear to complaints that there is little experimental proof of the worth of encounter groups.

If we are going to allow testimonial evidence, we have to consider other kinds of testimony as well. An unknown percentage of people come away disappointed or hurt. A fraction of a percent may suffer serious damage. Clearly, not everyone is pleased with the effects of their participation.

Some dissatisfactions with encounter group participation probably stem from individual differences in expectations about the group, vagaries in the composition of the group, and personality quirks of the people who come away unhappy. However, there are two liabilities of encounter group participation that all members must face. First, since openness and honesty seem so good, people may leave the group ready to change the world, only to find hurt and disappointment their rewards. Second, after a few meetings everyone in the group may be perceived as sensitive, warm, and understanding. This idea, coupled with a newfound faith in humanity, may contribute to a belief that just about anybody who has been in a group could be a successful encounter group **facilitator** (leader). This is tragic, because being a competent facilitator requires several skills.

Applying New Human Relations Skills outside the Group.   Unless all you want is a group-induced high, the encounter group is a laboratory *in* life rather than a substitute *for* life. Yet the social atmosphere and kinds of behavior fostered within an encounter group can be quite different from those fostered elsewhere. For this reason the attempt to exercise newly found skills can be difficult or frustrating. New concerns for sensitivity can be met with apathy or distrust. Some associates may be taken aback if the encounter group graduate's new frankness is interpreted as obnoxiousness. Other associates may regard his new approach to life as silly or as a put-on. These difficulties can be particularly pronounced when the person is the only one from his set who has taken part in an encounter group. Unless he remembers that *others do not necessarily share his new perspective,* he may be a "horror to behold" (Egan, 1970).

Unless the encounter group graduate remembers that others do not necessarily share his new perspective, he may be a "horror to behold."

The Fallacy that Anyone Can Conduct a Group. The intensity of feeling elicited within groups is hard to imagine. When emotions are strong, there is, perhaps, the greatest potential for developing understanding. But there is also the greatest potential for personal harm or damage. Whether an encounter group promotes new insights or personal disaster may depend to a large extent on the competence of the facilitator. First, the facilitator must have the skills necessary for recognizing social pressures and, when necessary, controlling or channeling them. Second, he must also be sensitive to the needs of all the group's participants and have some pretty good hunches as to who can take how much and under what conditions. Third, since many groups last for only a weekend, have infrequent sessions, or convene in a location far from the participants' homes, it is difficult or impossible for the facilitator to offer a follow-up service. For this reason it becomes important for him to know how to end the group properly.

The skills necessary to conduct an encounter group that meets objectives and proves rewarding are the product of training and experience. Sadly, many people are somewhat careless about who conducts their group. Although most people want to know the full credentials of the man who is about to perform an operation, drill their teeth, repair their television, or style their hair, they are amazingly apathetic about the qualifications of their encounter group facilitator. "Good intent" will not suffice. I know quite a few well-intentioned people whom I will not let remove my appendix!

Since in effect there are no laws concerning who can conduct groups, the high demand for groups results in a ripe opportunity for unqualified facilitators. Difficulties become apparent only when the skills of a good facilitator are sorely needed. Choosing to participate in a group and the selection of a group are personal decisions. The kinds of information potential participants might find of interest are the facilitator's background, training, and reputation and the rules he applies when conducting the group. These rules might include (1) what happens in the group is no topic for gossip, (2) if there is something a participant doesn't want to do, it is not fair for the group to try to wheedle him into it, and (3) there will be no physical violence.

The Humanistic Orientation:
Contributions and Limitations

The approach of this text (made explicit in Chapter Two) is that psychology follows certain rules, which distinguish science from other forms of human activity. Psychologists with a strong humanistic orientation do not always follow these rules but offer other rules instead. In a sense, trying to evaluate their offerings by traditional psychologists' criteria is improper.

I think that a main contribution of the humanistic psychologists is a refreshing set of friendly reminders and the offering of intriguing possibilities for future exploration. They remind us that much about man is *positive and assertive*; they remind us of man's *capabilities and talents*; they remind us that man is a *conscious* being; they remind us of a *discontinuity of the species*—that is, just as man does not look like rat or roach, he does not always behave like rat or roach. They remind us, in short, that psychologists might profit by looking at man in the same way that man looks at himself. Simultaneously, humanistic psychologists have highlighted a number of interesting issues that clearly deserve further consideration. Whether or not man is free, he sees himself as free. How does this perception affect his behavior? How do people set long-range goals and then try to achieve them? What is the psychologically strong and rich person like? How can forces in small groups be utilized to provide constructive experiences?

On the other hand, following the assumptions of this text, many of the ideas stemming from the humanistic psychologists are in sore need of scientific validation to buttress their intuitive validity. Some humanistic psychologists, such as Maslow, Moustakas, and Rogers, have either applied generally accepted techniques or developed entirely new ones for the validation of their claims. But, in general, the application of reliable, valid, rigorous techniques to the issues of humanistic psychology is conspicuously absent. I do not accept as fully satisfactory the excuse that humanistic psychology is too young to have developed an effective methodolgy. My impression is that, for the most part, the movement has been so excited by a continual stream of new ideas that little time is spent on careful evaluation. So what? So it is hard to separate the ideas that could grow, develop, and find application from those that only add to confusion.

My hope is that some of the concepts and principles reported here will be developed in such a way as to make them *precise, public,* and *provable.* I hope that many other concepts and principles that are often lumped under the heading of humanistic psychology (but not dwelt on in this text) will be recognized as half-baked, fraudulent, faddish, or inhumane if they are, as I strongly suspect. Although there is a certain democratic appeal in the idea that "there's room for everyone and every idea in humanistic psychology," an uncritical initial acceptance of every practitioner and every theory will so disgust professionals of all kinds and produce such disappointment in society at large that the whole humanistic orientation could be doomed to a very premature death. Fortunately, some of the strongest voices in humanistic psychology are those of responsible people.

CONCLUSIONS

Which approach to personality is most satisfactory? There are as many answers to this question as there are approaches. If we adopt the criteria of hard-nosed, objective scientists interested in assertions supported by experimental evidence, the social-learning approach looks rather attractive. If we are most interested in a complete and comprehensive theory that best describes the abnormal personality, the psychoanalytic theory comes to the fore. If we prefer rich theorizing that places less emphasis on the rules of science and more emphasis on philosophizing about the unique nature of man, the humanistic orientation gains in strength. In short, each approach has its strengths and weaknesses. Whether or not an approach appears satisfactory will depend largely on the criteria chosen for evaluation.

Many psychologists who deal with personality take an **eclectic approach,** picking and choosing terms and principles that seem to fit together to describe a particular case. Murphy (1947) has tried to do so in a highly formalized way and has pieced together a theory from the best features of a number of different approaches. For many psychologists—myself included—this eclectic approach is much less formalized. The considerations that repeatedly arise when I think about personality are:

1. the biological substrata, which provide both capabilities and limitations;
2. the biologically based and other needs, which provide forces that propel behavior;
3. the learning history of the person, particularly that having taken place during interaction with others;
4. conflicts or incompatibilities among the biological capacities and limitations, the personal motives, and the demands of society; and
5. *the immediate situation, which interplays with all else to produce the impression that a person has a certain kind of personality.*

The student of personality has a difficult task, since there is so much for which he must account. Many approaches have been tried, each with attendant advantages and disadvantages. The best way of identifying and integrating the complex array of forces that produce personality varies from theory to theory. In this text, I have only touched on some of the major approaches and concepts.

9.
Measures of Man

Take a thin, hollow glass tube with a bulge at one end. Fill the bulge, and a part of the tube, with mercury. The amount of space within the tube that the mercury will subsequently occupy will vary largely as a function of the intensity of an environmental quality labeled temperature.

When temperature is decreased to exactly that point at which water freezes, mark the level of mercury. When it is increased to exactly that point at which water boils, again mark the level. Label the former mark 0 and the latter 100. If you place 99 equally spaced marks between these two extremes, you will have a centigrade thermometer. Although the marking process is quite arbitrary (you could have labeled the extremes 32 and 212 and gone on to make a Fahrenheit thermometer), the resulting instrument nonetheless allows the user to reliably measure a varying environmental quality. It is thus called a *measuring* or *assessment* device.

Like the physicist, the psychologist also wants to make statements about the relative intensity of qualities. He, too, must therefore create assessment devices. But he needs instruments that will permit him to make statements about the psychological qualities of different people under different conditions. These instruments may be referred to as **psychological tests.**

The construction of psychological assessment devices is often quite complicated, but this is not necessarily so. Say, for example, that the psychologist wants to assess how much pain different people can tolerate. One technique would be to place a football cleat on his subject's shin and fasten it there with an inflatable tube with a pressure gauge, exactly like the devices physicians use to measure blood pressure. If the psychologist increases the pressure in this tube until his subject grunts or cries "uncle," he can, by referring to the pressure gauge, make a statement about the subject's tolerance for pain.

All psychological research involves variables that must in some way be measured. For this reason it is possible to construe every result of every experiment in psychology as obtained using a psychological test. But in this chapter we will discuss one certain class of psychological tests—specifically, those used by researchers and clinicians for measuring such elusive personal qualities as intelligence, interests, and personality.

It is possible to construe the results of every experiment in psychology as obtained using a psychological test . . .

. . . But in this chapter we will consider those tests used for measuring such elusive personal qualities as intelligence, interests, and personality.

Each of these tests provides a **standardized method** for making comparisons among people. That is, each test has specific instructions, contains a set series of questions that are asked in an invariant sequence, and is administered to different people under conditions that are as uniform as possible. Standardized methods are necessary if meaningful comparisons are to be made. If a test had no established instructions, involved presenting different questions to different people in a willy-nilly sequence, and was administered to different people under vastly different test-taking conditions, meaningful comparisons could not be made, for differences in scores could as easily reflect differences in the test and test administration as they could differences among people.

THE FUNCTION OF PSYCHOLOGICAL TESTS

As Cronbach (1960, 1969) observes, *psychological tests are used for making decisions.* The decisions may be about people, about scientific hypotheses, or about programs. For example, suppose that a psychologist is interested in the hypothesis that encounter groups will raise college students' **self-esteem,** that is, the extent to which each person sees himself as competent and worthwhile. First he may administer Coopersmith's (1967) self-esteem test to a large group of students. On the basis of their responses, he can select people with high or low self-esteem. *He thus makes a decision about people.* Next he divides the students who are low in self-esteem into two groups: one takes part in an encounter group; and the other does not. When he later readministers the self-esteem test to these students, he will be able to determine if the encounter group affected the participants' level of self-esteem. If their self-esteem relative to that of the nonparticipants is indeed raised, he would decide that his hypothesis was correct; if their self-esteem was not raised or was lowered, he would decide that his initial hypothesis was false. *He thus makes a decision about his scientific hypothesis.* If he concluded that his hypothesis was true, he might decide to initiate a series of encounter groups for other students with low self-esteem. *He thus makes a decision about a program.*

Those who use psychological tests most often direct their efforts toward making decisions about people. They are concerned with the general problem of making the most satisfactory match between the person and his environment. There are two ways of accomplishing this matchmaking (Cronbach, 1957). One is by *engineering* the environment so that a given person can perform effectively and happily within it. The second is by *selecting* either the right person for a given environment (as when the organizational psychologist chooses among a number of job applicants) or the right environment for a given person (as when the school psychologist must decide which curriculum will best fulfill the needs of a particular student).

VARIETIES OF PSYCHOLOGICAL TESTS

Decisions about people and what to do with them are not easy to make, but there are many different kinds of tests that may aid in the decision-making process. Some tests assess intellectual abilities, some assess needs and interests, and some assess personality. Although I will discuss each kind separately, psychological tests are typically used in combinations, or as **test batteries.**

Tests of Ability

A recent edition of the *Guinness Book of World Records* included the case of a woman who has been in a coma but kept alive since August 5, 1941

(McWhirter & McWhirter, 1971). Her environment requires of her only the most primitive biological functioning. Survival and comfort in most settings, however, require behavior that presupposes not only consciousness but certain capacities, talents, or *abilities*: to identify stimuli, to perceive relationships, to communicate with others, to cope with changing conditions, to profit from experience, and so on. These abilities can be measured by **ability tests.**

Although one can never assume a one-to-one correspondence between a test score and performance in a real-life situation . . .

. . . there are positive correlations between ability-test scores and levels of performance at real-life tasks.

Although *one can never assume a one-to-one correspondence between a test score and performance in a real-life situation,* there are positive correlations between ability-test scores and level of performance at real-life tasks. For example, IQ tests are designed to measure a person's general abilities, with higher IQ scores indicating greater assessed ability. Summarizing half a dozen or so studies, Cronbach (1960) notes that the average IQ score of people who receive Ph.D.s is 130, and the average IQ score of people who successfully complete four years of college is 120. People with an IQ score of about 110 have a 50-50 chance of graduating from college; those with an IQ score of about 75 have a 50-50 chance of graduating from high school. As IQ scores decrease, so do the number of occupational choices available. Mowing lawns and doing "simple" laundry are considered probable tasks for persons with IQ scores of about 40. Mischel (1968) reports that students who do well on tests of specific abilities (such as English or mathematics) tend to get better grades, although the same ability tests do not so closely correspond with performance when one is trying to forecast success outside the classroom. Mischel also notes that, in many cases, behaviors that are correlated with ability-test performance are themselves fairly consistent over time.

The measurement of an ability requires that the respondent exercise that ability for the benefit of the examiner. To do so, he must draw to some extent on what he already knows, even if it is only how to say "yes" or "no." Nonetheless, both *IQ tests* and *aptitude tests* are intended to measure the person's *capacities* or *potential* for successful performance, and this potential is believed to exist in the abstract and to be independent of prior learning. The distinction between IQ and aptitude tests is that, whereas **IQ tests** are designed to measure abstract abilities in their most *general form* (and hence are predicated on the belief that abilities do exist in a general form), **aptitude tests** are designed to measure fairly specific abilities, such as the abilities to judge or create art, to perceive mechanical relationships, or to work deftly with one's hands. Knowledge of potential is useful when the tester wants to determine how quickly a person is likely to acquire the new behaviors conducive to success in a given setting. For example, the person with the potential to become an artist may not know how to draw much of anything at the time of his testing but should quickly develop creative skills if he is sent to an art school. He might be a more attractive candidate to the school than someone who could, at the time of testing, use pencils, pastels, oils, and an engraving stylus in rather mediocre fashion but showed no evidence of potential for further improvement.

Since raw potential should not be affected by learning, repeated measures of a person's raw potential should suggest that it remains fairly stable over time. That is, IQ scores should not appreciably increase over time (during which learning could have occurred), and attempts to develop specific aptitudes should not appreciably raise aptitude-test scores. Consistent with this hypothesis, the evidence suggests that many scores on certain IQ and aptitude tests remain fairly stable over time. Learning experiences, which should by all intuition raise scores on IQ and aptitude tests, do not necessarily do so. But, as we shall soon see, some of this stability may be understood in terms of learning considerations.

An **achievement test** does not attempt to measure potential. Instead, it is used to assess the extent to which potential and learning have combined to produce a given level of proficiency. Such tests are particularly useful for determining a person's present level of competence. If, for example, the tester is trying to choose one of two people to paint a poster for tonight's big dance, an abstract potential to become an artist is probably less important than a present ability with poster paints.

Wesman (1968) suggests that the psychologist is fooling himself when he tries to draw distinctions among intelligence tests, aptitude tests, and achievement tests. He argues that learning is reflected in every test. Wesman's definition of intelligence is "the summation of the learning experiences of the individual." Aptitude and achievement tests, which deal with a narrow band of behavior, presumably measure only some of the person's learning experiences. In support of his argument that each "type" of test measures basically the same quantity, he notes that the very same questions could be accepted for inclusion on any or all of the three "types" of tests.

I have few doubts that Wesman is correct when he asserts that learning contributes to IQ and aptitude-test scores. Many of the questions asked on IQ tests, for example, are vocabulary items or presume experience with such so-called common objects as a telephone, an envelope, and an orange. A certain child may have the potential "brainpower" to identify and use these objects, but, if he were reared in an impoverished environment where such things were absent, he could never demonstrate his potential to the examiner. The more he learns, the better his demonstration will be. The finding that IQ and aptitude-test scores sometimes remain fairly stable over time could signify that people's environments and hence chances to learn useful new things also remain unchanging. For example, breaking out of a ghetto and into an environment that could provide learning experiences conducive to improved IQ-test performance is no easy task, as a few of you may realize. However, Skodak and Skeels' study (1949; reported in Chapter Six), certain investigations cited in Wrightsman (1968), and a few other researches suggest that, when there *is* a drastic improvement in the environment, the person's level of performance on both ability tests and real-life tasks has a good chance of improving.

Whatever the contribution of learning to ability-test performance, scores on ability tests and real-life performance are sometimes surprisingly discrepant. There are several reasons why a person may do well on a test but perform poorly in real life or do very poorly on a test but show satisfactory or even exemplary performance in his natural setting. First, tests themselves contain certain flaws, which may produce misleading scores. (Flaws of psychological tests will be discussed later in this chapter.) Second, the person who is physically ill, having an off day, or not motivated to apply himself to the test because he finds it dull and boring may score poorly, even though real-life success waits around the corner. Third, many considerations other than abilities will influ-ence performance in the natural setting. Motivation is one example. Herculean efforts on the person's part may to some extent compensate for a lack of abili-ties, or a low level of motivation may result in tremendous abilities going unutilized. Fourth, special educational procedures may result in a level of per-formance in the natural setting that is far superior to that which would be predicted on the basis of test results alone. Finally, two or more of these fac-tors can work together to produce very large discrepancies. Thus, although in general people who score higher on IQ, aptitude, and achievement tests may perform better in real-life settings than do people who do not score so well, this rule cannot be expected to hold true in each individual case.

Interest Inventories

Deciding on a line of work is one of the most crucial decisions a person can make. Perhaps you are one of the few who have already made a decision on a very sound basis and look forward with delight to the day you will start run-ning up the pyramid of success. But if you are still agonizing over this prob-lem, you are not alone. Although people are exposed to various occupational alternatives and, indeed, begin preparation for some of them during childhood, the issue looms particularly large when it becomes apparent that school will not provide a sanctuary for many more years. Furthermore, all around us we see many people who hate their work or repeatedly switch from one unreward-ing job to another.

Ability tests should be useful for vocational decisions, since it seems reason-able that, if someone's skills match the job requirements, he is likely to per-form well and find his work rewarding. But by itself ability is not enough to ensure good performance and personal satisfaction. What the person will find *interesting* and *intrinsically enjoyable* must also be taken into account.

Interest inventories are psychological tests designed to assess preferences and aversions that should contribute to success and feelings of satisfaction in dif-ferent jobs, educational programs, and recreational settings. These tests are based on the premise that simply asking a person to state what he would find enjoyable is likely to elicit replies that are unreliable, superficial, unrealistic, or based on faulty knowledge (Anastasi, 1961). For example, if a man sol-emnly declares "I want to be a doctor," his choice might have been based on the incomplete view of a physician as someone who makes a great deal of money and is respected by others. He may not have carefully considered other features of his choice, which include an exhausting training course, a few years of poverty, the performance of rather grisly tasks, the necessity for being reasonably sober and on call 24 hours each day, and the tremendous burden of being responsible for other people's lives. Each of these other considerations may be incompatible with his true interests. Through carefully formulated questions, the interest inventory can provide a clear general picture of the respondent's overall requirements for personal satisfaction.

There are several interest inventories, but the best-developed one is the Strong Vocational Interest Blank. It comes in two forms, one for men and one for women. Each contains 400 items, concerning occupations, school subjects, activities and amusements, and kinds of people and their peculiarities. For the most part the respondent replies to the items by indicating "Like," "Dislike," or "Indifferent," but he is also required to do such things as order some of these items in terms of relative attractiveness and choose among them when they are presented as pairs.

Afterward the psychologist compares the respondent's answers with the known answers of people within different fields. The object is to find the closest match. If a woman shares the interests of social workers, this should be a better occupational selection for her than the choice of office worker, which is known to attract women with quite different interests. With this interest inventory it is possible to compare men's responses with the known responses of men in 47 different occupations and women's responses with the known responses of women in 28 different occupations. Follow-up studies suggest considerable correspondence between assessed interests and eventual occupational choices and low but significant correlations between assessed interests and job satisfaction (Anastasi, 1961).

Changing interests pose a challenge for any interest inventory, so once again we cannot expect a one-to-one correspondence between how the test results suggest people will fare and how in fact they do fare. On the basis of test results a person could decide to pursue an occupation that requires many years of training, only to find on attaining that position that his interests have changed and it is no longer attractive. On the basis of Strong's (1959) reports, however, this would not seem to be a major problem. Changes in interests occur most often between the relatively early ages of 15 and 20; from 20 to 55 or so they remain fairly stable.

Personality Tests

Interest inventories and, in a sense, ability tests tell us something about personality, for they help to show in what ways the respondent is like all other people, like some other person, and like no other person. But now let us turn to tests that attempt to assess the underlying personal qualities that are believed to represent something other than sheer intellect and perhaps deeper than interests. Personality is very elusive. But, as Thorndike pointed out, if something exists, it exists in some amount; if it exists in some amount, it can be measured.

Personality tests attempt to measure personality characteristics, their relationships to one another, and the forces that produced them. Although personality tests take many different forms, they tend to fall into two broad categories known as *objective* and *projective*. The two types are most clearly distinguished in terms of the procedures involved for measuring personality. But there are also differences in the assumptions of these tests and in the orientations of the psychologists who favor one type over the other.

Objective-Report Tests

Objective-report tests are paper-and-pencil tests of the true-false or multiple-choice variety. They consist of a list of statements or questions (items). The respondent answers by checking one of a number of alternatives, such as "like me" or "unlike me" in the case of statements or "always," "sometimes," or "never" in the case of questions. These tests are objective in that the answers the respondents must give are easy to score or categorize and hence easy to reach agreement upon. If the respondent were allowed to answer freely in any words he chose, there would be hundreds of ways he could answer, and his answer could be easily misinterpreted or interpreted in different ways by different people. On the other hand, if his answer consists of an alternative such as "true," everyone inspecting the answer would be able to interpret it the same way.

The multiple-choice format offers other advantages as well. It facilitates quantification—that is, makes it easy to reduce the person's answers to numerical scores that are easily compared with the scores obtained by others. It also facilitates speedy scoring, either by hand or by computer. This consideration is important when one realizes that a personality test may contain several hundred items. The drawback of the approach is that, since the respondent is forced to choose one of a few highly specified alternatives, he may have trouble finding one that is indeed appropriate. Although he will eventually choose an answer, he might, if allowed to answer in his own words, have offered one that was quite noticeably different from any of those provided on the test.

Without question, the most widely used objective-report test is the Minnesota Multiphasic Personality Inventory **(MMPI).** The MMPI was developed in the early 1940s and has undergone refinement and development ever since. It is designed to measure those phases of personality that suggest existing or potential psychiatric disorders.[1] You may recognize it immediately from these items:

> *Evil spirits possess me at times.*
> *It is safer to trust nobody.*
> *Sexual things disgust me.*
> *I am a high-strung person.*

The MMPI contains 550 such items, to which the respondent replies "true," "false," or "cannot say." These items deal with such issues as habits, health, marriage and the family, occupation, education, sex, religion, politics, fears, morale, and mood. After the test is completed, it is scored by various scales, each of which consists of a number of items drawn from the test. There are four *validity scales,* which are used to decide whether the person completed the test satisfactorily, hedged by marking "cannot say" an unusual number of times, lied, or answered in a secretive or guarded manner. There are ten *clinical scales,* which consist of 33 to 78 items each. Scores from them indicate the degree of similarity between the respondent's answers and the answers given by people with known psychiatric disorders. The implication is that, if the respondent answers as these patients did, he may be suffering from the same disorder. Thus one scale (*D*) contains items that, taken together, indicate the extent to which the respondent is depressed and given to thoughts of suicide and death.

Certainly everyone will answer *some D*-scale items in a way that will suggest depression; this would be expected by chance alone. The same is true of the other clinical scales, virtually all of which measure undesirable qualities. The psychologist is thus interested in *how many* questions on each scale are answered in a given direction. This score can then be compared with those of people believed to be normal and those of people exhibiting various psychiatric disorders. In the case of the *D* scale, 20 to 28 of the 60 items can be answered in the direction of depression without indicating any serious problem.

[1] Neuroses, psychoses, and other forms of personal disorders (described in Chapter Ten).

How are items selected for such personality tests? Although the test constructor's ideas about personality may influence the selection, it is nevertheless quite possible to develop an effective test without referring to any well-formulated theories of personality (such as those described in the preceding two chapters). The MMPI is a good case in point.

Initially, 1000 items were selected from textbooks in abnormal psychology and psychiatry, from case histories, and from preexisting personality tests and examination forms. All the items were then responded to by a number of people diagnosed as having psychiatric difficulties of different types and by a larger number of people who were categorized as normal. Analyses of responses revealed the ways in which people in various diagnostic categories answered differently from one another and from the people classified as normal. For some items, different classifications were not associated with different responses; therefore these items were discarded from the test. Retained were the items that were answered differently by people of different classifications. The process of selecting test items according to their effectiveness in distinguishing among people (such as "normal" versus "depressed") is referred to as **empirical keying.**

Tests based on this empirical-keying method have proven to be quite practical. For example, Kleinmuntz (1967) points to studies suggesting that the MMPI is useful for detecting individuals with emotional problems in high school, the military, and industrial settings and for determining the severity of symptoms of present psychiatric patients.

As I have said, the MMPI is not based on any standard personality theory, but, since the items were chosen from earlier tests and case reports, each individual item may reflect somebody's speculations about personality. However, tests can be constructed with items that seem to reflect nothing in particular. This prospect has been pursued by Berg (1957, 1961). According to his **deviation hypothesis,** the item itself is unimportant, but how the respondent answers the item is very important. His hypothesis suggests that the person who gives unusual answers to a test item is likely to be unusual in other ways, too. An implication of this hypothesis is that personality tests need not contain verbal items—they could contain patterns or sounds instead.

There are literally hundreds of personality tests of the objective-report type. Some of them, like the MMPI, attempt to spot potential or existing psychiatric difficulties. Others are intended to measure only a very few phases of personality, and still others try to measure personality in broad perspective. Despite these differences, however, they are all characterized by easy scoring and easy quantification of results.

Perhaps it is sufficient that test results help us to make predictions about how people are likely to fare under given conditions. However, without assigning blame, I regard it as unfortunate that major theories of personality and well-developed objective-report tests are at best loosely related. This is because psychological tests could be very useful for testing hypotheses derived from these major theories, which are, after all, some of the most widely publicized theories ever offered. In the absence of suitable measures, many important hypotheses from these theories cannot be tested. Thus a full and proper evaluation of the theories cannot be made.

Projective Tests

Many projective tests feature vague, ambiguous stimuli, which the respondent is asked to describe.

Objective-report tests are highly structured: the respondent is asked a fairly specific question and is required to select one of a set of specified answers. **Projective tests,** on the other hand, are highly unstructured: they feature vague, ambiguous stimuli (such as inkblots) or indefinite, ill-defined tasks (such as drawing a man—any man), and the respondent is asked to describe the stimuli or perform the task. He is allowed to reply in his own words or to set about the task in whatever way he sees fit. The idea is that, since the stimuli and tasks are vague and indefinite, the respondent must draw heavily on his own needs, motives, and perceptions when reacting to them. In other words, his responses should reflect his personality. Projective tests are so called because the respondent is believed to "project" his own personality outward onto the test materials, much as a movie projector projects its pictures onto a screen.

In this area of psychological testing, as in all others, a wide variety of tests is available. Projective tests differ tremendously in format, content, procedures, and scoring systems. The two most widely used are the Rorschach Test and the Thematic Apperception Test.

The Rorschach Test. The **Rorschach Inkblot Test** was devised in the early 1920s by Hermann Rorschach, a Swiss psychiatrist. Rorschach recognized a need for a uniform technique for assessing personality within the clinical setting. He was also interested in a measure that would provide a more comprehensive overview of the person than did the specific instruments in use at that time. Rorschach decided upon inkblots for this purpose, since what the respondent reported seeing in them necessarily reflected himself. Rorschach devised a series of ten partially symmetrical inkblots, five of which are gray, two of which are gray and red, and three of which are multicolored.

There are several techniques for administering the Rorschach, but most of them go something like this: The cards containing the inkblots are presented in a set sequence, and the respondent is given instructions to tell what each one represents. The psychologist records the replies, along with his observations of the respondent's general demeanor, how he holds and orients the cards, and the amount of time the testing takes. Next the psychologist and respondent go through the cards again. The psychologist asks questions, seeking greater elaboration of the response ("Tell me more about the two cannibals dancing around the pot") and trying to determine how the respondent came to his answer. Then there may be a phase during which the psychologist discovers whether or not the respondent *can* see certain things in the inkblots ("Can't you see the bat?"). This part of the testing may be omitted if the psychologist believes it would "spoil" the respondent for subsequent testings by giving him a perceptual set to "see" what the examiner pointed out.

Earlier I noted that almost anyone can score objective-report tests. The scoring of projective tests tends to be complicated, and the scorer may have a difficult time deciding how to categorize a given response.

Proper scoring of the Rorschach involves consideration of not only the major content of the response (for example, a bat) but many other variables as well. These include the originality of the response, the parts of the inkblot that provided a basis for the response, and the qualities of the inkblot (form, shading, and color) that contributed to the response. This information is entered into specific categories and then summarized graphically on a scoring sheet producing a **psychogram.** This graph shows at a glance the number of times various considerations entered into the respondent's reactions. Interpretation of the psychogram and of the content of Rorschach responses is complex and cannot be dealt with here. But test users who like the Rorschach believe it provides information about the respondent's intellect, emotions, social relations, and perceptions. The extent to which the test achieves such objectives has been a source of unending debate.

The Thematic Apperception Test.   The second most popular projective test is the **Thematic Apperception Test (TAT).** Like the Rorschach, it consists of a series of cards containing ambiguous stimuli. However, the 20 stimuli of the TAT are far less ill defined than the inkblots. TAT pictures are representational works of art, very similar to the drawings used in some magazines. In one sense it is clear what they show. For example, one TAT picture portrays an older woman standing slightly behind a younger one. Nonetheless, to follow the test instructions to develop an imaginative story, the respondent must draw on his own needs and experiences.

TAT administration involves handing the subject the picture cards, one at a time, with instructions similar to these (Allison, Blatt, & Zimet, 1968, p. 99):

> I am going to show you a series of pictures, and I want you to make up a story about each one. I want you to tell me what is happening in the picture, what led up to it, and what the outcome will be. I also want you to describe the thoughts and feelings of the characters.

The psychologist attempts, as far as possible, to record each response in full, although in some cases he may spare himself this ordeal by having the respondent write down his own stories. (In either case, producing 20 stories is so demanding that most TAT testing involves use of only about half the cards.) Several scoring systems are available. Murray (1943), the TAT's originator, favored a scoring system that involved identifying the central character in the story and then categorizing the interplay between this character's dispositional forces (*needs*) and the situational forces acting upon him (*presses*). Murray's approach is largely qualitative and is based heavily on the actual content of the stories. More quantitative scoring systems have also been developed, as have specialized systems to deal with selected aspects of personality.

McClelland and his associates devised a scoring system for the TAT that has proven to be a particularly fruitful research tool (see Atkinson, 1958a). These investigators have been concerned with various motives or needs, in particular *nAch,* or **need achievement.** A person with a high need for achievement is described as having a persistent desire to succeed and to live up to standards of excellence. To assess *nAch,* psychologists ask respondents to write stories about four TAT-style pictures. The stories are then scored in terms of achievement imagery—that is, the concern for excellence shown by the people in the story. On the basis of their responses, examinees can be classified as either high or low *nAch.*

As a whole, the results of *nAch* research suggest that some people have a greater concern with excellence than do others, and this concern appears in a variety of ways. McClelland (1961) has found that people engaged in entrepreneurial endeavors tend to have higher *nAch* than people in other occupational groups. Veroff, Atkinson, Feld, and Gurin (1960) found that people who are better educated and more skilled tend to have higher *nAch*. Birch and Veroff (1966) note that people with higher *nAch* learn faster, perform more rapidly, and are more persistent under difficult conditions. Furthermore, when people with high and low *nAch* are given experimental tasks to perform, they are likely to approach the tasks quite differently. All in all, it would seem that the concept of *nAch,* which is generally assessed by the TAT, has a certain amount of value.

Projective Tests and Personality Theory.   Whereas objective-report tests are rarely based on a developed personality theory, projective tests are frequently based on strong theoretical foundations. Hermann Rorschach made assumptions about the unconscious processes of the individual, and Murray, who developed the TAT, had fairly definite ideas about personality (see Geiwitz, 1969). But the contribution of personality theory to projective tests is probably best illustrated in Blum's (1950) **Blacky Test,** which was devised to assess personality in light of psychoanalytic theory.

Blum wanted to construct scenes which would elicit responses that were derivatives of early psychosexual stages (orality, anality, the Oedipal conflict, fear of castration, and so on). To do so, he developed a series of pictures in which these responses could come to the fore. The use of people in these scenes was undesirable, partly because good taste dictated against portraying humans engaged in obvious oral, anal, and phallic behavior. More important, though, was the consideration that such scenes involving humans might strike "too close to home," arousing the respondent's defense mechanisms and thereby precluding exactly the reactions Blum found most interesting. To solve these problems, Blum pictured the capers of a dog of unidentified sex called Blacky. He noted that, although the use of a dog as a hero should minimize the respondent's defenses, the "canine medium, owing to the prevalence of animated cartoons and comic strips, still preserves sufficient reality so that subjects can identify fully with the cartoon figures and project their innermost feelings" (Blum, 1969, p. 23).[2]

In successive pictures the ungainly hero, Blacky, is shown nursing, chewing on its mother's collar, relieving itself, watching its parents copulating, exploring its sex organs, watching a knife about to fall on another dog's tail, admonishing a toy dog, watching its parents bestow love and affection on another, cowering before a stern superego figure, dreaming of perfection, and dreaming of love. After the respondent makes up stories about these pictures, he answers some specific questions and indicates which pictures he likes. These responses are then scored in psychoanalytically important categories, such as orality, anality, and the Oedipus complex.

The Blacky Pictures are perhaps best described as an experimental test suitable for research purposes. Critics point out that the test is clearly in need of further refinement. On the other hand, Blum (1969) suggests that the results of some completed studies using the Blacky Pictures offer encouragement both for the test and for the psychoanalytic theory of personality.

Objective and Projective Tests: Assets and Liabilities

Both the objective and projective approaches to personality have definite strengths and weaknesses. Since administering an objective test consists mainly in passing it out, it can be given on a mass scale and there is relatively little room for the test administrator to influence the results. Moreover, since the results are easy to quantify, they are easily plugged in to the mathematical formulas used for assessing the test's reliability and validity. Projective tests allow more room for the examiner to infuence the respondent's answers, require considerable effort to administer, and are difficult and time-consuming to score. On the other hand, projective tests allow the respondent the freedom to react in whatever way he sees fit, enable the psychologist to gain a firsthand impression of the respondent, and tend to be less loosely related to the ideas of major personality theorists.

[2] Blum is probably correct. Until I read a review of Blum's test which mentioned that Blacky's sex is unspecified, I had always thought of Blacky as "him."

Psychologists favoring objective tests claim that this approach tends to be more reliable and valid; psychologists favoring projective tests claim that their approach presents a comprehensive picture of people's innermost workings rather than a mere listing of personality qualities. The skillful clinical psychologist, however, is apt to use both types of tests in order to gain as much information as possible about the person he is testing.

CRITERIA FOR EVALUATING PSYCHOLOGICAL TESTS

We will now turn to some of the standards or *criteria* established for evaluating psychological tests. Information concerning a test's adequacy is usually presented openly and candidly in the manual prepared for use with that test. Such information can also be secured from the various test handbooks prepared periodically by Buros (for example, 1965, 1970). Psychologists, educators, and other test users must be sensitive to this information, for they must take a test's limitations into account before they make pronouncements on the basis of its results.

Psychological tests provide ways for making observations of behavior. In Chapter Two I pointed out that good observations are reliable and valid. Let us begin by considering the reliability and validity of psychological tests.

Reliability

A fundamental assumption of psychological measurement is that any obtained score (X) consists of two components, the true score on that quality (t) plus a certain amount of error (e). The error component comes from many sources, some of which can be dealt with (such as variations in test instructions and examination settings) and some of which cannot (such as the respondent's hunger, fatigue, or emotional state). Error may appear in terms of fluctuations in a person's test performance. For example, if on the same test a person has an IQ score of 110 on Monday and 120 on Tuesday, it is believed unlikely that his true IQ has changed but quite likely that the variables contributing to error have changed. Since the test user is far more interested in the true score than in the error component, tests that show less fluctuation are considered more satisfactory. You may recall that, when a method or instrument produces consistent, repeatable results, it is said to be *reliable*.

Since psychological tests are measuring instruments, just like rulers, one helpful method for communicating the idea of reliability is to draw an analogy between reliable and unreliable rulers, on the one hand, and reliable and unreliable psychological tests, on the other. Suppose you manufacture two rulers. One is made of brass, and its markings are carefully engraved. The other is a piece of rubber cut from a fatigued inner tube and is marked with a warm Hershey bar. Measures made with *either* ruler will contain both true-score components (related to the actual length of the measured object) and error components (resulting from the user's angle of vision, the care with which the ruler and the object are aligned, and so on). But the rubber ruler, which stretches, slips, sags, and has crude markings, allows for additional sources of error. Therefore readings made from it are less consistent or reliable.

Reliability can be expressed numerically in terms of correlations (Chapter Two). One way of assessing a psychological test's reliability is to administer it to the same group of people on two different occasions. The scores obtained by each person on the two administrations are then correlated. The higher the correlation, the greater the reliability, since high correlations suggest that the respondent's performance did not fluctuate over time. Reliability correlations obtained in this way are referred to as **test-retest stability coefficients.** Low correlations of this type suggest that performance on the test is affected by unsystematic fluctuations in the mood, motivation, or emotional state of the respondent or in the nature of the test setting. The test is unreliable if it allows for much in the way of error.

Consistency of results over successive administrations of the same test is only one type of reliability. Another is based on the **internal consistency** of the test. Internal consistency is a somewhat difficult concept to grasp, but it may be illustrated by turning once again to the brass and rubber rulers. Suppose you want to measure an object that is in fact 1 inch long. With the brass ruler you could come close to this result whichever of the 12 inches of the ruler you use for making the measurement. That is, whether you align the ruler and the object so that the object stretches from 0 to 1, 3 to 4, or 11 to 12, you could still come up with the result of 1 inch. The rubber ruler, which may be more fatigued, stretched, or bent out of shape between 3 and 4 than between 11 and 12, is likely to give you different results depending on where you start. It has less internal consistency because its 12 "inches" are all different sizes! This lack of consistency could be expressed by saying that, relatively speaking, the 12 inches on the rubber ruler do not correlate highly with one another.

To assess the internal consistency of a psychological test, the test is divided into parts (such as first half and second half), and scores obtained on the parts are correlated. High correlations suggest that the test measures one thing in a systematic way rather than one or more things in haphazard ways. There are many techniques for splitting up a test and many procedures, often complicated, for estimating internal consistency.

Validity

It is nice to know that a test produces consistent results, but it is also nice to know that it measures what it's supposed to measure. A test is *valid* to the extent that it serves its intended purposes. Several types of validity must be considered in evaluating a psychological test.

Face Validity

Face validity refers to the extent to which a test measures what it appears to measure. A test of artistic ability that involves drawing or evaluating sketches would have face validity. A test of artistic ability that involves assembling small motors or estimating the loudness of tones would not be face valid, because it would appear to measure something else.

Face validity is usually considered one of the less important types of validity. Whether or not a test seems face valid will depend on the assumptions of whoever is judging it. Furthermore, face validity can harm the test. For example, suppose you were applying for a job and knew that your personal and social adjustment were important considerations. You are given a face-valid test containing such items as "I cannot get along with people," "Sometimes I feel as if my head were packed with worms," and "I have never been a happy person." Since this test is face valid, it should be quite easy to see exactly how you should respond to such items if you want to be hired, and you could manage your answers accordingly. Better for the test user's purpose would be items that are less transparent, such as "I prefer spaghetti to macaroni," "Summer is my favorite season," and "Shakespeare was a good man." Nonetheless, in some cases face validity is important to get the respondent interested in the test. A face-valid test of artistic ability might interest the art-school candidate and motivate him to do the best job possible, whereas a test that asked him to do something unrelated could result in disinterest, low motivation, and a failure to perform to the best of his ability.

Content Validity

There are untold thousands of items that could be included on any psychological test. Since a test cannot possibly contain all these items, it must represent only a handful or sample. **Content validity** refers to the extent to which this sample faithfully reflects all items that could be included.

Why is content validity important? Suppose a test is intended to measure vocabulary skills. It cannot contain all the words in the dictionary. On the basis of how well the respondent can define the relatively few words included on the test, the psychologist hopes to make some prediction about that person's performance when he is confronted with entirely different words. For the psychologist to do so with any degree of success, the words on the test must be *representative* of all possible vocabulary items. If they aren't, disastrous mistakes could be made. For example, if a test of "general vocabulary" somehow contains only words that would be most familiar to seamen (batten, starboard, jib, forecastle, and so on), seamen would appear to be very good in "general vocabulary" but people in other walks of life would not. Predictions about seamen's and nonseamen's performance on a later, less partial vocabulary test would probably prove disappointing.

Content validation involves first establishing a large pool of items called a **domain.** (Ideally, the domain consists of every possible item that could be included on the test, but in practice this cannot be achieved.) Procedures are then used to ensure that the items drawn from this pool are representative of this domain. For example, several things may reflect general ability: vocabulary skills, mathematical skills, and manual dexterity. A content-valid test of general ability would thus contain some of each type of item. However, although there are some techniques available for increasing representativeness of test items, true content validation is difficult because of the problems in establishing a domain. This is particularly so in the case of personality tests, which must draw items from an unknown domain (Kleinmuntz, 1967).

Correlation with a Criterion Measure

Most frequently, validity is stated in terms of correlations. A psychological test of a given attribute is considered valid to the extent that it correlates highly with an accepted indicator of that attribute. These accepted indicators are referred to as **criterion measures.**

Sometimes the criterion is a behavioral measure, such as vocational performance. In this case the test becomes increasingly valid as test scores correlate more highly with vocational success. At other times the criterion consists of a different, presumably well-established and highly accredited test. If a new test correlates highly with an accepted test and the accepted test correlates highly with a behavioral measure, then the new test is likely to correlate with the behavioral measure. Why not stick with the old, well-proven test? Simply because the new test may be briefer, cheaper, or easier to administer.

Construct Validity

Hypothetical constructs, you will recall, are the invisible links that underlie and tie together a number of different forms of behavior. If a test is based on a theory, it may be intended for measuring a construct, such as orality. Starting with the theorizing about the construct, the psychologist makes claims about how different people should perform on the test or how the same person should perform on the test under different conditions. He then administers the test to the appropriate people and under the appropriate conditions. Finally, he examines the test results to see if there is evidence for his claims. Thus, in the case of a test of orality, the test constructor might theorize that people who have undergone harsh deprivations in earliest childhood are characterized by concerns with food, adopt passive-dependent modes of responding, and have certain immature ways of relating to others. If test results indicated that respondents who underwent harsh deprivation showed these characteristics whereas undeprived respondents did not, both the test and the construct gain credibility. First, the results suggest that the test measures something that can conveniently be labeled orality. Second, the results also support the idea of orality, since they suggest that people respond in the ways we would expect on the basis of theorizing about orality. The present example, you should note, is highly simplified, for the process of **construct validity** requires the careful assembly of evidence from many different sources (Cronbach & Meehl, 1955).

Test Norms

A person's test score tells nothing unless it is compared with the scores obtained by others on the same test. These other scores provide a yardstick or a standard of comparison. The set of scores used for this purpose is called the set of **test norms.**

Evaluating a psychological test includes consideration of whether or not its norms provide an appropriate yardstick for the test's intended purpose. If the norms are based on the performance of only a very few people, or if these people are somehow atypical, the usefulness of the test is open to doubt.

The problem of test norms can be illustrated in the following situation. A school psychologist wants to make a statement about a third-grader's level of reading achievement relative to that of other children of the same age. The psychologist administers his reading-achievement test, takes the child's score, and then finds the table of norms in the test's manual. Let us say that, by magic, we know that the child is an average reader. However, the psychologist is forced to refer to the test norms.

Suppose the scores providing these norms were based on the performance of children of bright, wealthy professional people. These children came from an intellectually rich and stimulating environment, had parents who encouraged and rewarded reading, and were taught by good teachers in excellent schools. There is certainly reason to suspect that, as a whole, the reading performance of these children would be quite high. By comparison, the child under investigation might be judged a *rather poor* reader.

On the other hand, suppose that the children who provided the test norms had poor, uneducated parents, received no intellectual stimulation, and were sent to overcrowded, undersupported schools. There is certainly reason to suspect that these children, as a whole, would not do well on a reading-achievement test. Using these norms, our "rather poor reader" might appear to be *well above average.*

How the child will be evaluated, then, will depend on the nature of the test norms. In the first case the norms were an inappropriate yardstick because they were based on the performance of advantaged children; in the second case the norms were inadequate because they were based on the performance of disadvantaged children. If the norms had been collected from children of many different backgrounds, the results of the child's testing might be more fairly appraised as "about average." For most purposes it is necessary that test norms come from a variety of sources rather than from a small, unrepresentative group. You can imagine the consequences of evaluating someone's score on a test of personal and social adjustment if the norms were based either on hospitalized mental patients or on Maslow's self-actualizers.

Special Problems

Anyone who wants to develop a psychological test of any type must face the problems of reliability, validity, and test norms. Anyone who wants to construct an interest inventory or personality test must face some additional problems as well.

Faking

Test results are often used for making a decision that will affect the respondent's life. Since the respondent is usually aware of the possible decisions (for example, to be hired or not to be hired) and prefers one to the other, he may try **faking**—that is, responding to the items in the way he believes will secure the more favorable result. Such attempts may come to nothing on an ability test, for, despite the strongest motivation, it is impossible for a respondent to tell who wrote the *Rubáiyàt* if he never heard of it. But respondents may have some ideas about how to manage their performance on a personality or interest test. **Faking good** refers to attempts to answer items in such a way as to appear stable, wholesome, and well adjusted socially. **Faking bad** refers to attempts to answer in such a way as to appear unstable, poorly adjusted, or unable to get along with others. Faking good is elicited when the respondent is being considered for a more pleasant environment (a better job, a better school, release from a mental hospital), and faking bad is elicited when he is being considered for such environments as the military.

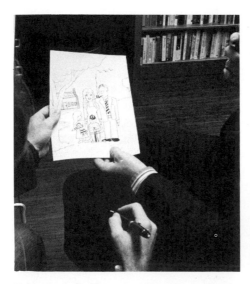 

Faking good refers to attempts to answer items in such a way as to appear stable, wholesome, and well adjusted socially . . .

. . . and faking bad refers to attempts to answer in such a way as to appear unstable, poorly adjusted, and unable to get along with others.

There are several techniques for minimizing the problem of faking. First, the test constructor can attempt to select items that have no face validity and hence give the respondent no clues as to which responses are most acceptable. Another technique is to administer the test to a number of people who have no vested interests in the results. These people take the test twice. The first time they are asked to answer as honestly and candidly as possible, and the second time they are asked to try as hard as they can to fake. All items that are answered differently under the two conditions are then discarded from the test, leaving only those that seem uninfluenced by faking. Other techniques involve including on the test specially devised items that betray attempts to fake. To detect faking good, the test may contain such items as "I have never told a lie," which cannot be honestly agreed with. People who agree with many such preposterous propositions are seen as striving to present themselves in an unnaturally favorable light. To detect faking bad, the test may include a number of items that appear to indicate serious maladjustment but in fact do not. Respondents who answer many of these items in a certain direction are seen as trying to disqualify themselves from whatever they are being considered for.

Response Sets

It might seem safe to assume that if you ask a person to check "agree" or "disagree" in response to the item "I prefer Bach to the Beatles," he would answer on the basis of his musical tastes. Yet such an assumption cannot be made, for it has been found that people have characteristic ways of responding that are based on something other than the content or meaning of the item. For example, a person who checks "agree" in response to "I prefer Bach to the Beatles" might also check "agree" if the item were worded "I prefer the Beatles to Bach."

People's tendencies to give certain types of answers whatever the question are called **response sets.** In psychological testing it is considered harmful when scores are affected by response sets, because the scores then reflect something other than the psychological quality intended to be under investigation.

Response sets take many forms. One is **acquiescence,** or a tendency to agree with an item no matter what it is. This phenomenon may account for why a person would agree with both "I prefer Bach to the Beatles" and "I prefer the Beatles to Bach." Another response set is **social desirability,** or the tendency to describe oneself as favorably as possible. Thus a respondent might agree with

"I prefer Bach to the Beatles" not because of his musical tastes but because this answer suggests a highly educated, cultured, refined, *socially desirable* person.

Procedures have been developed for minimizing the problem of response sets. To combat acquiescence, a high score on a test may require that the respondent answer half the items "agree" and the other half "disagree." Thus a person could not appear highly depressed simply because he automatically checked "agree" on a scale of depression. To minimize the problem of social desirability, the test can force the respondent to choose between answers of equal social desirability.

How Do the Measures Measure Up?

How well do psychological tests work? Are they reliable and valid? Are there adequate norms? Are they resistant to faking and response sets? The answers to such questions vary from test to test. Information about specific tests must be sought in each test's manual, in one of Buros' (1965, 1970) handbooks, or in a text that discusses testing in great detail (Anastasi, 1961; Cronbach, 1960, 1969; Kleinmuntz, 1967).

In terms of adequacy, even the better tests often fall short in one way or another. The better tests do seem reliable by both test-retest and internal consistency measures. The better tests have some validity, but not as much as most psychologists would like. True content validation is rare, and correlations with criterion measures can perhaps best be described as moderate. The better tests have adequate norms, but there is always a need for updating and improving these norms. Some of the better personality tests do appear resistant to faking and to the problems posed by response sets.

It is an exhausting project to construct and develop a psychological test. In light of the many difficulties involved, some of today's tests are surprisingly successful. But they are nowhere near perfect, and it is partly due to this imperfection that we can never expect a one-to-one correspondence between test scores and behavior in everyday settings.

HAZARDS OF PSYCHOLOGICAL TESTING

Properly used, psychological tests are helpful. But when they are misused, they are hazardous. To minimize the chances of misuse, there are certain restrictions concerning who may administer and interpret them. The belief is that, if tests are available only to properly trained professionals, the likelihood of their abuse is diminished. These restrictions may to some extent produce their intended result. But for various reasons psychological tests occasionally are misused, and the hazards of testing rise to the fore. Hazards include blind faith in the test, self-fulfilling prophecies, the indiscriminate use of tests, and the invasion of personal privacy. These problems are worth considering because, even though you may never administer psychological tests, you are likely to have them administered to you.

Blind Faith

Categorical statements are risky, but I will venture this one: *no psychological test is perfect*. All tests can produce misleading results.

The test user must never lose sight of his test's inadequacies, or he may be led to an unwise decision. For example, if he labels a child "mentally retarded" on the basis of the child's ability-test performance, that child may be assigned to a special school or class. This is fairly awesome when one considers that the test may be so unreliable that, if the "retardate" were given the test on a different day, he might be classified as "normal." Even more awesome to me would be the decision to keep somebody in prison simply because of the way he described a number of inkblots.

Tests do not make decisions—people make decisions. Tests can aid in the decision-making process. But if test results are uncritically accepted, the decisions based on them will not be wise ones.

Self-Fulfilling Prophecies

A **self-fulfilling prophecy** involves predicting an event in such a way that the prediction causes the event. You may have heard the story about the man who was told he was going to die. Supposedly, he became so upset after hearing this news that he suffered a fatal seizure.

In our earlier discussion of the self (Chapter Seven) you read about how other people's communicated expectations have a great deal to do with a person's behavior. Psychologists, teachers, and administrators may form expectations on the basis of test performances, and in this way psychological tests may contribute to self-fulfilling prophecies. A teacher may look at a child's test results and decide that he is low in ability and unlikely to learn. She may expend her teaching efforts elsewhere, on a child she expects to learn quickly. If the "dull" child learns slowly, it comes as no surprise. But his slowness might stem not from a real lack of ability but from how he was treated by the teacher.

In a study of self-fulfilling prophecies (Rosenthal & Jacobson, 1968), intelligence tests were administered to children. The children were then divided into two groups. Those in the experimental group were described to their teachers as likely to show rapid intellectual growth. Later, when the tests were again administered, the children in the experimental group did show such growth. Since the two groups were initially equal, there was no real basis for anyone to expect the experimental subjects to perform better than the control subjects. The teachers' expectations of intellectual development seem to have somehow contributed to the experimental children's surprising intellectual growth.

Test-Happiness

A few test users seem to operate on the philosophy that if it *can* be measured, it *should* be measured. I think of these people as "test-happy."

Since tests generally help psychologists make fairly specific decisions, the use of more than one test may aid them further in those decisions. But nothing at all is gained by the indiscriminate use of tests, and, unless you hold stock in the Psychological Corporation, Educational Testing Service, or some similar test-publishing business, quite a bit is lost. The test user wastes time, effort, and money. He may end up with so much information (sometimes conflicting information) that his decision making process is impaired, not facilitated. His snooping into the life of the respondent is maximized, not minimized. The respondent, on the other hand, becomes tired and disgusted with psychological tests.

Invasion of Privacy

One of the rights people are very jealous of is their right to personal privacy. Psychological tests, like army spies, phone taps, and secret credit bureaus, threaten this right. Psychological tests offend in two ways. First, they may demand information that people would just as soon not divulge. Second, once the information is obtained, it is stored somewhere, and *someone* has access to it. Some people do not seem to care much what they are asked or who knows their replies. Other people are very much concerned about both these issues. If submitting to a test were always voluntary, there would be little problem, for people preferring to maintain privacy could refuse to take the test. However, people are not always given that choice. Psychological tests may be required of individuals trying to gain admittance to a school, obtain a new job, or even maintain a long-held job.

Psychological tests, like army spies, phone taps, and secret credit bureaus, threaten the individual's right to personal privacy.

Invasion of privacy is a problem not easily dealt with. However, it can be minimized if a few simple rules are scrupulously followed. First, the investigator should beware of test-happiness. If there is no reason to know how someone performs on a test, he should not be given that test. Second, wherever possible (such as in research studies comparing groups, not individuals) the respondent should not put identifying marks on his answer sheet. Third, if names and test scores must be paired and retained, they should be kept safely out of the hands of unauthorized people (and the tougher it is for people to be considered "authorized" the better). Finally, when the answer sheets no longer serve a useful purpose, they should be destroyed.

CONCLUSIONS

Psychological tests are instruments for comparing people with each other and with themselves under varying conditions. Although every scientific psychological observation can be construed as the result of a psychological test, emphasis in this chapter was on tests specially devised for measuring abilities, interests, and personality. Such tests are useful for helping to make various kinds of decisions. Some psychological tests appear to do their intended job, but it is safe to say that we can never expect a one-to-one correspondence between psychological test scores and behavior in everyday situations.

Satisfactory measures of man do not materialize out of thin air. Their construction is time-consuming and difficult, since they must meet certain standards. They must be *reliable,* in that the results they produce must be consistent. They must be *valid,* in that they must assess that which they are supposed to assess. Adequate *test norms* must be collected, in order to provide standards for making meaningful comparisons about individual and group performance.

Tests vary widely in terms of the degree to which they fulfill these criteria. The test user must know the qualifications of the tests he administers. He must also be aware of the wide array of tests available to him and willing to select those most appropriate for his decision-making problem. He must avoid seeing his tests as perfect, using tests indiscriminately, and creating disastrous self-fulfilling prophecies. He must also always respect his respondent's right to personal privacy. For such reasons test users should be highly qualified and the access to tests and their results highly limited.

10.
Abnormal Behavior

According to Shakespeare, it can happen in the best of families. Richard, the hunchbacked Duke of Gloucester, accused George, the Duke of Clarence, of plotting against the king. The king, a cautious soul, had George incarcerated in the Tower of London. As the king wavered concerning the ultimate fate of their prisoner, Richard wheedled an order for George's execution. Before the king could have the order rescinded, Richard had George stabbed and then drowned in a barrel of wine. In the meantime, Richard married the influential Lady Anne (whose husband he had killed six months earlier). Anne withered away and died, presumably because of Richard's cruel treatment. At this point the king died. Richard, while publicly supporting the coronation of the rightful heir, circulated rumors that the heir and his brother (the next in line for the throne) were of illegitimate birth. They were placed in "protective custody" in the Tower, and, by popular acclaim, Richard became King Richard III. One of his first acts was to order the smothering of the two boys. Civil war ensued, and King Richard III, so evil yet so tragic, died on the field of battle.

Personal tastes and social rules generally allow for tremendous variability in human conduct, but these factors also set limits that separate appropriate and acceptable behavior from inappropriate and unacceptable behavior. Behavior that falls within the range of the appropriate and acceptable we may consider **normal** behavior, and behavior that does not fall within this range we may consider **abnormal** behavior.

It was once common to view all abnormal behavior as the result of "abnormal personality." The psychological processes held responsible were thought to be different from the psychological processes that account for normal behavior. The person with an abnormal personality was seen as conflict-laden, unhappy, and unable to live effectively and efficiently in his environmental setting. It is true that in many cases people who act abnormally do appear to have inaccurate perceptions, difficulties in reasoning, and severely impaired communications skills, all of which suggest distorted or abnormal psychological processes.

297

It is also true, as we shall soon see, that some people do live ineffective, ineffi-cient, and uncomfortable lives. But today it is becoming increasingly clear that many people who behave in unacceptable and unwanted ways give little or no hint of an "abnormal personality." Evidence is mounting that learning oppor-tunities, the immediate environment, and the condition of society contribute heavily to abnormal behavior.

Personal tastes and social rules generally allow for tremendous variabil-ity in human conduct.

A juvenile delinquent within a slum is a good case in point. According to the rules of society and the personal tastes of many citizens, the juvenile delin-quent's behavior is abnormal. Yet the delinquent may be living quite effec-tively in the slum setting. He may be able to perceive as clearly, learn as easily, and reason as well as any nondelinquent. His behavior is a purely predictable consequence of very normal learning processes. For example, perhaps he has never been taught that theft and aggression are bad; he has been repeatedly exposed to delinquent models; he has been encouraged by his friends to steal, get in fights, push dope, and so on; and he has discovered that the police in his neighborhood are so overburdened that, for him at least, crime does pay. He is, in other words, able to learn through imitation and reinforcement and is responsive to social standards. Given this environment, a person who is *not* delinquent might be suspected of having inaccurate perceptions and difficulties in reasoning.

Since the psychological processes contributing to abnormal behavior are sometimes indistinguishable from those contributing to normal behavior, and since external environmental variables also play a role in eliciting abnormal behavior, the present discussion is organized around the general topic of "abnormal behavior" rather than around the narrower topic of "abnormal personality." First, let us try to clarify the distinction between normal and abnormal.

DEFINITIONS OF ABNORMAL BEHAVIOR

Most of us have some intuitive ideas about what constitutes abnormal behavior. We could agree, for example, about the sniper who, after barricading himself atop the University of Texas bell tower, wounded or killed a score of people with gunfire. But in many cases such agreement is difficult to reach, because different people select different kinds of standards for defining the normal and the abnormal and tend to apply their chosen standards in rather inconsistent ways. Only in very rare instances (such as that of the Texas sniper) does behavior seem to violate everyone's standards at once.

What kinds of standards do people use for identifying abnormal behavior? Possibilities include *statistical standards, social standards,* and *personal standards.*

Statistical Standards

Behavior is often classified as abnormal because it is *quantitatively different* from normal behavior. Thus a certain amount of distrust, deceitfulness, or depression is considered normal, but an amount exceeding chosen statistical standards is considered abnormal. Normal behavior refers to a statistical average; abnormal behavior is that which noticeably departs from this average.

As an example, let us consider the extent to which college students hold themselves in high self-esteem, as assessed by a modified version of Coopersmith's (1967) self-esteem test. The hypothetical statistical distribution is shown in Figure 10-1. The horizontal axis represents self-esteem scores (high numbers indicating high self-esteem) and the vertical axis the number of cases (people with a specific score). Figure 10-1 suggests that only a handful of people have either very high self-esteem or very low self-esteem.

To see which people are abnormal by statistical standards, we first determine what "average" behavior is like (in this case a self-esteem score of 15) and then

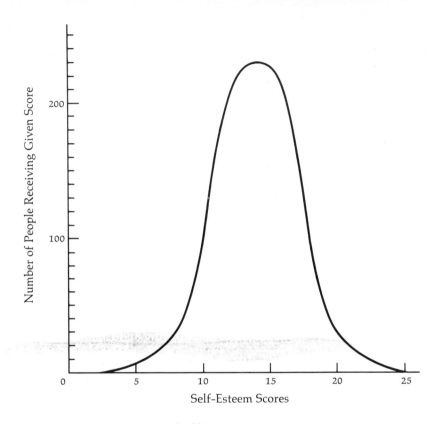

Figure 10-1. A Distribution of Self-Esteem Scores.

define as abnormal those people who clearly depart from this average. The trick here is to gain agreement concerning the cutoff point that separates the normal from the abnormal. In the case of Figure 10-1, for example, most respondents had scores between 13 and 15. If a respondent has a self-esteem score of 12, should he be considered abnormal or still within the realm of normality? What about a score of 11? Eleven is only one point less than 12 and 10 but one less than 11. In this manner it is possible to continue to the extremes of the graph without making a decision.

Departure from statistical standards provides a useful conception of abnormality when the norms (Chapter Nine) are well established and when a cutoff point is identified. Both these conditions can be met when the psychologist has a large number of cases and is willing to draw the lines so that, say, 5 percent of the observations are arbitrarily considered abnormal. Let me remind you, though, that any behavior that is defined as abnormal in this way is abnormal only in relationship to the available norms; thus the exact nature of the norms must be clearly specified. A person who is abnormal by one set of statistical standards is not necessarily abnormal by another. For example, by most norms a man would appear to be a bit unusual if he washed his hands 30 times each day. But those norms would not apply if we discovered that this man was a dentist.

Social Standards

Behavior is also regarded as abnormal if it conflicts with *socially agreed upon* standards. The abnormal person is the one who fails to meet the standards maintained by his community.

One set of social standards are those made explicit in a community's written laws. Indeed, the district attorney, policeman, or lawyer might suggest that an abnormal person is one who violates these written standards. The bad or wicked citizen who pushes drugs, steals, gets in fights, rapes, or murders is abnormal, whereas the law-abiding citizen is not. However, there are also very important *unwritten standards* within a community, which may or may not correspond to the written laws. In practice these unwritten standards may prove more useful for achieving agreement about who is behaving abnormally than are the legal standards set down in writing. For example, I know of no laws prohibiting a man from wearing cowboy boots, a wedding dress, and a crown and carrying a grandfather's clock wherever he goes. Nevertheless there would probably be considerable agreement within his community that he was not "normal."

Sociologist Howard Becker (1963) has offered a definition of abnormality (or "deviance") that is based on social standards but that makes more sense than one which suggests the standards are found in the written laws of the community. Becker suggests that from the perspective of any social group, a person who breaks that group's written or unwritten rules is likely to be considered a troublemaker or "abnormal." The important social standards reside not in dust-covered books but in the consensus of living people.

Personal Standards

A third set of standards useful for distinguishing between normality and abnormality are those that the person maintains for himself. The abnormal person is one who does not live so comfortably, effectively, or morally as his personal standards dictate.

From the perspective of the individual, these inner standards are probably the most important ones of all. For example, a person could be statistically average and could live up to all the rules established by the groups to which he belongs yet still describe himself as miserable, frustrated, and unhappy. Or, to take the opposite case, a forward-looking, avant-garde self-actualizer living in a tiny rural town might break enough of the local rules to be considered "some kind of nut" by his fellow townspeople. Although abnormal by social standards, it seems difficult to regard him as in the same category as someone caught pilfering the church collection.

Perhaps internalized standards for normality are at once the simplest and the most difficult for the psychologist to ascertain. They are the simplest, because he need only ask the person how he is faring relative to how he feels he ought to be faring. They are the most difficult, because the person either may not be able to explain at all or may offer an answer that is false or misleading.

Abnormal Behavior as Relative

Mental patients, criminals, delinquents, neurotic housewives, depressed college students, drug pushers, homosexuals, alcoholics, sadists—abnormal behavior is simply too complex and far-reaching to be defined solely as a violation of statistical, social, or personal standards. Yet each type of standard may appeal for a different purpose. Statistical standards may be particularly salient for the test user or the psychologist interested in a carefully controlled research project. Social standards may be appealing to the psychologist interested in the smooth coordination of activities among men. Personal standards may be especially relevant to the clinical psychologist who is trying to understand why his client feels that he is not living happily and effectively.

Given these different standards, it is quite possible for the same act by the same person to simultaneously be judged normal and abnormal, because *abnormal behavior is relative*—that is, not anchored in absolute standards. By statistical standards, a person can be abnormal only relative to the people who provided the norms. By social standards, he can be abnormal only relative to the group that established the social rules. By personal standards, he can be abnormal only relative to the standards that he himself maintains. It should

be apparent to you that different people maintain different standards, since
they may try to apply their personal standards to others, such as yourself.

Psychologists, sociologists, anthropologists, and explorers long ago concluded
that behavior considered wicked, evil, abnormal, or sick varies tremendously.
Whether or not behavior is judged to be abnormal depends on the time and
place in which the behavior occurs and on who does the judging. As for time,
you might wonder about a person in a Boston coffeehouse who boiled some
coffee beans, poured off the liquid, and then ate the beans with his fingers.
But in the first colonial coffeehouses in America, this behavior could be taken
as a sign of culture, refinement, and elegant living. As for place, someone
dressed in a drab, brown, dentist-like "Chairman Mao" outfit would likely
receive different welcomes in Peking and in Philadelphia. As for who is doing
the evaluating, a juvenile delinquent's shoplifting may not be abnormal according to his associates who live in the same slums and share the same rules.
Indeed, if he was highly skilled at crime, he might be considered a local hero.
But the police, the shopkeepers, and the society at large would probably make
a different judgment. In the discussion to follow, it should be remembered that
there are no absolute, permanent standards that define what is abnormal at
all times and in all places.

ORIGINS OF ABNORMAL BEHAVIOR

At one time many psychologists and psychiatrists believed abnormal behavior
to be the product of "mental disease." The mind of the person displaying such
behavior was thought to be different from the minds of people with "good
mental health," in the same sense that an inflamed appendix is different from
a healthy appendix. Elimination of the problem could be brought about, it was
thought, only if the underlying illness were "cured."

Historically, this orientation provided the first real basis for attempts to understand and deal scientifically with abnormal behavior. Earlier, behavior had
been seen as the product of demons, devils, and weak moral fiber.

According to the "disease" conception, abnormal behavior is merely a *symptom*
that reflects the presence of the underlying disease. Attempts to remove the
symptoms directly cannot remove the disease. Furthermore, any apparent success at mere "symptom removal" would be short-lived. Since the disease is
still present, the symptom must reappear or a new one take its place. Support-

The mind of the person displaying abnormal behavior was thought to be different from the minds of people with "good mental health," in the same sense that an inflamed appendix is different from a healthy appendix.

ing this view were some early and rather meager clinical reports that, when a symptom was removed (by means of hypnosis), another quickly replaced it.

However, Szasz (1961) suggests that the concept of mental disease is a myth. True, some forms of unwanted behavior can be traced to physical causes such as abnormal brain waves, infections, nutritional deficiencies, and hormonal imbalances. *But all these conditions are illnesses of the body, not illnesses of the mind. And these illnesses of the body account for only the smallest fraction of abnormal behavior.*

Perhaps the greatest challenge to the concept of "mental disease" comes from the successful use of learning principles for eliminating or modifying unwanted behavior. (Some of these techniques, such as the use of withdrawal of reinforcement to eliminate food stealing and the application of social-learning techniques to remove fear of snakes, were discussed earlier.) These investigations all point to the conclusion that *removing the so-called symptom may be equivalent to restoring normal behavior.* A symptom thus removed may not be replaced by another one. To the extent that this is so, the existence of an underlying "disease" loses plausibility.

The disease conception has had the wonderful effect of encouraging tremendous compassion for all people. Many of us feel more sympathy for murderers than for their victims. Compassion is still fine, but thinking in terms of "diseased minds" may no longer be helpful. In fact, it may be a distraction that draws attention away from other causes of unwanted behavior, such as our imperfectly contrived society.

If abnormal behavior is not best viewed as the result of a disease, how may it be construed? One trend is to regard much abnormal behavior as *ineffective solutions to the problems of living.*

This ineffectiveness is manifested in many ways: through inappropriate behavior, unsolved problems, poor social relations, a lack of ability to fulfill obligations, feelings of discomfort, distorted reasoning and perception, unwarranted displays of emotions, and, often, an inability to understand the reasons for all these things. Since the person may be experiencing intense inner conflicts, it is likely to be difficult for him to discover more effective solutions. Conflicts, as you may recall from Chapter Seven, can produce repetitive, rigid behavior, thus robbing the person of the flexibility required for new learning. Let us refer to people who cannot effectively cope with their problems of living as having **personal disorders.**

Why should one person be able to come to grips with his life while another person cannot? What causes these personal disorders? There are many possible origins. A distinction is commonly made between *organic* and *functional* disorders.

The causes of **organic disorders** are sought in malfunctions of the body, such as changes in blood chemistry, brain injury, or damage to the nervous or other systems. Thus, for example, the severe overuse of alcohol can cause brain malfunctions resulting in delirium, hallucinations, and an inability to take care of oneself. Treatment of the organic disorders sometimes relies on the use of powerful chemicals, which by changing the body's chemistry restore the ability for more effective behavior. At other times treatment relies on a proper diet, withdrawal of the toxic substances, and healing over time.

Functional disorders do not stem from the body's malfunctions. When found, physical malfunctions or ailments are a result of, rather than the cause of, the disorder. Functional disorders arise from a poor combination of personal needs and resources, on the one hand, and environmental conditions, on the other. Thus in a certain situation a person may behave abnormally because of per-

The severe overuse of alcohol can cause delirium, hallucinations, and an inability to take care of oneself.

sistent and perhaps overpowering needs or because he has not developed the resources required to respond more appropriately and effectively. Precisely what these needs and resources are and how they interact with environmental conditions to produce functional disorders depend on the view taken of personality. For example, psychoanalysts may suggest that a personal disorder stems from early-childhood needs and may see the person's resources seriously undermined by id-ego-superego squabbles that produce energy-wasting inner conflicts and an overreliance on one or more defense mechanisms. The more behaviorally oriented psychologist, on the other hand, might view the same problem as the result of inadequate or faulty learning and perhaps correctable through classical or operant conditioning.

VARIETIES OF PERSONAL DISORDERS

In one sense any personal disorder is unique to the individual. Yet there are enough similarities among certain cases that classification systems have been devised (most recently the one proposed by the American Psychiatric Association, 1968). These "diagnostic classification" systems can be incredibly complex. Unfortunately, man's systems for classifying nature's phenomena leave much to be desired, and the present diagnostic classification schemes are no exception. First, within some of the categories there is a wide range of seemingly inconsistent behavior. Second, people are often "mixed bags"—that is, they show characteristics of more than one of the supposedly different disorders. Third, an individual's behaviors that provide a basis for his classification may shift over time, making it difficult to keep the same label pinned on him. Finally, judging from a present lack of types of cases that were prevalent in the 1890s, the patterns of abnormal behavior seem to vary as a function of culture and social change, which suggests that a classification scheme is likely to be of only temporary value.

Diagnostic categories have themselves been organized in various ways. One is in terms of the presumed *origin* of the disorder—for example, whether it is believed to be organic or functional. Another way of organizing categories is in terms of the perceived *severity* of the disorder. At one extreme are the rather minor functional disorders in which the person's resources are almost sufficient to meet the challenging conditions; at the other extreme are functional or organic disorders that are totally incapacitating. However, certain classifications are not easily handled by either organizing system. Let us now consider five major classes of personal disorders: (1) minor maladjustments, (2) neuroses, (3) psychoses, (4) psychophysiologic disorders, and (5) antisocial personality.

Minor Maladjustments *(Transient Situational Disturbances)*

Ours is a complex, constantly changing world that presents challenge after challenge. It is unlikely that at all times a given person will have sufficient intellectual, emotional, and social resources to cope effectively with each new challenge. When ineffective coping behavior is not particularly strange or bizarre, does not keep the person from meeting his daily obligations, and does not prove too disruptive to others, the problem is one of **minor maladjustment**.

There is an endless list of challenges that could be met in ineffective and somehow disturbing ways. Dismissal from a job, a death in the family, induction into the military, retirement, an unwanted pregnancy, and discovering after a lifetime in the navy that you will not be promoted to admiral are only a few.

The specifics of the challenge vary, and so do the ways in which they are met. For example, a common occurrence is rejection in love. Some rejected people never lose sight of their own strengths and favorable qualities or of the fact that, since there are about one billion people of the opposite sex in this world, the chances are very good of meeting someone who is at least as lovable as the one who has recently been lost. However, others pass through a period of minor maladjustment. Some may react with bitterness and brooding, which may lead to a decline in work performance and a number of mannerisms that are irritating to the self or to others. Still other people may react by withdrawal. They refuse to initiate new contacts that could lead to future failure at love.

A happy ending to cases of minor maladjustment is in no way guaranteed, but in many instances the future looks bright. First, the person may soon develop the resources required for a happier existence. As an illustration, consider the man who has difficulty adjusting to retirement but soon acquires new interests that happily occupy his time. Second, the external conditions that gave rise to the problem may soon pass. This latter case is illustrated by the person who becomes dazed and disoriented during a disaster such as a tornado but quickly regains his composure once the danger is over.

Neuroses

Somewhat less temporary and more serious personal disorders than minor maladjustments are the **neuroses.** Neurotic behavior is likely to be noticeably different from "normal" behavior, it keeps the person from fully meeting his daily obligations, and it often proves disruptive to others. However, the person showing neurotic behavior is typically able to maintain social contacts, keep a job, and in other ways fulfill the minimal requirements for day-to-day survival in our complex society. Neurotic behavior is believed to be quite common. Estimates of the proportion of people who can be classified as neurotic rarely fall below 10 percent and have risen much higher.

Whereas minor maladjustments may take an almost endless number of forms, neuroses are believed to assume one of a relatively few distinct forms. Those described in this section were for the most part identified in Freud's day, although they have been periodically renamed ever since. Conditions change, and so, perhaps, do neurotic responses to problems of life. Psychologists are by no means presently agreed that "neurotic" behavior must assume one of the following sharply defined forms.

Phobic and Anxiety Neuroses

A certain amount of fear is useful for surviving in our occasionally dangerous environment. But when fears persist in the absence of objectively threatening external conditions, they are considered neurotic.

Phobias are strong, irrational, groundless fears that appear to be elicited by a specific, identifiable stimulus, such as open spaces.

Phobias are strong, irrational, groundless fears that appear to be elicited by a specific, identifiable stimulus. One person's phobia may involve a maddening fear of heights, another person's a continuing dread of closed spaces, and a third person's a terror of open spaces. The unrealistic fear may be of something that is not harmful (such as being rained on) or of something that is harmful but very unlikely. You could, for example, be squashed to death by a hippopotamus, bitten by a viper, or devoured by piranhas (Clarke, 1969), but the chances of any of these things happening are so slim that you probably don't worry much about them. The phobic person, however, may act as if these events are imminent.

Anxiety is a vague but continuing feeling of dread. Whereas the apparent source of a phobia is specific, the source of an anxiety is hard to identify. What the person knows is that he is apprehensive and worried and has a tight feeling in the chest, a dry throat, a palpitating heart, cold, clammy hands, and an upset stomach. These feelings persist at a low level but occasionally become intensified. Rational, realistic fears pass as external dangers disappear, but phobias and anxiety linger on. As we saw in an earlier discussion of snake phobia (Chapter Five), unrealistic fears can dominate the person's life as he takes more and more "safety" measures that hamper his movements and limit his capacity for a free existence.

What causes these fearlike reactions? Psychoanalysts point to a lack of cooperation among the id, ego, and superego. An irrationally feared external stimulus may represent a disguised fear of something within the self. For example, a fear of a wild boar could reflect a fear of one's own "wild" (id) impulses, a fear of falling could represent a concern about personal moral failure, and a fear of snakes could be a manifestation of certain worries about male sex organs. Anxiety, also, is believed to reflect fears of the impetuous id or of the severe and punishing superego.

It is also possible that phobias and anxieties are simply learned responses. You have already seen (Chapter Four) how, under some conditions, learned fears can be very strong and persistent. Solomon et al.'s (1953) dogs did not stop making avoidance responses to a light, and Campbell et al.'s (1964) subjects long feared a tone after a single pairing with a terrifying drug. Whether or not all phobias and anxiety are learned, it is interesting to note that many phobias can be *unlearned*. This finding would not be expected from psychoanalytic theory, which implies, for example, that teaching someone not to be afraid of snakes should do little good, since snakes are not what the person really feared in the first place.

Obsessive-Compulsive Neurosis

The **obsessive-compulsive neurosis** involves recurrent thoughts and repetitive behavior. Obsessions are thoughts that simply won't leave one alone, and compulsions are persistent and recurring patterns of behavior. Continually brooding about the number of railroad ties between New York and San Francisco would be an obsessive thought; actually going out and counting them would be compulsive behavior. Obsessions and compulsions come in an unending variety. The person may be obsessed with mental replays of a popular tune, with whether the oven or lawn sprinkler is shut off, or with how many angels can sit on the head of a pin. The compulsive person can polish his car night and day, be careful not to step on the cracks on the sidewalk (or to step on every crack), or, like me, check pockets for wallet, keys, sunglasses, and pen 10,000 times a day. Disturbing to the self and irritating to others, obsessive thoughts and compulsive acts block opportunities for more constructive activity.

To be sure, specific symptoms can be quite spectacular, as when unending obsessions about dirt and contamination are coupled with compulsive and unnecessary house cleaning. Less conspicuous, but perhaps equally dismal, is the obsessive-compulsive **life-style,** or general way of behaving. Shapiro (1965) has noted that obsessive-compulsive people usually behave in a rigid and inflexible way. They tend to be isolated from close social contacts and to have a strong sense of the "should." They also have difficulties with the direct expression of emotions; that is, they appear to rely on indicators of how they *should* feel. Thus, an obsessive-compulsive might say "I am going to get married today, *so I guess that means* I'm pretty happy."

From the psychoanalytic perspective, obsessions and compulsions are viewed as a *defense* against unacceptable impulses. By thinking about the opposite of an impulse ("I hope my house isn't burning down") or by acting in a way that seems to suggest the opposite of the impulse (checking lights and stove, removing all paper and rags, checking lights again, and so on), the impulse itself ("Burn, baby, burn!") is never expressed. Social-learning theorists, on the other hand, could see obsessive-compulsive behavior as the result of early learning experiences. The person who, thanks to incessant scrubbing, is as "neat as a pin" might have simply been taught standards of cleanliness only too well. Still another possibility is to view the obsessive-compulsive action as a rigid behavior that originates in an approach/avoidance conflict and prohibits the person from adopting new and richer ways of responding.

Conversion Hysteria

Conversion hysterias, or the "hysterical neuroses, conversion type" (originally called hysterias and later called conversion reactions) involve behavior that suggests a physical illness or disability. Although the "symptoms" may be very convincing to the untrained eye, they do not have organic causes and in some cases flagrantly violate known laws of medicine. For example, a man could have his legs paralyzed in a way that is inconceivable to a neuroanatomist. The paralysis could make sense only when one considers that the man is supposed to get on an airplane in preparation for his first parachute jump.

There are two types of conversion hysterias: autonomies and inactivations. **Autonomies are involuntary muscular movements,** such as tics, twitches, throbbings, and shakes. They are believed to reflect an inability to express certain subjectively unacceptable impulses in an open and direct manner. Thus anger or sexual excitement may be expressed in a tic or a twitch. **Inactivations refer to such reactions as blindness, a loss of sensitivity, or paralysis.** Because the person cannot perceive or perform normally, frightening perceptions and activities are made impossible. Although the fame of the reluctant bride with paralyzed legs seems to be diminishing, we can still find this type of reaction in the case of impotent men whose disability keeps them from unconsciously frightening sexual activity.

The psychoanalysts seem to have had more to say about hysteria than have the learning theorists. However, it is worth note that the "sick" role in our society can be highly reinforcing when it exempts one from unwanted tasks or duties.

Dissociative Hysteria

In Chapter Eight you learned that repression provides a convenient way of dealing with one's inadequacies, stupidity, or wickedness. The experimental studies cited in that chapter suggest that repression is a very normal process. But when whole segments of one's identity, activities, or past maneuverings in time and space are blocked from awareness, the repression is considered a neurotic **dissociative hysteria** (officially called hysterical neurosis, dissociative type). This condition may involve simple **amnesia**—that is, blank periods that the person can't describe. McNeil (1968) describes the case of a man who disappeared from Detroit and was later discovered in San Francisco by a relative. The man's Detroit past was not accessible to his consciousness, even when he was confronted with his former wife and children.

In certain extremely rare but spectacular cases the person does not make a single move from one life to another but shifts back and forth between two seemingly different "personalities." These are cases of **multiple personality.** The best known is the case of "Eve" (Thigpen & Cleckley, 1957). One personality ("Eve White") was conscientious and moralistic. The other ("Eve Black") was wanton and self-indulgent. Eve White was spared Eve Black's wickedness, and, to some extent, Eve Black was spared the stern admonitions of Eve White's overdeveloped conscience. This is, you must admit, an interesting solution to the problem of being above reproach on the one hand and self-indulgent on the other. Thigpen and Cleckley report that eventually a single personality developed that had some capacities for seeking pleasure while still maintaining some minimal standards for conduct. This third personality, by the way, called herself Jane.

Psychoses

The most extreme personal disorders are the **psychoses.** In these cases needs, resources, and external conditions are so poorly matched that there appears to be a loss of contact with reality. The psychotic's inability to accept and deal with conditions as they exist typically affects his perception, thinking, and expression of emotion. Perceptual distortion may appear in **delusions** (that is, a misconstrual of the world), and **hallucinations** (subjective impressions of stimuli that are not physically present). Thus the psychotic may see an innocent passerby as a government agent out to "get him" or hear his long-dead mother calling from the corner of a darkened room.

Disturbed thought processes may appear in the form of reasoning based on wrong assumptions, poor logic, or both. Thus the psychotic may develop plans for wild and hopelessly doomed business projects, offer an intricate and lengthy description of why a stray matchbook is ultimate proof of a plot against him, or deduce that some form of bizarre activity will redeem him on Judgment Day.

The psychotic may also display a seeming lack of emotions, an exaggeration of emotions, or highly inappropriate emotions. Thus he may quietly stare off into the distance day after day, swing between deep depression and euphoria, or laugh when other people are crying and cry when other people are laughing. The psychotic, in short, appears to have severely impaired perceptual and judgmental abilities, poor communication abilities (since he operates on different assumptions than the people with whom he tries to communicate), and little in the way of social skills (since he behaves inappropriately in many situations, including social interactions). Psychoses are generally so extreme that it is difficult or impossible for the psychotic to manage his daily affairs. At some point he or others find his behavior so personally unacceptable or socially disruptive that a period of hospitalization generally results.

Schizophrenia

People classified as **schizophrenic** are primarily characterized by strange, bizarre, and seemingly unsystematic patterns of thought. The schizophrenic's speech consists of thought fragments arranged in sentences that make no apparent sense. It is as if the schizophrenic were preoccupied with several streams of thought at once and spoke randomly chosen bits and pieces from each stream, producing an indecipherable mishmash of words. The apparent thought irregularities are so prominent that schizophrenia is usually referred to as a **cognitive disorder,** although there are other indicators as well. For example, the schizophrenic's behavior suggests that he finds it very difficult to accept or express feelings, especially warm feelings about himself and others. Such emotional isolation may represent a defense against being hurt by others.

The apparent thought irregularities are so prominent that schizophrenia is usually referred to as a cognitive disorder.

The picture described above is one of simple schizophrenia. There are many other forms involving more than bizarre thought patterns and some emotional dampening. For example, in **catatonic schizophrenia** there is very prominent withdrawal. For months on end the catatonic schizophrenic may remain mute, immobile, and virtually unresponsive to stimulation. His existence may be so passive that assistance is required for him to sustain life. In effect, the catatonic schizophrenic responds to the challenges of life by withdrawing from life. In some spectacular cases he assumes the posture of a fetus in his mother's womb. This behavior must be the ultimate in regression.

Strikingly different from catatonic schizophrenia is **hebephrenic schizophrenia,** which is characterized by uncontrollable displays of intense emotions. The hebephrenic is given to loud, raucous, and often "silly" outbursts.

Paranoid schizophrenia involves delusions. Unlike the delusions of the pure paranoid (which superficially may appear quite logical), those of the paranoid schizophrenic are immediately recognizable as such. For example, he may believe that people from another dimension are forcing him to masturbate, that the center of the world consists of hamburger, or that he is living in a time and place that have never existed.

What combination of needs, resources, and environmental conditions produce schizophrenia? Geneticists have linked the disorder to heredity, but it appears that a person will inherit only a *tendency* to become a schizophrenic; he will not actually become one in the absence of certain other conditions. The psychoanalysts have some ideas, as when they suggest that the catatonic reaction represents a regressive response. But for the most part the causes of schizophrenia remain shrouded in mystery. Fortunately, new advances in pharmacology help people weather and finally abandon schizophrenic behavior, although the ways in which these drugs create their miracles are not completely understood.

Affective (Mood) Disorders

Changes of mood are natural and acceptable. But when they produce extreme highs and lows or have little or no correspondence with objective conditions, they reflect **affective disorders.** Extreme lows are referred to as **depression.** The depressed person is discouraged, fatigued, listless, unable to concentrate, and has little or no appetite. Tired, withdrawn, and gloomy, he may turn his thoughts to suicide. However, depression comes in all degrees, and it is not until it is so acute that it severely disrupts daily functioning that the depressed person can be considered psychotic.

Extreme highs in moods are referred to as **manic states** or reactions. They consist of periods of elation, euphoria, optimism, and the expression of tremendous energy. Wild plans and impulsive behavior, such as shopping sprees,

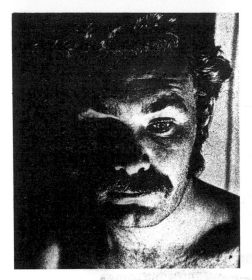 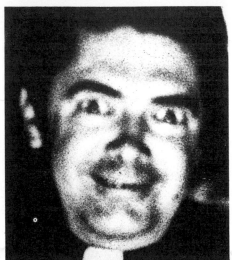

When changes of mood produce extreme · · · *they are considered affective disorders.*
highs and lows or have little correspond-
ence with objective conditions . . .

daring stunts, and grandiose ambitions, may result. However, since judgment is impaired, the consequences can prove disastrous. McNeil (1968) cites the case of a man who, during a manic period, almost succeeded in establishing a chain of computer dating services. But because of judgmental difficulties, he was unable to maintain his initial success. In such cases fortunes dwindle, debts pile up, and partners, family, and friends are disappointed. Yet it is interesting to consider how the originators of unrealistic schemes are regarded when, through some quirk of fate, they reap money and fame.

Affective disorders often involve swings between mania and depression. This problem is the **manic-depressive psychosis.** In a sense, the person is an emotional Yo-Yo, traveling repeatedly between the euphoric highs of mania and the lowest depths of depression.

Great strides have been made in the control of affective disorders. Depression responds to new "mood-elevating" drugs and electric-shock treatments. The manic reaction can also be controlled by new drugs, but it is sometimes difficult to get people to take medication that will ruin their high. Occasionally, affective disorders disappear in the absence of treatment. However, even after years of seemingly satisfactory adjustment, the formerly manic-depressive person may again exhibit mania or depression.

Paranoia is a relatively rare disorder characterized by "systematized" delusions—systematized in the sense that they are intricate, elaborate, and, on the surface at least, quite logical. Perhaps the chief distinction between "pure paranoia" and related disorders such as paranoid schizophrenia is that, whereas the paranoid schizophrenic's story is immediately identifiable as unrealistic, the paranoid's story may at first glance appear quite reasonable.

A paranoid delusion may be highly specific, in that it is based on one central belief such as "They are out to get me" or "I am the first of a new breed of man." However, the single idea may have implications that extend into all spheres of life. Jobs are lost and so are associates, since the paranoid's suspicious or overbearing behavior drives other people away.

One way paranoia can be understood is as the result of an overreliance on certain mechanisms of defense. For example, the person who believes he is being persecuted may be projecting his own hostile impulses outward onto someone or something else. Thus, through projection, "I hate him" becomes "He hates me." Delusions of grandeur might be traced to denial. That is, the person can spare himself full recognition of his inadequacies by concentrating on his imagined superiority.

Psychophysiologic Disorders

Formerly referred to as psychosomatic reactions, **psychophysiologic disorders are physical illnesses that result from the psychological challenges of living.** Tensions, conflicts, and worries may be translated into skin eruptions; excessive business pressures may lead to the development of ulcers; continuing exposure to severe stress may precipitate fatal heart attacks. No part of the body seems immune from such psychologically caused damage.

Psychophysiologic disorders are not to be confused with **hypochondriasis,** in which the "sufferer" complains about imaginary ailments, or with the earlier described conversion hysteria, which is a form of neurosis. The conversion hysteric gives the appearance of a seemingly plausible physical ailment that is simply not there. On the other hand, the person who has undergone a psychophysiologic reaction does have a "real" illness. You are just as dead from a psychologically induced heart attack as you are from strychnine poisoning, and psychophysiologic ulcers are products, not figments, of the imagination.

Antisocial Personality

When a person is poorly socialized and persistently responds to the challenges of living by engaging in deceitful, irresponsible, lawless, and impulsive behavior, he is said to have an **antisocial personality.** This classification includes a wide variety of people, ranging from those who are simply crude and untamed to those who are suave and sophisticated but hide their defects behind a charming facade. Cleckley (1955) described these latter antisocial types as wearing a "mask of sanity." The mask becomes transparent, however, when someone tries to form emotionally close ties with them and inevitably meets with disappointment.

Repeated law infraction is not sufficient cause to consider someone an antisocial personality, since breaking society's written rules may result from membership in a delinquent group whose members show a certain amount of social responsibility for one another. Antisocial personalities are marked by a lack of such responsibility, as well as by other characteristics. First, they appear to have exaggerated tendencies to succumb to momentary impulses and to seek gratification in the here-and-now. Second, many are bright and manage to avoid getting caught by the law. If they are caught, they may do a good job of feigning remorse and repentance or describing very convincingly the "mental illnesses" responsible for their misconduct. In prison or in a mental institution, they may quickly become model inmates and thereby be granted an early release for good conduct. Once free, however, they soon revert to their previous behavior. Neither guilt, the internal punisher, nor the adverse reactions of others seem to change their actions.

The causes of persistent antisocial behaviors are very much open to speculation. There are probably many contributing factors at the biological, individual, and social levels.

PSYCHOTHERAPY

Personal disorders are upsetting to the individual and disruptive to the society. What can be done to help someone with a personal disorder cope more effectively with his life circumstances? One possibility is the use of drugs that restore biological functioning and make normal behavior once again possible. But in many cases the disorders have no known organic origins, or effective drugs that provide a permanent solution are not available. Another possibility is to change environmental conditions so that they will match better with the person's needs and resources. But this cannot always be arranged, and when it can (such as by sending the person to a mental hospital), it is not always advisable. What remains are techniques that attempt to bolster the person's own resources for living a satisfactory and rewarding life.

Psychotherapy is the process by which trained practitioners (psychotherapists) help the person to discover a more effective, richer, and more rewarding life. The psychotherapist's methods depend on his training, his theoretical orientation, and his perception of the problem. In addition to "talk therapy" (that is, therapy built on conversations between the therapist and client), there are literally dozens of approaches. Some, involving play, participation in impromptu dramatic skits, or dancing, have received moderately wide acceptance among psychologists. Others, involving massages, deliberate screaming, or exercise and diet, seem to have a much more limited appeal. Here we will touch on a few of the most common forms of psychotherapy.

Individual Therapy

Individual therapy involves a person (called either a patient or a client) and a therapist working together on a one-to-one basis.

In **individual therapy** a person (referred to as either a patient or a client) and a therapist work together on a one-to-one basis. The procedure is largely conversational, although it is the client who does most of the talking. The atmosphere is *permissive*, in that the client is encouraged to speak and show his emotions freely. In some cases the therapist takes a passive role, simply encouraging the client to explore his feelings; in other cases he takes a more active role, interpreting and explaining his client's behavior and sometimes pointing to alternatives that the client has left unexplored. Often the psychotherapist does not follow an inflexible procedure but modifies and adapts his techniques to fit the particular situation.

Psychoanalytic Approaches to Therapy

In psychoanalytic therapy the therapist (psychoanalyst) meets with the person (patient) several times a week over a period of two or more years. The analyst attempts to uncover the patient's most important inner needs, conflicts, and feelings, which are presumed to have been pushed into the unconscious by repression and other mechanisms of defense. To explore this hidden mental life, the analyst encourages **free association**—that is, talking about anything that comes to mind, no matter how trivial, stupid, incoherent, irrelevant, and loosely organized it happens to be. This technique is believed to encourage a temporary failure of repression, thus allowing significant material to rise to the surface. The analyst is also interested in hearing about such things as dreams, accidents, and mistakes, which in part represent the workings of the unconscious.

During the sessions the psychoanalyst attempts to be as neutral and as noncommittal as possible. To do so, he sits behind the patient (who is reclining on a couch) so that his own facial expressions cannot be seen although he can clearly see those of the patient. This procedure encourages **transference,** a process by which the patient transfers to the analyst important feelings of love and hate that he has maintained toward significant people in his life (such as parents).

The result of these procedures is that the patient comes to recognize his inner needs, defenses, and conflicts; to understand how they were formed; and to regard them in a new and more mature light. The slow, laborious process of psychoanalysis is considered necessary to effect this change. That is, if the analyst somehow discovered in the very first session that an obsessive-compulsive neurotic's problem stemmed from severe toilet training, it would do absolutely no good to tell him so, remind him that he is no longer being toilet trained, and ask him to please place his childhood experience in proper perspective. Instead, the problem must be slowly and painstakingly uncovered and the strong feelings developing through transference used for corrective emotional experiences.

True psychoanalysis in the Freudian style requires tremendous time, money, and luck in finding an analyst (since psychoanalysts these days are few and far between). The training of an analyst requires many years, and each analyst can handle only a few patients at a time. More common are forms of therapy based on true psychoanalysis but sped up by various expedients. For example, the therapist may prompt and probe, rather than rely on the time-consuming method of free association, which may produce hours of talk that is for all intents and purposes meaningless. Whether these expedients speed the process or detract from its ultimate value seems to depend on whom you ask.

Client-Centered Therapy

Client-centered therapy, also called nondirective therapy, was developed in the 1940s under the guidance of Carl Rogers. Rogers, you may recall, is one of the main figures in humanistic psychology (Chapter Eight), and his psychotherapeutic technique seems to reflect the optimistic and positive orientation of the humanistic approach. First, instead of the 400 or so sessions and $20,000 necessary for full psychoanalysis, client-centered therapy generally requires only about ten sessions and is often available free at college counseling centers. The implication is that many problems in living are fairly easily solved, and it is unnecessary to find someone who has had many years of psychoanalytic training to help discover these solutions. Second, the client-centered approach is based on the premise that the client has, within himself, the potential for constructive change.

This form of psychotherapy takes place in a highly permissive conversational setting. The therapist faces the client and encourages him to say what he pleases. Thus the course of the discussion is for the most part controlled by the client. The therapist seeks to understand the way the client views and interprets the world and does not try to make everything the client says fit in with his own preconceptions about personality and adjustment. The therapist offers neither advice nor interpretations but seeks continual clarification of the client's thoughts and feelings. An important part of this process is restating thoughts and feelings that the client has himself partly expressed but does not seem to fully appreciate the significance of. For example, if the client nonchalantly says "Oh, I got mad at that guy" and then quickly proceeds to another thought, the client-centered therapist might say "You say you became angry with him?" thereby focusing the attention back on the anger. Through this process it becomes possible for the client to explore his own perceptions, motives, and feelings and to develop an understanding and acceptance of himself. The result is more effective behavior.

Many psychologists follow the client-centered approach. As a psychotherapeutic technique, it is brief and, according to the testimonials of both practitioners and clients, seems to be effective in many cases, especially when the disorder is a minor one. Furthermore, client-centered therapy is one of the few "talk" therapies that has been evaluated for effectiveness by means of a controlled study (Rogers & Dymond, 1954) and found to be worthwhile.

Behavior Therapy

Behavior therapy (also called behavior modification) operates on the assumption that abnormal behavior represents learned responses and is therefore susceptible to change through classical conditioning, operant conditioning, and social learning. Since I have already discussed how learning principles have been used to encourage appropriate behavior and discourage inappropriate behavior (food stealing, dressing in the attire of the opposite sex, and so on), there is no need to elaborate here on the general procedures and the seemingly striking successes. Behavior therapy, however, is not above criticism. Its effectiveness seems rather limited when the problem is unspecific and diffuse. Applying behavior therapy to a person who is afraid of snakes is one thing, but what do you do with the student who comes in with a very vague, global problem, such as feeling bored, restless, and dissatisfied, and who has no idea what he would like to do next in life?

Group Therapy

In **group therapy** one or more therapists work with several clients simultaneously. Therapy groups take many different forms. Some are psychoanalytically oriented, some are client centered, some are basically inspirational (like sales meetings), and some are indistinguishable from encounter groups (Chapter

Eight). Most groups, however, seem to represent a sort of compromise among these various approaches.

Group therapy involves one or more therapists working with several clients simultaneously.

Group therapy dates to the beginning of the twentieth century, but its development was spurred in the 1940s by a shortage of therapists, on the one hand, and an overabundance of people seeking therapy, on the other (Rosenbaum & Berger, 1963). But although it began primarily as an economy measure, group psychotherapy offers some distinct advantages for the participants. First, it provides the therapist with the opportunity to see firsthand how the person interacts with others. He may thus discover an intriguing social behavior that the client might not be able to describe or might somehow "forget to mention" in individual therapy. Second, the people within a therapy group often prove helpful to one another. They usually accept one another and offer support and encouragement, share experiences that prove useful to one another, and offer helpful reactions when a member shares his thoughts, feelings, and plans.

Many therapy groups consist of a number of complete strangers. When the group first meets, each member is grappling with his own problem, which is not connected with the problems of others. Thus Georgia's divorce, Fred's getting fired, Merv's drinking, and Joann's private disgrace are all separate and personal crises. When the group contains married couples, or families, this independence of problems no longer holds, and the therapist must deal with the intricately intertwined problems of closely related people. If Georgia is getting divorced because her husband, Fred, was fired, and Merv is drinking because of Joann's private disgrace (which was spending a weekend with Fred, unbeknownst to Georgia), things get very, very complicated very, very fast. The responsible therapist is particularly challenged when he is dealing with such groups. In addition to being sensitive to the individual problem of each person, he must be sensitive to how their problems are interdependent. Any successes or failures he has helping one person sort out his or her life will strongly affect the lives of the others.

Group therapy is not expected to work in all cases, because certain minimal social skills are a prerequisite for participation. Then, too, this type of therapy offers certain disadvantages. As the focus of attention shifts from member to member, issues arise that may not be of use to one specific member. Furthermore, since many people are present, it may be difficult to express oneself as freely and candidly as is possible in the more private individual therapy. Nonetheless, group therapy does provide some unique advantages, and some of its limitations can be overcome if it is used concurrently with individual therapy.

Hospitalization

Most psychotherapy takes place in clinics, counseling centers, and the offices of private practitioners. Nonetheless, there are enough instances in which people are so disorganized that they cannot take care of themselves or are highly disruptive to others that our numerous mental hospitals are often crowded to capacity. If the hospital is fully staffed and can support modern treatment programs, it will offer a carefully controlled environment that provides therapy during most of the waking hours. There are many ways to operate a hospital so that the patient spends more time being treated than sitting around doing nothing, but one that is rapidly gaining favor is the application of behavior-therapy techniques on an around-the-clock basis.

One form of this approach is the **token economy.** Tokens, such as poker chips, have reinforcement value because they are exchangeable for goods and services. Patients may acquire tokens by behaving in ways that are acceptable to the therapists, just as in our larger economy money may be acquired by behaving in ways that are acceptable to others.

On the wards, tokens are dispensed as reinforcers for good behavior. Dressing oneself, brushing one's teeth, cleaning one's room—all will be rewarded on the spot, thus shaping a set of personal and social skills. The token economy may be more effective than a series of brief, intensive learning sessions. Since the patient is monitored continually, instances of the behavior to be modified may occur spontaneously and hence provide an opportunity for the reinforcement to be administered. Similarly, around-the-clock control ensures that the patient will not be inadvertently reinforced for making unwanted responses.

A token economy differs tremendously from what we think of as a ward for the "sick." When all mental-hospital patients are seen as "sick" and given set standards for living, all behavior—abnormal as well as normal—is rewarded and hence maintained. In the token economy the patient's standard of living can be tremendously raised over the minimum standards when he behaves in approved ways. Under these latter conditions acceptable behavior is strengthened but unacceptable behavior is not.

Mental hospitals provide a place for the management and treatment of people who cannot be effectively handled elsewhere. But in addition to the problem of overburdened facilities, there are other considerations that discourage the liberal use of hospitalization. Hospitalization forces a break with employer, family, and friends, which means that, upon release, the person will have the problem of reestablishing his former life. This task may be made particularly difficult if his associates consider his hospitalization as ultimate proof that he is dangerous or hopelessly fouled up. Furthermore, the hospital setting is so different from the normal environment that it may impair the process of learning to readapt to the normal environment. The "normal" behavior learned inside the hospital may not persist upon release. For example, avoidance-conditioning procedures are sometimes used within the hospital to train alcoholics to avoid booze, but conditions are so different on the outside that there is always a chance that the new avoidance response will be quickly lost. If the new learning had taken place in the alcoholic's natural setting, this problem would be less likely to occur. Finally, there is a chance that the person will become highly socialized into the hospital setting, find it comfortable, lose motivation to leave, and remain there for life.

The Effectiveness of Psychotherapy

Psychotherapy consumes tremendous time and money. Does it work? It is easy to find practitioners who will assure us that psychotherapy is successful, and it is easy to find people who have undergone psychotherapy and describe the experience as useful. Nevertheless there is a lack of carefully controlled studies showing that psychotherapy is effective.

Careful studies with experimental and control groups are required, since, although some people seem to be better off after psychotherapy, it is possible that they would have improved even in the absence of this treatment. To settle the issue, an experiment is required.

Certainly the idea of an experimental test of the effectiveness of psychotherapy is not original. For example, Rogers and Dymond (1954) conducted an experiment that some psychologists take as favorable to client-centered therapy. However, conducting a study to the satisfaction of all interested parties is very difficult when the experiment deals with psychotherapy. First, a great deal of time and money would be required. Second, there is an ethical consideration concerning the acceptability of assigning people to a control group. How can a therapist tell someone who is thinking about suicide that he has been assigned to a control group and will receive no therapy? Third, there is not always agreement as to what constitutes "improvement" or becoming "better off." For example, in the case of marital disharmony, is it "better" to decide to stay together or to decide to part? What if the disharmony seems very temporary? What if it seems very permanent? Since it is not clear what constitutes improvement, it is impossible to devise a satisfactory measure of improvement.

I'm not saying that psychotherapy does no good. But if you want more proof than reassuring reports from therapists and clients alike, the effectiveness of psychotherapy remains to be proven.

CONCLUSIONS

Behavior that violates personal tastes or social rules is often referred to as abnormal behavior. At one time it was common to explain all such behavior in terms of abnormal psychological processes. Although it is true that in some cases people who engage in abnormal behavior give evidence of distorted perceptions and reasoning, it is becoming increasingly clear that learning opportunities, the immediate environment, and society contribute heavily to much abnormal behavior.

The position taken in this chapter was that, although abnormal behavior is sometimes accompanied by distorted or abnormal psychological processes, it is not the product of a "mental disease." Instead, a limited amount of abnormal behavior has its origins in the malfunctions of the body, and a broad spectrum of abnormal behavior has its origins in an unfortunate combination of personal needs and resources, on the one hand, and environmental conditions, on the other. The definition of "resources" depends on the approach one prefers for understanding personality.

The classification systems devised for categorizing abnormal behavior leave much to be desired. Nonetheless, they are useful in labeling seemingly similar cases. Discussed here were minor maladjustments, neuroses, psychoses, psychophysiologic disorders, and antisocial personalities. These disorders vary in terms of both severity and the patterns of behavior involved.

Psychotherapy is the process by which trained practitioners assist the person to live a more efficient, effective, and rewarding life. There are many forms of both individual and group therapy. The specific procedures involved in the different forms reflect different assumptions about man, about personality, and about personal adjustment. Psychoanalysis is based on the psychoanalytic theory of personality, client-centered therapy is based on Rogers' theorizing about the self and on the humanistic orientation to man, and behavior therapy is based on the view that abnormal behavior represents learned responses. Group therapy combines these different orientations to various degrees. Although psychotherapy seems to involve many satisfied practitioners and users, its effectiveness has not been publicly demonstrated by means of an experimental test satisfactory to all psychologists.

11.
Attitudes

It is 2:30 A.M. A small group of people huddles in front of a television set. In front of them are overflowing ashtrays, smeared glasses partially full of amber-colored liquids, and a tray containing the sad remnants of fancy snacks. They sit almost immobile, their wide eyes staring unblinkingly as the announcer flickers before them. They are bent slightly forward, heads cocked at an angle to better take in every word. "It is clear now," says the announcer, "that the election is over, and the state has a new governor." The picture switches to a wild, boisterous party where a flushed but smiling man is unsteadily working his way toward a rostrum. At first the reaction of the viewers is stunned silence. Then one of the women bursts into tears. Next to her a man begins muttering oaths and at least twice hits the palm of one hand with a fist formed by the other. Someone sprints to the TV set and switches channels, only to find a different view of the same rowdy celebration. Glass in hand, he stalks, muttering, from the room.

Clearly these persons' actions tell us something about themselves, in particular their views concerning the newly elected governor. They have conveyed a strong negative attitude about the result of the elections. These people do not have to tell us that they voted for the defeated candidate that day.

People, policies, things, events—all elicit attitudes. Attitudes are an important part of each person's unique makeup and an important force within each group and society. Since attitudes reflect the joint operation of individual psychological processes and social influences, they have long been a focal point for social psychological research.

Many definitions of attitudes have been offered. Most of them are similar in that the term **attitude** somehow designates a tendency to respond in a predictable or characteristic way. Personality is also used to account for people's tendencies to respond in characteristic ways. Both attitudes and personality are personal consequences of the systematic forces that act on each of us, and both are something that the person carries with him from place to place. The distinction is that, whereas personality is broad and pervasive, attitudes are relatively narrow and specific. Theoretically, personality is object-free and is shown everywhere the person goes, but each attitude is relatively object-specific and elicited by a limited range of stimuli. In the discussion to follow, I will use the term **attitude holder** to designate a person who has an attitude and the term **attitude object** to designate the people, policies, things, or events about which the attitude is formed.

Attitudes are an important part of each person's unique makeup and an important force within each group and society.

Since personality accounts for more general tendencies to respond, it should be possible to guess some of a person's attitudes by referring to his personality. For example, we might expect the person brought up with a strong, inflexible sense of right and wrong to have negative attitudes toward hippies, marijuana, and premarital sex, whereas another person, whose personality developed in a more permissive and flexible environment, would be expected to have more tolerant attitudes toward each of these breaks with tradition.

But perhaps the distinction between personality and attitudes is to a large extent artificial. When does an "attitude," which refers to a fairly specific predisposition to respond, shade over into "personality," which refers to a more general way of responding? It is hard to draw the line. Nevertheless, personality theorists and attitude theorists have developed somewhat different perspectives and terms.

PERSPECTIVES ON ATTITUDES

There are two major thrusts in the study of attitudes. The one you are most likely to have already heard about is public-opinion polling, or **survey research,** such as that conducted by the Gallup, Harris, and Roper polls. This approach deals with attitudes as they are found. It involves estimating the proportion of people within a group, community, or society who have a particular attitude, such as for or against a certain political candidate. The group, community, or society under investigation is called a **population.** Since the survey researcher cannot interview each person within the population, the project begins by selecting a relatively small handful, or **sample,** of people for questioning. On the basis of the proportion of different attitudes of the people within the sample, it is possible to estimate the proportion of these attitudes within the population. The most difficult part is selecting a sample that faithfully reflects the attitudes held within the population. After one or two spectacular failures, survey researchers seem to have learned well how to do this. There are well over 200 million Americans, but with sophisticated, present-day methodology the responses of 2000 or so people can give the researcher a good indication of such things as who is likely to be our next President.

The second major thrust in attitude research does not deal with attitudes as they are found. It involves the experimental investigation of the conditions that cause people to form or change their attitudes. In this approach emphasis is on understanding the dynamic relationships between causes and effects, rather than on obtaining a clear picture of attitudes that have already been formed. Within this approach are two general explanatory themes. One draws most heavily on psychological processes within the individual. That is, it concentrates on the ways the person acquires, processes, and organizes information, and it stresses mental activity such as emotions and thoughts. The second explanatory theme is more social in nature, drawing heavily on relationships between two or more individuals. Included in this theme are already discussed processes such as imitation, social reinforcement, and conformity.

Both survey research and experimental investigations have made important contributions, but here again I find it more exciting to describe the experimentalist's search. Let us begin with a brief consideration of three major perspectives that have proven useful in this search: attitudes as socially learned responses, attitudes as functional, and attitudes as multicomponent.

Attitudes as Socially Learned Responses

A simple way of viewing attitudes is as *socially learned responses.* For example, the sixth-grader who voices political, religious, and social views similar to those of his parents may simply be imitating them.

If you are willing to consider attitudes as one more form of verbal behavior, it is easy to understand how they may be formed and changed through imitation and social reinforcement. Thus, as you have already seen, through the judicious use of such reinforcers as "Yes" and "Good," Hildum and Brown (1956) were able to influence attitudes toward the Harvard philosophy of education; Insko (1965) attitudes toward the creation of an Aloha Week; and Cialdini and Insko (1969) attitudes toward experimental and clinical psychology. Studies such as these suggest that many attitudes may be viewed simply as the product of a learning history. Each person has been rewarded for stating some attitudes and punished for stating others. Exactly which attitude statements are reinforced will depend on the groups to which the person belongs, the attitudes considered important by these groups, and the extent to which the members of the groups consider conformity necessary.

However, once again we find the social-learning approach a bit too spartan for many psychologists' tastes. It can be correctly pointed out that people's attitudes often seem to violate the known laws of learning. For example, religious martyrs have been known to express very strong attitudes, even following the negative reinforcer of torture. To understand things like this, additional concepts have been offered.

Attitudes as Functional

Daniel Katz (1960) has proposed a **functional approach** to attitudes, which suggests that people form and maintain an attitude because it serves a useful personal purpose for them. Katz identifies four basic functions: *the utilitarian function, the ego-defensive function, the value-expressive function,* and *the knowledge function.* Any given attitude, however, may serve more than one function.

The Utilitarian Function

A traditional theme in psychology is that people strive to maximize the personal gains or rewards that they secure while keeping the losses or punishments to a minimum. We have seen this theme before in the expectancy-incentive approach to motivation (Chapter Four) and will see it again in a major theory of social interaction presented in the next chapter. Here, let us note that attitudes can be useful for securing direct rewards. Thus someone who believes he needs welfare checks to survive may endorse a political candidate who maintains that the government should be one big, all-giving cornucopia, whereas another person, who is already hurting from shelling out large taxes, may choose a candidate who promises to keep welfare expenditures to a minimum. Attitudes such as this are said to fulfill the **utilitarian function.**

The Ego-Defensive Function

In the discussion of psychoanalysis (Chapter Eight) you read about psychological processes called defense mechanisms, which serve to keep people from a full and clear awareness of unpleasant conditions. Katz suggests that certain attitudes can serve such an **ego-defensive function.**

Attitudes can be used to deny the reality of a situation, project the attitude holder's own shortcomings onto someone else, or explain away unpleasant conditions. For example, a failing student may think of an instructor who "gave" him a poor grade in unprintable terms or loudly complain that the instructor's exams are picky, ambiguous, and unfair. With such attitudes the student could protect himself from his own incompetence by drawing attention to the instructor's real or imagined flaws. Or, by adopting the attitude that complaining students are highly defensive, an instructor can protect himself from the knowledge that he is incompetent or gives picky, ambiguous, and unfair exams.

The Value-Expressive Function

Some things we judge attractive, desirable, and of great worth, whereas other things we judge repugnant, undesirable, and worthless. Values refer to such judgments when they are based on abstract concepts or broad classifications.

Within our society it is common for peace, freedom, success, courage, and the "American way of life" to be positively or favorably valued and for war, failure, cowardice, and "un-American activities" to be unfavorably or negatively valued. Katz suggests that people find satisfaction in expressing their values. This **value-expressive function** of attitudes is fulfilled by maintaining and expressing attitudes consistent with personal values. For example, the pacifist values friendly international relations and peaceful solutions to international disputes and finds distasteful poor international relations and solutions to disputes that are based on might and bloodshed. Consequently, he may criticize or condemn the professional soldier, who is seen as likely to engage in behavior of a general type that the pacifist disavows. At the same time the pacifist may express favorable attitudes toward a Quaker who refuses to serve in the military but chooses alternative national service instead.

The Knowledge Function

People strive to make sense out of the world, and Katz suggests that attitudes may help with this effort. For example, national troubles may be "understood" in terms of Communist subversion, and suspicious attitudes toward Communists in general could make rational and understandable an otherwise incomprehensible commitment of American military forces. When attitudes allow the attitude holder to make sense out of the world, they are said to be fulfilling the **knowledge function.**

Attitudes as Multipurpose

The various functions that an attitude can fulfill are by no means mutually exclusive. Prejudicial or bigoted attitudes toward members of minority or "out" groups are a good case in point. The prejudice shown by some poorly educated, unskilled, lower-class whites who are in socially and economically insecure positions can serve utilitarian, ego-defensive, value-expressive, and knowledge functions simultaneously.

First, the arrival of a group of poorly skilled blacks raises the possibility that there will be more workers than jobs. This situation can result in lowered wages and less job security for the equally unskilled white. Prejudicial activity aimed at keeping the blacks from obtaining jobs can have the *utilitarian function* of bolstering the white's job security. Second, the "I am better than you" attitude can have the *ego-defensive function* of giving someone a painfully lacking sense of security. Third, prejudice against blacks can serve the *value-expressive function* for any person who has been indoctrinated in a heritage of white supremacy. Finally, the person can make some sense out of his observations that blacks are treated shabbily if he draws the conclusion that "Blacks must be bad to deserve this treatment." In this way prejudicial activities can also serve the *knowledge function*.

Attitudes as Multicomponent

The term *attitude* initially referred to visible cues that signified an intent to act in a certain way. For example, a person who bows signifies a willingness to submit to the requests of another, but a person who stands with legs apart, chin jutted forward, and arms tightly crossed over his chest may signify defiance. Similarly, a person who says "I fully endorse candidate X" is communicating a readiness to vote for candidate X and perhaps actively assist with his campaign. Less subtly, we are likely to consider a punch in the nose a clear indicator of an attitude. Although this **behavioral component** of attitudes is still considered very important, present-day theorists note that attitudes have *affective* (emotional) and *cognitive* (intellectual) components as well.

The **affective component** of an attitude is the feeling or emotional component. It consists of the positive or negative feelings that the attitude object elicits. War, mad bombers, polluters, hypodermic needles, fish with bones, and drug pushers make me feel anxious and unhappy, whereas San Francisco, the Smithsonian Institution, fancy restaurants, and Christmas vacation make me feel well-off and happy. Feelings of pleasure and displeasure, of liking and disliking, of happiness and sorrow are internal and subjective and cannot be measured directly. However, they can be inferred from physiological indicators (trembling, sweating, and so on), responses to attitude questionnaires, and the things people say.

The **cognitive** (also called belief) **component** is the intellectual aspect of attitudes. It consists of what the attitude holder sees, knows, or reasons about the attitude object. For example, a person may "see" that unemployed people are lazy and irresponsible, "know" that they are not interested in supporting themselves, and "reason" that the only way to get them to contribute to society is to take them off the welfare rolls. Although the cognitive component of attitudes refers to what we think of as knowledge, thought, and reason, the underlying processes involved do not necessarily involve logic or fact.

The cognitive component often has to do with the perceived usefulness of something for promoting or preventing various ends. Thus a person may believe that the passage of tough new antipollution laws will result in a healthier environment, whereas the absence of such laws will speed up the death of the planet. The perception of these relationships is intellectual, but the emotions aroused by the anticipation of improving or deteriorating environmental conditions are affective.

How are any or all of the components of a given attitude formed or changed? In what ways do the components fit together? It seems reasonable to expect the behavioral, affective, and cognitive components of an attitude to be interrelated in some logical and easily understandable way. Believing something is useful, liking it, and acting favorably toward it would seem to fit together, as would believing it useless, disliking it, and acting unfavorably. For example, if I believe that Brand X toothpaste is useful for fighting tooth decay, I should like it and use it in a conscientiously applied program of oral hygiene; but if I believe that Brand X toothpaste destroys tooth enamel and leads to an early need for dentures, I should dislike it and refuse to use it.

Although such neat packages of behavior, affect, and belief can be found, the various components of an attitude do not always fit together so nicely.

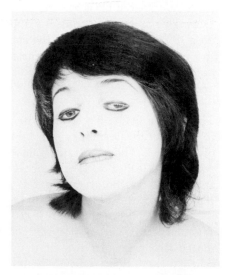

It seems quite possible for people to feel one way...

...but act another way.

Attempts to infer an entire coherent package given one component of an attitude can lead to miserable failure. For example, a salesman may *act nicely* to blacks. But we might be wrong if we guessed that he *liked* blacks and *believed* they were good. He could hate them and see them as troublemakers but act "nice" because he wanted to make a sale. Or, to consider another example, we may see a housewife using a particular brand of coffee. But she may not like this brand or believe it is the best available—she may merely have borrowed it from Mrs. Olson next door.

Despite such problems, it seems as if there are many cases in which the components of an attitude are systematically related—although not always in ways that appear logical or rational. As we progress through the chapter, you will read of several theories suggesting that attitudes consist of two or more components that fit together neatly and in such a way that a change in one will result in a change in the other. Before turning to these theories, however, let us consider a simple procedure by which positive and negative affect can be influenced.

EXPOSURE AND LIKING

In 1967 a speech class at Oregon State University was the scene of a mystery. During each meeting someone appeared enveloped in a big black bag and sat on a table near the back of the class. There were no clues as to the identity of the bag's occupant. Initially the students' reactions to the bag were hostile. Later hostility gave way to curiosity and finally to an attitude of friendship and liking.

The person in the bag did not dispense money, love, approval, or free tickets to the local theater. He or she did not deliver a stirring speech about his or her own virtues. There was no dramatic announcement that the person in the bag was a local leader, folk hero, or well-loved public figure. The bag just sat there, and over time the students grew to like it. One possible explanation is that repeated exposure to the bag led to the fondness.

The black bag incident occurred almost a century after psychologists first speculated that exposure to a stimulus may lead to a liking of it. During the past century there have been numerous but sporadic tests of this exposure-liking hypothesis. Some of these studies were concerned with the formation of esthetic preferences. It was found, for example, that exposure to various musical selections led to improved ratings of them (for example, Moore & Gilliland, 1924;

Mull, 1957). Other studies were conducted within the field of consumer motivation. In this context Becknell, Wilson, and Baird (1963) found that their female subjects had increasingly favorable reactions to made-up "brand names" after those names were shown repeatedly. Still other studies attempted to untangle word frequency (the approximate number of times a word appears in print per so many million) and "goodness of meaning" (favorability) in order to understand why more frequent or common words are easier to recognize than others. For the most part these studies found a close positive correlation between the frequency of appearance of a word and its rated goodness of meaning (Frincke & Johnson, 1960; Johnson, Thomson, & Frincke, 1960).

Let us pick up the story at about the time Zajonc (1968) reformulated and revitalized the familiarity-liking hypothesis. The way he (1968a, p. 1) stated it, "*Mere repeated exposure of the individual to a stimulus is a sufficient condition for the enhancement of his attitude toward it.*" By **mere exposure,** he is referring to conditions that make the stimulus accessible to the individual's perception. Zajonc then reviewed past studies and introduced new ones in support of this **exposure hypothesis**—evidence that, as he notes, seems to conflict with such common-sense notions as "Familiarity breeds contempt" and "Absence makes the heart grow fonder."

One line of evidence supportive of the exposure hypothesis is correlational and suggests that things or events with a high frequency of appearance in the environment (that is, greater exposure) receive more favorable ratings than things or events with a lower probability of appearance. Most of the correlational studies use the Thorndike-Lorge (1944) word count to obtain an estimate of exposure. This monumental volume reports the relative frequency with which words appear in print in the English language. It is assumed that, in general, the higher the frequency count as indicated in the Thorndike-Lorge compilation, the more frequently the individual has been exposed to the word or its referent.

Johnson et al. (1960) took two words from each alphabet category in the Thorndike-Lorge count. Subjects then rated the words. The correlation between frequency of exposure and rated "goodness" was +.63. This correlation is highly significant, as were two additional correlations obtained when they repeated their procedures using different words. In a variation of this study the same investigators presented subjects with 30 pairs of words in which one of the pair had a relatively high frequency and the other a relatively low frequency. Subjects were instructed to encircle the "most pleasantly toned word." In 26 of the 30 pairs of words the high-frequency member of the pair was chosen by the majority of the subjects as most pleasantly toned. The actual *sound* of the word probably had little to do with the pleasantness ratings. Frincke and Johnson (1960) presented subjects with pairs of words of different frequencies that sounded alike but were spelled differently and meant different things (such as team/teem and straight/strait). Subjects again chose the high-frequency member of the pair as the most "pleasantly toned," even though the two words sounded the same!

Zajonc (1968a) chose from the Thorndike-Lorge count the names of ten countries and had high school students rank these countries in order of preference. A correlation of +.89 between frequency and preference was obtained. Similar results were found using the names of American cities as stimuli. Zajonc had other subjects rate on seven-point like-dislike scales how much they liked a variety of trees, fruits, vegetables, and flowers. In all cases correlations between frequency and liking were positive and greater than +.80. Other studies have shown that more common adjectives receive higher ratings of goodness (Zajonc, 1968a; Harrison, 1968a), more common first names receive higher likability ratings (Harrison, 1969), and more frequently cited religious, occupational, political, and ethnic groups tend to receive more favorable ratings than less frequently cited groups (Harrison, 1969; Zajonc, 1968a). Moreover, similar exposure-favorability correlations have been found in some non-English-speaking countries as well.

Although it is suggestive, this wealth of correlational evidence certainly does not prove that "mere repeated exposure of an individual to a stimulus is a sufficient condition for the enhancement of his attitude toward it," for, as you know, correlational studies do not indicate causal direction. It is quite possible, for example, that something appears frequently in the environment *because* it is liked. On the other hand, if an experimenter can vary exposure and thus influence ratings, the hypothesis receives strong support.

Nonsense words are words that the experimenter concocts when he wants to make sure that they will initially be unfamiliar to his subjects. Johnson et al. (1960) had subjects rate 20 nonsense words on good-bad scales. The words were then shown to the subjects either once each or ten times each. Again the stimuli were rated, and results showed a significant relationship between exposure and favorability.

Zajonc repeated this experiment with some changes in procedures that included a comparison of stimuli shown in five different frequencies. Each subject saw two words once, two words twice, two words five times, two words ten times, two words 25 times, and two words not at all. The subject viewed each word, listened to the experimenter pronounce it, and pronounced it himself. He then was told that the words he had just seen were adjectives in a foreign language and was asked to rate them. The results were in full support of the exposure hypothesis. However, after a large number of exposures, it took more exposures to appreciably improve ratings than it would have taken had the stimulus previously been exposed only a few times. In other words, for improved favorability to be produced with a reasonable number of exposures, the stimulus must be fairly "unexposed" or novel to begin with. Substantially the same exposure-favorability relationship was obtained in an additional study that used Chinese ideographs (picture words). Other investigators have duplicated Zajonc's results. For example, Figure 11-1 shows the favorability ratings given the Chinese ideographs after they had been shown 0, 1, 3, 9, and 27 times (Harrison & Crandall, 1971).

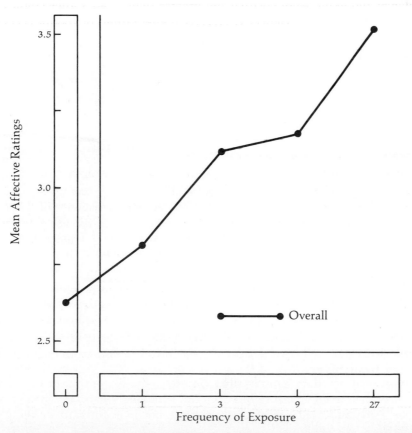

Figure 11-1. Mean Favorability Ratings of Chinese Ideographs as a Function of Frequency of Exposure (drawn from data presented by Harrison & Crandall, 1972).

Such "exposure" results are often taken to conflict with results showing that, when subjects are given a choice of looking at something they have never seen before or looking at something that has been seen over and over again, they will look at the novel or *low-frequency* stimulus (Berlyne, 1960, 1966). To consider these findings as conflicting, though, one must show that paying attention to a stimulus indicates a liking for it. I have no doubt that this is sometimes the case, but consider what would happen if you were put in a small room with a sack of familiar-looking dollar bills and a very novel 15-pound sewer rat. Chances are you would pay more attention to the rat. Does this mean that you like it more than the money? Where strange or unusual stimuli are involved, people often pay attention to things because they are *anxious* or *worried about them*, rather than because they like them (Harrison, 1968b; Harrison & Hines, 1970; Saegert & Jellison, 1970).

Limitations of the Exposure Effect

My own research interests, which I have been booming for the past few pages, might be rubbing your intuition the wrong way. You are probably wondering about good old-fashioned *boredom*. Don't people get sick and tired of seeing the same thing again and again and again? As far as I know now, simply increasing the number of exposures does not seem sufficient to produce a negative reaction of this sort. In one study (Zajonc, Swap, Harrison, & Roberts, 1971) we presented the Chinese ideographs in frequencies of 0, 3, 9, 27, and 81 following our usual procedures of showing all the stimuli one by one in a random sequence and then obtaining ratings. We found no evidence of decreasing favorability at the maximum number of exposures, even though this number exceeded that used in previous experiments by a factor of more than three. However, when the stimulus is extremely simple (Saegert & Jellison, 1970) or is presented again and again without any let-up or interruption, its ratings may eventually decrease (Berlyne, 1970). For example, Figure 11-2 shows what happened when the ideographs were presented in uninterrupted sequences and then rated immediately, before another ideograph was shown (Harrison & Crandall, 1971). Here, as exposure increased, liking initially increased but then decreased.

It may be that boredom temporarily *suppresses* the liking that has built up as a result of continued exposure but does not completely undo it. Thus someone may be "sick and tired" of his daily routine but look forward to being back home after a weekend away.

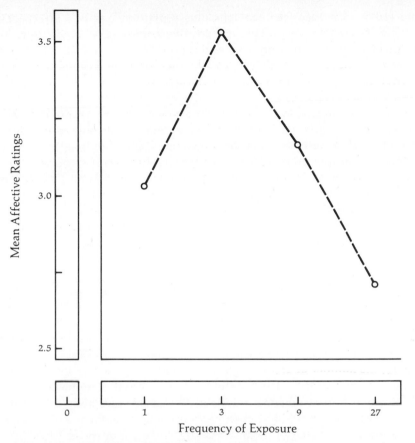

Figure 11-2. Mean Favorability Ratings of Chinese Ideographs as a Function of Exposure in a Repetitious Sequence (Harrison & Crandall, 1972; reproduced by permission of the American Psychological Association).

Two Explanations of the Exposure Effect

Why does repeated exposure to a stimulus seem to raise ratings of that stimulus? I favor the explanation that, when a novel stimulus is initially encountered, it elicits a certain amount of conflict, which is unpleasant. This unpleasantness is reflected in low favorability ratings and in exploratory behavior aimed at eliminating the unpleasantness. Subsequent exposure to the stimulus reduces the conflict, which in turn raises liking and decreases curiosity. I and others have completed several studies that I think support this interpretation (Harrison, Tutone, & McFadgen, 1971; Matlin, 1970).

Berlyne (1970) has theorized that stimulus repetition has two effects. First, there is **positive habituation.** Through positive habituation, exposure reduces worrisome uncertainty and conflict, resulting in a feeling of comfort. The second factor is **tedium,** by which a highly exposed stimulus becomes dull, unexciting, and unpleasant. With repeated exposure of the stimulus, both positive habituation and tedium increase, but at different rates depending on a number of variables. For example, if stimuli are shown in interrupted or mixed sequences, positive habituation will be ascendant and exposure will lead to liking (Figure 11-1). On the other hand, if stimuli are shown in monotonous, repetitious, uninterrupted sequences, positive habituation is important for the first few exposures but later on tedium gains the upper hand (Figure 11-2).

Advertisers and politicians have long been aware of the effects of exposure. We will trace some further implications of the exposure hypothesis in the next chapter when the discussion turns to interpersonal attraction.

THE CONSISTENCY THEME

Prominent among attitude theories are **consistency theories** which propose that attitude formation and change can be understood in terms of principles of psychological consistency. Although these theories differ in their specifics, each suggests that people strive in one way or another to impose some semblance of order on the component parts of an attitude or among different attitudes. As Bem (1970) notes, however, the consistency sought and often attained is not necessarily rational or "logical" in the Aristotelian sense.

Each consistency theory begins by defining basic irreducible parts or elements. These elements may be components of a person's attitudes, his attitudes themselves, or even his friends and enemies and *their* attitudes. Each theory also describes the psychological relationships among the elements. Conditions are specified under which the relationships are consistent—that is, psychologically stable and unlikely to change—and alternative conditions under which the relationships are inconsistent—psychologically unstable and likely to change. When change occurs, it is in the direction of consistency. In effect, the human mind will operate to eliminate inconsistency, and in the process attitudes are formed and changed. Although the attitude holder may be able to make things "fit together" nicely, this impression of order may require distorted perceptions and a misjudgment of evidence. Here we will consider three such attitude theories based on consistency: cognitive dissonance theory, balance theory, and Newcomb's *ABX* system.

Festinger's (1957) **cognitive dissonance theory** (or dissonance theory for short) has been perhaps the most important attitude theory to date. At least, more experiments have been based on this theory than on any other. The basic elements of it are cognitions. According to Festinger (1957, p. 3), "Cognitions can be described informally and intuitively as any knowledge, opinion, or belief about the environment, about oneself, or about one's behavior." **Cognitions,** then, are simply *items of information* that a person has. They include the knowledge that the Surgeon General has determined that cigarette smoking is hazardous to your health, the belief that an increased pomegranate crop would bolster the local economy, and the perception that there is a car with red lights and sirens following you closely.

Cognitions can be unrelated or related. In the latter case, which is of interest to dissonance theory, the relationship can take one of two forms. First, the two cognitions can fit together nicely, in that one psychologically *follows from* or is *implied by* the other. For example, the cognitions "I have just agreed to pay $100 a month for this car" and "This is a very nice car" would seem to fit together. It *follows from* the expense involved that the car should be good. Another example is to be found in the two cognitions "My country, right or wrong" and "I support our government's foreign policies." An unconditional endorsement of the country *implies* favorable attitudes toward any specific governmental policy. In these two cases the relationships between the cognitions involved are described as relationships of **cognitive consonance.** Formally stated, given two related cognitions *A* and *B*, if *A* implies *B* (or *B* follows from *A*), they stand in consonant relationship.

The second type of relationship is one of **cognitive dissonance.** In this case the cognitions do not fit together so nicely. One cognition is the *opposite* of what would be expected given the other cognition alone. For example, the cognitions "I have just agreed to pay $100 a month for this car" and "This car is a worthless lemon" would be dissonant. Given the immense expense, a "lemon" is the opposite of what one would expect. Another example is the relationship between the cognitions "My country, right or wrong" and "Involvement in the Vietnam War was a tragic mistake." "My country, right or wrong" implies that no national policy could be considered "a tragic mistake." Formally stated, given two related cognitions *A* and *B*, if *A* implies the *opposite* of *B* (or if *B* follows from the *opposite* of *A*), they stand in dissonant relationship.

When two cognitions are consonant, the relationship between them is psychologically consistent, stable, and not conducive to change. When two cognitions are dissonant, the relationship between them is psychologically inconsistent, unstable, and likely to result in change. Dissonance is described as an uncomfortable, drivelike state that people will strive to avoid or minimize. One way this **dissonance reduction** can be done is to distort one of the cognitions so that it appears consonant with the other. For example, in the case of the expensive car that proved to be a lemon, the person could deny the evidence and decide that his car is really great, a cognition more compatible with the knowledge that he will be making large monthly payments for the next three years.

Having purchased an expensive car that proved to be a lemon, a person might deny the evidence and decide that his car is really great.

Most of the time a person must deal simultaneously with more than two related cognitions. In this case the intensity of the dissonance depends on the personal relevance and strength of the different cognitions and the proportion of dissonant cognitions. For example, recently I tried camping. This activity required considerable planning, expense for equipment, and, for me, effort. At first I was tremendously disappointed. The campsite did not have a floor of pine needles but of volcanic grit; there was no shade, and the three surrounding campsites were occupied by constantly arguing families. Wildlife consisted mainly of noxious insects and marine creatures that affixed themselves to your body when you tried to go swimming. The temperature did average a cool 65°, but this was because it was based on the average of 105° during the day and 25° during the night. Or so it seemed. Anyway, what I found at this recreation area was dissonant with the cognitions that I had undergone considerable trouble, effort, and expense to get there.

However, over the course of the next few days, new cognitions were added. There was a feeling of relaxation from being away from my desk. Nights were clear, allowing a view of the heavens seldom afforded to those who live near cities. My cigarettes were left at home, and this, coupled with exercise, led to a healthy feeling. Conscientious daily excursions provided new delights, and occasionally large mammals appeared that somehow excused the presence of wasps and mosquitoes. Also, I secured a boat, which allowed exploration of the lake. All these new cognitions were consonant with the knowledge that this was my vacation, for which I had gone through a lot of planning, trouble, and expense. "All in all," as they say, the trip was successful and worth it. In this instance dissonance reduction was strikingly similar to the defense mechanism of rationalization (Chapter Eight). In both cases people seek justifications for actions that initially fail to produce an appropriate result.

In the discussion to follow, I will describe two focal points for dissonance research: postdecisional dissonance and the effects of lying. Before embarking on this, let me emphasize that dissonance theory is a very general theory and has been applied to many intriguing situations. For example, Aronson and Mills (1959) have noted that people undergo initiations to enter a group because they see membership in that group as attractive and worthwhile. If they undergo a severe initiation and then discover that the group is worthless, dissonance should arise, for a valueless group does not follow from the "high price of admission." Aronson and Mills conducted a study showing that dissonance arising from undertaking a severe initiation to gain entrance into a dull, boring, and worthless discussion group was reduced by distortedly perceiving the group as exciting and worthwhile—a cognition more compatible with the price of admission. Further support for the dissonance-based hypothesis that "suffering leads to liking" has been presented by Gerard and Mathewson (1966).

Postdecisional Dissonance

Whenever a person is trying to make a choice, he is likely to discover that each alternative has some good features and some bad features. When a choice is finally made, dissonance may arise. Dissonance theorists suggest that the _bad features of the chosen alternative_ and the _good features of the rejected alternative_ will be dissonant with the knowledge of the choice. This is **post-decisional dissonance.**

Suppose you are a woman about to entertain an attractive gentleman, Mr. Wright (pun intended), for the first time. You have dated him before but don't know much about him. You are undecided whether to prepare an exotic foreign meal (let's say sukiyaki[1]) or a standard American meal (let's say roast beef[2]). Being an intelligent, rational person, you compile a list of the advantages and disadvantages associated with each. (These are, of course, the advantages and disadvantages _I_ consider associated with each.)

SUKIYAKI

A. _Advantages_	B. _Disadvantages_
1. Cheaper ingredients	1. Takes more effort
2. Shows refined tastes	2. Not everyone likes unusual foods
3. Proves mastery of difficult skills	3. Easier to ruin
4. Shows willingness to do something special	4. May be too showy

ROAST BEEF

C. _Advantages_	D. _Disadvantages_
1. Easier to prepare	1. More expensive
2. No one finds it objectionable	2. No one finds it that exciting
3. Difficult to ruin	3. Does not demonstrate culinary skills
4. Can save some for tomorrow's lunch	4. Will have to eat leftovers for next three days

After you buy the ingredients and start to prepare the meal, all cognitions concerning the unattractive features of the chosen alternative and all cognitions concerning the attractive features of the rejected alternative should be dissonant. Thus, if you chose sukiyaki, the cognitions in columns B and C should be dissonance producing. To reduce this dissonance, you may ignore or start to distort the cognitions in these columns. For example, you may argue to yourself that sukiyaki isn't really that hard to ruin because, after all, few people know what it is supposed to taste like in the first place. Furthermore, you could begin adding new elements to column A (for example, "A sukiyaki dinner is healthful because it is low in cholesterol") and column D (for example,

---

[1] Very thin slices of beef cooked in a marinade with a variety of carefully pared and sliced vegetables; served with rice and hot rice wine (saki) or tart plum wine; mandarin orange slices for dessert.

[2] If you don't know this one, take him out to dinner.

"A decent roast beef contains too much waste in the form of fat and bone"). If you do a good enough job with this type of argument, you should come to like the idea of serving him sukiyaki *more* than you did before you made your choice.

Not all choices will result in dissonance. Choosing $10 over a poke in the eye would not produce dissonance. When something very good is chosen over something very bad, there is little dissonance, for the choice follows from a knowledge of the values. Dissonance arises when the two alternatives are somewhat equal in attractiveness.

Brehm (1956) had women rate small appliances in terms of overall attractiveness. Each subject was then told that she could keep one of the articles, but, since there were not enough of each to go around, the experimenter would have to limit her choices to one of two articles. In the *high-dissonance* condition each subject had to choose between two equally attractive articles. In the *low-dissonance* condition the two alternatives were of unequal value. In the *no-dissonance* condition subjects were simply given one of the items without making a choice. Next, some subjects were given propaganda sheets, which helped to reduce dissonance by drawing their attention to possible consonant elements. All subjects again rated the articles. The most salient result of this study was that subjects in the *high-dissonance* condition, who had the opportunity to reduce dissonance by seeking out new cognitions, rated the chosen alternative more favorably and the rejected alternative less favorably *after* having made their choices. This finding suggests that dissonance may be induced after one has chosen between two equally attractive alternatives but that this dissonance may be reduced when new, consonant cognitions are discovered.

Other successful studies have been conducted using this general approach. Brehm and Cohen (1959) found that children's choices of toys were followed by enhanced ratings of the chosen toy and less favorable ratings of the rejected toy. More recently, Knox and Inkster (1968) used an entirely different approach for studying postdecisional dissonance. At a racetrack, bettors estimated the chances that their horse would win before and after they had placed their bets (that is, before and after having made a firm decision) but before the race had been run. After placing their bets, cognitions that their horse would be likely to lose would be dissonant with their choice, as would be cognitions that other horses might be likely to win. After placing their bets, bettors thus raised their evaluation of the chosen horse by increasing their conviction that it would win.

Lying

A second focal point for dissonance research is the effects of lying. In these studies the investigator induces the subject to express a **counteropinion**—that is, a point of view opposite to (dissonant with) what he really or privately believes. For example, giving a speech in favor of racial integration within all public schools by means of busing is dissonant with the convictions that children should be sent to schools with their "own kind" and that principles of democracy can be satisfied if we maintain "separate but equal" schools. If the public statement or "lie" cannot be explained away or withdrawn, dissonance reduction should be apparent in a change in the private belief.

It has long been known that, if people are induced to state things they don't believe privately, the result is attitude change in the direction of the argument. But why should this change stem from dissonance reduction? Perhaps when a person is induced to argue for a position he doesn't hold, he merely carefully examines that position for the first time and comes to recognize its merits. Or perhaps the attitude change is a result of the *incentive* initially offered for expressing the counteropinion. In a sense this incentive (such as money or praise from the experimenter) could constitute a reward for the stated point of view. If this were true, one might expect that, the greater the incentive, the more attitude change.

Evidence for the dissonance explanation comes from a particular kind of study. According to dissonance theory, the amount of dissonance aroused by a lie is partially a function of the amount of justification available for telling the lie. If there are good excuses for lying (such as "I am making my friend happy" or "If I don't lie, I won't get the job"), dissonance will be weak, and there will be little motivation for changing the private belief. If there are no such excuses, dissonance will be great, and there will be stronger motivation for attitude change. Thus dissonance studies involve varying the justifications for lying, with the prediction that the smaller the justification, the greater the dissonance and attitude change.

Justifications in these experiments consist of monetary rewards. Paid well for a lie, a person can justify that lie by saying to himself that he really didn't mean it and was only doing it for the money. But if he is coaxed into lying without being given much in a way of justification, there should be strong forces for attitude change. Thus, although **incentive theorists** predict **greater** attitude change in the direction of the lie when there are high rewards, dissonance theorists predict greater change when there are low rewards.

Cohen (Brehm & Cohen, 1962) paid subjects $10, $5, $1, or 50¢ for writing an essay expressing a counteropinion. He found the greatest change in attitudes toward the counterposition or lie in subjects who were paid 50¢, the second greatest in subjects paid $1, the third in subjects paid $5, and the *least* in subjects who had received the highest pay of $10. Similarly, Festinger and Carlsmith (1959) put their subjects through a long, dull, and completely unrewarding task. Afterward subjects were paid either $1 or $20 for lying by telling a stranger that the task had been fun, interesting, and exciting. Those paid $1 for lying convinced *themselves* that the task was exciting, but those paid $20 did not.

These experiments certainly provide an interesting test of dissonance theory. The only trouble is that not everyone has been able to produce the same kinds of results. Some studies provide evidence for the "incentive" prediction of a positive relationship between the amount paid for lying and the degree of attitude change (Elms & Janis, 1965; Janis & Gilmore, 1965; Rosenberg, 1965).

The incentive-dissonance controversy is a lively one (see Elms, 1969). However, a study by Carlsmith, Collins, and Helmreich (1966) may provide some partial answers. They suggested that variations in procedures from one study to another may account for the seemingly conflicting results. There are many such variations, but Carlsmith and his associates saw one as particularly crucial: whether or not the lie was expressed anonymously or face-to-face. Under conditions of anonymity little dissonance should be produced. Here the subject's lie is seen only by the experimenter, who knows that the subject does not really endorse the view. According to Carlsmith et al., under these conditions subjects may regard the lie as no more than a demonstration of an intellectual ability to adopt a new position. There is sufficient justification for the lie and thus little dissonance or attitude change. On the other hand, when subjects tell the lie to someone who does not know he is witnessing a lie, dissonance is created.

In the Carlsmith et al. study subjects were paid 50¢, $1.50, or $5 for expressing a counteropinion. Some subjects expressed this lie in private essays and others in a public confrontation. The experimenters expected and found that, under face-to-face conditions where there was supposed to be greater dissonance, *less money* was associated with *more attitude change* in the direction of the counteropinion. However, when the counteropinion was expressed anonymously (that is, under hypothesized nondissonance-arousing conditions), *more money* was associated with *more attitude change*. An implication of this study is that under conditions of little dissonance, greater incentives lead to more attitude change.

Dissonance Reduction in Rats?

Lawrence and Festinger (1962) suggest that, within the field of learning, certain "resistance-to-extinction" findings are not easily explained by traditional learning theories. For example, the basic premises of these major theories as they were initially formulated would lead one to conclude that more reinforcement, faster reinforcement, and less effort expenditure should lead to better learning. However, by the resistance-to-extinction measure of learning described in Chapter Four (that is, the persistence of the response once all reinforcement has been withdrawn), the contrary conditions of partial reinforcement, delay of reinforcement, and greater effort expenditure lead to better learning. To be sure, some of these effects have long been recognized, and the major learning theorists have revised their theories and tacked on new assumptions and dangling clauses in attempts to account for them. But Lawrence and Festinger suggest that these effects can be accounted for more simply and

The cognition that there is no reward is dissonant with the effort expenditure.

elegantly by dissonance theory. They suggest that organisms that have worked harder, waited longer for rewards, or received few rewards experience dissonance. For example, receiving a nice treat should follow from the cognition that one has run a maze. The cognition that there is no reward is dissonant with the effort expenditure.

To reduce such dissonance, new consonant elements can be added. Specifically, under conditions of delayed reinforcement, partial reinforcement, and greater effort expenditure, the learner finds new justifications for his actions by seeking "extra attractions" in the course of the experiment. Thus, if we take certain liberties by imputing human motivations to animals, we can envision a rat running to the end of a maze during a learning trial and, finding it empty, saying to himself "Gee, this is a pretty place to be!" or "That exercise was really good for my health!" Later, when all reinforcement is withdrawn during the extinction trials, these extra attractions the animal has found to reduce dissonance may be sufficient to maintain his behavior. Animals that had not experienced dissonance and had not found these extra attractions would "give up" or "extinguish" sooner.

It's fun to think about a disappointed rat rationalizing his effort expenditure or denying the poor fruits of his labors. From my perspective it is no more far-fetched to assume thinking rats than to assume nonthinking, just behaving, people. However, Lawrence and Festinger's theory accounts for only a narrow range of learning phenomena, whereas the more awkward theories that they criticize have much broader scope. At present it is not clear that this dissonance explanation is superior to the unwieldy ones associated with the more comprehensive theories.

Balance Theory

Heider (1946, 1958) has developed a consistency theory that is based on principles of **homeostasis.** That is, there is an assumed "normal state," and when conditions depart from this state, there will be a tendency for them to return to it. The normal state involves a **balanced** relationship among some combinations of feelings or beliefs.

Dissonance, the opposite of consonance, is seen as a drivelike state that the organism strives to reduce. **Imbalance,** the opposite of balance, is not quite so unpleasant. Imbalance is psychologically inconsistent, but the forces to reduce it are mild, representing nature's way of organizing things (as the Gestalt laws

of perceptual organization represent nature's way of organizing sensations).
In the end, consistency or balance is created out of imbalance, and in the process come attitude formation and change.

Heider begins by adopting the perspective of the perceiver, *P*. The basic elements of the system are people (*P*, *O*, *Q*, . . .) and objects (*X*, *Y*, *Z* . . .). When
the elements are in some way related to one another, a **bond** exists among them.
Relationships may be either **unit relationships** *U* or **sentiment** or "liking" **relationships** *L*. A unit relationship is formed whenever two or more elements are
seen as belonging with or related to each other. They involve a mere connectedness between the elements, such as "Jack and Jill went up the hill" or
"Father Timothy distilled this keg of brandy." Sentiment relationships also
imply connectedness but refer additionally to a state of liking or disliking,
such as "Popeye likes spinach" or "Luthor hates Superman." I will indicate
the direction of unit and sentiment relationships by plus (+) and minus (−)
signs. With respect to unit relationships, a plus sign indicates a connection or
positive association (the Supreme Court (*U*+) the U. S. Constitution), whereas
a minus sign indicates disconnectedness, disassociation, or disavowal (the
Confederate States of America (*U*−) the United States of America). With
respect to sentiment relationships, the plus and minus signs refer to liking
and disliking, respectively. The two types of relationships are often hard to
discriminate, and it sometimes seems as if there are no real differences between
them. So here, for simplicity, let us talk only about positive (+) and negative
(−) bonds.

The Case of Two Elements

If we take two elements (**dyadic relationships**), a state of balance exists if the
bonds between them are both positive or both negative. If the signs of the
bonds differ, there will be a state of imbalance and a likelihood that the attitude
holder's perception of the relationship will change. That is, the bonds will be
perceived in such a way that they both become positive or both become negative. Let us consider the bonds between two hypothetical characters, Dick and
Ted:

1. Dick likes (+) Ted.
2. Ted likes (+) Dick.

Since both bonds are positive, this is a balanced relationship. But suppose you
heard that Dick walked out on (−) his partner Ted. This rumor would produce
a state of imbalance in your mind, for it is not psychologically consistent with

the second bond that Ted likes (+) Dick. To eliminate the imbalance, you could deny the rumor (and reaffirm your belief that Dick did not walk out) or change your perception of Ted's feelings about Dick, which would make both bonds negative:

1. Dick walked out on (−) Ted.
2. Ted now hates (−) Dick.

Three-Element Relationships

The most noted contribution of balance theory comes from its statements about three-element, or **triadic, relationships.** *In cases that involve three elements, a state of balance exists when all three of the bonds are positive or when two of the bonds are negative and one is positive.* Thus if two bonds are positive and one negative, or if all bonds are negative, imbalance and conditions for change exist.

To consider balanced relationships first, the simplest case would be when all bonds are positive. Take, for example, the elements Sue, money, and a new job:

1. Sue likes (+) money.
2. Sue's new job pays (+) big money.
3. Sue likes (+) her new job.

Then there is the case of Karl, home protection, and Doberman pinschers:

1. Karl is very concerned about (+) protecting his home.
2. Doberman pinschers are good (+) for protecting the home.
3. Karl likes (+) Doberman pinschers.

Still balanced, but somewhat less simple, are cases in which two of the bonds are negative and one is positive:

1. Sue likes (+) money.
2. Sue's new job pays (−) little money.
3. Sue hates (−) her new job.

Or:

1. Karl is very concerned (+) about home protection.
2. Toy poodles are no good (−) for home protection.
3. Karl dislikes (−) toy poodles.

Again, in all these cases the perceived relationships among the bonds are balanced, psychologically stable, and unlikely to change. Conditions for change appear when all three bonds are negative or when any two signs are positive and one is negative. For example:

1. I am against ($-$) dishonesty in state government.
2. Candidate X is against ($-$) dishonesty in state government.
3. I do not like ($-$) candidate X.

1. Sue likes ($+$) money.
2. Sue's new job pays ($-$) practically no money.
3. Sue likes ($+$) her new job.

1. Karl is very concerned ($+$) about home protection.
2. Doberman pinschers are very good ($+$) at home protection.
3. Karl hates ($-$) Doberman pinschers.

As with two elements, balance is created by changing or misinterpreting one of the bonds. In this case balance consists of perceiving the entire relationship in such a way that all bonds are positive or two are negative and one is positive. For example, regarding my views on honesty in state government, candidate X's views on honesty in state government, and my views of candidate X, I could achieve balance by considering honesty in state government unimportant *or* liking candidate X or perceiving candidate X as a lying hypocrite who does not really endorse honesty in state government. In the case of Sue, if she likes money but is content with her new low-paying job, the perceiver might believe that Sue lost some interest in money *or* that the pay was actually pretty good by her standards *or* that she really did not like the job. In the case of Karl's disavowal of those fabulous watchdogs, the perceiver might believe that Karl is soft on burglars *or* that Doberman pinschers are not good watchdogs *or* that Karl really likes Doberman pinschers more than he admits.

Several lines of evidence support balance theory. Although not all these studies have produced entirely favorable results, most of them suggest that balanced relations are more natural than imbalanced or unbalanced (that is, incomplete) relations.

1. There are studies suggesting that people like or prefer balanced states. Jordan (1953) described balanced and unbalanced three-element relationships and found a significant preference for the balanced relationships. Scott (1963) found that both college students and noncollege students preferred balanced relationships among nations, although he also found that some people were more tolerant of imbalanced relations than were others. Price, Harburg, and

Newcomb (1966) had subjects indicate "pleasant" and "uneasy" feelings about eight triadic relationships. In this study each subject was asked to think of himself as P, one of the elements in a relationship involving two people, P and O, and an impersonal entity X. Balance predictions were supported, but *not* in the case of a balanced relationship in which the bond between P and O was negative. As Aderman (1969) notes, this finding of a lack of preference for a balanced relationship in the case of P $(-)$ O has been repeatedly found when the subject is instructed to take the viewpoint of P. It is not found when the subject responds as an outside observer of hypothetical situations in which he is not supposed to be involved. Aderman himself hypothesized that the reason for this former finding was that subjects implicitly assumed that they would have future interactions with O; since they were told that they did not like O, they rated the relationship as unpleasant. Aderman found that subjects *did* like the balanced but negative bond relations when it was made clear that they would not later have to interact with the disliked person O.

2. There is evidence that people will complete or fill in missing links in ways that are consistent with balance principles (Morissette, 1958) or express a desire to see one of the bonds changed so as to produce balance (Rodrigues, 1967). An important result of this tendency to fill in missing links to produce balance will soon be discussed when we consider Newcomb's *ABX* theory.

3. There is some evidence suggesting that balanced relationships are easier to learn than are imbalanced relationships. Zajonc and Burnstein (1965a, 1965b) had subjects memorize all the bonds in a triadic relationship and counted the number of errors made before all the bonds were learned. P and O were two hypothetical men, and the remaining elements in the different experiments were integration, birth control, and *Newsweek*. Results suggested that balanced relationships were more easily learned, but only when the issues were relevant to the relationship. This type of finding, too, may suggest a naturalness of balanced relationships.

3. Newcomb's ABX System

Newcomb (1956, 1961) has offered a consistency theory that in many ways is similar to Heider's theory about three-element relationships. Newcomb's theory is also based on principles of homeostasis, which he refers to as **strain toward symmetry.** In Newcomb's theory the relationship between two people is important.

In Newcomb's **ABX system** *A* and *B* are people, and *X* is anything or anyone about which an attitude may be formed. Between the two people is a state of attraction (+) or disliking (−). The bonds between each person and the object are attitudes, or "orientations," which are also similar to Heider's sentiment relationships of liking (+) and disliking (−).

The conditions of homeostasis are the same as for Heider's three-element relationships. That is, if all the bonds are positive or if two of the bonds are negative, the relationship is balanced. If all the bonds are negative or if two bonds are positive and one negative, something is likely to change. But perhaps Newcomb's conditions of balance can be summarized more succinctly. People who already have similar attitudes should find each other attractive, and people who already find each other attractive should develop similar attitudes.

The Acquaintance Process

According to Newcomb's system, people who have similar attitudes should find each other attractive, and people who already find each other attractive should develop similar attitudes.

Newcomb (1961) has ingeniously collected evidence in direct support of his theory. For two years he rented a large house in a university town. He invited men students who did not initially know one another to live there without cost, making their payment by devoting a few hours each week to psychology experiments. Newcomb predicted that, as these initial strangers came into contact, those with similar attitudes would develop friendships. He also predicted that, after friendships had blossomed, the partners in the friendships would tend to develop similar attitudes. Both hypotheses received some confirmation.

One particularly interesting finding was that his subjects liked others who had feelings toward them that were similar to the feelings they had toward themselves. This means, reasonably enough, that if a subject liked himself, he liked people who liked him. But it also means that if he disliked parts of himself, and the other person showed this disliking also, he tended to *like* his critic. These theoretically self-evident but intuitively hard-to-swallow findings have been supported by others (Backman & Secord, 1962; Broxton, 1963). Additional studies showing a relationship between attitude similarity and interpersonal attraction will be presented in the next chapter.

Dissonance, Balance, and American Public Opinion

Newcomb's study of the acquaintance process certainly suggests that the operation of consistency principles is not limited to the laboratory situation. Let us now consider how these principles might have real and important implications for public opinion and social change. For example, those in the late 1960s who advocated an immediate cessation to the Vietnam hostilities necessarily sought the support of a large group of so-called middle Americans. But virtually every principle of cognitive consistency seemed to work against their attempts to obtain support from the uncommitted or from those committed to a military solution.

Let us begin with dissonance theories and here I will draw from memories of a talk given by Leon Festinger at the University of Michigan. Consider the cognition "I (or someone close to me) fought and suffered in the Vietnam War." This would be consonant with the cognition "The Vietnam War is necessary and just." If a protester comes along and offers the cognition "The Vietnam War is neither necessary nor just," there will be dissonance. Since there is reason to believe that people tend to avoid dissonance-inducing evidence, or to reconstrue it in such a way as to make it compatible with preexisting beliefs, we would expect those who made sacrifices in the war to be reluctant to accept this latter cognition. With the large number of troops that were at any time in Vietnam, and with the specific men changing yearly, the number of people sharing the cognition "I (or someone close to me) fought and suffered in Vietnam" becomes immense. The cognition "The Vietnam War is neither necessary nor just" would also be dissonant with such cognitions as "America is always right," "All Communists are bad," and "My hard-earned taxes are used to support the Vietnam War." Thus we should not be surprised to find many Americans avoiding the dissonance-inducing assertions of the war protesters or reducing dissonance by finding either new "reasons" to support the war or new ways to deprecate and reject the protesters.

Turning to balance theory, one finds further reasons why these protesters' task was difficult. In any large social movement different people participate for different personal motives. Although in the late 1960s some people condemned the war for ethical reasons, there were also some who did so because they flagrantly rejected the American way of life, preferred non-American political systems, or wanted to show rebellion for rebellion's sake. These protesters are more colorful than the others and hence more newsworthy. If they denounce the President and call for the downfall of the government, they do not make themselves attractive to the people whom they must persuade in order to elicit a change in national attitudes. After making themselves disliked by means, say, of burning a flag, it is not surprising that they failed to elicit support on the critical issue of withdrawal from the war. Agreeing with these "spokesmen" would produce for the average American the imbalanced two-pluses-and-one-minus state of affairs.

This type of problem was anticipated by the organizers of the earliest antiwar demonstrations. They begged and pleaded with demonstrators to present themselves in such a way as to be persuasive. It was correctly perceived that, if peace advocates appeared to be hippies, beats, acid heads, and Commies, they would alienate exactly those people whose support was most severely needed and encourage them instead to adopt opposite views. Despite these exhortations, a minority was more interested in demonstrating its independence than in being persuasive. It was this group that the television cameramen found most interesting to film, with the net effect, perhaps, of presenting war protest "leaders" as unsavory troublemakers. Furthermore, on at least one occasion, demonstration organizers implored certain people who had repeatedly alienated the public in the past *not* to come and support their rally. But the undesirables showed up, demanded the stage, and doubtless impressed the TV audience with what remarkably unlikable people advocated immediate disengagement from Vietnam. It is true that persuasive demonstrations might not be much fun for those looking for excitement. But anyone who is seriously interested in a social issue should carefully weigh the relative value of venting one's spleen against that of producing social change.

Is the task of most protest movements hopeless? Difficult, perhaps, but not hopeless. New cognitive elements are always being added, and new balanced structures are continually being completed. At some point, for example, the easiest way for leaders to reduce dissonance about a war might be to decide it is worthless and abandon it.

Limitations of Consistency Theories

A tendency to reduce inconsistency seems to account for a wide range of attitude phenomena. Consistency theories—particularly cognitive dissonance theory—have generated a tremendous amount of experimental research, and for the most part the results have been flattering to the theories. Yet there are two major problems with these theories.

First, people often seem to be more tolerant of inconsistency than the theories would have us believe. For example, the cognitions "I am for law and order" and "I am breaking the law" would appear to be dissonant. We would expect that the person would either adopt a more moderate law-and-order position or refrain from breaking the law. Yet Wrightsman (1969) found that people who apparently took a relatively strong law-and-order position were *less* likely than others to obey a law that required them to purchase and display a vehicle registration sticker. Certainly a need for consistency the way I have been discussing it could not have been the major factor at play.

Second, consistency theories often do a poor job of predicting what form inconsistency reduction will take. This problem can be illustrated by the *ABX* system. For example, I know two women who like each other but have radically different political views. According to *ABX*, the first one should change her political views *or* the other one should change her political views *or* they should find each other less attractive. But what form will the balance restoration take? We can only presume in a case such as this that the weakest bond will give; but since we do not know the weakest bond, this is not much help. The problem is complicated if we consider that people may deal with inconsistencies in ways that the *ABX* and balance theories do not readily accommodate. In the case of the two women, for example, the imbalanced situation has remained stable for more than 25 years. I inquired about this, and they told me that they simply never discuss politics with each other, although they do talk about cooking, camping, and the arts, which both find highly attractive.

Another way that people "cheat" is by redefining the attitude object so that agreement can be reached (Brown, 1961, 1965). In illustration, Brown describes a televised confrontation between a musical-comedy star and a drama critic who were good friends. The star liked his new comedy and the critic did not. Neither one changed his attitude toward the show, and they did not terminate the friendship. Instead, they resolved the conflict by concluding that there were *two* comedies: the one on opening night (which both disliked, since the bugs had not been worked out) and the one after opening night (which both liked, since wonderful changes had been introduced). Disagreement concerning one attitude object was replaced with agreement concerning two. Thus, since it is not always clear what route inconsistency reduction will take, the consistency theories cannot always be applied correctly.

CONCLUSIONS

A person's attitudes, like his personality, are personal consequences of living in a lawful universe. Both denote a readiness to act in certain ways. But whereas personality is elicited in every situation in which the person finds himself, each attitude is elicited by a relatively narrow range of things and events.

First we considered some primary perspectives on attitudes. Attitude research has two major thrusts: survey research, which involves assessing attitudes as they are found, and the experimental investigation of attitude formation and change, which involves determining cause-effect relationships. Several perspectives have contributed to the search for understanding attitude formation and change. First, attitudes may be viewed as socially learned responses. Second, attitudes may be viewed as functional, in that they can serve a useful purpose for the person. Third, attitudes may be seen as multifaceted—for example, composed of action, feeling, and belief components. The basic questions concern what causes changes in people's action tendencies, feelings, and beliefs, and how the components of an attitude are interrelated so that a change in one results in a change in the others.

The simplest form of attitude change would appear to be a result of repeated contact with the attitude object. For many types of stimuli, repeated contact seems to lead to more favorable ratings of it. Although conditions can be created such that very repetitious (that is, tedious or boring) contacts can eventually lead to a decline in rated favorability, the "familiarity breeds liking" principle seems to be a useful one.

Conspicuous among attitude theories are those that are organized along principles of psychological consistency. The theory of cognitive dissonance, balance theory, and the *ABX* system all describe certain basic elements and specify the relationships among them. The details of these theories vary, but each suggests that attitude holders tend to arrange the elements in stable, predictable patterns. Each of these theories has generated interesting research. However, in many cases people would seem to be more tolerant of psychological inconsistency than these theories would suggest, and in most cases the theories do not do a good job of specifying what form inconsistency reduction will take. When experimenters correctly predict the form that dissonance reduction or balance restoration will take, they usually carefully block off alternative routes. This luxury is not possible if we are interested in the results of dissonant or imbalanced situations as they are found.

4

Interpersonal Processes

Throughout this text you have seen how each person is influenced by the presence and actions of others. In the concluding chapters we will view these processes as mutual and reciprocal. When two or more people are affecting each other's behavior, they are participating in **social interaction.** Studying interaction, our focus shifts from the individual to the processes that go on between and among individuals. As psychologists we should not forget, though, that each and every participant is a unique person with his own special characteristics.

THE CONCEPT OF SOCIAL INTERACTION

Stimuli, you will recall, are changes in the physical environment that are in some way detected by the organism. Responses are behaviors that the organism emits, often seemingly in response to an identifiable stimulus. Thus a child's

363

roller skate left at the top of a flight of stairs is a stimulus, since it reflects light of a different wavelength from that reflected by the surrounding carpet. If you step to avoid the roller skate, you are making a response.

People also reflect patterns of light that differ from those reflected by the surrounding furniture or landscape. They cause further detectable changes by moving around, touching things, and making noises. As stimuli, people elicit responses from others. Those responses are themselves detectable and hence can provide a new source of stimulation.

If we observe two people together, we are likely to find that the first to act provides a stimulus that elicits a response from the second. If the second person's response in turn stimulates a response from the first person, we have the simplest instance of social interaction. In many cases the cycle continues until each person has elicited reactions from the other a number of times.

The problems of accurately observing people are multiplied many times when they are interacting with others. Occasionally in psychology behavior can be "frozen" for analysis, much like the action in a snapshot. For example, psychological-test results can provide a "still" picture of certain aspects of the person at one particular point in time. But social interaction is an ongoing, flowing process that cannot be frozen. The observer studying interaction must attend to several people at once, each of whom has available a wide range of response alternatives.

Studying interaction requires looking at *combinations* of people's behavior. The complexity of this task is easy to illustrate. If each person in a *two-person group* could make only *one* of *two* responses (for example, to say "hello" or to look the other way), there would be *four* response combinations that might emerge. If each could make one of *five* possible responses, the number of combinations would be 25. If each of the two could choose one of 100 responses, there are 10,000 combinations. Remember, this is only a two-person group. In a three-person group, if each could select one of 100 responses, there would be 1 million combinations. In a four-person group, such as a Wednesday night bridge party, if we can limit each individual's response options to 100, there would be 1 billion combinations.

Of course, in the four-person group, hoping to have to cope with only a billion possible response combinations is a bit wishful. The number of responses available to each person is likely to be more than 100, even though earlier events would probably have imposed some limitations on the subsequent number of likely responses. Then, too, pointing to a combination of responses tells us nothing about who made the opening gambit and who responded. In the four-person group, person *A* may lead off and elicit responses from person *B* or person *C* or person *D*; from persons *B* and *C*, *B* and *D*, or *C* and *D*; or from persons *B*, *C*, and *D*. Persons *B*, *C*, and *D* could have the same opportunities as person *A*. This consideration raises the total number of possible combinations to a fantastic figure.*

Clearly, scientific investigations demand that social interaction somehow be reduced to something manageable. One technique is to watch for certain responses and declare all else irrelevant. A second technique is to devise a classification scheme so that whatever happens can be fit into one of a manageable number of categories. A third technique is to rig the situation such that constraints are imposed on the interacting people, which limits the number of response alternatives available to each of them. All these procedures involve the loss of some information or the use of a somewhat "artificial" experimental situation. But in return they help us get reliable information about the processes that go on between and among people.

OVERVIEW OF PART FOUR

Chapter Twelve discusses some of the basic directions people take when they come into contact with one another. We will consider some of the conditions under which people form and maintain mutually rewarding relationships, as well as alternative conditions under which people inflict punishments and penalties on one another. Chapter Thirteen describes some of the processes that operate within the small group. Communication, leadership, group morale or spirit, and performance in groups provide the focal points for discussion. Chapter Fourteen concludes with a consideration of social psychological findings that are particularly pertinent to some of the problems of our heavily criticized society.

* My calculator self-destructed when I was working on this problem.

12.
Moving toward, with, and against Others

A man named C. L. Clark spent the greatest proportion of his life as an unwilling guest in a series of prisons, most of which catered to hardened criminals. In his autobiography, *Lockstep and Corridor* (1927), he tells about one inmate who provided a compelling source of attraction for another. After being released, this latter prisoner went to great lengths to break *into* the prison to visit his friend after he was denied entry by the prison authorities. Clark's illustration is admittedly a bit extraordinary, but it is not at all uncommon to hear of cases in which people are propelled toward each other despite hurdles and obstacles. For example, how far have you traveled to be reunited with a friend? What sacrifices have you made when promised an intriguing date?

Moving toward another person is one of the basic directions an individual may take when he is confronted with someone. In this chapter we will first consider some of the conditions that contribute to this process of **interpersonal attraction.** Next we will discuss **cooperation,** or how people sometimes **move with** one another, each behaving in such a way as to promote a mutually rewarding relationship. Finally, we will take up the less pleasant case of **aggression,** in which people **move against** others, behaving in ways that inflict harm and punishment.

MOVING TOWARD OTHERS: INTERPERSONAL ATTRACTION

Let us begin by considering some of the bases for interpersonal attraction—that is, why people may be propelled together. Two major issues are involved. First, what are some of the most general reasons that people might seek to associate or **affiliate** with others? Second, why is the association process selective, in that some people seem to provide compelling sources of attraction, others seem to be sources of indifference, and still others seem to be potent sources of repulsion?

Why is the association process selective, in that some people provide more compelling sources of attraction than others?

Motivational Bases for Associating with Others

The strength of people's tendencies to associate with others have been traced to a number of variables. Some are personality variables, which represent enduring characteristics of the individual. Some are personal requirements or needs, which arise under special conditions. Still others are to be found in the demands and constraints enforced within a specific social setting. We can refer to these variables, respectively, as *enduring motives*, *passing needs*, and *situational demands*.

Enduring Motives and Movement toward Others

Considerable theorizing and research suggest that there are consistent differences among people in the extent of their general motivation to associate or affiliate with others. One classic distinction you may have heard of is that offered by the Swiss psychiatrist Carl Jung. Jung noted that some people tend to be shy, withdrawn, and self-contemplative, whereas others tend to be sociable and outgoing. The former he labeled **introverts** and the latter **extroverts.** Something in the same vein but which has generated more in the way of research is the concept of **need affiliation,** which is measured by evaluating stories given in response to pictures such as those used in the projective Thematic Apperception Test (Chapter Nine). Researchers in this area have offered systematic evidence that people have a general tendency to affiliate with others and that the strength of this tendency varies from person to person. Birch and Veroff (1966) note that, compared with people with low need affiliation, people with high affiliative needs are more likely to behave in ways that secure approval from others.

At least one study suggests that people with strong affiliative needs are more likely than other people to give in to pressures exerted by their friends (Walker & Heyns, 1962). One explanation is that people with strong affiliative needs are especially sensitive to the possibility of disapproval or rejection for failing to conform with their friends, whom they hope to be with again and again in the future. Disapproval or rejection from a group of strangers one is unlikely to ever see again is nowhere near so great a penalty for nonconformity.

Closely related to the concept of need affiliation is the concept of **need for social approval,** which is another personal motive that may propel one person toward another. This need is typically measured by means of a 33-item objective personality test called the Crowne-Marlowe Scale. An intriguing correlate of need for social approval has been reported by Crowne and Strickland (1961). In their study they first classified their subjects as having high or low need for social approval. The subjects were then put through a learning task similar to that used by Greenspoon (Chapter Five) in which subjects were simply required to emit words. Under one set of conditions subjects received positive reinforcement in the form of social approval ("Mmm-Hmmm") each time they emitted a plural noun. Those with high need for social approval emitted more plural nouns than subjects with low need for social approval. Under other conditions subjects received negative reinforcement in the form of disapproval ("Uh-Uh") after they emitted plural nouns. "Uh-Uh" had a greater punishing or deterrent effect on the high- as opposed to low-need subjects. Using a different learning task, Millburn, Bell, and Koeske (1970) also found that social approval was a particularly effective reinforcer when administered to subjects with high need for social approval. However, unlike Crowne and Strickland, they did not find that disapproval was a more effective negative reinforcer for subjects in the high-need category. In this experiment disapproval seemed to spur high-need subjects on to greater efforts! Both studies suggest, however, that people assessed as having a high need for social approval are especially sensitive to the reactions of others and should prove to be exceptionally "good learners" in studies in which praise and approval are used as reinforcers.

On the whole, studies of need affiliation and need for social approval suggest that some of the antecedents of moving toward others may be found in measurable, more or less enduring characteristics of the person. As for the origin of these motives, once again you can take your pick of personality theories.

Learning-oriented theorists can point out that moving toward someone can be viewed as a learned response. Just as when someone approaches a strange dog, he can be rewarded by a playful romp or punished by a not-so-playful nip, he can be rewarded or punished for approaching other people. The antecedents of persistent tendencies to affiliate with others can thus be sought in earlier rewards and satisfactions associated with being with others.

Psychoanalytically oriented theorists have identified at least two major antecedents of continuing affiliative tendencies. First, seeking others could reflect persistent, unsatisfied needs arising during childhood. As a result, the person would continually seek out others for the love and approval not obtained during earliest infancy. Affiliative behavior resting on this motivational base should be easily identified, since it is likely to be unsuccessful. As we saw in Chapter Eight, the social skills of people with persistent, unsatisfied childhood needs are apt to be immature, and attempts to approach others are generally met with failure. A second set of antecedents may be found in a highly successful passage through the trials and tribulations of early psychosexual stages! Successful development fosters a sense of trust and security. Goldman-Eisler (1948), for example, found in a study of college students that those who had been cared for generously in infancy were characterized by a warm sociability. Movement toward others resting on this motivational base should also be easy to identify, for it should be mature and successful.

Humanistically oriented psychologists also comment about people's tendencies to affiliate with others. Maslow (1954), for example, considers receiving attention and love an important prerequisite for human well-being. Moving toward others can also be described as a major aspect of realizing human potentials. That is, within encounter groups descriptions of personal growth usually involve some reference to warm, successful contacts with others.

Passing Needs and Movement toward Others

Association with others has also been traced to personal needs created by specific situations. When conditions are such that people are understimulated, uncertain, afraid, or unable to cope on their own, they are likely to seek out others. People may thus be attracted to others because they expect them to be stimulating, informative, reassuring, and helpful!

Other People as Stimulating. A certain amount of stimulation seems important for survival in comfort. In the discussion of motivation (Chapter Four) we saw that animals engage in activities that lead to increased levels of stimulation; that people often seem to show preferences for "fun," "exciting," and stimulating activities such as mountain climbing, athletic contests, and hobbies; and that prolonged periods of low levels of stimulation can lead to irritability, muddled reasoning, hallucinations, and possible physical deterioration of the nervous system. Since people provide almost unending variety, they can serve as rich and pleasant sources of stimulation.

Since people provide almost unending variety, they can serve as rich and pleasant sources of stimulation.

Stimulation from others may be particularly important during certain periods of life. As indicated in Chapter Six, research by Spitz (1945, 1946, 1965) suggests that children raised for an extended period under conditions of highly limited social stimulation tend to suffer intellectually, emotionally, and sometimes physically. On the other hand, despite dramatic reports to the contrary, there is some evidence suggesting that adults can undergo periods of social isolation without any devastating effects (Schachter, 1959).

Other People as Informative. Several lines of evidence suggest that people feel uncomfortable when there are important gaps in their knowledge, and they will seek information to close these gaps. Other people can serve as a useful source of such information. In times of civil, natural, or military disaster, for example, people may seek out others in an attempt to discover what happened and what is likely to occur next.

Other People as Reassuring. When conditions are stressful or upsetting, people may move toward others for comfort and reassurance. Schachter (1959) informed a group of subjects that they were about to receive electric shocks. Some of them were told that the shocks would be strong and painful(high-fear condition), and others were told that, at worst, the shocks would be very mild tingles (low-fear condition). All subjects were allowed to wait for this shocking experiment either alone or in the presence of others. Under conditions of high as opposed to low fear, subjects expressed greater preference for waiting in the presence of others. A subsequent study in the same series suggested that, when people were told they could not discuss the impending experiment (in other words, could not gain friendly reassurances from the other persons), the preference for waiting with others declined.

Other people can provide a source of comfort, but they can also provide a source of embarrassment. If you were to receive a painful inoculation in the arm, you might gain a certain amount of courage from others. On the other hand, if you were to receive an equally painful inoculation in that other common place for doctors' needles, the presence of others could increase your anxiety. Sarnoff and Zimbardo (1961) conducted a study similar to Schachter's. When their subjects anticipated a fearful shock, they preferred to wait in the presence of others. However, when the subjects anticipated performing infantile and foolish tasks such as sucking on rubber nipples, they preferred to wait in isolation.

Other People as Helpers. Affiliative behavior can be instigated by the simple discovery that other people are useful or necessary for accomplishing a task. Two or more people, by coordinating their efforts, can complete jobs that could not be done by an individual. As you will discover in the next chapter, "assistance" from others is not invariably beneficial. But, for the most part, such tasks as having a piano to move can prove sufficient motivation for seeking out others.

Affiliative behavior can be instigated by the simple discovery that other people can be helpful.

Situational Demands and Movement toward Others

Thus far our search for the bases of movement toward others has centered on enduring and transient personal motives and needs. Now let us consider how external variables contribute to different degrees of affiliative behavior. Two main sets of such variables are (1) social prescriptions and (2) physical layouts.

Social Prescriptions. Socially imposed rules and regulations that take effect in specific situations can encourage or discourage movement toward others. For example, the guards at Buckingham Palace are ordered to stand at attention and maintain their post in a military manner, ignoring all distractions. This means that they must not visibly respond to catcalls, jeers, grimaces, foreign children stamping on their toes, or women who make attractive offers. Admittedly, most social roles offer a little more flexibility, but in many cases one of the strings attached to fulfilling a role is maintaining a prescribed distance from other people. Psychoanalysts, for example, are supposed to remain detached and distant from their "patients," and people who work for large organizations (such as police departments, welfare bureaus, schools, universities, and hospitals) may be officially admonished not to become "personally involved" with individual clients and their problems. Similarly, different amounts of affiliative behavior are encouraged at a cocktail party, at home, and during meditation hour at a monastery.

Physical Layouts. With the possible exception of a maximum-security solitary-confinement cell, it seems as if physical layouts cannot absolutely prohibit or enforce affiliation. For example, there are cases such as that of the lonely prisoner in which people are drawn together despite formidable physical barriers, and other cases where people physically jammed together (for example, in the same office or apartment) do not speak to each other for days on end. On the other hand, the arrangement of objects in physical space can certainly make easy or make difficult and hence encourage or discourage affiliative behavior. Friendships among office workers can be discouraged if their desks are separated by shoulder-high filing cabinets, and in school it may be easier to strike up an acquaintanceship in a small seminar room than in a cavernous lecture hall. Sommer (1969) reports a number of studies which relate physical layouts to the distance people maintain from each other.

An attempt to initiate and maintain a conversation can be taken as evidence of movement toward others. Sommer (1969) reports a study in which he systematically varied the distance between two couches. He found that people sitting across from each other conversed freely when the distance was about 5½ feet, but communication was dramatically curtailed when the distance was increased. The results of this study are intriguing when we consider the furniture arrangement in some American living rooms: the couch is at one end of the room and the easy chairs at the other.

Attraction as Selective

The motivation and capability to form associations and friendships are generally displayed in a highly selective fashion. Each of us can list people we find attractive, people we find repulsive, and people who leave us indifferent. Why should some individuals have more drawing power than others? The answer seems to lie in the *degree of contact* and in *interrelationships of personal characteristics.*

Degree of Contact

Propinquity refers to nearness or closeness in space. Numerous studies have found a direct, positive relationship between propinquity and friendship or mate selection. In clusters of homes and apartment complexes, residents are more likely to strike up friendships with the people next door than with the people several doors away. In dormitories, strangers assigned to the same room are likely to become good friends, and strangers assigned to adjacent rooms are more likely to become friends than are strangers living several rooms apart. Furthermore, there is at least some support for the old notion that a young adult will eventually marry the boy (or girl) next door. These findings *cannot* always be explained away by saying that the initial friendship motivated the people to locate themselves near each other: in many studies the pairs of friends were initially strangers thrown together by the whims of a capricious housing authority or experimenter.

Certainly some form of contact is a prerequisite for being attracted to or repelled by another person. It is difficult to envision anything but a reaction of indifference toward someone whom we have never met and know nothing about. But why is it so likely that once people are brought into proximity, they should generally find each other attractive? Why shouldn't they be equally likely to leave each other cold or find each other repulsive?

When people are thrown into contact, they can either coordinate their efforts and live together harmoniously or hinder and frustrate each other and endure in misery. The rewards for friendship and the punishments for feuds, rivalries, and conflicts should clearly favor becoming friends with nearby people. Persons thrown into contact may thus quickly learn to accommodate to one another, which can provide satisfactions and reinforcement for continued association. However, as we saw in the case of the person in the black bag (Chapter Eleven), attraction may develop from contact or "exposure" even when there are no specifiable reinforcements. Could it be that one person learns to like another simply because the other person has been seen day after day?

Zajonc (1968a) presented subjects with pictures of men taken from an old college yearbook. Some pictures he showed once, some twice, some 5 times, some 10 times, and some 25 times. He then asked the subjects to indicate how much they thought they might like each man "as a person." Results showed that men whose pictures had been presented a greater number of times were rated as more likable.

An implication of this finding is that people who are constantly in the lime-light should be more popular than those who escape the public eye. To examine this implication, I prepared a list containing the names of 240 people (Harrison, 1969). Two hundred of the names were of public figures—that is, Americans who appeared on the covers of *Time* and *Newsweek* magazines during the years 1966, 1965, 1961, 1956, and 1941. Forty names were chosen from each of these years to ensure differences in exposure. Presumably, people who appeared on the magazine covers years ago would be less familiar today than those who were so publicized more recently. The remaining 40 names were fictitious ones made up by combining first and last names chosen at random from a telephone directory.

Sixty subjects took part in this study. Half of them rated the public figures on a seven-point familiar-unfamiliar scale and the other half rated them on a seven-point like-dislike scale. The overall correlation between subjectively estimated familiarity and likability was +.63, which is very substantial. More-over, for all six groups of names (1966, 1965, 1961, 1956, 1941 and fictitious) the correlations were in the predicted direction, and for four of the five groups of real people the correlations were statistically significant. Further research provided supporting evidence. First, the relationship between the exposure of public figures and their popularity was also found when objective estimates of exposure replaced subjective ratings of familiarity. Second, using other subjects I found that well-known religious, occupational, political, and ethnic groups tended to be rated as more likable than lesser-known groups in the same categories, although the magnitude of some of these correlations left something to be desired. All these findings, however, suggest some relation-ship between exposure or contact and liking.

Saegert, Swap, and Zajonc (1971) conducted an experimental study in which they varied the exposure of actual persons. Subjects reporting for this experi-ment were told that it was a study of taste perception. During the experiment they moved from room to room, where the different taste solutions were located. Half the subjects tasted pleasant soft drinks; the other half, unpleas-ant solutions of vinegar, quinine, and citric acid.

In the course of moving from room to room, each subject found herself with other subjects. For each girl, another girl was seen ten times, five times, twice, or once. Afterward, each subject rated the others in the experiment. The results showed that the most frequently encountered girls had the highest ratings. This was true whether the contact took place in the setting of the pleasant-tasting solution or that of the unpleasant-tasting solution and even though the subjects were not allowed to talk with each other when they met in the different rooms. Apparently, repeated contact can lead to attraction, even if it occurs in the presence of unpleasant stimuli.

Contact and Race Relations. The relationship between contact and attraction raises an intriguing possibility. Can interracial contact reduce prejudice between racial groups?

Brophy (1945) found that, the more times a white sailor had shipped with a black seaman, the less prejudice he showed. Similarly, research reported by Wilner, Walkley, and Cook (1952, 1955) compared the attitudes of whites living in segregated housing with the attitudes of whites living in integrated housing units. Those living in the integrated projects (and having more contact with blacks) showed less prejudice. Mann (1959) assigned blacks and whites to six-person discussion groups. He found that over successive meetings these group members became less sensitive to racial considerations.

At present there is considerable evidence that interracial contact reduces prejudice (Amir, 1969). But a close examination suggests that this relationship may be limited in certain important ways.

First, interracial contacts can take place in many different settings, such as the work setting, the recreational setting, or the residential setting. Whereas contact within one setting can reduce prejudice *within that setting,* it does not necessarily result in lessened prejudices within other settings. Thus, thrown together in combat, white and black soldiers may develop some respect for each other as fighters but still carefully avoid each other at the garrison or away on leave. Minard (1952) has found that blacks and whites work effectively side by side in the coal mines of West Virginia but maintain separate lives outside the mine. Something similar has been found in department stores (Harding & Hogrefe, 1952), where whites who show favorable attitudes toward black co-workers on the job maintain their prejudices off the job.

A second important consideration is that not all interracial contacts lead to lessened prejudices. For example, the slave owners of the Old South certainly had considerable contact with blacks; yet they were less favorable toward blacks than were the Northern abolitionists, some of whom had never seen a black. To take a more recent example, we would not necessarily expect interracial contact in the course of a ghetto uprising to lead to lessened prejudices.

Amir (1969) has identified some of the conditions under which interracial contacts are likely to reduce prejudice. The first condition is when the minority person's social status is at least equal to that of the prejudiced person he contacts. MacKenzie (1948) found that, among American war veterans, only 5 percent of those who had had contact with unskilled, low-status blacks voiced favorable interracial attitudes; the corresponding figure for veterans who had had contact with skilled, professional, high-status blacks was 64 percent. Thus, for interracial contacts to reduce prejudice, minority-group people must not be kept uneducated and chained to poor-paying, menial, subservient *low-status* occupations.

Interracial contact is also likely to have beneficial effects when "someone in authority" or the "prevailing social climate" favors such contact, when the contact is prolonged and intimate rather than quick and casual, and when the people in contact are working to reach common ends. On the other hand, when people are competing for scarce resources, when they are angry or frustrated, and when there are conflicting attitudes and standards, interracial contact can lead to increased prejudices and tensions.

Interrelationships of Personal Characteristics

A popular approach to the problem of interpersonal attraction involves examining the *interrelationships* of the characteristics of people who are drawn to each

According to the similarity hypothesis, people are attracted to those who somehow resemble themselves.

other. In what ways do the personal characteristics of the two people contribute to attraction?

According to the **similarity hypothesis,** people are attracted to those who somehow resemble themselves. To the extent that this is true, we would expect people who come from the same social class, are roughly equal in intelligence, and share a number of interests to be attracted to each other.

The **contrast hypothesis** suggests that "opposites attract." If this were true, we should expect someone tall, good looking, intelligent, and rich to fall in love with someone short, ugly, stupid, and poor. Although such relationships may occasionally develop, there is very little systematic evidence supporting this hypothesis, so it will not be discussed in detail here.

Another hypothesis based on the differences between people is the **complementarity hypothesis,** which holds that certain different-appearing needs of two people may mesh together in such a way that an association will be rewarding for each of them. For example, the "good woman" and the "bad man" may fall in love because each can satisfy important needs of the other. At the risk of oversimplification, the good woman may find the bad man attractive because he appeals to her hidden sexual longings or because she finds the possibility of reforming him an irresistible temptation. The bad man may find the good woman attractive because she provides an exciting challenge to his seductive abilities or because he perceives her as capable of exerting a beneficial and stabilizing influence on his life.

Similarity and Attraction. Newcomb's (1961) *ABX* system (described in some detail in the last chapter) is one of several lines of theorizing suggesting that similarity provides an important basis for attraction. Newcomb's theory deals with similarity in terms of attitudes. If we consider attitudes as the *independent* variable and attraction as the *dependent* variable, people with similar attitudes should find each other attractive, and people with dissimilar attitudes should find each other not so attractive. In support of this hypothesis, Newcomb found that friendship formation among male students was predictable on the basis of similarity in attitudes. Byrne and his associates (Byrne & McGraw, 1964; Byrne & Nelson, 1965) have also found a relationship between attitude similarity and degree of attraction.

Similarities in attitudes can even outweigh other important factors in attraction. For example, whites can develop a liking for blacks if the blacks are presented as sharing the whites' attitudes, although we cannot always expect attitude similarity to completely erase initial prejudice (Byrne & McGraw, 1964).

Newcomb's system is easiest to understand when we consider one attitude at a time. In hobby clubs, for example, we can find people drawn together because of one shared interest, such as stamp collecting, ham radio, or archery. But most people are probably not attracted to or repelled by each other on the basis of one attitude. Since we cannot expect agreement or disagreement on all issues, what is likely to happen?

Byrne and Nelson (1965) asked subjects to read another person's alleged answers to an attitude questionnaire. In actuality, these answers had been prepared by the experimenters, who varied the extent to which the expressed attitudes conformed to the subjects' own attitudes. After reading the questionnaire, each subject rated the attractiveness of the person who had allegedly expressed the attitudes. Byrne and Nelson examined the effects on ratings of both the *total number* of attitudes similar to the subject's and the *proportion* of attitudes similar to the subject's. They found the second variable most highly related to interpersonal attraction. That is, as the proportion of attitudes similar to the subject's increased, the rated attractiveness of the person who allegedly expressed the attitudes also increased. This finding is sufficiently well documented that, in studies in which an experimenter wants to vary the degree of attraction between two people, he need only tell each subject that the other person has attitudes similar to (or dissimilar to) the subject's own.

Studies of attitude similarities and dissimilarities provide only one line of evidence that people find most attractive those who are similar to themselves. Miller, Campbell, Twedt, and O'Connell (1966) report various studies suggesting that friends are similar in socioeconomic class, religion, values, and interests. Richardson (1939), Reader and English (1947), Izard (1960), and Cattell and Nesselroade (1967) have found that people who are attracted to each other may have similar personalities.

Similarity among Friends: Real or Imagined? There is considerable evidence that a person will find attractive someone who is similar to himself. But is this similarity in all cases real, or is it sometimes imagined? Some studies suggest that people who are on friendly terms may *perceive* themselves as more similar than in fact they are, whereas people on unfriendly terms may falsely see each other as dissimilar. For example, studies that simultaneously examined the actual attitudes of spouses and each spouse's perceptions of the other's attitudes have found that perceived similarity is greater than actual similarity (Byrne & Blaylock, 1963; Levinger & Breedlove, 1966). On the other side of the coin, when marital satisfaction is low, spouses may tend to underemphasize their similarities and exaggerate their differences.

A third party who knows both friends may make the same judgmental errors about their similarity. Miller et al. (1966) examined 95 pairs of females and 90 pairs of males who chose each other as friends. Each member of the pair was rated on a personality scale by himself and by an outsider who knew both him and his friend. The investigators could thus determine the extent to which each pair of friends was actually similar in terms of personality (by comparing the self-ratings of the two persons) and the degree to which the two persons' personalities were perceived as similar by others who knew them.

This study did not find much evidence for true similarity, since there was little correspondence between the self-ratings made by each member of a pair. However, the pairs of friends had **reputational similarity,** in that people who knew them rated them as similar. Miller et al. note, however, that people who are attracted to each other have indeed been shown to be similar in a number of ways. But, they suggest, similarity in personality is not so clearly proven. Explaining reputational similarity, the authors suggest that, because friends are similar in a number of other ways, people have a tendency to see them as having similar personalities, too.

The studies just reported do not preclude real similarities as contributors to interpersonal attraction, but they do suggest that similarities among friends are in some cases more imagined than real. That is, the degree of similarity among people may be distorted by errors in perception and judgment.

Complementarity and Attraction. The complementarity hypothesis suggests that two people can have rather different-appearing needs that fit together to provide a basis for mutual attraction. These needs are considered complementary in that the satisfaction of one need has some bearing on the satisfaction of the other. For example, if one spouse has strong needs for nurturance (nourishing, aiding, and protecting a helpless person) and the other spouse has strong needs for succorance (seeking aid, protection, or sympathy), the first derives satisfactions from being able to freely give love, care, and protection, and the second finds gratifications in being a recipient of all this attention.

Tests of the complementarity hypothesis have emphasized mate selection, although Douvan and Gold (1966) report that preliminary evidence has been obtained suggesting that complementarity may enter into the formation of friendships among student nurses. In studies of married couples, Winch, Ktsanes, and Ktsanes (1954, 1955; Winch, 1958) found that people with needs to be dominant or assertive tend to marry people with needs to be submissive or receptive. However, Kerckhoff and Davis (1962) suggest that the importance of complementarity varies depending on the stage of the relationship. In their study of pairs of college students who were seriously considering marriage, they obtained measures of similarity, complementarity, and progress toward marriage. They found that early in the relationship, similarities were important in progress toward marriage, whereas later on complementarity gained in importance.

The complementarity hypothesis seems to confirm all intuition and is supported by the results of a handful of studies. Yet at least a baker's dozen of investigations have produced results that are *not* complimentary to the complementarity hypothesis (Berscheid & Walster, 1969). Schellenberg and Bee (1960), for example, found that premarried and married couples tended to have similar, not complementary, needs. But despite the disturbing lack of verification, the complementarity hypothesis is by no means ready for discard. It is generally conceded that the hypothesis is extremely difficult to test, partly because of the problems involved in discovering and measuring the complementary needs that might be relevant to attraction and partly because of the fancy and sophisticated methods required for an appropriate and complete statistical analysis. Possibly new advances (such as the statistical procedures described by Hope, 1969) will aid in the search for different-appearing needs that mesh and thereby contribute to attraction.

MOVING WITH OTHERS: COOPERATION

Thus far, emphasis has been on the variables that propel people into association. Now let us consider how, once brought together, people may exercise capacities for coordinating activities. If two or more persons coordinate their efforts to produce mutually beneficial results, they are moving *with* each other. This movement together is referred to as cooperation, which has been of great interest to a number of psychologists for the last decade or so. To understand how psychologists have dealt with cooperation, it is first necessary to consider a general theory of social interaction. This theory is closely related to the expectancy-incentive theories of motivation described in Chapter Four. It is a popular theory, because it has proven eminently suitable for generating experimental research. Although the theory had its initial basis in economics, we'll pick it up in the form developed by psychologists Thibaut and Kelley (1959).

Cooperation involves the coordination of efforts for mutually beneficial results.

A Theory of Social Interaction

Whenever a person accepts the opportunity to respond to another person, he has many options available and is, in effect, confronted with the issue of selecting a response. The other person is faced by the same issue: he, too, must choose a response. Thibaut and Kelley (1959) suggest that the responses chosen by each person will *combine* in some way to affect each party's level of happiness or satisfaction. Feelings that result from the combination of different people's individual responses are referred to as the **outcomes of the interaction.**

As an example, let's consider that time at the end of a first date when the opportunity arises to arrange a subsequent outing. We'll assume for purposes of illustration that there are only two responses available to each person: *willingness* to date again or *reluctance* to date again.[1] There are thus four pos-

[1] Only for simplicity must we ignore other response alternatives, such as hedging, and other considerations, such as variations in the ways willingness and reluctance may be expressed. For example, an invitation followed by a polite "no" would be expected to have one set of consequences, whereas an invitation followed by raucous laughter would be expected to have another.

sible combinations of behavior: (1) both can indicate willingness; (2) the first person can indicate willingness and the second reluctance; (3) the second can indicate willingness and the first reluctance; and (4) both can express reluctance. Each of these combinations will have real consequences for both persons, who will probably consider all the possible combinations before making their own response.

If both persons indicated a willingness to date again, each would feel attractive to the other. The personal outcome for each of them would be rewarding.

If one person indicated willingness and the other reluctance, the willing person would likely feel rebuffed and hurt. The reluctant person might feel slightly sorry about his or her refusal but consider this light sorrow a small price to pay for avoiding a repeat date. Each person's personal outcome would therefore be dissatisfying, but more so for one than for the other.

If both persons indicated reluctance, neither would feel attractive to the other. But they might both find some comfort in the knowledge that they did not find the other person attractive either. Each would be spared the discomfort of being refused. In this case the outcome would be neither particularly pleasant nor particularly unpleasant.

Thibaut and Kelley suggest that the outcomes people experience or anticipate will exert a compelling influence on their social behavior. Very simply, people will choose the response they think will produce the best outcome for themselves. Outcomes contain two components, *rewards* and *costs*. **Rewards** refer to all the positive aspects of the outcome (joys, pleasures, delights, and so on) and **costs** to all the negative features (expended efforts, embarrassment, frustration, loss of "face" or esteem, and so on). The concept of a "best outcome" is, of course, highly relative. Sometimes it is the one that provides the most rewards; at other times it is the one that incurs the fewest costs. Although determining the value of an outcome is no simple task, Thibaut and Kelley suggest that outcomes have measurable values. Anything that can be measured can be assigned a number.

The basic elements in the theory are the response alternatives available to each person, the possible combinations of these responses, and the possible outcomes. All of this information can be conveniently represented in a table called a **matrix**. The response alternatives available to one person are listed horizontally, and those available to the other are listed vertically. The dating example can be illustrated in a two-by-two matrix—"two-by-two" referring to the fact that each person has two available responses (Table 12-1).

MAN'S RESPONSE

		Willing	Reluctant
WOMAN'S RESPONSE	*Willing*	Woman: +5 Man: +5	Woman: −5 Man: −1
	Reluctant	Woman: −1 Man: −5	Woman: 0 Man: 0

Table 12-1. Response Alternatives and Outcome Values: The Question of a Second Date.

In Table 12-1 the columns designate the man's responses and the rows designate the woman's responses. To determine the values of the outcomes for each person under each combination of responses, we need merely look at the intersection or crossing point for the column and the row. "Plus" outcomes range from +1 for slightly favorable to +5 for very favorable. "Minus" outcomes run from −1 for slightly unfavorable to −5 for very unfavorable. The values of the outcomes in this illustration are arbitrary, being based on my own subjective evaluations. Subjectivity is acceptable here, incidentally: although the outcomes are represented in terms of hard numbers, the numbers represent the direction and intensity of subjective feelings.

Table 12-1 is simply another way of stating that if both people indicate a willingness to date again, each will have a favorable outcome; if one person expresses willingness and the other reluctance, the willing party will feel hurt and rebuffed and the other a little regretful; and if both express reluctance, each person's disappointment is mitigated by the realization that they are "let off the hook." According to this matrix, the most satisfactory (and hence compelling) outcomes will result if each person indicates a willingness to date again. Each person should therefore be motivated to arrange a subsequent date. In this case, as in expectancy-incentive theories, the motivation to behave in a certain way comes from *expecting* that one response alternative is likely to lead to an *incentive* (now called an outcome). However, in the present case more is demanded from the individual, because he must also anticipate what the other person is likely to do. For example, whether or not the man brings up the subject of a subsequent date may depend in part on his anticipation of the woman's response. If he expects her to be receptive, he should be motivated to ask; but if he anticipates rejection, he may choose not to ask and hence spare himself embarrassment.

This type of approach can be applied in one way or another to account for almost any form of interpersonal behavior. For example, one could maintain, as Thibaut and Kelley do, that people are initially attracted to those who provide them with the best outcomes and that an association between people will be maintained as long as the outcomes received within the relationship are better than the outcomes expected from alternative relationships. Similarly, it is possible to account for social power or influence by saying that one person has more control over the outcomes than does the other. For example, the boss can motivate a high level of performance by offering good pay and discourage a low level of performance by threatening dismissal. He can ensure almost uninterrupted good outcomes for himself by keeping good employees and rapidly replacing unsatisfactory ones. Most employees, on the other hand, can attain good outcomes for themselves only by doing what the boss demands. In effect, the boss controls the fate of the individual employees, but they do not control the fate of the boss. Although explanations based on this kind of theorizing are sometimes supported by accumulated evidence, they may also be based on unproven assumptions.

Application of the Approach

There are certain problems inherent in trying to apply Thibaut and Kelley's approach to social interaction. It is difficult to specify the responses available to each person and to determine the values of the various outcomes to each of the people involved. Furthermore, when the number of interacting people increases beyond two or three, it is necessary to say good-bye to helpful little tools such as Table 12-1. Despite these limitations, however, this approach has a very important strength: conditions can be *created* with a *clear designation of response alternatives* and a *careful specification of the outcomes*. That is, it is quite possible for an investigator to do experimental research within a theoretical framework such as that proposed by Thibaut and Kelley.

Here is a simple example. Two volunteers appear for an experiment. Each is seated before a control panel with one red and one blue button. The experimenter then explains that, on signal, each subject must press one of the two buttons. On the basis of the two subjects' choices, each will be paid some money. They are given a matrix to help them with their decisions (Table 12-2). This is a direct translation of Thibaut and Kelley's approach into a simple experimental situation. The buttons provide the response alternatives, and monetary prizes provide the outcomes. This type of situation is described as an **experimental game**—"experimental" for rather transparent reasons and "game" because the two players can win or lose prizes in varying amounts.

PLAYER II'S RESPONSE

	Red	Blue
Red	Player I: +3¢ Player II: +3¢	Player I: −1¢ Player II: −1¢
Blue	Player I: −1¢ Player II: −1¢	Player I: +3¢ Player II: +3¢

PLAYER I'S RESPONSE

Table 12-2. An Experimental Game.

To secure the best outcomes in this particular experiment, both players should choose the same (for example, red) alternative. If each chooses a different alternative, they both lose. In this situation it should be easy for two people to coordinate efforts to produce the most favorable outcomes (3¢ each); unless they are irrational, their behavior would quite likely fall in line with Thibaut and Kelley's predictions.

Learning to Coordinate Efforts

In an experimental situation like the one just described, the two participants would probably be able to coordinate activities for their mutual advantage, even if they were not allowed to talk. In fact, people sometimes learn to coordinate activities when they are unaware of each other's presence.

Sidowski, Wycoff, and Tabory (1956) sat each of two subjects at individual control panels that had two response alternatives. Also present was a counter or scorekeeper. An electrode was fastened to each subject's wrist to deliver an electric shock. Subjects could not see each other, and neither was aware of the other's presence. They were told that the object of the experiment was to score as many points as possible. They were instructed to push whichever button they wanted whenever they wanted. Scores and shocks were received on the basis of the *other* person's response choice. For example, if the first subject pushed the left button, the second subject might be shocked; if the first subject pushed the right button, the second subject might receive a score. Subjects quickly learned to accommodate and deliver to each other the favorable outcome of a score as opposed to the unfavorable outcome of a shock, even though each was unaware of the other's existence.

The Use of Games for Studying Cooperation

Experimental games take many different forms. They become interesting if the responses can be defined as representing socially significant behavior. If, for example, one response in an experimental game can be defined as selfish and the other as altruistic (aimed at helping another at the expense of oneself), the experimenter has a game with which he can examine the determinants of selfishness and altruism.

Experimental games have been used most extensively for studying cooperation.

Experimental games have been used most extensively for studying cooperation. Each of the two players is given two response alternatives: one is cooperative, since its selection promotes gains for both players; the other is noncooperative, since its selection promotes personal rewards at the expense of the other person. The most frequently used experimental game that provides cooperative and noncooperative responses is the **Prisoner's Dilemma Game,** which is, for the typist's sake, usually called the PDG.[2]

PLAYER II'S RESPONSE

		Red	Blue
PLAYER I'S RESPONSE	*Red*	Player I: +5¢ Player II: +5¢	Player I: −4¢ Player II: +6¢
	Blue	Player I: +6¢ Player II: −4¢	Player I: −3¢ Player II: −3¢

Table 12-3. Example of the Prisoner's Dilemma Game (PDG).

Table 12-3 shows the response alternatives and a pattern of outcomes characteristic of the PDG.[3] The essential qualities of the game are that if both participants choose to cooperate, both receive moderately favorable outcomes. If one cooperates but the other does not, the noncooperative person receives a highly favorable outcome at the other person's expense. If both fail to cooperate, both receive low outcomes. Typically, each pair of subjects plays the PDG a number of times, and the two participants are not allowed to talk during the experiment.

Despite the seeming attractiveness of the outcome for choosing the noncooperative response, cooperation is the best choice in this game. This is because *both* players may choose the noncooperative response, with the result that neither wins very much. If one person tries to take advantage of a cooperative partner, the partner is able to retaliate by becoming noncooperative himself.

Experimental games such as the PDG are useful precisely because they provide a carefully controlled situation for assessing behavior. Yet, frankly, they involve a highly artificial setting, stripped of virtually all the trappings we associate with normal social interaction. Are experimental games so far removed

[2] The idea behind this rather strange name is explained by Luce and Raiffa (1957).

[3] The outcomes given are representative of those that have been used in the PDG. The exact value of the different outcomes can vary within certain formal limits and still fulfill the assumptions and intent of the game (Gallo & McClintock, 1965).

from the natural setting that they tell us nothing about real-life behavior? Or can they as well tell us something about behavior outside the laboratory?

Although, as we shall see, there is some evidence suggesting that a person who chooses to cooperate in experimental games may also show a cooperative orientation in other ways, attempts to find relationships between game behavior and other behavior have not always been successful. We must be very careful about generalizing from behavior in experimental games to behavior in other situations (Sermat, 1970).

Antecedents of Cooperation

preceding

The area of experimental games is extremely rich in research, and investigators have examined many different factors that might contribute to cooperative behavior: the precise nature of the game and of the outcomes associated with the different combinations of responses, the personal characteristics of each player, the relationship of the players to each other, the course of interaction among the players, and cooperative versus noncooperative group atmospheres (for summaries and reviews of these studies see Gallo & McClintock, 1965; Vinacke, 1969). Here we'll consider a few of the ways that the antecedents of cooperation have been sought in the individual player and in the nature and behavior of the "other" player.

Personal Characteristics and Cooperation

Deutsch (1960) studied the effects of **authoritarianism** on cooperation in the PDG. The authoritarian person tends to be hostile toward outgroup individuals and emphasizes power, toughness, and obedience in social relations. The non-authoritarian, on the other hand, tends to be flexible, is accepting of others, and prefers social relations based on mutual respect. Deutsch found that authoritarian people tended to be less cooperative when playing the PDG. In a subsequent study, which used a different type of game, Smith (1967) also found systematic differences between authoritarian and nonauthoritarian players.

Lutzker (1960) and McClintock, Harrison, Strand, and Gallo (1963) investigated the effects of internationalism and isolationism on choices in the PDG. Internationalism and isolationism are assessed by means of an attitude questionnaire. The **internationalist** shows trust for people of other nations, promotes communication among nations, and prefers friendly negotiated solutions to international conflicts as they arise. The **isolationist,** on the other hand, shows a distrust for people of other nations, prefers to minimize communication between the United States and potentially hostile nations, and is quick to suggest the use of forceful military solutions when troubles arise. Findings of these studies indicate that internationalists are more cooperative in the PDG than are isolationists.

Most definitions of personal adjustment suggest that withdrawal, ineffective social responding, and conflict with others indicate poor adjustment, whereas an alertness to changing social stimulation, an ability to cope with others, and an ability to secure mutual satisfactions with others suggest quite the opposite. Might we not, therefore, expect personal disorders to be associated with an inability to work with others for mutual rewards?

Travis (1966) had 15 pairs of schizophrenics and 15 pairs of nonpsychotics play several experimental games, some of which were similar to the PDG. Within these games one of the response alternatives was "withdrawal," which was basically a cop-out from the whole procedure. Because he used a number of different games, Travis could measure more than simple cooperation and noncooperation. He found that the nonpsychotics were more cooperative, more trustworthy, more forgiving, and more likely to interact with each other. Travis' hypotheses were based on clinical observations about the social difficulties of schizophrenics. His contribution was to provide support for these ideas within a carefully controlled experimental situation.

The studies just described and a handful of others suggest that some people tend to be flexible and tolerant and to behave cooperatively, whereas others tend to be inflexible and intolerant and to behave somewhat selfishly. Different people have different orientations to life, and their orientations are sometimes reflected in the ways that they play experimental games. We must note again, however, that attempts to find relationships between game behavior and personality measures of players have not always been successful.

Nature and Behavior of the "Other Person"

Cooperation, by definition, involves two or more people. It seems quite reasonable to hypothesize that whether one person chooses to cooperate with another is likely to depend partly on the nature and behavior of the other person.

Nature of the Other Person. Certainly, we would expect friends to be more cooperative than strangers. Exploring this hypothesis, Oskamp and Perlman (1966) obtained pairs of players who were best friends, acquaintances, disliked each other, or were completely unknown to each other. These subjects were selected from two different colleges: one may be described as a small, friendly liberal arts college with a highly cooperative atmosphere; the other may be described as having a less cooperative atmosphere, stressing in its curriculum such competitive fields as business and politics. In part, Oskamp and Perlman found, as you might expect, that pairs of friends were most cooperative. However, this was true only for the subjects from the liberal arts college. Subjects from the second college were *least* cooperative when they participated with their friends. What happened here?

Oskamp and Perlman believe that the answer is to be found in the social standards fostered by the two different schools. In the liberal arts college there were conformity pressures for students to cooperate for mutual advantage. This would give pairs of friends a history of cooperation. The second college had a competitive atmosphere. In this case friendship served as a "permission" for rivalrous and competitive behavior. Some support for this interpretation comes from another study by Oskamp and Perlman (1965). In this study they created cooperative and competitive standards within small groups and found that these standards led to increased or decreased levels of cooperation in an experimental game.

Swingle and Gillis (1968) have also found that the relationship between friendship and cooperation is not simple. They chose school-age subjects who liked each other, disliked each other, or had no specified relationship with each other. Initially, subjects playing with friends were more cooperative. However, Swingle and Gillis arranged that halfway through the experiment the partners became *more* or *less* cooperative than they had been earlier in the game. When the subject's partner was a friend and the friend suddenly became more cooperative, the subject would become more cooperative too. On the other hand, if the friend suddenly became less cooperative, the subject would respond in kind and decrease his level of cooperation. Sudden increases or decreases in cooperation by partners who were not friends did not make so much difference. In Swingle and Gillis' study, it appears again that friendship is not a ground for unconditional cooperation. In some cases people will be more willing to cooperate with friends, but if the friend chooses to abandon cooperation and begin rivalry (which in the experimental game I would venture is *friendly* rivalry), the person will respond in kind.

Behavior of the Other Person. Imagine that you are playing the PDG with someone you know nothing about. How would his behavior affect yours? It seems reasonable that if he made the cooperative choice and allowed you to win, you would reciprocate. Thus you would both continue to make modest gains. On the other hand, if he were noncooperative and forced you to lose (meanwhile racking up tremendous outcomes for himself), you might decide to become noncooperative yourself and teach him a thing or two.

To test the hypothesis that cooperation leads to cooperation and noncooperation is returned in kind, various investigators have rigged the experimental situation so that the two players interact with a simulated partner, rather than a real one. The subject believes he is playing the game with the other person present, but in fact his outcomes are a result of his response choices and selections carefully made by the experimenter. In this way the experimenter can control what the "other player" seems to do.

Bixenstine, Potash, and Wilson (1963) had one group of subjects participate with simulated partners who made cooperative choices 83 percent of the time and another group of subjects participate with simulated partners who made cooperative choices only 17 percent of the time. There were no differences in the overall level of cooperation. McClintock et al. (1963) had subjects participate with partners who made cooperative choices either 85 percent, 50 percent, or 15 percent of the time. Again the level of cooperation of the alleged partner had no effect on the subject, whether he was internationalistic or isolationistic. McKeown, Gahagan, and Tedeschi (1967) found no differences in subjects who played with simulated partners making cooperative choices on 90 percent, 50 percent, or 10 percent of the plays. These findings would seem to contradict what psychologists refer to as the **norm of reciprocity** in social relations. This norm suggests "Do unto others as they do unto you" and would seem to apply in many situations. For example, favors are likely to be returned, and people seem to like those who like them. Applied to cooperation, we would expect that one person would be cooperative to the extent that the other person is cooperative. Why, in these experiments, should a cooperative simulated partner fail to elicit reciprocal cooperation from the real player?

One analysis (Zajonc, 1966) suggests it is because, in these particular experiments, noncooperation results in the best personal outcomes. The responses made by the simulated partner are unconditional, in the sense that they do not depend in any way on the real player's choice. They are fixed in advance by the experimenters, and nothing the subject can do can change them. His best strategy is to be uncooperative.

If the simulated partner is unconditionally cooperative, the real player can take advantage of his alleged partner without risking punishment in return. The real player soon discovers that, whatever he himself does, the partner will be cooperative and let him win. Winnings are greatest when he makes the non-cooperative choice. On the other hand, when the simulated partner is not at all cooperative, the real player discovers that he cannot coax cooperation from him, for again the alleged partner remains uninfluenced by the real subject's behavior. Here, too, the noncooperative choice makes sense, for it will minimize the losses that the real player sustains. Unconditional, blind cooperation on one person's part may therefore not be the best way to elicit cooperation from another.

There is, however, evidence suggesting that conditional cooperation on one person's part may elicit cooperation from the other. Solomon (1960) used a conditionally cooperative simulated partner. If a real player was cooperative, the simulated partner would also be cooperative; if the real player was non-cooperative, the partner would retaliate in kind. Under these conditions it becomes clear to the real player that, if he wants to do well in the game, he must allow the alleged partner to do well also. Cooperation is rewarded whereas noncooperation is not, and players learn to make cooperative responses.

Not all studies suggest that simple tit-for-tat cooperative behavior will induce cooperation (Komorita, 1965). However, several investigations support the general idea that cooperation may be brought about during a series of steps during which one person indicates a willingness to repay cooperation with cooperation. By his series of responses, each person may slowly influence and adapt to the other, with the result that both begin coordinating efforts for mutual rewards (Vinacke, 1969).

A Cautionary Note

There is an abundance of studies relating different variables to cooperation. Those just described were selected because they present a fairly consistent pattern of findings. First, some people seem to have a cooperative attitude in general, which may be reflected in their behavior in experimental games. Second, cooperation is affected by friendship, but not always in the same way. In some cases people are more likely to cooperate with friends than with strangers, but if their friends show a competitive rivalry, they will feel free to respond in kind. Finally, whether or not a person will be cooperative will depend to some extent on the level of cooperation of the other person; but if the other person is unconditionally cooperative (a human doormat, so to speak), the pattern of outcomes may favor noncooperative activity.

Noncooperative activity can have advantages, as sports enthusiasts and businessmen are quick to point out.

These results should remind us that people will not always be motivated to coordinate their efforts with others. Perhaps this is just as well, for noncooperative activity can have advantages, as sports enthusiasts and businessmen are quick to point out. Competition can promote healthy change (for example, when two firms strive to develop superior products) and can lend an interest to life. Two prizefighters who decided to forget about the fight and split the purse would not be in business for long.

The casualties of noncooperative activity need not be severe. Yet there are cases in which people interact in such a way that someone really does get hurt. We will turn now to those situations whereby people dish it out with no friendly intent at all. This is movement against another, or aggression.

MOVING AGAINST OTHERS: AGGRESSION

If you are on the planning committee for a church bazaar or college fair, you would do well to consider investing $25 or so in an old car that looks fine but has enough mechanical difficulties to have been retired to the junkyard. Borrow a sledgehammer and some goggles, and then let people have three swings at the car for a nominal fee. You'll make a small fortune! Of course, it is only in rare cases that such activities meet with social approval. In a public parking lot the same activities that would be fun at a carnival would be considered violent and worthy of a jail sentence.

The Nature of Aggression

Definitions of aggression typically involve both behavior and intent. A strictly behavioral definition might define as aggressive those activities that inflict harm or discomfort on something or someone. Emphasis would be on the behavior itself, rather than on the objective damage accomplished. Thus, although two soldiers who bayonet each other could be defined as aggressive, so could a screaming, flailing child held at arm's length by an annoyed adult.

A strictly behavioral definition falls short, however, because we know of many cases in which one person inflicts harm on another in a way that does not seem to satisfy the requirements of aggression. If the pilot of a small plane suffers a stroke and falls forward onto the controls, it is quite likely that his action will lead to harm for the plane's occupants, but it is unlikely that we could convince anyone that this was an instance of aggression. For this reason, aggression is better defined as behavior with the intent of inflicting harm or damage. This, however, implies that there is some way to measure intent. Although in some cases aggressors proudly announce their intent, in other cases they are reluctant to discuss this behavior and its motives.

Hidden and Disguised Aggression

There are many forms of behavior that psychologists regard as hidden or disguised aggression. To the casual observer, the aggressive component of this behavior may be so hidden or disguised that it is difficult to recognize.

First, the intended victim or target of aggression may be disguised when the person directs his aggression away from one target and toward another that is usually less formidable. This is called displaced aggression. The sales manager, bawled out by the company president, cannot safely aggress against the president, but he can take it out on the junior salesmen. Or, an adolescent with aggressive feelings toward his father may turn his aggression toward someone else, such as a teacher or policeman. At still other times the ultimate victim may be an inanimate object. In a now almost forgotten series of advertisements for muscle-building equipment, a 98-pound weakling has sand kicked in his face by a 200-pound bully. No idiot, the weakling returns home and kicks over a chair. The process of displacement can make the original instigator of the act difficult to discover.

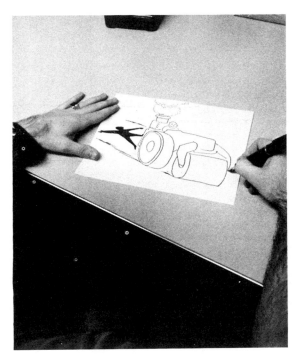

Aggression can appear in the form of fantasy.

Second, aggression can appear in the form of fantasy rather than in overt behavior. Thus, although a student can't do much about his landlord's irritating demands, he can daydream now and then about various horrible fates for the landlord. Fantasy aggression ranges all the way from rather crude thoughts about disembowelment and dismemberment to refined thoughts about psychological torture and all the legal and subtle ways that it is possible to "get even" with someone or "make him sorry" for what he has (or has not) done.

Finally, psychoanalysts suggest that aggression can be disguised by unconscious mental processes. As we saw in Chapter Eight, it is possible that accidents and mistakes reflect hidden motives. Thus an accidental shooting that results from toying around with a gun believed to be unloaded, a car accident in which the passenger is killed but the driver escapes virtually unscathed, an accident in which a child is injured due to a sudden inattentiveness on the mother's part, and the mistake of forgetting to send the landlord the rent could all be construed as involving aggression. Indeed, psychoanalysts might find evidence of aggression where there is neither visible intent nor harm accomplished. Through reaction formation, aggressive impulses could be converted into overly courteous and solicitous behavior, and through projection aggressive intent could be attributed to somebody else.

Aggression, then, encompasses many different forms of thought and behavior. No single definition is going to be perfect, but it is necessary to draw the line somewhere. For our present purposes, we shall go along with Berkowitz (1969, p. 3), who defines aggression as "behavior whose goal response is the inflicting of injury on some object or person. . . . The behavior may be overt (physical or verbal) or may be implicit (as in the case of thoughts). . . ."

The Frustration-Aggression Hypothesis

Much behavior is aimed at attaining an objective or goal. The course toward the goal may be either clear or filled with obstacles. Obstacles that keep one from speedily reaching a goal are called **frustrations.** According to both Freud and a number of experimental psychologists (for example, Dollard, Doob, Miller, Mowrer, & Sears, 1939), frustration is a cause of aggression. The greater the frustration, the greater the aggression, and we would expect the aggression to be directed toward the frustrating person or object. For example, suppose you were a college man looking forward to a wonderful date this evening (goal). As you are preparing for the date, you discover that your roommate left a note saying he borrowed your best clothes and car and will return them tomorrow (frustration). If you become angry with your roommate, you would be supporting the **frustration-aggression hypothesis.**

Initially the frustration-aggression hypothesis was stated in rather sweeping terms, suggesting that aggressive behavior always presupposes frustration and that frustration always leads to aggression. However, the hypothesis has been restated in the more modest form that frustration raises the probability of aggression (Berkowitz, 1958, 1969). Evidence for the hypothesis typically involves inspecting or manipulating frustrations of various strengths and then measuring aggression.

Dollard and his collaborators have given many examples that they claim supported the frustration-aggression hypothesis, as have many others. One of the more intriguing and controversial of the early studies (controversial because it is open to many different interpretations) had to do with the price of cotton and the number of lynchings in the South (Hovland & Sears, 1940).

Wealth is a common goal, and anything that blocks the path to riches should be a source of frustration and subsequently aggression. Hovland and Sears reasoned that in the South, which was for some time highly dependent for wealth on the value of a single commodity, cotton, decreases in the price of cotton should be highly frustrating and hence result in aggressive activity. To investigate this hypothesis, they examined fluctuations in the value of cotton in 14 Southern states between 1882 and 1930 and related these variations to the number of lynchings occurring in the same areas during the same years. The obtained correlation of $-.67$ suggests, in accordance with the frustration-aggression hypothesis, that, as the price of cotton decreased, the number of lynchings increased.

The frustration-aggression hypothesis has received some support from a number of different experimental studies. Barker, Dembo, and Lewin (1941) allowed children to play with a number of attractive toys. They then introduced frustration in the form of a wire barrier that kept the children from the toys. The children could still see the attractive toys but were forced to make do with less appealing playthings. During this frustration period constructive play diminished. Some children began smashing the available toys, others made threatening movements toward the experimenters or made assaults on the barrier.

College students received a number of frustrations at the hands of Sears, Hovland, and Miller (1940). First, the students had to remain awake for 24 hours, which was frustrating because it kept them from needed sleep. The experimenters introduced additional frustrations by discouraging conversations, prohibiting smoking, failing to produce promised amusing activities, and canceling a meal. As the experiment progressed, aggression increased, although it took unpredictable forms. Some subjects began making direct verbal attacks on the experimenters, who were, indeed, the frustrating agents. Others expressed aggression in thinly disguised ways, such as by drawing pictures of brutally mutilated psychologists.

Is the frustration-aggression relationship limited to man? Azrin, Hutchinson, and Hake (1966) taught pigeons to obtain food by pecking at a key. Then frustration was induced by withholding the food. When another pigeon was present, the frustrated bird would angrily attack it.

The frustration-aggression hypothesis suggests that keeping people from reaching goals leads to aggression.

Despite these and other findings generally taken as favorable to the frustration-aggression hypothesis, the theory has several severe limitations. First, frustration appears to be a basic condition of human existence, and, very fortunately for all of us, most people do not react aggressively each and every time they are inconvenienced. Second, there are considerable differences among people in terms of tolerance for frustration. Some persons seem to react violently to the slightest provocation, whereas others remain calm, stoic, and even friendly in the face of very trying circumstances. Finally, as we saw in the discussion of displaced aggression, the victims or targets of aggression vary, and the frustration-aggression hypothesis cannot fully account for this fact. To understand who will act aggressively in what ways and in which situations, learning variables must also be taken into account.

Learning and Aggression

Modern social-learning theorists such as Bandura (Bandura & Walters, 1963; Bandura, 1969) suggest that most aggression can be understood in terms of learning considerations. Thus aggression will be encouraged when there are aggressive models to imitate and when aggressive responses are reinforced. Through modeling and social reinforcement, we learn when to aggress and how to aggress.

Bandura and Walters note that, if we compare different societies, we find differences in aggression that can be understood more easily in terms of learning conditions than in terms of the frustration-aggression hypothesis. A high level of aggression is shown among the headhunting Iatmul. In this society children are raised surrounded by aggressive models who approve of aggressive actions. The killer is a hero. Decapitation and scalping of enemies are rewarded by immediate victory celebrations and an improvement in social standing. On the other hand, a low level of aggression is shown among the Hutterites. In this society there are no killer heroes, only pacifistic models. Aggressive behavior is almost never rewarded. The differences between these two peoples do not seem to be accounted for in terms of differences in frustration, for the pacifistic Hutterites undergo severe and presumably frustrating socialization procedures.

Within our own society, suggest Bandura and Walters, the aggressiveness of children is clearly related to the patterns of rewards offered by the parents. That is, parents of aggressive children usually encourage or reward aggression. Parents of children who are nonaggressive do not reward aggression—but they do not necessarily punish it, either. As noted in Chapter Four, the role of punishment is rather complex, particularly when it is used as a method for weakening or eliminating aggressive responses. Geen (1968) and Gentry (1970) have found that being attacked elicits aggression. Punishment itself may be interpreted as an attack and may therefore elicit further aggression.

The Effects of an Aggressive Model

In 1931 the gangster film predominated at most American movie houses. In 1932 a gangster film was extremely hard to find. They had been almost completely banished by one Will H. Hays, president of a committee established to impose virtue and decency on the film-going public. Hays was reacting to voluminous protests from the Daughters of the American Revolution, the American Legion, and a host of women's groups, businessmen's clubs, and civic organizations. Griffith and Mayer (1957, p. 269) report:

> It was useless for Mr. Hays to reply that gangster films moralized against crime and were grim object lessons that it did not pay. . . . everybody knew that Edward G. Robinson in the title role of *Little Caesar* (1930) had become an ideal for emulation by hordes of young hero worshippers.

Despite this and subsequent campaigns, movies, television, and comic books still abound with violence. Was the D.A.R. correct in asserting that violence in the mass media could contribute to aggression in society?

Two theories offer very different predictions about the effects of exposure to violence. The **catharsis theory**, derived from early frustration-aggression concepts, suggests, among other things, that watching aggressive action should serve as a harmless release for pent-up aggression (Dollard et al., 1939). In effect, observing violence should have the beneficial effect of allowing the person to "blow off steam," thereby harmlessly draining off aggressive tendencies. The second hypothesis, derived from social-learning theory, suggests quite the opposite. Observing violence will provide the viewer with an aggressive model. If the social-learning theorists are right, viewing aggressive action should have the deleterious effect of encouraging aggression in the viewer.

In a recent study by Hanratty et al. (1969), small children were shown a short movie. The film began with Do-Do, a clown, standing stationary in the center of the screen. Another actor appeared. Circling Do-Do, he expressed great anger, telling Do-Do that he was about to be shot, hit, and beaten. This aggressive actor then proceeded to make good his threats. Later each child was taken to a small house trailer and told to wait in a certain room. When he entered, he found either Do-Do or an inflated clownlike doll standing there, surrounded by the toy tools of violence. Compared to children who had not seen the aggressive movie, these children exhibited more aggression, although all were reluctant to physically attack the large human clown.

Animated cartoon characters can have similar effects. Mussen and Rutherford (1961) showed children a nonaggressive cartoon movie of a frog and a duck playing cooperatively. Another group of children saw a cartoon in which an "animated weed attempted to choke a flower, and a panda bear struggled to destroy the weed." The latter cartoon stimulated aggressive behavior in play.

Also bearing on the relative worth of the catharsis and social-learning hypotheses is a study by Bandura, Ross, and Ross (1963), who compared groups of children exposed to (1) a live aggressive model, (2) a film of a human model engaged in aggressive activity, and (3) a film of a cartoon model engaging in aggressive activity with a control group of children who had not been exposed to aggressive models. Ratings of subsequent behavior showed that subjects in all three experimental groups were more aggressive than the control subjects. The effect was most pronounced for subjects who had viewed the filmed aggression. These subjects were rated as almost *twice* as aggressive as the controls.

Exposure to live or filmed aggressive models is likely to encourage aggressive behavior.

The studies just described are only a few of those that suggest exposure to live or filmed aggressive models is likely to encourage aggressive behavior (see Baron & Kepner, 1970; Berkowitz & Geen, 1966; Mallick & McCandless, 1966). These, coupled with studies suggesting that aggressive behavior follows the laws of reinforcement cited in Chapters Four and Five (Bandura & Walters, 1963), make the argument for the catharsis hypothesis seem very weak indeed.

The Interplay of Frustration and Learning

Considerable evidence suggests that an aggressive model to imitate and reinforcement following aggression may go a long way toward producing aggression. Yet it is also clear that frustration is an antecedent of aggression. How can the frustration-aggression and social-learning hypotheses be integrated?

One possibility is that frustration produces a motivational "push" for aggressive behavior, but that the emission of aggressive responses depends on other conditions as well, such as *cues* or other external stimuli that actually trigger the aggressive responses (Berkowitz, 1965; Berkowitz & LePage, 1967; Geen, 1968). Thus, once aggression is learned in response to a set of stimuli called cues, the level of aggression may rise as a result of frustration—*but only if those cues are present*.

A study by Davitz (1952) shows how frustration may serve to energize previously learned responses. First, Davitz observed groups of children playing together. Half the groups then underwent a series of sessions during which they were reinforced for acting aggressively; the other groups underwent training in which they were reinforced for friendly, constructive play. Next the children saw the beginning of a movie and simultaneously were given a candy bar. The frustration procedure consisted of interrupting the movie and taking the candy bars away. Subsequent observation of the children, again in a free-play situation, suggested that children trained to be aggressive were more aggressive following frustration, whereas children trained to be cooperative were more cooperative following frustration.

The results of this study by no means imply that frustration is unrelated to aggression, for frustration did enhance the aggressiveness of those children trained to be aggressive. But we also have to take into account the finding that children coached in constructive play were more cooperative following frustration than were the children coached in aggression. This we can do by considering frustration as producing increased motivation, which strengthens the dominant response. If aggression is the learned response to the available cues in the situation, then frustration will yield increased aggression. But if another response, such as cooperation, is dominant, this response would be strengthened instead. In our society competition and aggression may be well-learned responses to cues associated with many of the conditions that we think of as frustrating.

Aggressive cues may arise from many sources, one of which is violent films. Berkowitz (1965) and Geen (1968) propose that observing a violent film provides the viewer with stimuli that are highly related to aggression. These stimuli trigger aggressive responses, but the response may be so weak as to be unobservable in the absence of strong motivation. A source of motivation that can strengthen the response is frustration.

Implications for Reducing Violence in Society

The foregoing studies suggest two possibilities for reducing aggression in society. One possibility, to be inferred from the research of the social-learning theorists, is that we will have less violence if we create learning conditions less congenial to learning violence. Thus we might want to reduce the number of aggressive models in the mass media and create a system of rewards that favors cooperative, as opposed to aggressive, activities. We could, for example, incorporate some of the suggestions Skinner (1948b) offered for creating a utopian society. In the family, for instance, nonaggressive behavior could be rewarded but reinforcement would not follow aggressive acts. Again we should remember that punishment following an aggressive act may be particularly ill advised for use in this context.

A second set of possibilities for reducing the level of aggression within our society is to be inferred from the frustration-aggression hypothesis. Simply put, if we can remove or weaken frustrations that are likely to be accompanied by aggression-eliciting cues, aggression should decrease. Certainly it is difficult to envision a world that does not include for everybody a number of hurdles, stumbling blocks, and dead ends. On the other hand, there would seem to be a number of frustrations that are systematically applied to selected segments of our population. Here I am referring to the discriminatory practices that keep minority-group members from reaching goals supposedly available to everyone.

One final problem: how do we reeducate our present-day fellow Americans so that there will be fewer crimes of violence? They have had years of learning to respond violently when certain cues are present. Here, I think, some of Berkowitz' contributions are of particular interest. Perhaps we can try to identify and minimize the number of aggression-eliciting cues, such as weapons (Berkowitz & LePage, 1967). In a sense, an aggressive response that is never emitted is as little a problem as an aggressive response that has never been learned.

CONCLUSIONS

In this chapter our discussion turned to three directions a person's behavior may take when he is allowed the opportunity to contact another. First, he can move toward another and seek to establish friendly contacts. Second, he can move with another and coordinate activities for mutual rewards. Third, he can move against another, behaving in such a way as to inflict harm.

The antecedents of movement toward others have been sought in enduring personal characteristics, passing needs, and the behavioral requirements imposed by specific situations. The antecedents of the relative attractiveness of different people have been sought in interpersonal contact and in the interrelationship of the characteristics of friends or mates. First, it is clear that repeated contact with another person can contribute to raising his or her attractiveness, although we cannot expect each and every contact to lead to this result. Second, the best evidence suggests that people will be attracted to those who are similar to themselves, although the degree of similarity of friends may be overestimated because of errors in judgment. Finally, the apparent differences of people may contribute to mutual attraction if these differences satisfy complementary needs.

Movement with another involves the coordination of activities for mutual satisfactions. This movement together is called cooperation. In the discussion of cooperation, we first turned to a general approach to social interaction developed by Thibaut and Kelley. Highly compatible with this approach is research on behavior in the context of experimental games. These games provide one technique by which complex interpersonal processes can be examined in a rigorous and methodical way. Experimental-game research has produced a rather bewildering array of findings, but there are certain seeming consistencies within the overall pattern of results. First, it would appear that some people have a measurable cooperative orientation, which is reflected in an experimental-game situation. Second, people are more likely to cooperate with their friends, but only if their friends are willing to cooperate in return. Third, unconditional cooperation on one person's part does not necessarily elicit reciprocal cooperation from the other person. Instead, the development of cooperation between two people is apt to be a slow process during which each party must influence and adapt to the other.

Movement against another is a form of aggression. Aggression is a complex phenomenon, for many psychologists believe that it can appear in some heavily disguised ways. An important hypothesis, once endorsed by psychoanalysts and experimental psychologists alike, is that frustration, or the thwarting of goal-directed activity, leads to aggression. However, this hypothesis has some very severe limitations, since it does not account for individual or cross-cultural differences in reaction to frustration or for the form that the aggressive activity takes. It is necessary to look beyond the frustration-aggression hypothesis to learning variables.

It has been clearly demonstrated that exposure to aggressive models will increase the likelihood of aggression and that aggressive behavior, like so many other forms of behavior, gains strength and direction by the application and withdrawal of rewards. Thus recent theorizing suggests that aggression is a learned response that is elicited by specific cues, such as those provided by an aggressive model or those to be found in many of the situations that we consider frustrating. Frustration itself may have the motivational effect of strengthening an aggressive response once it has been tenuously elicited by the appropriate cues.

13.
Behavior
in Small
Groups

The British Secret Service was in the business of turning out agents and operatives (spies and saboteurs) for duty behind enemy lines in World War II. Since there was no lack of volunteers, they could afford to be quite selective about those chosen for field assignments. To ferret out the most promising candidates, all nominees underwent extremely rigorous testing. Some of this testing involved actual field problems (such as getting across a river without getting wet) given to teams of candidates for solution. The groupstacle (group obstacle) course, described by Morgan (1957), required that a team of six men carry a 10-foot log over a 400-yard area. It was necessary to move the log over a 10-foot-high wall, under a heavy tarpaulin stretched on the ground, over a tree branch 20 feet off the ground, and across a deep, muddy stream. The time limit was 45 minutes.

The course record Morgan reports was 4 minutes 16 seconds. In highly efficient teams there was enthusiasm, good humor, loyalty, and friendship. Success and satisfaction were the rewards for membership. Other, less coordinated teams could not finish within the allotted time. In these teams there was hostility, distrust, and dissension. Frustration and disappointment were the rewards for participation. Let us now turn to the study of behavior within small groups such as these six-man teams.

A group consists of a collection of people, each of whose behavior is highly dependent on the behavior of the others. This interdependence means that each person's rewards and satisfactions are contingent not only on his or her own behavior, but on the behavior of other group members as well. Each person has a part to play—a part that must be coordinated with the parts to be played by the other group members. When each member fulfills his part correctly, the group functions smoothly and produces favorable outcomes for all. In most groups the members are highly aware of each other and to some extent appreciate that everybody's behavior and outcomes are highly interdependent.

A group consists of a collection of people, each of whose behavior is highly dependent on the behavior of the others.

Small groups are distinguished from larger groups on the basis of the chances each member has for face-to-face interaction with each other member. For a group to be considered small, everyone within the group must have the opportunity to interact on a personal, face-to-face basis with everyone else. Although small groups can be distinguished from each other in a number of ways (size, performance, announced objectives, composition in terms of the members' ages, sex, backgrounds, and so on), it would appear that there are several processes that operate in similar ways in many different small groups. Here we will consider the flow of communication within the small group, the differentiation of group members and the emergence of leaders, the forces that bind group members together, and the effects of group membership on performance. The study of such small-group processes is called **group dynamics.**

COMMUNICATION

Communication may be defined as the transmission of information and affect from one organism to another. It is the most basic process within a group, since all other processes depend on it.

Human communication rests heavily on the spoken language and generally takes place through the exercise of learned verbal skills. Communication through speech is referred to as **overt** communication. The importance of language and the tremendous premium placed on it in our culture have been stressed earlier in this text (Chapters Six through Eight). However, our heavy emphasis on the content of spoken and written communication may make us insensitive to alternative modes of communication. These other modes are referred to as **covert communication.**

Covert Communication

Covert communication provides what is called in common parlance "vibrations" or "vibes." Psychologists are more apt to describe it, however, as the transmission of information by postures, gestures, and tenor of voice. On occasion, covert communication provides the only source of information available. Della Femina (1970), for example, describes advertising salesmen's concentration on smiles, grimaces, attention, and inattention when trying to evaluate the receptivity of potential but silent customers. More typically, covert communication is coupled with overt communication. In some cases postures, gestures, and tenor of voice enhance and add to the spoken words; in other cases they seem to express thoughts and feelings that contradict the spoken words.

Forms of Covert Communication

Three major forms of covert communication are proxemic, kinesic, and paralinguistic.

Proxemic Communication. How people space themselves with respect to one another can serve a communicative function. **Proxemic communication** refers to this transmission of information via spatial arrangement. For example, you can communicate one thing to the door-to-door salesman by standing clear of

Covert communication is the transmission of information by postures, gestures, and tenor of voice.

the doorway once you have opened it and another thing by physically blocking the entryway with your body.

Scheflen (1968) has examined proxemic communication within the context of courting. The person who sits close communicates something different from the person who sits far away. In the case of a couple sitting close, the approach of a second man may cause the first to shift his position so as to present a human wall between the woman and his potential competitor. For example, he may cross his legs in such a way that one shin forms an obstacle between the intruder and the woman. He is, in effect, saying "I am interested in you" to the woman and "Stay away" to the man. Although his positioning communicates both attraction and jealousy, none of the three may be consciously aware of his message.

Kinesic Communication.   The transmission of information through motions of the body and limbs is called **kinesic communication.** It includes such activities as waving, making threatening gestures with a fist, jumping to express excitement or joy, making faces, and making obscene gestures. Scheflen suggests that sexual interest may be expressed kinesically by changes in the body and repetitive or ritualistic motions. For example, when someone is sexually "interested," his torso becomes more erect, the potbelly is sucked in, slumping disappears, and the leg muscles tighten (a condition seen in "cheesecake" photos and associated with the professional model or athlete). Sagging facial muscles are tightened, and the complexion may become flushed or more pallid. The ritualistic motions take the form of preening: women check their clothing, makeup, and hair, and men may buff their shoes on their trouser legs, pat their hair into place, and adjust their neckties.

Paralinguistic Communication. The transmission of information through the manner of speaking is called **paralinguistic communication.** It involves the tone of the voice and the rate of speech. Sometimes people speak in nice, round, pear-shaped tones; their voices exude strength and confidence. At other times you might notice people's voices trembling and soaring. They stutter, stammer, hem and haw, or possibly even lose coherence. Such faulty speaking can suggest stress or a lack of confidence. On the other hand, as Abrahamson (1966) notes, a "polished" presentation does not necessarily indicate confidence and conviction. Under trying conditions, an extremely polished delivery may only signify prior rehearsal.

Does Covert Communication Communicate?

Interest in covert communication has been reawakened by many humanistic psychologists, particularly those interested in encounter groups (Chapter Eight). Some of these psychologists suggest that overt communication, or the spoken language, often serves to distort or mask true feelings. By becoming sensitive to proxemic, kinesic, and paralinguistic cues, we can increase our awareness and understanding of others.

But is covert communication really useful, or is it highly limited, either because it is unreliable or because it is decipherable only by highly trained observers? Early research suggested that people could reach *agreement* about the significance of covert cues, but there was considerable doubt about whether people could draw accurate conclusions. However, approaching this issue experimentally is quite difficult, and the earlier studies on which these conclusions of nonaccuracy were based may have suffered methodological shortcomings. More recently it appears that people can accurately interpret covert communications. Thompson and Meltzer (1964) have found that subjects can judge emotion from facial cues, and work by Ekman and his associates (Ekman, 1964, 1965; Ekman & Friesen, 1969) has certainly produced encouraging results.

In one study, Ekman (1964) provided untrained subjects with action photos of a number of different people. He then played recordings of speeches by the same series of people. His untrained subjects proved fairly reliable at indicating who in the photographs was doing the speaking. To do so, they had to correlate the nonverbal cues in the pictures with the verbal cues on tape. In a later series of experiments, Ekman (1965) found that the head and face provide cues about the kinds of feelings a person is experiencing but do not impart much information about the intensity of the feelings. On the other hand, cues from the body transmit information about the intensity of the feelings, although little about their nature. In combination quite a bit of information is transmitted.

Movement of the limbs and facial expressions can actually give the person away. For example, when someone says "Glad to see you" (when he really isn't), a frown or look of distaste may briefly flash across his face. Some people seem particularly good at detecting these true-feeling leakages, even though the clue may last only a fraction of a second (Ekman & Friesen, 1969).

Communication Flow within the Small Group

Properties of the individual group members and properties of the group itself will determine the amount of communication and the direction of its flow within a group. We can almost visualize a group as a network of two-way radio stations. Some broadcast a great deal; some mainly receive. Some are linked by clear channels, but the channels between others are weak, full of static, or nonexistent. Some stations are given greater priorities than others. Let's now consider the development of **communication networks** among people who are meeting for the first time around a rectangular table in a meeting room.

Spatial Arrangement and Communication Networks

A very simple variable that will affect communication is propinquity, or closeness in space. It is simply easier to communicate with someone who is sitting in an adjacent seat or across from you than it is to communicate with someone who is seated far away (Sommer, 1969).

At a table, certain positions seem to be **high-talking seats**—that is, whoever occupies them seems to issue more than the average number of communications. There are also **low-talking seats**—that is, positions whose occupants tend to initiate fewer than average communications. High-talking seats may gain their distinction because they happen to be psychologically closer to the

A very simple variable that will affect communication is propinquity, or closeness in space.

other seats present than are the low-talking seats, or they may acquire their importance in some other way (like the throne at King Arthur's Round Table). In any event, people seem to have the ability to identify them. Research by Hare and Bales (1963) suggests that dominant personalities tend to choose high-talking seats, whereas less dominant people defer. This implies that people with the ability to influence others by means of verbal communications may select a position within the group that allows them to more easily exert their influence.

Social Status and Communication Networks

Social rank is also an important determinant of the flow of communication. People seen as influential or as of high status within the group issue and receive more communications than do people of lower status. In the discussion of leadership we will find that social status is reflected not only in the rate of communication but also in the content of communication.

It appears that, within a group, communications tend for the most part to be directed toward people of equivalent status. Hurwitz, Zander, and Hymovitch

(1960) studied communication patterns at a mental-health conference and found that high-status people did a lot of talking but tended to direct their messages toward other high-status people. Riley, Cohen, Toby, and Riley (1954) found something similar in a study of preadolescent girls. Results such as these suggest that people feel more comfortable communicating with equal-status people.

Communicating with people within their class, low-status people run less of a risk of being embarrassed or rejected. Higher-status people, by maintaining an "in" group that remains aloof and distant, do not risk their exalted positions. Police chiefs, doctors, and military officers, for example, generally refrain from self-criticism and try to give the impression that the situation is well in hand when they are talking to subordinates or clients, although they may be willing to wring their hands in despair when discussing the same points with their equals. Technical jargon may be useful here, for it allows high-status professionals to talk to each other while remaining indecipherable to outsiders.

When status boundaries are broken, it would appear that people of lower status seek the attention of higher-ups (Hurwitz et al., 1960). Perhaps this finding can be understood in terms of the **congruity principle.** The congruity principle and its ramifications are complex, but all you have to know here is this: things, such as people, can be ranked on a positivity or favorability scale. Assume that there are two people, one positive (high-status) and the other negative (low-status) and hence far apart on the positivity scale. According to the principle of congruity, if an association is formed between them (perhaps in this case initiated by friendly questions on the part of the low-status person), they will be drawn together in terms of their positions on the scale. The end result is that the low-status person will have his positivity or favorability raised, and the higher-status person will have his positivity or favorability lowered. Thus, assuming that the low-status person does not expect a rejection (which according to the congruity theory would propel the pair farther apart), he has everything to gain by attempting to associate with the high-status person.

Consequences of Communication Networks

The telephone company is justly proud of its elaborate communication network. If you wanted to call between San Francisco and New York but the direct lines were busy, it is quite possible that your call would be automatically shunted down to Los Angeles, up to Denver, down to New Orleans, over to Miami, and only then up to New York. The geographical origin of the call, the destination of the call, and the number of way stations involved make little difference to the cables, relays, and amplifiers making up the telephone system. On the other hand, the origin of a communication, the destination of the communication, and the number of way stations make a great deal of difference when the network consists of a number of people constituting a small group. Each of these considerations will affect the group's effectiveness and the levels of satisfaction experienced by its members.

The effects of various human communication networks and positions within them have been studied by Bavelas (1948, 1950), Leavitt (1951), and others (for example, Shaw, 1954, 1964). Typically in these experiments, small groups of five or so people are seated at a circular table and separated from each other by partitions. The experimenter establishes the communication network by dictating who may communicate with whom. For example, as a participant you may be able to pass messages to the person directly on your left, or any messages you intend for him may have to pass through other people first. In these sessions the goal is to solve problems that require a pooling of the information that the different members of the group possess. Many different types of communication networks have been constructed, each of which specifies how many hands a written message will have to pass through before it reaches the desired recipient. For example, in one five-person network called the circle, each person could pass messages to the two adjacent people. Messages designated for the other two people had to pass through the hands of one of these people first.

Leavitt (1951) is one of the investigators who varied the **centrality** of certain positions within small-group communication networks. Within a network a position is said to be **central** to the extent that a large proportion of messages must pass through it. In a five-man circle arrangement, no position is more central than another. Everyone can communicate directly with people in the two adjacent positions and with the people in the remaining two positions through only one intermediary. In more central networks, one position (which we will designate C) became increasingly important to the flow of communication, in the sense that the person in position C was required to handle an increasing number of messages, serving, so to speak, as a switchboard or clearing house. In the network that was most central of all, all messages between all group members had to pass through the hands of the person in position C.

Leavitt found that people seemed more satisfied in the less central networks, where they could independently communicate with one another without having

A position is said to be central to the extent that a large proportion of messages must pass through it.

to go through the person in position *C*. This was not true for the person in position *C*, who came to be identified as the leader and enjoyed his influence and importance. A later experiment (Cohen, Bennis, & Wolkon, 1962) extended these results. These investigators found that when a person was moved from a position of low centrality to one of high centrality, his satisfaction increased; if the person was moved from a position of high centrality to one of low centrality, his satisfaction dropped.

But what about the efficiency and effectiveness with which the assigned problems were solved? Although the less centralized networks were more satisfying to most group members, the early research suggested that the less central arrangements were less efficient. The same independence that made them satisfying inhibited their organization into a highly effective performing unit. In the Leavitt research the *least* centralized networks involved the passage of more messages and the making of more mistakes before reaching the solution.

However, the inferiority of less centralized networks would appear to depend on the task at hand. Shaw (1964) has persuasively argued that the centralized networks are more efficient when the task is simple and when the role of the person in the most central position is one of merely distributing messages. On the other hand, when the task is complex and requires a greater flow of messages, the less centralized networks show superiority. One possible explanation is that in the centralized network the person in the most central position becomes overburdened when there is a complex problem that requires the passage of many messages and a careful sorting of information. The less centralized networks can reduce the demands made on this person by allowing the exchange of messages directly or by developing a communication network that is more efficient for the task at hand than the network imposed by the experimenter.

In summary, the channeling of communication within the small group has implications for both member satisfaction and group efficiency. Centralized communication networks, in which one person serves as a switchboard and controls information flow, are less satisfactory to group members, presumably because they curtail personal independence. The exception is that the member in the most central position is highly satisfied because of his influence and status. More centralized networks, which are better organized, are more efficient when tasks are simple. When tasks are complex, the more centralized networks can prove less efficient, perhaps because the person in the central position cannot handle the burden placed on him.

SOCIAL DIFFERENTIATION AND LEADERSHIP

Placed together in a group, people engage in social behavior that distinguishes them from one another. This is the process of **social differentiation.** R. F. Bales (1950a, 1950b; Bales & Strodtbeck, 1951) has carefully observed this differentiation process within the small group. Rather than try to reduce social interaction to manageable proportions by applying constraints to his subjects (as the experimental-games researchers do by forcing their subjects to push buttons and as the communication networks researchers do by specifying who may communicate with whom), Bales attempts to reliably observe, quantify, and analyze the natural flow of communication.

The group under investigation comes into a room that is equipped with a one-way mirror. Observers in an adjoining room can see the subjects but cannot be seen by them. Sound is transmitted to the observers via an intercom.

Bales and his followers call the smallest decipherable unit of social behavior a **behavior act.** There are four broad classes of behavior acts, and each class

Placed together in a group, people engage in social behavior that distinguishes them from one another.

contains three categories. Thus all behavior acts can be placed into one of 12 categories. The classes of acts are organized in terms of the decreasing favorability of the interpersonal relations involved. Categories 1-4 show positive regard for the person (persons) toward whom the communication is directed. Categories 5-9 are emotionally neutral and include behavior acts relevant for the completion of a task confronting the group. Categories 10-12 specify behavior that signifies tension, disagreement, or hostility. Here are Bales' 12 categories:

1. Shows solidarity
2. Shows tension release
3. Agrees
4. Gives suggestion
5. Gives opinion
6. Gives orientation
7. Asks for orientation
8. Asks for opinion
9. Asks for suggestion
10. Disagrees
11. Shows tension
12. Shows antagonism

The observers behind the one-way mirror record each behavior act.[1] Typically they observe groups of strangers who have had no prior history of association with one another. Under these conditions the group is, of course, initially unstructured and without a leader. As the members begin to interact, the frequency, direction, and content of the communications begin to take on characteristic forms. Some people tend to be task oriented (emitting behavior that falls into categories 1-3 and 9-12), whereas others tend to be socioemotionally oriented (emitting behavior acts falling into categories 4-9). In the case of task-oriented members, activities are directed toward the objective task at hand ("Hey, you guys. Let's stop clowning around and see about putting out this fire!"). Socioemotionally oriented members direct their acts toward the social relations within the group. We find them intervening in disputes ("Let's keep it cool!"), helping people save face ("Well—uh—I think I can see Joe's point"), and in general trying to minimize tensions and ensure that everyone is happy.

Although we cannot expect a given person to act the same way in each group he enters, Bales and his associates have found that people have certain characteristic ways of acting in small groups. For instance, when individuals' behavior in a number of different small groups was compared, they showed a characteristic *rate* of participation that was maintained as they moved from group to group. That is, people who do a lot of talking in one group are likely to do a lot of talking in another.

Let's concentrate now on those people who for one reason or another talk more than others. The contents of their communications tend to fall into the task-orientation categories (suggestions, information, opinions). Many of their remarks are directed to the group as a whole, rather than to individual members.

When the different members are rated after the session, this type of high talker is seen as having contributed heavily to the discussion and having given useful guidance. If we define leadership as influencing and guiding others, an incipient leader has emerged, and his leadership is recognized by the group. In many, if not most, groups, two leaders will eventually emerge. One is the task leader, who provides ideas and helps the group achieve its goals. The other is the socioemotional leader, who maintains and improves human relations within the group.

Is a high rate of participation merely one symptom of a "commanding personality"? Or does a high rate of participation actually help to *produce* the leader?

[1] More than one observer is used so that reliability estimates can be obtained.

We have already seen that a person assigned to a position of high centrality in a communication network is more likely to be chosen as leader (Leavitt, 1951). Additional evidence that a high rate of participation provides a basis for leadership comes from Bavelas, Hastdorf, Gross, and Kite (1965). Four subjects were seated around a conference table, and each had before him an individual signal panel visible only to himself. The group was given a human relations problem to discuss. Each person was told that, if his individual comments were helpful, his green light would illuminate; if his comments were worthless or deleterious, his red light would illuminate. Using these signal lights as reinforcers, the experimenters were able to induce a person with a low rate of participation to contribute more and a person with a high rate to participate less. Next there was a session during which group members rated one another. Once again, high-talking participants were seen as leaders. But in this experiment the rate of participation was artificially manipulated, so that the personalities of the different people could not be responsible for their standing within the group. The leader was literally the man who was given the "go-ahead" for a high rate of contribution.

In this study the experimenter gave the leader-to-be the go-ahead. But in other instances the group itself may, by manipulation of social approval, encourage a person to participate more fully. As he does so, he may gain the social influence necessary to be considered a leader. We will consider this possibility again.

Leadership and Social Influence

Studies such as those just described suggest an interrelationship among rate of participation, influence, and rated leadership. **Leadership** has been defined in a number of ways, and certainly "social influence" is one of the most commonly used criteria (Gibb, 1969). Gibb agrees with Pigors' (1935) suggestion that the leader is differentiated from others in the group in that his "will, feeling and insight control others in the pursuit of a common cause," and Gibb argues that his own research supports this definition. The O.S.S. Assessment Staff, which was involved with the groupstacle course described at the beginning of this chapter, notes: "There was nothing novel in our conception of leadership. We thought of it as a man's ability to take the initiative in social situations, to plan and organize action, and in so doing to invoke cooperation" (O.S.S., 1948, p. 301; cited in Gibb, 1969).

Although leaders are differentiated from others in terms of influence, perhaps the term *influence* should not go unqualified.

Schjelderup-Ebbe (1922) identified the various hens in a flock and then observed their behavior toward one another. He discovered that every interaction between two hens took on a characteristic pattern. When there was conflict, one hen would peck at the other and the other would defer. After observing all the hens, it became apparent that they could be ordered in terms of the number of other hens that could peck them into submission. Some hens were highly effective, getting most of the remainder of the flock to defer. Others were highly ineffective, giving way to the onslaught of all others. Certainly the hen to whom all others deferred exerted the greatest social influence. Could we call this hen a leader?

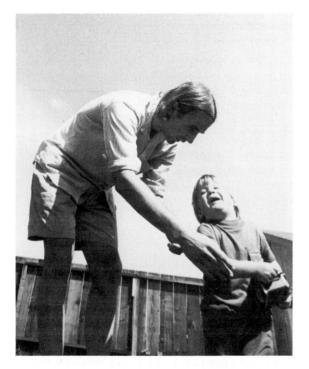

Leadership?

Gibb argues that not all social influence represents leadership. First, he notes that in a relationship such as that between master and slave, the unidirectional influence that the master exerts on the slave cannot be considered leadership. Leadership involves a *two-way* influence process. Although it is likely that the person regarded as leader will exert more influence on his followers than any individual follower will exert on him, the leader is to some extent responsive to the needs and demands of the followers. Second, Gibb insists that, in the case of leadership, the leader's influence is *voluntarily accepted* by the follow-

ers. That is, we must view leadership as something that the group confers on a
person by voluntarily accepting his influence and recognizing him as leader.
In the case of the hens we find a unidirectional influence and a lack of voluntary recognition on the part of other hens. Here it seems more appropriate to
speak of **domination** than of leadership. On the other hand, in many groups
of humans we do find a two-way interplay between leader and follower such
that the followers recognize and accept influence from a person who is sensitive to the needs and demands of the group.

Gibb's qualifications seem reasonable, for they seem to capture the spirit of
leadership as most of us think about it. Yet they also raise some fairly knotty
problems. When individual A induces individual B to do what he wants, is this
a case of leadership? Or is it a case of domination, such as in Schjelderup-Ebbe's
flock of hens? Sometimes the answer is clear, but at other times it isn't.

Small military bases, where there are perhaps one officer and a small number
of enlisted men (for example, radar outposts and small Coast Guard bases),
well illustrate this problem. Under relaxed conditions the officer deals with the
enlisted men on a first-name basis ("Look, Jim. We'd better overhaul that
engine because it's running pretty rough"), and the "orders" may be voluntarily accepted. Under less relaxed conditions the influence takes another form
("Seaman, you will overhaul that engine right now and that is an order!"). The
form of influence the officer exerts could represent domination, leadership, or
some combination of the two.

Origins of Leadership Influence

In the studies by Bales, influence seems to come from a high rate of participation in task-relevant or socioemotionally relevant classes. Certainly there are
other bases for influence as well. Some leaders may say only a little but be
quite able to make it stick. French and Raven (1959) note that a person may be
able to exert influence over a group because he has the ability to provide generous rewards, because he has a high level of expert knowledge, because he
has been appointed by a respected authority, or because he has coercive power
(which may not qualify as leadership influence).

A popular conception is that a leader is someone who has a general, all-around
ability to coordinate people and "get things done." In other words, leadership
is often seen as a gift of the individual that can make itself known in virtually

any situation. Thus a truly great leader should with equal facility be able to take over the helm at General Motors, become Head of the Joint Chiefs of Staff, assume the Presidency of the University of California, or become an effective Speaker of the House of Representatives. Early studies of leadership attempted to examine the attributes of the leader to see if he was bigger, stronger, or more sociable than his followers.

To many psychologists today, this "great man" theory of leadership is not necessarily true. It is becoming apparent that, although the individual's abilities do have some importance, they must combine with the needs and properties of the group to produce effective leadership. Consequently, the person who makes the best leader under one set of circumstances does not necessarily make the best leader under a different set of circumstances.

If we think of a leader as someone who has *somehow acquired skills* that will be of use to a *particular group in a particular situation*, perhaps the interrelationship of participation, influence, and rated leadership can be understood as follows. Let us ask ourselves under what conditions a group will encourage a person to talk. First, it seems likely that when a person has some knowledge about a task or problem confronting the group, he will be encouraged to speak out. Second, he is more likely to be rewarded for participating in the group discussion if he subscribes to group standards than if he deviates from these standards. Third, if he is kind and sensitive to others, people should be pleased to hear from him and hence reinforce his utterances.

There is evidence that people with expert knowledge are seen as influential or as leaders (Collins & Raven, 1969). There is also some evidence that people who subscribe closely to group standards are more likely to be considered important to the group than are people who deviate from group standards (Schachter, 1951). Finally, according to the "principle of supportive relationships" (Likert, 1961), effective and accepted small-group leaders tend to be more friendly, sympathetic, and understanding with subordinates than do less effective leaders. Thus it appears that people with leadership potential behave in such a way that others encourage them to talk. They then begin to exert a differential amount of social influence, which in turn defines them as leaders.

To specify the conditions for successful leadership, then, we might proceed by looking for the types of verbal behavior that a group is likely to reinforce. When this behavior is permitted and encouraged, its rate will increase, and the leader-to-be will be given the opportunity to exert his social influence.

COHESIVENESS

Some groups are absolute drags: nothing ever gets done, and meetings are boring. Other groups are effective and efficient and have a certain sparkle. The former groups provide an unappealing picture, whereas the latter are quite attractive.

Some groups are effective and efficient and have a certain sparkle.

Such differences in group spirit have been under consideration for well over a hundred years. One of the earliest interests was that expressed by militarists, who discovered that groups high in "spirit" or "morale" were more successful as fighting units than were loosely knit aggregates of replacements. Indeed, in this context group spirit has occasionally been endowed with almost magical properties. Certain generals of World War I, for example, mistakenly believed that "esprit de corps" could more than compensate for an enemy's immense superiority in firepower. Today few such illusions are harbored, but differences in group quality are seen as having important implications for the functioning of military and civilian groups alike. The term **cohesiveness** is now used to refer to the spirit or "groupiness" of a group.

Whatever we call it, however, the quality under consideration seems to remain spiritous in the sense that it is not very easy to pin down. Fortunately, Cartwright and Zander (1960, 1968) suggest that we can define the cohesiveness of a group in terms of the *attractions* that it offers to the members. That is, cohesiveness is the sum of all the attractions for all the members of the group. Cartwright (1968) notes that, given this definition, it is possible to measure cohesiveness in several ways. First, a high-cohesive group (which offers many attractions) should be rated more favorably than a low-cohesive group (which offers few attractions). Second, since some of the attractions are likely to come from association with other members in the group, people within a highly cohesive group should rate each other more favorably than would people within less cohesive groups. Third, since attraction should lead to involvement in the group, cohesiveness should also be measurable by asking group members how much they "identify" with the group—that is, how personally involved they feel with the group members and activities. Finally, cohesiveness should be measurable by asking the members how much they would like to remain in the group. Of course, the investigator could observe rather than ask. He could, for example, simply record the time at which group members left a meeting. A speedy departure would suggest that the group offered little in the way of attractions. Willingness or reluctance to remain within the group has been a common measure of cohesiveness.

Cohesiveness is a construct—just like "habit" or "personality"—but one that is used to account for group, rather than individual, phenomena. In Chapters Two and Nine we saw that constructs gain validity if they can be defined by a set of convergent operations. What this means in this specific case is that the construct of cohesiveness becomes valid if the various measures interrelate in such a way as to all point to the same direction. Thus in high- as opposed to low-cohesive groups we would expect more favorable evaluations of the group by its members, more favorable evaluations of the members by one another, a strong personal involvement in the group, and a reluctance to leave the group. This is indeed a tall order. How does cohesiveness stack up? Reviewing studies that have used multiple measures of cohesiveness, Cartwright (1968) concludes that the different measures do interrelate, although not very highly.

Cohesiveness is significant in two ways. First, since high-cohesive groups are considered "better" groups, they are of interest in themselves as end states. Thus the *antecedents* of cohesiveness are important. Second, since high-cohesive groups are more lively and have more sparkle than low-cohesive groups, cohesiveness itself may have implications for other group processes, such as productivity and problem solving. For this reason the *consequences* of cohesiveness are also considered important.

Antecedents of Cohesiveness

Important contributors to cohesiveness are the rewards and satisfactions that the group offers the individual members. In terms of drive-habit theory (Chapter Four), these rewards and satisfactions would reinforce participation in the group, and their effects should appear in such measures of cohesiveness as a high degree of personal involvement and a reluctance to leave the group. In expectancy-incentive terms, a group that provides more satisfactions provides more incentives for group participation. Thus Thibaut and Kelley (1959) theorize that, to the extent that the outcomes within a group are favorable, and to the extent that they are superior to the outcomes obtainable from membership in competing groups, the group will tend to be attractive to its members.

Several early studies (Exline, 1957; Marquis, Guetzkow, & Heyns, 1951) found a positive relationship between need satisfaction and "morale." More recently, Collins (1963) has reported that the perceived favorability of outcomes is positively correlated with cohesiveness. In the business setting, Ross and Zander (1957) found that employees were more likely to remain in an organization if they believed that their needs would be satisfied. Katz and Kahn (1966), describing the effects of different ways of organizing work groups within a coal mine, suggest that conditions which eliminate conflict within the group, allow members to pick their own associates, recognize and increase interdependence within the group, and provide an equitable distribution of rewards lead to increased cohesiveness. Each of these conditions, it may be argued, raises the group members' level of satisfaction. The conclusion to be drawn from this theorizing and from these studies is that the rewards experienced within the group contribute heavily to its cohesiveness.

The rewards a group offers its participants come from many sources, such as safety, friendship, prestige, and success. Cartwright (1968) suggests that the several sources of rewards for group participation may operate singly or in combination. For example, groups may provide important social and emotional rewards for the participants, sponsor activities that the participants find intrinsically satisfying, and serve as a means for achieving ends unattainable by any individual.

First, if a group is warm and friendly, it can prove a source of attraction by satisfying social and emotional needs of the individual members. Groups that feature this type of attraction would include those established for the unlucky in love and for people who have been stigmatized, such as by hearing loss or blindness, and who need special channels for satisfying their social and emotional needs.

Second, a group may be attractive because it engages in activities that the individual members find intrinsically satisfying. Hobby clubs fall into this category. For example, sports-car clubs can offer meets where members get to see new and exciting cars; they can hold rallies that prove to be exciting challenges to the individual members; they can have swap meets where two members can trade parts that they need for their respective cars; and they can provide a source of knowledge that members find useful when confronted with automobile-related problems.

Third, groups may prove attractive because they provide a useful means to ends that are important to each individual member but that cannot be attained by the efforts of any individual member alone. Groups can raise barns, sponsor cake sales for a worthwhile charity, or barrage the local Congressman with letters and petitions that are favorable or unfavorable to some impending legislation.

Although it seems pretty much accepted that the incentives or rewards offered to group members are an important antecedent of cohesiveness, other variables, such as cognitive dissonance, may also be significant. In Chapter Eleven we discussed experiments by Aronson and Mills (1959) and Gerard and Mathewson (1966) that showed that groups of *low* value were perceived as more attractive by subjects who underwent severe initiations to gain entrance. Of course, we do not know how much the subjects in these experiments would feel attracted to these worthless groups if the groups remained worthless over the course of several meetings.

Consequences of Cohesiveness

Using several techniques to vary cohesiveness, Back (1951) found that greater cohesiveness led to greater involvement in the work of the group, more attempts on the part of individuals within the group to exert influence on one another, and an increased acceptance of influence from others within the group. Perhaps it is the greater involvement and flow of influence that serve to increase conformity within the high-cohesive group. Festinger, Schachter, and Back (1950) found greater uniformity of opinion in more cohesive as opposed to less cohesive groups. You will recall that Schachter (1951) varied cohesiveness and observed group reactions to nonconformists. Rejection of the deviate was more striking under conditions of high cohesiveness.

Back's research suggests that cohesiveness encourages participation and give-and-take. The other two studies suggest that cohesiveness leads to greater conformity. In a sense, all three emphasize a greater coordination among group members. Does this greater coordination within high-cohesive groups lead to more effective problem solving and greater success at getting things done? Not necessarily.

Schachter, Ellertson, McBride, and Gregory (1951) brought together groups of girls and assigned them work. The experimenters varied the attractiveness (cohesiveness) of the groups by telling some subjects that the other members of their group were particularly likable and telling the other subjects that there was no particular reason why they should find the others within their group attractive. During the work session notes were passed to the girls. These notes called for either a work speedup or a work slowdown. The investigators hypothesized that in the cohesive groups, which should be characterized by a greater receptivity to influence attempts (Back, 1951), there should be greater receptivity to the attempts to influence them to speed up or to slow down. Results suggested a greater receptivity on the part of the high-cohesive groups, but only in the case of the message to slow down. Why did the high-cohesive groups not respond readily to the speedup communication? Subsequent research by Berkowitz (1954) illuminated this issue. In the experiment by Schachter et al., subjects in the high-cohesive groups were unable to increase production because they were already working at maximum speed! Berkowitz found that, by using another task at which a speedup was possible for high-cohesive groups, the speedup plea had the expected effect.

The greater sensitivity to group standards in high-cohesive groups obscures any clear relationship between cohesiveness and performance in the form of productivity. Standards may favor high or low productivity, and if they favor low productivity, high cohesiveness is a disadvantage as far as "getting things done" is concerned.

Norms of low productivity sometimes develop in the industrial work setting. The overall plan of the concern is high productivity, but this plan is thwarted when the standards of the work group call for low productivity. Apparently in these situations the workers believe that raising their productivity will place them in jeopardy, since management will discover that they *can* produce more and will then demand that they *do* produce more. After this fashion, minimal standards come to define maximum performance. In a low-cohesive work group, on the other hand, individual workers may decide to "go out for themselves" and impress management by producing more than their fellow-workers.

The relationship between cohesiveness and a group's ability to provide comfort for its members and remain organized in the face of attack is less obscure. Research by Seashore (1954; reported in Cartwright & Zander, 1968) suggests that members of cohesive groups are less likely to feel nervous or jumpy in group activities and more often find security and comfort in their group membership. French (1941) compared the reactions of unorganized groups of people who did not know one another (low-cohesive) with organized groups of people who knew one another and had worked together in the past (high-cohesive). Under conditions of frustration, the low-cohesive groups tended to split up. The organized groups did not split up and seemed better able to express their aggression and hostility. Such hostility in the face of attack may serve a useful function. Pepitone and Reichling (1955) found that following an attack from an outsider, high-cohesive groups were more able to express hostility than were low-cohesive groups. The expression of hostility in such a case is useful, for it allows the group to block or remove the attacker. Pepitone and Reichling suggest that, in high-cohesive groups, members provide one another with social support that allows them to express their hostility.

PERFORMANCE IN GROUPS

People working in groups often perform quite differently from people working alone. You have already seen some evidence of this fact in the earlier discussion of coaction (Chapter Five). There it was suggested that, when people work on individual, *independent* tasks that are easy for them, their performance benefits from the presence of others. But what happens when people work in a group on an *interdependent task*—that is, a task in which each one's performance affects progress toward an objective or a goal in which the whole group has a stake? When we consider people working together on an interdependent task, we are dealing with **group performance.**

There are certain potential advantages to banding together to get things done. First, there can be a pooling of individual skills and abilities. If the task involves manual efforts, there are simply more arms and legs; if it involves solving a problem, there are more heads, each of which probably contains at least a few good ideas. Second, there can be a division of labor within a group, such that each person works on only one small part of the overall project. Third, the group members can offer encouragement and support for one another. Fourth, in the group setting people can stimulate one another and coax forth new ideas. Finally, as Jones and Gerard (1967) observe, in the group

*There can be a division of labor within a group, such that each person
works on only one small part of the overall project.*

setting people may stop and think before they act, which would prevent them
from doing something rash or foolish. This factor could contribute to the overall quality of the group's product. Kelley and Thibaut (1969) cite a variety of
studies that suggest certain advantages to working in groups.

On the other hand, there are certain problems that must be surmounted if
working in groups is to be effective. One major problem is that of organizing
or coordinating the people within the group so that they can function as an
effective unit. The importance of organization was illustrated in two incidents
in my neighborhood that involved moving a piano from one home to another.
Each piano weighed between 800 and 1000 pounds. The first was moved by
eight straining and struggling friends who took about an hour to accomplish
the task. The second was moved by two professionals who delivered pianos
daily. It took them about ten minutes. The group of two professionals appeared
to be of about average brawn compared to the group of eight friends. The
difference in efficiency was due to the smooth coordination of efforts in the
team of professional movers.

For performance in a group to be efficient, rules for action must be formulated
and enforced. Each person must understand the task at hand, agree on a solu-

tion, and be willing to fulfill his part. Such organization is difficult and takes considerable time—time to communicate, time to resolve conflicts of interest, time to bring uncooperative people into line. Although the performance of a group can be impressive, the time and effort spent on organization must also be taken into account in any evaluation. Tasks such as piano moving *require* working in groups, but many jobs can be accomplished by *either* an individual or a group. In some of these cases a person may discover that it is quicker and more efficient to forget about committees and task forces and to tackle the task by himself.

The problem of organization is complicated by evidence suggesting that a high degree of organization within the group is not always an asset. Earlier in this chapter I described the effects of different communication networks. The more centralized or organized networks were more efficient at solving simple problems but less efficient at solving complex problems. Perhaps as the problems became complex, people in the key positions within the group became unable to cope with the burden placed on them.

Let us consider another factor that could make it difficult for a *highly organized* group to deal effectively with complex problems. Complex problems call for new and novel solutions. In a group—particularly a well-organized, cohesive group—there are pressures to conform. The flow of innovative and potentially successful solutions to problems can be constrained by pressures for conformity. Good ideas may be summarily rejected, or people may be afraid to offer them because they fear ridicule and rejection. Thus within a group conformity pressures may reduce the likelihood of hitting upon the most promising course of action.

Brainstorming represents an attempt to deal with the constraining effects of pressures for conformity. The aim of brainstorming is to elicit from the group as wide a range of ideas as possible. This is done by encouraging and approving the offering of any and all zany, bizarre, far-out possibilities. (In one brainstorming session in which I participated, a group of apparently anemic eraser-chewers devised a plan for a pencil with a chocolate-coated, vitamin-packed eraser.) Later the ideas resulting from brainstorming can be weighed, evaluated, and modified to fit the requirements of reality, but initially the group is supposed to impose no censoring whatsoever. Hypothetically, this procedure is particularly helpful in the organizational setting, where there are believed to be strong pressures for conformity and conservative courses of action. Osborn (1957), father of brainstorming, maintains that under brainstorming conditions people can think up twice as many ideas as they can when working alone.

Unfortunately, there is considerable doubt as to the effectiveness of brain-storming. Taylor, Berry, and Block (1958) gave problems to groups of four members and then compared their performance with that of four control individuals who worked on the problems alone. Subjects were asked to do such things as list the practical advantages or difficulties that would be encountered if we each had three thumbs, figure out ways our educational system could handle 50 percent more students, list the problems that would arise if people averaged 6'8" and weighed twice as much as they actually do now, and devise ways to coax more Europeans to visit the United States. The *control* subjects devised more solutions to the problems, and the quality of their solutions was adjudged higher. Dunnette, Campbell, and Jaastad (1963) gave problems for brainstorming to 48 research scientists and 48 advertising personnel employed by a large Midwestern firm. Again there was a superiority of individual performance. Although people in groups were supposed to brainstorm freely and without criticizing one another, the group setting seemed to exert a certain inhibiting influence. The findings of these two studies, which cast doubt on brainstorming as a technique for removing inhibitions and encouraging the offering of novel solutions, do not suggest that one man working alone necessarily did a better job than four men working together. What they do suggest is that, with the type of problems involved, the individual working alone performed more satisfactorily than did the individual working in a group.

In sum, although there are certain widely publicized advantages to working in groups, performance within the group setting may be impaired when there is a lack of organization or faulty organization and when group standards inhibit the flow of novel and perhaps useful ideas. Brainstorming, a popular technique sometimes used to deal with this latter problem, may not be effective.

When Are Two Heads Better than One?

The question "Which is better—the individual or the group?" is not an easy one to answer. But with reference to problem solving, Kelley and Thibaut (1969) have specified certain conditions under which the performance of the group will be *worse* than the individual performance of the best-performing member, about *equal* with the individual performance of the best-performing member, and *better* than the individual performance of the best-performing member. According to their analysis, the relative superiority of working in groups would seem to depend on the nature of the task or problem. Each of Kelley and Thibaut's points are supported by the results of experimental research, but here we will concentrate on the points themselves.

*Group Performance as Poorer than That
of the Best-Performing Member*

Fauchaux and Moscovici (1958; reported in Kelley & Thibaut, 1969) gave groups of subjects very complicated problems and compared their efficiency with that of subjects working alone. The distinguishing feature of these problems was that there were many possible solutions and many ways of approaching them; but once an approach was taken, it involved a complicated series of steps, each of which was based on the preceding one. The solution demanded consistency of approach and continual reference to earlier steps. The interacting group's performance was inferior to that of a collection of individuals.

In this experiment, Kelley and Thibaut point out, success required following a consistent strategy or approach. Since there were so many different approaches to the problem, it was difficult for the people in the group to reach agreement about the best way to proceed. Ideas offered by the different people tended to disrupt the ideas of the others. Thus, suggest Kelley and Thibaut, with very complicated problems that do not have one right solution, the group tends to handicap the most proficient members. Each member is trying to follow an intricate chain of reasoning, which becomes confused when someone else offers other ideas.

*Group Performance as about the Same as the
Performance of the Best-Performing Member*

Under certain conditions the performance of the group is at the same level as that of the "best" person within the group. According to Kelley and Thibaut, this will occur when there are few steps to the solution of the problem and when the solution, once offered, is easy for the other people in the group to identify.

Suppose you were with a group of prisoners held captive in the third story of a fortress. You have managed to loosen the bars in the window, and a very strong ship's rope has been smuggled in with which you can make your descent. The rope is 4 inches thick and can easily support 1000 pounds. But the descent to the ground is 40 feet, and the rope is only 20 feet long. The 20-foot drop is no solution, because if you weren't hurt seriously you would at least have a good chance of twisting an ankle and becoming an easy target for recapture.

Since the rope described is a big fat one, the solution is to unravel the rope's strands and put them back together in such a way as to make the rope twice as long but half as thick as it was originally. This is called an **insight** problem, for it requires viewing things in a new way—in this instance, seeing one fat rope as two skinny ropes. The solution provides an "Aha" or "Eureka" experience and, when found, suddenly becomes "obvious" to all.

Now back to the prisoners. Let's assume that each one will eventually derive the solution by himself but that it will take each one a different amount of time. The fastest figures it out in 20 minutes, the second fastest in 50 minutes, the third fastest in 70 minutes, and the slowest prisoner in 100 minutes. Individual performance can be expressed in terms of the average amount of time taken to derive the solution, which in this case would be $(20 + 50 + 70 + 100)/4$, or 60 minutes. But in the group setting the answer provided by the fastest thinker would be immediately accepted by all the others. All would, in effect, have the solution in the same amount of time as the fastest, which in this example is 20 minutes. Thus the average savings in terms of think-time-per-person is 40 minutes, and the slowest member of the group has saved 80 minutes. This extra 160 minutes of think-time-for-the-group can be quite useful for solving the next problem, which is how to get through the barbed-wire barricade along the beach armed only with Ping-Pong paddles.[2]

Since only one person can be the most proficient in the group, all other members profit when group performance is raised to be in line with his. Again, though, the preconditions noted by Kelley and Thibaut are that there are few steps to solution and, once found, the solution is easy for all members to grasp.

Group Performance as Better than That
of the Best-Performing Member

If no one has the complete solution but each person has something to contribute toward it, group performance can exceed the performance of any individual within the group. For example, in preparing an advertisement, one person may have a creative idea, another the skills to write effective copy, and a third the talent necessary to provide a good illustration. Together they could come up with a good product, whereas alone they might produce a poor product or nothing at all. Faust (1959) had subjects unscramble series of anagrams, or

---

[2] Use the paddles as shovels to dig a passage under the fence.

words in which the letters had been scrambled. (For example, Theda Bara, the name of an old-time movie heroine, was an anagram for Arab death.) After solving one anagram, the group could proceed to the next, but only then. Members of the group could thus pool their abilities and insights. One person could solve the first anagram but not the second, whereas someone else could solve the second but not the first. Hence in this experiment there was superior performance within the group setting. According to the Kelley and Thibaut analysis, this superiority of groups would seem to appear when tasks or problems can be broken down into a number of smaller subtasks or segments and when the various members of the group have different but complementary skills.

CONCLUSIONS

In this chapter the focus turned to some of the processes that go on between and among people who constitute a small group. Perhaps the most basic process of all is communication, here defined as the transmission of information and affect from person to person. Communication is accomplished overtly by the use of the spoken or written word and covertly by spatial arrangement, posturing, gesturing, facial expression, and tenor of voice.

Within a small group, communication does not proceed on a haphazard basis but flows along established channels. People tend to direct their communications toward people who are nearby and toward people of equivalent social status. Considerable research has focused on the consequences of various networks of communications channels. In the studies described here, researchers varied the centrality of certain positions within networks. Within these networks, a position is central to the extent that a large proportion of communications must pass through it, and a network is centralized to the extent that it has a central position. In general, people seem to be more satisfied with less centralized networks that allow them to freely communicate with each and every other member, rather than having to go through rigorously prescribed channels. The important exception to this is that in highly centralized networks the person in the most central position, who serves as a clearing house for messages, enjoys his position of influence and prestige. In terms of performance considerations, it would appear that, when the tasks confronting the group are simple, the more highly organized and centralized networks are more efficient for getting things done. On the other hand, when the task is complex and requires a heavy flow of communication, less centralized networks tend to be more efficient.

Next we turned to the topic of social differentiation and leadership. Bales and others have shown that, when people are put together in a group, they will behave in ways that distinguish themselves from one another. Some people participate more than others. Of these high participators, those who direct more communications to the group as a whole and issue more task-relevant communications will later be perceived as having greater influence and occupying a leadership role. In many groups two leaders eventually emerge: a task leader, who provides guidance and helps the group to attain its objectives, and a socioemotional leader, who tries to prevent or minimize interpersonal tensions and strife. Additional research suggests that participation leads to greater influence rather than merely being a symptom of a "commanding personality."

Gibb has persuasively argued that leadership can best be defined in terms of the differential exercise of influence. This argument is supported by findings that more influential people are more likely to be rated as leaders. The term *influence*, however, should not go unqualified, for when people use brute force to coerce compliance from others we do not think of them as leaders. Influence, in the context of leadership, is a two-way process. Although the leader may exert more influence over the followers than the followers exert over him, the leader is influenced by the followers' needs and demands, and the followers in effect confer leadership on an individual by voluntarily accepting his influence attempts. For a person to emerge as a leader, his abilities must combine with the needs and the properties of the group.

Groups vary tremendously in terms of quality. Cohesiveness refers to the "spirit" or "groupiness" of a group. It is generally defined in terms of the attractions a group has for its members. Cohesiveness appears to have its antecedents in the rewards or incentives the group provides for its members. These include social and emotional rewards, intrinsic satisfactions from engaging in group activities, and the attainment of goals that are not readily accessible to individual members. Cohesiveness also has important consequences. Cohesive groups are marked by a high rate of participation and strong pressures toward conformity. Perhaps largely because of this, the relationship between cohesiveness and the performance of the group is not simple. If the group's standards favor a high rate of productivity, a high-cohesive group may outperform a low-cohesive group. If group standards favor a low rate of production, cohesiveness may decrease the group's level of productivity. Finally, a cohesive group appears to be a strong group. Cohesive groups seem to better withstand external threats and stresses without disbanding. They are likely to react to threats by expressing hostility, which is useful because it allows the group to take action aimed at blocking or removing the attacker.

Finally, turning to the issue of accomplishing tasks and solving problems, we examined the relative superiority of the individual and the group. There are a number of reasons why one would expect groups to be more efficient and effective than individuals. Individual resources can be pooled, the task can be split up into manageable segments, group members can egg each other on, and the presence of others can have the beneficial effect of forcing each person to think before he acts. On the other hand, a great deal of time must be spent preparing a group to tackle a problem, and special care must be taken to ensure that conformity pressures do not keep important but unusual contributions from being offered. Because of these latter factors, it is necessary to think long and hard before enlisting a committee or task force to deal with an issue that might be handled by one person alone.

A question of special interest is under what conditions group performance is superior to individual performance. In an insightful analysis (we can only speculate as to whether they did this together or alone), Kelley and Thibaut (1969) suggest that, when the problem is very complex and cannot be mastered in a step-by-step fashion agreeable to all, the ideas interjected by the different group members disrupt others' chains of reasoning, thereby resulting in a level of performance below that expected from the group's best-performing member working alone. When the problem at hand requires few steps and the answers are easy to verify, group performance is likely to rise to the level of the best-performing member of the group. Finally, when each member of a group has something to contribute but no one person can provide a complete solution, the level of performance by the group will exceed that of the group's best-performing members.

14.
Psychology and Social Issues

My introductory science teachers always impressed me when they argued that science is *amoral*—that is, supposedly uninfluenced by value judgments. These days I am not at all convinced that science is, ever was, or should be amoral. I am *not* suggesting that the findings of scientific studies should reflect the prevalent fancies, biases, and misconceptions of the supporting society, for such "findings" would not be findings at all. For example, one government once hoped to discover that acquired characteristics could be transmitted genetically to subsequent generations. The useful implication was that, once a generation had been indoctrinated along official lines, indoctrination of subsequent generations would be simplified, since some tendency to behave in prescribed ways would be inherited at birth. However, genetics does not work that way, and no amount of wishful thinking or erroneous results can change that. Dogged pursuit of evidence to support a fanciful theory wastes resources and obscures a real understanding of any issue.

What I *am* suggesting is that the issues scientists address and the approaches they use reflect the needs, values, and interests of their society. Society dictates what kinds of research will be tolerated, encouraged, or generously rewarded, and research results are frequently taken into account when projects and policies are planned.

Some people labor under the impression that research (the careful analysis of a problem) and relevance (importance for real people living in a real world) are mutually exclusive. Perhaps this is because careful researchers tend to be conservative, in the sense that they do not promote each new finding as a cure-all for the nation's ills. But as we have seen in preceding chapters, carefully controlled experimentation can either immediately shed light on the problems of interest to all of us or provide a body of knowledge that later

437

proves to be highly useful for this purpose. As an example, consider that the "academic" psychologists who in the 1920s and 1930s identified the basic phenomena of learning provided a basis for principles now being used to help people leave mental hospitals.

Psychologists, as professionals and as members of society, are concerned with problems of society.

Much of this text has been concerned with topics such as conformity, socialization, personality, abnormal behavior, attitudes, attraction, cooperation, aggression, communication, leadership, and group performance, all of which have implications for both the individual and society. Each of these topics is time honored, and many have proven relevant since the dawn of history. In the present chapter we will turn to some of the research and theory that have developed as a result of highly contemporary social issues. There are two main reasons for the recency of these developments. First, the behavior in question may have only recently been identified, as in the case of people's reluctance to help a stranger in distress. Second, the behavior in question may have been with us for quite some time but only recently been defined as "problem" behavior because of a change in society's values. War, for example, has been with us for quite some time, but recent years have seen a growing appreciation that it involves considerably more in the way of destruction, hardship, and death than in the way of prancing around in a fancy uniform.

RESPONSIBILITY FOR OTHERS

Are you your brother's keeper? How often have you found yourself in situations in which your behavior affected the fate of someone in distress? The last decade has seen a growing interest in identifying the conditions under which a person will offer another aid, stand idly by, or add to the distress.

Assuming Responsibility

You have probably heard stories in the tradition of the little Dutch boy who sacrificed himself by keeping his finger in the dike so it wouldn't break and drown others. On the other hand, perhaps you have also heard stories in the Kitty Genovese tradition. In New York City in early 1964, Miss Genovese was stabbed to death, slowly and brutally, over a half-hour period. Although many people watched the murder from their apartment windows, not one went out to help or even phoned the police.

Why do some people help others? Why do some people refuse to help others? This is a salient issue in contemporary psychology.

The Effects of a Helping Model

Earlier you read that aggressive models can encourage aggressive behavior. It should come as no earth-shaking announcement to read that models who help, rather than hurt, other people can encourage **helping behavior.**

In a study by Bryan and Test (1967), a woman was stranded by the side of a busy street, standing next to a car with a flat tire. The trunk of her car was open, and next to it was an inflated spare tire. Under one set of conditions approaching motorists first passed another stranded car. At this site was a man who was helping a woman by changing the tire. Under control conditions approaching motorists did not pass this helping model. About 60 percent more motorists stopped to offer help under conditions in which the tire-changing scene had been earlier encountered.

Models also seem to affect people's willingness to help the financially needy. In a further study by Bryan and Test, researchers were located in a shopping center near a Salvation Army kettle. They recorded the number of people dropping donations into the kettle under two different conditions. In one condition a model offered a donation in plain sight of potential contributors; in the other there was no such model. Where the donating model was present, 69 passersby dropped donations into the kettle; under control conditions only 43 donations were made. A later study (Wagner & Wheeler, 1969) demonstrated that, whereas helping models encourage this type of helping behavior, non-helping models discourage it. In this study Navy men were asked to make a contribution to a worthy cause. In one condition subjects first heard a model agree to make a substantial contribution; in another condition (control) subjects could not hear the model's response when the contribution was solicited; in a third condition subjects heard the model clearly refuse to make a contribution. Subjects exposed to the generous model made larger contributions than control subjects, and control subjects made larger contributions than subjects exposed to the model who selfishly refused to make any contribution whatsoever.

The speed with which a helping model offers help also seems to be of some importance. Research by Piliavan, Rodin, and Piliavan (1969) suggests that in a continuing stress situation (involving a person who is unable to rise from the floor of a subway car), a helping model who appears on the scene promptly will elicit more helping behavior from bystanders than will a helping model who appears some time after the emergency begins. It is nice to know that one is likely to make out well in an emergency if a Johnny-come-quickly helping model is on the scene. But, of course, when help is needed, usually someone other than an experimenter's accomplice has to be the first to offer.

Group Size and Helping Behavior

Each year sees many, many murders in New York City. The slaying of Kitty Genovese became sensational because of the large number of people (38) who witnessed it but did nothing. It seems reasonable to hypothesize that the larger the number of people who *could* come to someone's help, the more likely one or more *will* try to help. In effect, this woman had at least 38 chances for life, but not one paid off. But perhaps she would have been better off if there were fewer witnesses.

Darley and Latané (1968) brought subjects into the laboratory to take part in a group discussion. Although the sizes of the groups varied, each participant was stationed in an individual cubicle and the discussion took place through

Perhaps a person in distress is better off if there are few witnesses.

an intercom system. During the discussion the experimenter did not listen but was stationed near the cubicles. Before the experiment began, one of the participants (a confederate of the experimenter) indicated that he had health problems and might have a fit or a seizure.

During the discussions the confederate did indeed seem to have a "seizure," which was clearly heard by the real subjects as he monopolized the intercom. The seizure began mildly with gagging and gasping but became increasingly severe until the "victim" lost coherence. Darley and Latané were interested in just how far the simulated seizure would have to progress before one of the real subjects sought out the experimenter to report the emergency. They found that, as the size of the group increased, it took longer for someone to leave his cubicle in search of help. There was, then, a negative correlation between the number of people who *could* offer help and the likelihood that a given individual *would* offer help.

Latané and Darley (1969) have described a number of other studies, all of which point to this type of conclusion. In one study it was found that people in groups are less likely to report a liquor-store robbery than was a solitary witness. In another study, by Latané and Rodin (1969), subjects overheard a woman injure herself in an accident. Although 70 percent of the solitary subjects intervened, only 40 percent of the groups of strangers contained even one person who went for help.

Why should people be less willing to come to the aid of another when other bystanders are present? A popular interpretation of the Genovese incident was that people are becoming apathetic—that is, emotionally withdrawn and indifferent to the events around them. The Genovese murder was seen as another symptom of a cold, impersonal, and uncaring society. Latané and Darley do not agree with this explanation. They point to evidence that most people seem concerned with the welfare of others. Also, they note that dealing satisfactorily with an emergency is a very complicated task, and many factors will influence the decision to help and the efficiency with which help is carried out. One factor is likely to be social norms—norms that, in our society, encourage people to "play it cool" and "mind their own business." The more people present, the stronger these norms and the more likely risking "losing your cool" by taking action will elicit adverse reactions from others.

A second possibility (which is by no means excluded by the first) is that, as the number of bystanders increases, each individual will become less likely to act because of **diffusion of responsibility** (Darley & Latané, 1968). That is, the personal responsibility felt by each person may decrease. The attitude forms that "someone" (else) will help the poor victim. Since all the witnesses are likely to develop the same attitude, no help is forthcoming. On the other hand, if the witness believes he is the only one who *can* help, he cannot so easily evade his responsibility and therefore *will* help.

The results of additional investigations have suggested that the relationship between group size and helping behavior can be complicated by additional variables. As mentioned earlier, Piliavan et al. (1969) studied people's willingness to help someone who was unable to rise from the floor of a subway car. They found that a sick victim was more likely to receive help than a drunkard, that men were more likely than women to aid the fallen man, and that there was some tendency for the victim to receive help from a person of the same race. They did *not* find a strong relationship between the number of witnesses and the speed of helping but correctly note that there are several ways to account for the difference between their results and those reported earlier by Latané and Darley. An evaluation of the merits of the different reconciliations awaits further research.

Staub (1970) examined the reactions of children who, either alone or in pairs, heard another child in distress. These children were from kindergarten, first, second, fourth, and sixth grades. Helping behavior increased between kindergarten and second grade but decreased between second and sixth grades. It is possible that the initial increase in helping behavior resulted from an increasing ability to recognize and appreciate that someone was in need of help and that the subsequent decrease resulted from the development of inhibitions through the learning of social norms to remain uninvolved. Indeed, some subjects felt that, if they left the room to get help, it would anger the experimenter. In another study (Staub, 1969) children were explicitly given permission to behave in ways that could secure help, and helping behavior increased.

Staub (1970) also found that children in *pairs* were more likely to help than were children alone. However, this result does not necessarily conflict with the findings of Latané and Darley. First, Staub used children as subjects, and, as we saw in Chapter Six, people's behavior changes with age. Second, in Staub's experiment the children knew each other, whereas in many helping experiments the subjects assembled into groups of two or larger were initially strangers. In the presence of a friend as opposed to a stranger, it may not be quite so important to mind one's own business. Evidence to this effect has been secured by Latané and Rodin (1969), who found that groups of friends were more likely to help an apparently injured lady than were groups of strangers.

Yielding Responsibility

Many people object when someone abandons his personal principles and convictions because of social pressures—especially when those principles represent important moral rules (for example, the Ten Commandments). Those of us who prize personal freedom are repulsed by the idea of a society composed of people who routinely ignore personal scruples and comply with the demands of a dictator. A good example is to be found in Orwell's book *1984*, which describes a society in which people obey the numerous and imposing demands of one Big Brother.

Could our society develop into a collection of automatons? Certainly one variable affecting this likelihood would be the extent to which Americans are willing to yield self-determination and comply with objectionable demands—that is, to practice **obedience.** Here we will consider how obedience can result in behavior that violates the internal standards that hold us responsible for not harming one another.

Milgram (1963) placed advertisements in a newspaper to seek participants for a paid psychological experiment. When each subject arrived at the scene of the experiment, he found another subject waiting. This "other subject" was, in fact, a confederate of the experimenter. It was explained to the pair that the experiment was concerned with the effects of punishment on learning. The confederate was told that he would be the learner, and the real subject was told that he would assist the experimenter by administering electric shock to the alleged learner. The learner, of course, did not receive electric shocks but had been carefully coached to pretend that he was undergoing pain and distress.

Wires were attached to the "victim," and the subject was seated before a fancy shock generator. This apparatus had switches for delivering 30 different dosages of shock, ranging from 15 to 450 volts. The switches for administering high voltages were given added meaning by means of dramatic labels such as "danger—extreme shock."

The learning task began, and, as the learner consistently either failed to respond or gave a wrong answer, the experimenter commanded that more intense shocks be given. If the subject followed orders and administered increasingly greater shocks, the victim began to complain, refused to answer, and finally made no response at all.

Obedience was defined as the amount of shock the subject would administer upon demand. Initially it was expected that few subjects would obey as the shock demanded became intense. However, Milgram found that all subjects obeyed orders up to 300 volts, the point at which the victim stopped responding. Five subjects stopped obeying at 300 volts. Four more subjects ceased following orders at 315 volts. Twenty-six of the 40 subjects (that is, 65 percent) obeyed to the end.

In short, these subjects, many of whom were respectable businessmen and professionals, were terribly obedient. They could not be called *blindly* obedient, however, because they were too well aware of what they were doing. Their actions suggested that they abandoned responsibility for the welfare of the victim, but other evidence showed that they remained sensitive to the violations of their consciences. Apparently this experiment produced a severe approach/avoidance conflict (Chapter Seven). The external demand was to go ahead and shock the victim, but the internalized standards of responsibility for others were telling them not to do it. It is not surprising, then, that Milgram noted many signs of nervousness during the experiment and clear signs of relief when it was over. Subjects were described as fumbling for cigarettes, mopping their brows, and rubbing their fingers over their eyes. During the experiment one man pushed his fist into his forehead and muttered "Oh God, let's stop!" and yet continued to the very end. Milgram described this same man as being reduced from a poised and cheerful businessman to a "twitching, stuttering wreck who was rapidly approaching a point of nervous collapse." (It is not clear, however, that the experimenters themselves felt such tensions as they cooly gave orders to the tense and unhappy subjects.)

Milgram's first experiment was conducted at a very prestigious university. Perhaps the subjects were willing to obey for this reason. Discussing their obedience, some subjects noted that, since the experimenter was affiliated with the university, he must be competent, well meaning, and of high integrity. To examine this factor, Milgram (1965a) duplicated the study but within the setting of a sparsely furnished suite in a run-down building located in a nearby industrial town. Despite the fact that the experiment was no longer visibly connected with a prestigious university, obedience was not decreased.

Factors Decreasing Obedience

Because the procedures of Milgram's experiments were stressful for his subjects, his research was considered by many to be cruel and inhumane. On the other hand, obedience is a phenomenon of real concern, for it can lead to the commission of atrocities "with regret" but as commanded by authorities. It is important to discover the conditions under which obedience is decreased and reliance on internal standards and convictions is increased.

Milgram (1965a) thus set out to examine some of the conditions leading to *dis*obedience. In earlier experiments he had observed that some of his subjects had been quite reluctant to look at their victims. This finding suggested that it might be more difficult to follow orders if the victim were brought close.

Milgram thus created four experimental conditions, in which the subject was brought increasingly closer to the victim he was punishing. In the *remote feedback* condition the victim was placed in another room and could not be seen or heard by the subject, although at 300 volts the victim pounded on the wall. In the *voice feedback* condition the victim's complaints could be heard. In the *proximity* condition the victim was only 18 inches from the subject as the shock was administered. In the *touch proximity* condition the victim was again 18 inches away, but this time the subject was commanded to press the victim's hand down on the electrode so that he could be properly shocked. Results showed that, as the victim was brought closer to the subject, there was greater refusal to comply with the inhumane orders.

The physical presence of the experimenter was also very important for continuing obedience (Milgram, 1965a). Subjects were most obedient when the experimenter sat just a few feet away, less obedient when orders were given over a telephone, and least obedient when the demands to increase shock were presented via a tape recording. Furthermore, when the experimenter was not physically present, subjects sometimes administered lower shocks than ordered but did not admit this to the experimenter. Apparently such "cheating" was an easy way to reconcile the experimenter's commands and the conscience's demands. Finally, as in other conformity studies, further research (Milgram, 1965b) showed that, when there was group support for disobeying, obedience was decreased.

INTERGROUP RELATIONS

Two or more groups, like two or more individuals, can "move together" and cooperate for mutual advantage. When this type of **intergroup relationship** prevails, acceptance, goodwill, and comfort are generated. This happy state of affairs can be identified in the relations of groups of all sizes. We find it when two couples go out to dine and when two nations jointly sponsor mutually important projects.

Two or more groups, like two or more individuals, can also "move against" each other and conflict. When this occurs, mistrust, suspicion, and ill will are generated. Alas, this state of affairs can also be identified in the relations of groups of many different sizes. We can find it in neighborhood feuds, prejudicial and discriminatory practices within a community, and open warfare among nations.

When intergroup relations are tense or conflict laden, they become important issues to both the individual group members, who are likely to be the victims of the conflict, and to the society, which is charged with ensuring harmony among its various factions. Let us now consider some of the conditions that either foster or relieve intergroup tension and conflict.

A salient issue in psychology is the discovery of techniques by which interpersonal and intergroup hostility and tensions may be reduced.

The Sherif Studies: Creating and Eliminating Conflicts among Small Groups

Considerable insight into the development and reduction of intergroup conflict has been provided by a series of studies by Muzafer Sherif (reported most recently in Sherif & Sherif, 1969). Sherif took a historical approach, observing the whole process of group formation, the development of intergroup conflict, and the reduction of that conflict. His subjects were groups of preadolescent boys who did not know they were being studied while they attended a summer camp. Initially the boys were strangers to one another. All were described as normal preadolescents from roughly similar backgrounds. Sherif thus ensured that preformed friendships or prejudices would not enter into the results and that the boys' behavior would be relatively typical. Three experiments were conducted in different years and in different locales and hence varied in certain ways, but the basic procedures and findings were quite similar.

In the experiment emphasized here, there were three parts. Each part involved the manipulation of rewards, or, in Thibaut and Kelley's scheme, outcomes

(Chapter Twelve). In the first phase Sherif created conditions to form two sets of previously unacquainted boys into distinct, cohesive groups. In the second phase he created conditions encouraging conflict between the two groups. In the third phase he attempted to replace conflict with an atmosphere of friendly intergroup cooperation.

Formation of Groups

A precondition for studying intergroup conflict is to form two groups to conflict. Sherif hypothesized that this could be accomplished by placing the boys in contact and then offering them "fun" activities that required coordination of efforts for successful completion. Two collections of boys arrived at the camping region, each unaware of the other's existence. They were then given the chance to camp out in the wilderness away from the base camp, but the stipulation was that they must take the initiative and assume responsibility for the success of the project. They had to become organized to pitch camp, cook, and perform other campsite duties. This highly attractive "fun" activity thus involved the coordination of efforts to reach mutual goals.

This project did indeed have the anticipated effect. Boys began expressing interest in and friendship for the other boys within their group. As in Bales' laboratory studies (Chapter Thirteen), Sherif found a differentiation of members followed by an emergence of leaders. Group standards developed, and there were conformity pressures to obey these standards. Sherif and Sherif reported several indicators of "group identity," including special jargon, ingroup jokes, special nicknames for group members, and rather fierce names such as "Rattlers" and "Eagles" for the groups themselves. By several measures, cohesive groups had been developed.

Creation of Intergroup Conflict

The boys formed into groups when the best rewards came from cooperative activity. Sherif next hypothesized that intergroup conflict would be induced if the two groups were brought together under competitive conditions in which both groups were striving for rewards that only one group could attain. Thus a series of games and contests was arranged in which each group competed for points, which the ultimately winning group could later redeem for handsome prizes. To remind each group of their standing, total scores were posted daily.

Rivalry was heightened by ensuring that the two groups' scores were kept very close and by additional techniques that stressed the competitive nature of the two groups. For example, the experimenters provided refreshments for a joint meeting of the two groups and then arranged it so that one group arrived first and hogged all the desirable refreshments, leaving only the dregs for the other group.

Once conditions were created so that only one group could gain, tensions mounted quickly. Each group derogated the other (meanwhile singing praises of themselves), and the members of each group were reluctant to voluntarily associate with the members of the other. The intergroup contacts that occurred were marked by open conflict, including name calling, garbage hurling, and raids on each other's camps. In one instance, disturbingly similar to an international arms race, one group assembled green apples for ammunition "just in case" the other group attempted an attack.

Elimination of Conflict

In accordance with the theory that the distribution of rewards is an important contributor to intergroup relations, Sherif hypothesized that conflict could be eliminated if each group were offered rewards for cooperating with the other. He therefore established **superordinate tasks**—that is, tasks highly important to each group but requiring mutual cooperation for completion. For instance, since the camp water supply was important to everyone, the two groups cooperated and searched for the breakage point after the water main broke. Similarly, after the experimenters arranged for a food truck to break down, a towline was attached and the two groups of boys literally pulled together for their awaited meal. Such cooperation on one or two superordinate tasks did not eliminate all the tensions, but cooperation on a *series* of such tasks resulted in a clear change in intergroup relations. Boys from the two groups began cooperating with one another even in the absence of a superordinate task. Friendships formed between the members of the two groups, and the groups took a certain amount of pride in doing favors for each other.

Kid Stuff?

Sherif's research suggests that, if conditions can be created so that members of two conflicting groups are compelled to work together to accomplish tasks of importance to both groups, there will be a reduction of intergroup tensions. But his investigation concerned preadolescent boys. Can his findings be applied to help alleviate conflicts among opposing groups of adults?

There are at least three lines of evidence suggesting that Sherif's results are of general applicability. First, the camp research has served as a model for dealing with labor-management disputes (Blake & Mouton, 1962; Blake, Shepard, & Mouton, 1964). After assembling representatives of the two sides into encounter groups, these researchers introduced superordinate tasks that led to the reduction of antagonism. Second, a reexamination of the interracial contact hypothesis (Chapter Twelve) seems to further bear out Sherif. You will recall that when blacks and whites ship together on a steamer, work together in coal mines or department stores, or fight a common enemy on the battlefield, interracial conflicts are reduced. In all these cases members of usually conflicting groups are working together to achieve common goals. Finally, in time of hardship, various normally opposing factions seem quite able to forget their differences and band together for survival. Describing life under the harsh conditions imposed by a concentration camp, Kogon (1960, p. 312) notes:

> Nationality, class, party and group ties exerted a crucial influence on the individual and collective attitudes of the prisoners toward one another. But all the differences were fused into a militant unity with but slight shades of differentiation when the camp stood against the SS (guards). . . .

Such observations suggest that it should be possible to discover superordinate tasks (hopefully other than those imposed by a common enemy) that would be helpful for reducing conflict between racial groups, pro- and antiestablishment groups, or even hostile nations. But this is no easy job. Glowing slogans such as "Let's work together for a better America" or "Let's move forward together" will not work. Sherif and Sherif (1969) argue that a useful superordinate task *must* clearly require cooperation, *cannot* be based on fancy talk, and *may not* be imposed by one group on the other.

International Tensions

If you are less than 35 or 40 years old, tense international relations have been a continuous part of life since your birth. The idea of a war that could result in all-out nuclear destruction has made people jittery and anxious, and in these days when a medium-sized conventional bomb costs far more than a home entertainment console, defense appropriations draw tremendous amounts of public funds away from other purposes such as school, hospital, and highway construction. Furthermore, varying theories concerning how to handle international tensions and crises have led to severe divisions within our own society.

Some days the international situation seems more relaxed than on other days, but for the most part at least a moderate level of tension prevails. Expensive weapons are continually developed and stockpiled, and no one seems particularly surprised when one pair of nations or another edge toward the brink of disaster. Let us now consider some psychologists' ideas about the causes and management of international tensions, using for illustration the relations between the United States and Russia. In some very important ways these two nations sometimes seem like two people making noncooperative responses in a Prisoner's Dilemma Game or like Sherif's Rattlers and Eagles after intergroup conflict had been induced. Both countries seem to have emphasized the goals that cannot be obtained by both sides simultaneously. These goals may be a piece of land somewhere or a "way of life" (Bronfenbrenner, 1961), which is far less tangible but perhaps far more important. A popular philosophy in *both* countries thus seems to be "Either we win and you lose, or you win and we lose."

Earlier (Chapter Twelve) I noted that the development of cooperation between two people is often a painstaking task in which each person attempts to influence and adapt to the other. The same may be true of the development of cooperation among nations. In the case of international relations, this process may have been made difficult by the views each side has developed of the other.

During a tour of the Soviet Union an American psychologist named Urie Bronfenbrenner (1961) used his fluent Russian to become intimately acquainted with the views of as many Soviet citizens as possible. He found that they were genuinely satisfied with their way of life and that they believed themselves to be a peace-loving people led by well-intentioned leaders. He also found that they seemed to have a very distorted view of America and Americans. His Russian acquaintances maintained that, although many of America's common people are decent and sensible, influential Americans are militaristic and warlike. They believed that many of America's common citizens despised their wicked government, which lied to them and exploited them. The American leaders, said these Russian citizens, were pursuing foolish and insane policies that could force the peace-loving Russians into an unwanted war.

Perhaps, like Bronfenbrenner, you detect a curiously familiar ring to these charges. This is because many of his Russian acquaintances had the same view of themselves that we have of ourselves and the same views of us that we have of them. Many Americans see themselves as a peace-loving people led by well-intentioned leaders. Many of us also maintain that, although the Russian people are decent, the influential Russians are militaristic and warlike. In our view it is the Russian leaders who lie to and exploit the people and whose foolish and insane policies could lead us down the road to nuclear disaster. Like Sherif's Rattlers and Eagles, each international "team" thinks of itself in glowing, favorable terms and of the other team in derogatory, unfavorable terms. By choosing illustrations carefully, each side can find specific examples to support their views. Bronfenbrenner referred to each side's view that "We are good and they are bad" as the **mirror-image phenomenon.**

The mirror-image phenomenon is reflected in the judgments we make of each other's actions. Since actions are in some ways objective (both the United States and the Soviet Union have been known to send troops into other countries), the differences in judgments are likely to appear in such factors as the suspected *motive* for the action. Thus, from our perspective, if we invade Wallonia, we are doing so to preserve the peace; if the Russians invade the same country, it is but one more example of their shameless intent to overrun the world. The tendency to think this way seems to appear fairly early in life. American schoolchildren, asked why Americans and Russians plant trees, responded that Americans plant trees for shade and beauty, whereas Russians plant trees to hide the view and to make work for the prisoners.

Oskamp (1965) identified 50 actions, both friendly and hostile, that had been taken in recent years by *both* the United States and Russia. He listed them in two different questionnaires. In one the actions were attributed to America; in the other, to Russia. American college students then evaluated how favorably they felt about the American and Russian actions. The same actions were far more likely to be rated favorably if the United States was described as the instigator than if Russia was described as the instigator.

Bronfenbrenner notes that the mirror-image phenomenon makes communication and negotiation difficult. Each side views the other as untrustworthy. Hence each reacts by being tough (so as not to be tricked), and the other side reacts in kind. What can be done to break the stalemate? As Osgood (1962) notes, from World War II through the early 1960s, thought on this issue was largely dominated by two alternatives, one militaristic and the other pacifistic.

The tough, militaristic stand, based on the assumption that all-out war was eventually inevitable, involved starting the war ourselves, slugging it out, and letting the winner (presumably us) take all. The idea was to carefully pick a time when the balance of power was most in our favor and then sock it to them before they could effectively sock it to us. With timing, secrecy, and luck, their casualties were expected to be greater than our casualties, and we would therefore be the winner.

Aside from ethical considerations and the ludicrous possibility of each side starting a war to prevent the other side from doing so, there are serious problems with the militaristic alternative. Even if it were possible to make preparations in secrecy, a sneak attack would provide little in the way of advantages, because each side possesses formidable "second-strike" capacities—that is, abilities to retaliate from underground bunkers, ships at sea, and perhaps even satellites after the homeland has been thoroughly pasted. Given the high expected casualty rates, it is unlikely that either side would be a "winner" in any sense at all.

The pacifistic, or "chicken," alternative involved total disarmament on our part, with the hope that the Russians would follow suit. (We would have to go first because we cannot control what they do.) The idea was that after we rendered ourselves defenseless, the Russians would be nice to us, perhaps because we would have finally proven that we are peace-loving and trustworthy or perhaps because of sheer good sportsmanship on their part. According to some proponents of this approach, even if Russia took advantage of a disarmed America, "Better Red than dead."

This alternative, like the first one, does not seem to provide much of a solution at all. As Osgood notes, there is no guarantee that, if one side disarmed, the other side would respect its interests and rights and scrupulously refuse to take advantage of the situation. Within each country there are many people who would not care to take such a chance and would seem to prefer death to a "sellout." This attitude is evident in the hostile reception that many Americans gave the "Better Red than dead" slogan. As Bronfenbrenner (1961) notes, although the differences between the two nations are sometimes more perceived than real, there *are* some real differences between our way of life and theirs; many of us feel strongly about our system, which gives the individual a great deal of freedom vis-à-vis the government. The result is a political climate within each country that makes a solution based on wholesale self-disarmament entirely unfeasible.

The Gradualist Approach

Osgood (1962) has offered a plan that he hopes will keep us from becoming *either* Red or dead. The name of his plan is *Graduated Reciprocation in Tension Reduction,* or **GRIT** for short.

International tensions have built up slowly over time as the result of incident after incident involving the threat and application of force. Osgood suggests that this process can serve as a model for its own reversal—that it should be possible to throw the international arms race into reverse gear. This feat can be accomplished by initiating and responding to actions that *reduce* tensions rather than increase them. He further suggests that the United States take the initiative by making friendly moves toward the Russians.

Osgood's approach is not the same as the usual pacifistic approach, for he insists that the series of events aimed at reducing tensions must be both *graduated* and *reciprocated.* By graduated he means that the initial steps should be small ones involving very minor risks, whereas later the steps toward a true peace would become increasingly more dramatic and pronounced. By reciprocated he means that each time one side makes a move toward peace, the other side must respond in kind.

According to GRIT, the tension-reduction process begins with the United States announcing and then initiating a few "low-risk" actions—that is, actions that could not be taken advantage of by the Russians in such a way that our national security or international commitments would be endangered. As Osgood describes it, these actions must not reduce our capacity to inflict punishment on any enemy that attacked us.

Some examples of such low-risk actions are the closing of useless but visible military bases, the sharing of secret medical information or information gained in space, and the lightening of restrictions that keep Americans from traveling and trading within Communist nations. Osgood argues that the steps taken must be *well publicized, real,* and *verifiable* and that the reasons why they are being taken made perfectly clear.

According to GRIT, once we take the initiative, it is imperative that the Russians *respond in kind.* Only then is it possible to take more dramatic steps. As each side continues to make more pronounced overtures, tensions should be reduced, negative stereotypes diminished, and the stage set for cooperation. But at every point appropriate steps must be taken to protect ourselves from attack, and the speed, number, and size of our friendly moves are gauged on the basis of the Russian responses.

Osgood recognizes that the implementation of GRIT is no simple matter, for it would have to be sold not only to the Russians but to those among us who would interpret the necessary friendly acts as concessions or signs of weakness. (In a fictional account of the progress of GRIT, Osgood described attempts to impeach the U. S. President.) He also concedes that building momentum for the tension-reduction cycle would be difficult in light of the history of U. S.-U. S. S. R. relations. After all, the United States did send a military expedition into Russia only three short years after the Bolshevik takeover, and the Russians did fail to restore self-determination to certain nations that they "liberated" during World War II. Osgood thus expects strong feelings within each country against making concessions to the other. Yet he persuasively argues that GRIT is a good plan, for it allows us to *take the initiative in reducing international tensions while maintaining national security.*

True GRIT: The Kennedy Experiment. It is impossible to conduct a fully acceptable experimental test of a hypothesis such as Osgood's. There is no way to take sets of nations consisting of two large powers armed to the teeth and a number of smaller powers serving as pawns and then randomly assign them to either experimental conditions in which GRIT is applied or control conditions under which nature has its way. However, a *partial* test of Osgood's GRIT hypothesis (no control group) took place between June 10 and November 22, 1963, and has been referred to as the Kennedy Experiment (Etzioni, 1967, 1969).

In a speech delivered at American University, President Kennedy reminded the nation of the disadvantages of the emotional and financial damage being wreaked by the state of American-Russian relations. He then indicated a dedication to improving these relations. To actually begin the process, he announced that nuclear tests in the atmosphere had been discontinued and would not be resumed unless other nations conducted such tests first. Although this was a clear move toward lessening international tensions, it was also a low-risk action. A nuclear test ban does not undermine national security when one's nuclear arsenal already contains as much explosive force as would be provided by an ankle-deep layer of dynamite spread over the surface of the entire country. (See Osgood, 1962, for some interesting figures about our state of military preparedness at that time.)

A possible weak point in GRIT is the assumption that the Russians will respond in kind. Should we really expect them to be motivated to do so? Perhaps we should, given that they have had particularly stern lessons concerning the disasters of war. Approximately 25 million Russians died in World War II. About 1.1 million died virtually under the nose of now-Premier Alexei Kosygin (Salisbury, 1969), and then-Premier Nikita Krushchev was by no means unacquainted with the horrors of battle (Krushchev, 1970). Whether or not memories of this earlier holocaust were responsible, Russia did respond to Kennedy's announcement. The day after Kennedy's speech appeared in full in *Izvestia* (itself a rare event according to Etzioni), the U. S. S. R. agreed with our request that U. N. observers be sent to Yemen.

Next the United States ended a lengthy dispute by agreeing to seat the Hungarian delegation in the U. N. Krushchev subsequently announced that he would halt the production of strategic bombers. Limited bans on nuclear tests were put into effect, discussions on joint exploration of space began, new East-West trade agreements were considered, and proposals were offered for the establishment of new consulates and the removal of travel restrictions within each country. According to Etzioni, the relaxing effects of this chain of events were apparent in the headlines and editorials of the newspapers of each country.

Thus, when procedures were applied that sounded suspiciously like GRIT, the Russians quickly responded to American initiatives and the Americans to Russian initiatives. A cycle of actions leading to lessening international tensions began to replace the cycle of actions that led to increasing tensions. The Kennedy Experiment ended before all conficts were removed. We don't know what would have happened if it had not been "slowed down with the approach of an election year, halted with the assassination of President Kennedy, and undermined by the escalation of the Viet Nam War" (Etzioni, 1969, p. 551). On the whole, though, the available results suggest that Osgood's plan is highly workable.

APPLYING RESEARCH FINDINGS

It is one thing to obtain findings on problems of personal and social relevance; it is quite another thing to apply those findings on a large-scale basis. Psychologists, like other scientists, can offer ideas, but whether or not they will be implemented depends on the receptivity of the people who can put them into effect. Our society's decision makers may not be aware of the researcher's recommendations, or the researcher may prove inept when he tries to persuade them that his ideas will work.

Indeed, there are many reasons why recommendations based on scientific analysis may go unheeded. A decision maker may object to them on legitimate technical grounds or consider them too risky. The decision maker may like the proposal but not be able to implement it because of priorities. For example, someone could devise a really splendid plan for educating disadvantaged children, but this plan could gather dust because all available funds must be used simply to keep the regular but mediocre school services in operation. Finally, we must not forget that decision makers are themselves individuals and, in our society, personally responsible to an electorate. Thus it is also possible for recommendations to go unheeded because the decision maker finds them personally objectionable or because the electorate is perceived as hostile toward the plans. The apparent fate of the President's Commission on Obscenity and Pornography illustrates what happens when recommendations conflict with prevailing values and standards.

The Pornography Commission's Report: A Case History

Representational works of art that explicitly and graphically portray overt sexual activity have been with us since earliest recorded history. The extent to which such sexual material has openly flourished has varied tremendously over time and in different societies. Denmark, for example, currently allows such **pornography** to be openly and freely available, whereas in our own society pornography is distributed surreptitiously or in the guise of "documentary," "educational," or "artistic" material. Whether or not we should follow Denmark's lead and repeal laws prohibiting the sale of pornography is controversial. Advocates of permissive legislation argue that removing censorship would be consistent with American principles of individual freedom and freedom of the press. Some even argue that this material could be developed to serve useful educational and possibly therapeutic purposes. Opponents of permissive legislation argue that the ready availability of pornography would contribute to the degeneracy of the society and would promote irresponsible sexual relations, an increase in illegitimate pregnancies, soaring rates of venereal disease, and a rising flood of sex crimes. If pornography does produce such deleterious effects, they certainly should be taken into account when considering the repeal of prohibitive legislation. In one survey a number of people indicated that the legalization of pornography ought to depend on whether or not it has harmful effects on behavior (President's Commission, 1970).

In 1967 a Presidential Commission was established to consider the problem of censorship. On September 30, 1970, their report was submitted to the Presi-

*In considering whether or not pornography should be legalized, it would
be useful to know whether it has a deleterious effect on behavior.*

dent and the Congress of the United States. (All material reported here is from
press releases of the same day.) This report delineates, among other things,
who uses or "consumes" pornography (which the Commission delicately refers
to as explicit sexual materials) and how they seem to be affected by it. The
report also lists specific recommendations offered by the Commission.

The Consumers

The Commission found that, despite prohibitive legislation, explicit sexual
material is widespread in the United States. Does pornography appeal primarily
to the unsavory and the immature? About 85 percent of all adult American
men and 70 percent of all adult American women have had firsthand contact
with it. Generally this material describes or pictures socially acceptable forms
of sex (such as heterosexual intercourse) rather than the statistically unusual
forms of sex many people consider strange, unusual, unnatural, or perverse.

The people who patronize "adult" bookstores tend to be neatly dressed,
middle-class, middle-aged, white married males. It was very rare to find minors
in these establishments, even when the laws did not specify that they had to

be at least 21 for admission. In some ways these patrons seemed to have fewer sexual inhibitions than nonpatrons, but overall they appeared to enjoy sexual intercourse neither more nor less than did nonpatrons, and they were no more likely than nonpatrons to engage in forms of sex that are condemned by society.

The Effects

Experimental studies confirm that exposure to explicit sexual material can be sexually arousing for *both* men and women. Yet for most people contact with this material did not influence level of sexual activity. Of those whose behavior was affected, some reported a decrease, whereas a slightly larger proportion reported an increase. In the latter case this increase generally took the form of masturbation or additional experiences with an already established partner.

Pornography, then, does not seem to goad people into casual affairs or unnatural acts. In fact, it can promote improved sexual relations. This statement is borne out by the claims of professional counselors and by the findings of certain experiments sponsored by the Commission. Some married couples participating in these experiments found that exposure to explicit sexual material improved their marital relationship.

In Chapter Eleven you saw that, as stimuli become familiar, they lose their ability to command attention. In Denmark, when pornography was legalized, the Danes themselves were initially avid consumers. But within a few months their interest slacked off, and the vendors had to rely on foreigners for business. The Commission's studies also suggest that repeated exposure to explicit sexual material may result in disinterest. Over time, initially arousing material lost its ability to be exciting. Repeated exposure did not seem to affect people's judgments of "rightness" and "wrongness" but did seem to reduce their fears that pornography had a deleterious effect on behavior.

As for crime, a majority of professionals who deal with people (psychologists, psychiatrists, sex educators, social workers, counselors, and so on) believed that exposure to explicit sexual material does not have an adverse effect on individual conduct, although chiefs of police did not concur with these other professionals' opinions. In Denmark sex offenses *decreased* following the legalization of pornography. An analysis of crime statistics and the results of their own experiments and surveys led the Commission to assert (1970, p. 32): "Empirical research designed to clarify the question has found no evidence to date that exposure to explicit sexual materials plays a significant role in the causation of delinquent or criminal behavior among youth or adults. The Commission cannot conclude that exposure to erotic materials is a factor in the causation of sex crime and delinquency." Similar commissions in other countries have also concluded that voluntary exposure to erotic material does not demonstrably damage the individual or the society.

The Recommendations

Some of the studies on which the Commission based its report can no doubt be faulted on one ground or another. But it is clear that this expensive, qualified, hard-working Commission found scant evidence that exposure to explicit sexual materials promotes irresponsible sexual activity. It does not seem that the repeal of prohibitive laws would result in an increase in illegitimate pregnancies, venereal disease, and sex crimes. Rather, the repeal of repressive laws would be in accordance with principles of freedom of expression and freedom of the press. Moreover, it would also result in the development of useful educational materials and materials that could enhance the fading love lives of long-established couples. Thus (p. 57):

> The Commission recommends that federal, state and local legislation should not seek to interfere with the right of adults who wish to do so to read, obtain or view explicit sexual materials. . . . The Commission recommends that federal, state and local legislation prohibiting the sale, exhibition or distribution of sexual materials to consenting adults should be repealed.

Cautiously, the Commission did *not* recommend that explicit sexual material be made available to adolescents or children. This was not because they found that it warped young minds but because they did not obtain sufficient information to draw a conclusion about the effects of pornography on minors.

The Commissioners, however, were not unanimous in their support of these recommendations. Two cried "A Magna Carta for the pornographer!" Another Commissioner, the founder of Citizens for Decent Literature, wrote "Credit the American public with enough common sense to know that one who wallows in filth is going to get dirty. This is intuitive knowledge. Those who spend millions of dollars to tell us otherwise must be malicious, misguided or both." The President sided with these dissenting Commissioners and discarded the recommendations.

The Commission's Report is controversial because it offers evidence that conflicts with cherished intuition. Weighing millions of dollars of research money and countless hours of effort, on the one hand, against long-established beliefs, on the other, the beliefs won.

But science does not exist in a vacuum; it exists in a society that has a history, a set of needs, and a particular type of political atmosphere. Researchers can only conduct their studies in the best way they know how. Prevalent social attitudes, particularly as reflected among those whom we have elected to represent and govern us, provide strong checks so that findings and recommendations are not always directly translated into new governmental policies. This is how it has been and how it is likely to remain. Whether this system is good or bad I leave for you to decide.

PSYCHOLOGY AS A SOCIAL ISSUE

Psychologists observe and, more than occasionally, try to manipulate people. In their observations they may knowingly or unwittingly infringe on a person's right to personal privacy. In their experiments they may lie, cheat, or deceive a person or subject him to unpleasant conditions. Clinical psychologists, school psychologists, or industrial psychologists may pry deep into an individual's privacy and then make recommendations that could have dramatic effects on his subsequent life. Given these circumstances, it is not surprising that there is great concern with the ethical propriety of psychologists' behavior.

All psychologists must consider the role of psychology in society and be sensitive to how psychology can affect each of society's members. A simple belief that psychology will ultimately lead to some form of good is not sufficient to release anyone from these concerns.

Special Concerns of the Researcher

I am thoroughly convinced that the largest proportion of psychological research is totally harmless. In these studies anonymous people are observed during their daily, public activities, willingly answer the questions of an interviewer, or cheerfully volunteer for a straightforward experiment.

Ever glance at a stranger? The same behavior is shown by psychologists in their studies of seating arrangements. Here, too, people who do not know they are being watched are watched by people who do not know whom they are watching; and here, too, it is hard to identify any disastrous consequences. Ever ask someone for his views? In attitude surveys many people are more than glad for the chance to express their opinions. Ever want to try something new and different? In many experiments a person freely devotes an hour of his time and in return undergoes an experience that provides a break from his daily routine and that may, in some very small way, shed some additional light on the nature of man.

Everything in this world is not fun and games. Psychologists may argue that man cannot be understood if we do not consider his reactions to unpleasant conditions. Understanding these conditions can lead to conquering them. Thus some experiments involve creating unpleasant conditions or leading the subject to anticipate that such conditions will be encountered. In a small percentage of studies psychologists have embarrassed or insulted subjects; led them to believe that they were somehow stupid, incompetent, or even perverted; or given them electric shocks or other painful stimuli in varying degrees of intensity. The results of these studies are invariably of great interest, and the rougher the treatment the greater the interest. The investigators responsible generally try to justify their experiments on the ground that they provide important new knowledge that will ultimately lead to some social good. Nonetheless, can such rough procedures ever be condoned? Does it make a difference if the experiment is only *mildly* unpleasant rather than *severely* unpleasant? Does it matter if the subjects initially volunteered and then freely completed the experiment? There are no set answers to these questions.

Relatively frequently, experiments involve deception in one form or another. Experimenters have lied glibly, cheated at games, made false promises, misrepresented their confederates as other subjects, and in many other ways created conditions that were not as they appeared. In some cases the deception is rather minor (as when subjects are told that made-up words are meaningful), and in other cases it is not (as when fake smoke is poured into a room to give the impression that the building is on fire). After the experiment the researcher almost invariably cheerfully owns up to his dishonesty, and many people claim to have enjoyed the ruse. But is deception ever justified? Does the justification depend on the nature or the extent of the deception? Is it sufficient that the psychologist goes one step further than the advertiser by admitting to his deception, explaining it, and then trying to undo it? None of these questions have very easy answers either.

At one extreme is the position that no research should be conducted, because somehow, somewhere, someone just might be imposed upon or hurt. Given this extreme position, one should not teach, sell shoes, put out fires, or drive an automobile either. At the other extreme is the position that any procedure can be justified on the basis of some ultimate good. Given this position, the researcher would and should soon end up in jail.

For the most part psychologists are neither afraid to conduct any experiments nor willing to conduct ruthless experiments. Most prefer to make a careful appraisal of the potential damages that could be done by an experiment and weigh these factors against the expected value or usefulness of the results. In many cases, if the proposed experiment involves fraud, stress, or pain, the project is abandoned, no matter how interesting the potential results.

Special Concerns of the Clinician

The experimenter may deliberately create unpleasant conditions for his anonymous subjects and then later try to undo them. The clinical psychologist may be less likely to create such conditions but more likely to deliberately meddle in the lives of specific individuals. Psychological testing involves prying deeply into people's personal lives. Psychotherapy involves trying to change a person.

Kleinmuntz (1967) provides a very good discussion of the ethical problems associated with psychological testing. Usually tests are administered to make a decision about a person (for example, to hire him or not to hire him). In a sense a psychological-test score is quite similar to a resumé of work experiences or a grade in a class. But psychological tests may tap very personal and sensitive issues. Even given that the information obtained is held in strictest confidence, is it ethical to pry into a person's life like this? Then again, is it ethical *not* to test him, when his scores may indicate that he will probably find failure and disappointment in the given position?

A person goes to a clinical psychologist or other psychotherapist for help because he finds himself feeling or acting in ways that are unacceptable. To deal with such a person, a psychotherapist must be able to decide in what ways the person should behave to lead to a better life and must then induce the person to behave in these ways. Can we ever tell a person how he should act? Is it fair to ask a person to relinquish some of his self-determination (such as it is) and yield to the ministrations of a psychotherapist? Is the issue complicated if the person clearly asks for help and is willing to do what he is told because he himself believes it will give him a better life?

Ethical issues are not simple ones. They must be confronted by responsible people in every walk of life. Professionals from all fields may point out in their own defense that their intentions are good, that they have undergone thorough training, and that they are sensitive to ethical concerns. Ultimately ethical judgments result from balancing one set of goods and evils against another. The upshot is invariably a value judgment, and each person must make his own.

CONCLUSIONS

Researchers have always been influenced by the interests and needs of their society. As members of society and as professionals, psychologists have shown concern for the problems that can affect us all. Since many, if not most, of society's woes have to do with human behavior, psychological research should prove very useful. Much psychological research has real implications for real people living in a real world, and some of these implications have been introduced in every chapter of this book. In this final chapter we turned to some recently defined problems that center around the interdependence of people.

In some situations a person's behavior can affect the fate of somebody else. First we considered conditions under which people will assume responsibility for their fellowman and offer aid to someone who is needy or in distress. Helping models have been shown to elicit helping behavior from observers. Unfortunately, such helping models are not always present, and, in an emergency, it is necessary for someone to go first if help is to be offered.

Research by Latané and Darley has shown that, as there is an increase in the number of people who could offer help, the chances that a given individual will help tend to decrease. Apparently as the size of a group of bystanders increases, each person feels less personal responsibility for aiding the victim. Moreover, in our society strong norms for "keeping your cool" and "minding your own business" prevail, and people are less likely to risk action when others are present because they expect adverse reactions for their troubles.

Next we turned to those conditions under which people abandon responsibility for others by obeying commands to inflict pain and punishment. Even though we would like to see ourselves as a nation of kindly souls who would refuse to obey unjust, unreasonable, and repulsive demands, the evidence hints otherwise. However, obedience can be reduced when the victim is brought closer to the harm-doer, when the authority issuing the orders diminishes his surveillance, or when there is social support for healthy defiance.

Intergroup relations have implications for all the members of all the groups involved. Some of our most pressing problems involve tensions and conflicts between different groups. Sherif's research with preadolescent boys provides a good model for understanding the origin and reduction of intergroup conflict. Sherif has shown that cohesive groups can be formed when there are goals requiring all potential members to coordinate their efforts. Conflict is induced when two thus-formed groups are placed in a situation in which they must compete for rewards that only one group can attain. Finally, this resulting conflict can be reduced when the two groups are faced with a compelling series of tasks that require for completion a high degree of cooperation among the members of each of the groups. Sherif's findings would seem applicable not only to preadolescent gangs but also to labor-management quarrels and the conflicts that can divide the various factions of a society.

International tensions are worrisome and expensive and can cause divisions within each society. In this chapter we examined some aspects of American-Russian relations. Cooperation between the United States and Russia appears to be inhibited by each side's distorted perceptions of the other, and thinking on the problem was long dominated by the worthless alternatives of all-out war or complete one-sided disarmament. A relatively recent and seemingly workable alternative is GRIT. According to this plan, the United States takes the initiative for peace by making a friendly move toward the Russians. The move, however, may not be one that endangers our national security. GRIT assumes that the Russians will respond in kind. Subsequent peace moves by each side are based on the quantity and quality of the other side's responses.

Psychologists, like other scientists, can offer recommendations, but whether or not they will be put into practice depends on many factors. Recommendations may be poorly presented or may be rejected because of expense, priorities, or legitimate technical flaws. They can also be rejected because of the personal needs and values of the decision maker or because of the prevailing political climate. An example of findings rejected on the latter basis is to be found in the apparent fate of the President's Commission on Obscenity and Pornography. Millions of dollars and countless man-hours were spent trying to discover if the repeal of laws prohibiting sexually explicit material would increase wanton sexual behavior, raise the crime rate, or contribute to moral decay. The Commission found no evidence of such deleterious effects, and a large majority of the Commissioners recommended that legislation prohibiting the distribution and use of such materials be repealed. These recommendations were subsequently rejected. In this case long-held intuitive beliefs and the political atmosphere appeared to prevent the acceptance of the recommendations of a scientific committee.

Finally, I pointed out that in some ways psychology itself can be considered a social issue. The psychologist's professional activities raise many problems of ethics. On the one hand he may poke, pry, fool people, apply stressful conditions, or try to change someone's way of life. On the other hand he may be starting to find and apply some solutions to problems that have been with us for quite some time. The ultimate evaluation of the psychologist's activities is up to you to make.

Glossary

Ability tests. Psychological assessment devices that purport to assess the examinee's "potential" for learning and performance.

Abnormal. Anything that falls outside the range of the appropriate and acceptable, as defined by personal tastes and social standards.

ABX system. A form of balance theory proposed by Newcomb that involves the relationship between two people, *A* and *B*, and their attitudes toward an attitude object, *X*.

Achievement tests. Psychological assessment devices that purport to measure the extent to which present abilities and past learning have combined to produce a given level of performance.

Acquiescence. In psychological testing, a person's predisposition to agree with a statement or question no matter what its nature.

Adolescence. A special, socially defined period of several years that helps the person complete the transition from childhood to adulthood.

Affective component. In attitude theory, the emotional or "feeling" part of an attitude.

Affective disorders. A form of neurosis or psychosis characterized by extreme moods.

Affiliation. The process of seeking out and being with other people.

Aggression. Overt responses (physical or verbal) or implicit responses (thoughts) involving inflicting injury on an object or person.

Aging. Normal detrimental changes over time that impose limitations and result in the loss of previously held abilities.

Ahistorical perspective. An orientation to behavior that emphasizes the immediate, contemporaneous forces acting on the organism, rather than past events.

Ambiguous stimuli. Vague and ill-defined stimuli that cannot be perceived as coherent unless the perceiver draws heavily on his own needs and experiences.

Amnesia. The repression of fairly lengthy segments of one's life such that they cannot be recollected.

Anal stage. In psychoanalytic theory, the second psychosexual stage of development, during which the anus is supposedly highly sensitized and the retention and elimination of feces provide erotic gratification. The main developmental issues during this stage are cleanliness training and the struggle for power and autonomy.

Antisocial personality. Person characterized by deceitful, irresponsible, lawless, impulsive behavior.

Anxiety. A fearlike reaction of vague and unspecific origin.

Anxiety neurosis. A form of neurosis characterized by vague but persistent feelings of apprehension, strengthened occasionally by waves of panic, fear, and dread.

Approach/approach conflict. A competition among responses resulting from a choice between two attractive alternatives that cannot be simultaneously realized.

Approach/avoidance conflict. A competition among responses elicited by a stimulus that has both attractive and unattractive features.

467

Approach gradient. Variations in motivation to approach a thing or event as it becomes more accessible or nearer in time.

Approach response. Moving toward a person, thing, or event.

Approach tendency. A behavioral predisposition to move toward an object, situation, or set of conditions.

Aptitude tests. Psychological assessment devices that purport to measure fairly specialized abilities, such as the ability to create works of art or to perceive mechanical relationships.

Art. In psychology, an activity of psychologists that involves creatively applying various principles to problems of people and human relations.

Attitude. A belief, feeling, or action that is elicited by a stimulus.

Attitude holder. A person who maintains an attitude.

Attitude object. A person, thing, or event that elicits an attitude.

Audience studies. Studies that examine the effects of passive spectators on learning or performance.

Authoritarianism. A hypothesized personality variable believed to account for the degree to which a person emphasizes power in social relations, subordinates himself to authorities, adheres to conventional values, and adopts harsh and punitive views.

Authority figures. People such as parents and policemen who are perceived as having an imposing amount of power and influence over the individual.

Autokinetic effect. Illusory motion of a stationary pinpoint of light in a darkened room.

Autonomies. Involuntary muscular movements, such as tics, twitches, throbbings, and shakes.

Availability. In motivation, the accessibility of a response.

Avoidance/avoidance conflict. A competition among responses arising when there are two unattractive alternatives, one of which must be accepted.

Avoidance gradient. Variations in the motivation to avoid something undesirable as a function of its nearness or likelihood.

Avoidance response. Moving away from a person, thing, or event.

Avoidance tendency. A behavioral predisposition to move away from an object, situation, or set of conditions.

Balance. In attitude theory, a relationship among two or more elements or cognitions that is "normal" and hence unlikely to change.

Balance theory. In the study of attitudes, a consistency theory that operates along the principle that there is an assumed "normal state" among attitudes or cognitions and that when conditions depart from this normal state there will be a tendency for them to return to it.

Behavior. The actions and reactions of living organisms.

Behavior act. In R. F. Bales' system, the smallest decipherable unit of social behavior.

Behavioral component. In attitude theory, that component or part of an attitude that represents a predisposition to behave in a certain way.

Behavioral dependence. A condition of the organism such that its behavior is modifiable by the presence and actions of others.

Behavioral interdependence. A condition of two or more organisms such that their behavior is modifiable by the presence and actions of each other.

Behaviorism. An orientation to psychology suggesting that, since psychologists, as scientists, must deal with observables, they must focus their attention on behavior.

Behavior modification. An unusually successful form of psychotherapy that involves the application of learning principles to reduce or eliminate unwanted behavior and to encourage wanted behavior.

Biological age. Age as assessed by events within the organism.

Blacky Test. A projective technique specifically devised to assess components of personality that are of interest to the psychoanalysts.

Blind walk. An exercise designed to reawaken people's sensitivity to touch, smell, and sound, which are often ignored as a result of heavy reliance on vision. A person is blindfolded and then led to sites rich in nonvisual stimuli.

Bond. In attitude theory, a relationship between two cognitions.

Brainstorming. A process claimed to overcome the inhibiting pressures of group membership on the offering of new and novel solutions by encouraging group members to offer all suggestions, no matter how seemingly unworkable, zany, or bizarre.

Castration anxiety. An exaggerated fear of harm to the genitals that may later become an irrational fear of harm to any part of the body.

Catatonic schizophrenia. A form of schizophrenia characterized by extreme withdrawal.

Catharsis theory. A poorly supported theory suggesting that observing an aggressive model should provide a harmless release for pent-up aggression.

Centrality. In group dynamics, the extent to which a person within a group handles a disproportionately large number of communications.

Child psychologist. Developmental psychologist who specializes in the study of age-related changes during the early years.

Chronological age. Age as assessed by calendars and clocks.

Classical conditioning. A learning process whereby the pairing of an initially neutral stimulus with one that reliably elicits a response results in the initially neutral stimulus eventually eliciting an identical or similar response.

Client. Person dealt with by a psychotherapist.

Client-centered therapy. (Also called nondirective therapy or Rogerian therapy) A form of individual psychotherapy in which the therapist encourages his client to explore and clarify his own thoughts and feelings and through this process discover and accept his real self. It is based on the assumption that the client has within himself the potential for constructive change.

Clinical psychologist. An artful practitioner in the area of clinical psychology.

Clinical psychology. A branch of psychology in which a practitioner deals directly with people and their personal and social problems with the goal of understanding them and assisting them to live as effectively and happily as possible.

Closure. (1) In perception, the process of perceiving stimuli as whole, continuous, complete figures. (2) In research on problem solving and repression, the completion of an interrupted or unfinished task. (3) In Gestalt therapy, the completion of earlier "unfinished business" that prevents the person from living a happy and effective life in the present.

Coaction. The behavior of two or more people or animals engaging in identical tasks in the presence of each other.

Coefficient of correlation. A numerical statement that expresses the direction and degree of closeness of the relationship between two variables. Coefficients of correlation are often referred to simply as "correlations."

Cognitions. (1) Thoughts or mental images. (2) In cognitive dissonance theory, items of information, such as the knowledge that cigarette smoking can be harmful, the belief that one's choice of a new car was a wise one, the conviction that heroin is bad, or the perception that flowers are in bloom.

Cognitive component. In attitude theory, that component or part of an attitude that is intellectual.

Cognitive consonance. In cognitive dissonance theory, a case involving two (or more) interrelated cognitions that are compatible such that one logically follows from or is implied by the other.

Cognitive disorders. Disturbances of thought processes and patterns.

Cognitive dissonance. In cognitive dissonance theory, the case of two (or more) interrelated cognitions that are incompatible with each other such that one cognition is the opposite of what would be expected from a knowledge of the other cognition alone.

Cognitive dissonance theory. A consistency approach to attitudes suggesting that the coexistence of two or more incompatible cognitions will produce an unpleasant tension state, which the organism will seek to reduce by changing one or more of the cognitions or by redefining their relationship to one another.

Cohesiveness. A term used to refer to the "groupiness" of a group. Less informally, it is defined as the result of all the forces that attract all the group's members to one another.

Common sense. Shared beliefs about behavior that intuition or custom suggests are true but that are not necessarily supported by the results of scientific inquiry.

Communication. The transmission of information and affect from one person to another.

Communication networks. In a group, the channels encouraging or impairing the flow of information among specific group members.

Comparative psychologist. A psychologist who attempts to relate regularities in behavior to the differences among species.

Competence behaviors. Behaviors believed to indicate or encourage independence, self-reliance, and a zest for accomplishment.

Complementarity hypothesis. A hypothesis concerning interpersonal attraction suggesting that certain different-appearing characteristics of two people will fit together in such a way as to make their association rewarding for both.

Concept formation. The lumping of stimuli into coherent categories on the basis of an identifiable set of rules.

Concrete operations period. In Piaget's theorizing, the second stage of intellectual development (2–11 years) characterized by an increasing ability to solve concrete problems.

Conditioned response. In classical conditioning, the learned response.

Conditioned stimulus. In classical conditioning, a stimulus that does not reliably elicit the response to be learned at the beginning of the learning procedures.

Confederates. Accomplices of an experimenter who have been secretly instructed to behave in certain ways in the presence of the subjects participating in the experiment.

Conflict. (1) A competition between incompatible responses. (2) A state of tension and hostility between two or more people or groups.

Conformity. Regularities in behavior among the people in a group.

Congruity principle. A principle stating that stimuli can be placed on a positivity-negativity scale. When two such stimuli are seen as associated with each other, they will be drawn together on the scale; when they are seen as dissociated (as a result of one rejecting or disavowing the other), they will be propelled apart.

Conscience. In psychoanalytic theory, that component of personality that punishes the person for doing something wrong.

Conscious. (1) Aware. (2) The "content of the mind" (habits, wishes, impulses, conflicts, feelings, and perceptions) of which the individual is aware at a given point in time.

Consistency theories. (1) Theories suggesting that man seeks to create order in himself. (2) In the study of attitudes, theories suggesting that people seek to create order among the component parts of their attitudes and among various interrelated attitudes.

Consonance. See *cognitive consonance.*

Construct. See *hypothetical constructs.*

Construct validity. Validity arising from a complex web of evidence that events happen in ways one would expect if the construct or the measure of a construct is useful.

Contact hypothesis. The hypothesis that contact with people from other identifiable groups will lead to increased liking of them.

Content validity. In psychological testing, a form of validity that indicates the extent to which the items included on the test faithfully represent all the possible items that could be included.

Contrast hypothesis. In theories of interpersonal attraction, the poorly supported hypothesis that opposites attract.

Control group. In an experiment, those subjects that are treated identically as the experimental subjects except that the experimental treatment or manipulation is not applied. Their behavior provides a gauge or yardstick for evaluating the behavior of the experimental group.

Controls. Procedures for ruling out alternative explanations of the results of experiments.

Conversion hysteria. A form of neurosis in which problems of living are inadequately met with behavior suggestive of a physical illness or disability. There is no organic cause for this malady, even though the neurotic sincerely believes that it is real.

Cooperation. The coordination of efforts for mutual rewards.

Cooperative response. A response aimed at providing rewards for others as well as for the self.

Core identity. The "real inner you" or center of personality that is formed earliest in life and provides a sense of continuity and coherence over time.

Correlation. (1) A relationship between two variables such that, given the value of one variable, it is possible to say something about the value of the associated variable (see *positive correlation; negative correlation*). (2) An abbreviated reference to a coefficient of correlation. (See *coefficient of correlation.*)

Costs. In Thibaut and Kelley's theory of social interaction, all the negative consequences of making a response (effort, embarrassment, self-sacrifice, and so on).

Co-twin control. A method for investigating the effects of heredity through a comparison of two people of virtually identical genetic composition (such as one-egg twins) who have been reared in different environmental settings.

Counseling psychologist. See *clinical psychologist.*

Counteropinion. A point of view opposite to that which a person maintains.

Covert communication. The transmission of information and affect by postures, gestures, facial expressions, and tenor of voice.

Criterion measures. In psychological testing, assessments of actual performance in a situation of interest (for example, grades in medical school) that provide a yardstick for gauging the success of a psychological test (for example, a test for predicting who will do well in medical school).

Cues. Parts of a stimulus or stimulus pattern that contribute a disproportionately large amount to the coherence of the total perception.

Data. "Facts" and "figures" that are the result of observations and that provide the basis for drawing conclusions.

Decay theory. In the study of learning, a seemingly erroneous theory suggesting that responses are extinguished or "lost" as the result of disuse.

Defense mechanism. A psychological process that serves to protect the person from unwanted habits, impulses, wishes, perceptions, and feelings by distorting them or blocking them from awareness.

Delusions. Misperceptions and misinterpretations of things and events, especially cause-effect relationships.

Denial. A defense mechanism involving a failure to accept unpleasant or unwanted conditions and seeing in their place happier conditions that are only the product of imagination.

Dependency. Relying on others.

Dependent variable. (1) That which varies or changes as a result of changes in the independent variable. (2) In an experiment, the behavior assessed by the experimenter.

Depression. A form of psychosis characterized by gloominess, pessimism, listlessness, fatigue, and an inability to concentrate.

Derivative. In psychoanalytic theory, behavior that had its origin in an early psychosexual stage of development.

Desensitization. Procedures used to help remove anxiety or to extinguish phobic reactions.

Determinism. The fundamental assumption of science that there are lawful relationships among causes and effects.

Development. Systematic changes over time.

Developmental psychologist. A psychologist who relates regularities in behavior to the systematic forces acting on the person or animal as he or it progresses through life.

Deviant. (1) A person who does not conform. (2) A person who is statistically rare. (3) A person who violates the standards of a group.

Deviation hypothesis. In psychological testing, the hypothesis that the content and format of test items are unimportant but the way in which the respondent replies to the item is all-important. This hypothesis suggests that the person who answers test questions in unusual ways is also likely to behave unusually in other ways.

Diagnosis. Process of defining or categorizing the nature of a problem.

Diffusion of responsibility. A process whereby personal feelings of accountability are diluted when the person is in contact with other people, whom he views as also accountable or responsible.

Discrimination. The process of distinguishing one stimulus from another.

Displaced aggression. Aggression that is directed toward a relatively "safe" target rather than the intimidating target that infuriated the aggressor.

Dispositional variables. Those forces contributing to behavior that have their origin inside the organism. Dispositional variables help to account for why the same person acts in similar ways in different situations and why different people act in different ways in the same situation.

Dissociative hysteria. A form of neurosis in which whole periods of time or whole facets of personality are blocked from recollection.

Dissonance. See *cognitive dissonance.*

Dissonance reduction. The process of redefining the relationship between two or more psychologically incompatible or dissonant cognitions in such a way that they become compatible or "consonant" with one another. (See *cognitive dissonance; cognitive consonance.*)

Domain. In psychological testing, all the possible test items that could be included on the test.

Dominant gene. A gene that produces an observable effect on the offspring.

Dominant response. Response most likely to occur under stated conditions.

Domination. Social influence through force that is involuntarily accepted by the influenced party.

Drive. A broad motivational state that energizes behavior.

Drive-habit theory. A theory of motivation suggesting that activity is energized by "drive," which results from the absence of comforts or necessities or the presence of unpleasant stimuli. The direction of behavior is determined by habit, which is a stimulus-response connection usually formed through learning.

Dyadic relationships. (1) The relationship between two people. (2) In attitude theory, the relationship between two elements or cognitions.

Eclectic approach. An approach to personality that involves picking and choosing from different theories terms and principles that seem to fit together nicely to describe and explain a particular case.

Effect dependency. Relying on others for care, for protection from deprivations and punishments, and for rewards and satisfiers.

Ego. (1) "Self" or "me." (2) In psychoanalytic theory, the system of the mind that coordinates need satisfaction with objective conditions. Ego is the rational, problem-solving part of the personality.

Ego-defensive function. In attitude theory, use of an attitude to protect the attitude holder from a correct perception of grim conditions.

Ego ideal. In psychoanalytic theory, that component of the superego that provides internal rewards for behaving in a morally correct or exemplary fashion.

Ego psychologists. Psychologists who stress behavior we think of as direct, purposeful, adaptive, realistic, and strong as opposed to wishful, fanciful, dreamy, or "sick."

Electra complex. In psychoanalytic theory, the daughter's attachment to her father and resentment of her mother initiated by events during the phallic stage of psychosexual development.

Empirical keying. In psychological testing, the selection of items for a psychological test solely on the basis of the item's ability to discriminate among respondents.

Encoded. Entered into the nervous system.

Encounter groups. Small groups used as a vehicle for helping participants to better understand their own personalities and ways of interacting with others.

Environment. (1) All situational forces. (2) Everything that impinges on the individual but that he does not consider a part of his self.

Erogenous zones. Areas on the surface of the body that are unusually sensitive to erotic stimulation.

Error. (1) In psychological testing, that component of a test score that does not reflect the psychological quality or attribute the test is designed to assess. (2) In open systems theory, a technique for attempting to adapt to information overload by means of the faulty processing of input.

Escape response. A response that extricates the organism from a painful or unpleasant situation.

Expectancy. (1) Any anticipation. (2) In motivation theory, an anticipation that an action will produce certain consequences.

Expectancy-incentive theory. An approach to motivation suggesting that organisms anticipate or expect that an action will produce a certain result and that each result has a certain value to the organism.

Experiment. A procedure for understanding cause-effect relationships that involves actively manipulating a hypothesized cause and then measuring its influence on the suspected effect.

Experimental game. A research technique for the study of social interaction typically based on economic models of social behavior. Each of two or more players has available two or more response alternatives, and on the basis of their mutual choices various wins and losses are incurred by each player.

Experimental group. In an experiment, those subjects that receive the experimental treatment or manipulation (for example, an injection of a drug).

Experimenter bias. (1) A tendency on the part of an experimenter to "see" his subjects as behaving in the way he hopes they will behave. (2) Unintentional behavior on the part of the experimenter that encourages the subject to behave in a way that proves satisfactory to the experimenter.

Exposure hypothesis. The hypothesis that mere repeated exposure to a stimulus is a sufficient condition for improving the favorability rating given that stimulus.

Extinction. The disappearance of a learned response. In classical conditioning, extinction results from repeated presentation of the conditioned stimulus without the unconditioned stimulus. In operant conditioning, extinction occurs when reinforcement no longer follows emission of the response.

Extrovert. A sociable and outgoing person.

Face validity. In psychological testing, a quality of a test such that it appears to measure that which it was designed to measure.

Facilitator. The trained professional in an encounter group who serves as a resource for group members to draw upon.

Faking. In psychological testing, responding to a test in such a way as to present a distorted view of one's self.

Faking bad. In psychological testing, attempts on the part of the examinee to cheat by answering test items in such a way as to convey the impression that he is unfit.

Faking good. In psychological testing, attempts on the part of the examinee to cheat by answering test items in such a way as to convey the impression that he is able and well adjusted.

Familiarity. Extent to which something is known or familiar as a result of prior contact.

Feedback. Information concerning the results of actions.

Filtering. In open systems theory, a technique for coping with information overload by means of selecting some, but not all, input to process.

Formal operations period. In Piaget's theorizing, the final stage of intellectual development (age 12) characterized by an ability to deal with abstractions and solve abstract problems.

Frame of reference. The product of past experiences, present needs, and social pressures that helps the person to structure, organize, and interpret stimuli.

Free association. In psychoanalytic therapy, a procedure in which the patient is encouraged to talk about anything that comes to mind without trying to organize or censor the material.

Frustration. The blocking of goal-directed behavior.

Frustration-aggression hypothesis. The hypothesis that the blocking of goal-directed behavior will elicit a response aimed at inflicting injury or pain.

Functional approach. (1) An approach to understanding behavior in terms of the uses or purposes it serves for the behaving organism. (2) In attitude theory, an approach suggesting that people maintain attitudes because these attitudes serve useful purposes for them.

Functional disorders. All personal disorders believed to have been caused by a faulty combination of personal resources, on the one hand, and demands of living, on the other.

Games. See *experimental games.*

Generalization. The opposite of discrimination.

Genes. Genetically transmitted biochemical substances that establish codes governing the offspring's characteristics.

Genital stage. In psychoanalytic theory, the last stage of psychosexual development, which begins at puberty with the advent of mature sexual longings.

Genotypic traits. Relatively enduring characteristics or attributes of an individual that show themselves in a variety of situations and under different conditions.

Gestalt psychologists. Originally, a group of German psychologists whose primary interests were perception and thought processes. They believed each organism was equipped at birth with abilities that allowed him to make sense of the environment.

Gestalt therapists. A group of humanistic psychologists whose orientation to personality and psychotherapy draws heavily on psychoanalysis and Gestalt psychology. Their method of treatment involves imparting a sense of closure for important life tasks.

GRIT (Graduated Reciprocation in Tension Reduction). A plan formulated by C. E. Osgood that suggests international tensions can be reduced if one side initiates a few "low-risk" friendly actions. The other side will reciprocate, the first side can make additional overtures, and an upward spiral of improving relations will commence.

Group dynamics. (1) Interpersonal processes within the small group. (2) The study of interpersonal processes within the small group.

Grouping. In perception, a tendency to see separate elements as belonging together.

Group performance. The level of accomplishment attained by individuals working together.

Group psychotherapy. A form of psychotherapy in which the practitioner meets with a group of "patients" or clients collectively rather than on an individual basis.

Groups. Collections of individuals who have some sort of specified interrelationships with one another.

Habit. A stimulus-response connection that is usually the result of learning.

Habit strength. (1) Roughly, degree of learning. (2) Hypothetical construct accounting for differences in the likelihoods of responses.

Hallucinations. Subjective impressions of sights, sounds, or odors that are not physically present.

Hebephrenic schizophrenia. A form of schizophrenia in which bizarre and disorganized thoughts are coupled with outbursts of uncontrollable emotion.

Helping behavior. Social behavior with the intent of aiding another person.

Heredity. The processes by which characteristics are transmitted from parent to offspring at the time of conception.

High-talking seats. At a table, those positions where the occupants are likely to be active and voluble and to initiate a large number of communications.

Homeostasis. The tendency of a system to be self-regulating such that following disruption it will return to its "normal state."

Humanistic psychology. An orientation to psychology that challenges traditional psychological assumptions about the nature of man, the kinds of questions that should be asked about man, and the techniques useful for understanding man. From this perspective man is viewed as a conscious, free, whole being who sets important goals and then works hard to obtain them.

Hypochondriasis. A reaction in which a "sufferer" complains of a wide variety of imagined aches, pains, and illnesses.

Hypothesis. A tentative explanation of a relationship, often derived from a theory.

Hypothetical constructs. Intellectual tools or "ideas" that are believed to account for the relationship between two or more observables.

Hysteria. See *conversion hysteria.*

Id. In psychoanalytic theory, the earliest system of the mind. Responsible for seeking out pleasure and avoiding pain, the id is often described as raw, untamed, and instinctual.

Identification. (1) A general process of assuming the attributes of others, which is an important part of socialization. (2) A defense mechanism that involves assuming someone else's attributes, which are somehow more acceptable than one's own.

Identification with the aggressor. Assuming the attributes of someone who is capable of and perhaps likely to inflict harm. This is defensive in that the identifier (1) may now view himself as possessing some of the power of the aggressor, thus reducing the imbalance of power, and (2) may now consider himself as "above reproach" from the aggressor's standpoint, since he is now similar to the aggressor.

Identity. Roughly equivalent to "self" or the answer to the question "Who am I?"

Illusion. The perception of a stimulus as something that it is not.

Imbalance. In attitude theory, a relationship among two or more elements or cognitions that is not "normal" and hence is likely to change.

Imitation. Process involving a model, who behaves in a certain way, and a follower, who behaves in a similar way after observing the model.

Inactivations. Losses of perceptual or motor abilities as shown in such things as blindness, a loss of sensation, or paralysis.

Incentive. (1) Inducement to behavior. (2) The value accorded the consequences of an action.

Incentive theorists. In attitude theory, theorists who suggest people will change their attitudes when rewarded or "bribed" for so doing.

Independent variable. (1) Suspected antecedent or "cause" of behavior. (2) Those changes in the environment, internal or external, that are responsible for or contribute to changes in behavior. (3) In the experiment, the independent variable is the variable the experimenter deliberately manipulates.

Individual therapy. A form of psychotherapy in which the professional works with each person privately on a one-to-one basis.

Industrial psychologist. A psychologist involved in the search for and application of principles of behavior useful in the man-machine setting.

Information. Anything that helps to reduce uncertainty.

Informational social influences. Pressures from others to accept information they provide as evidence of reality.

Information dependency. Relying on others for information useful for perceiving, interpreting, and understanding the world.

Information overload. In open systems theory, the bombardment of the system by more potential input than can be efficiently processed.

Input. In open systems theory, information or material entered into the system for processing.

Insight. A sudden understanding.

Insight problem. A problem that requires for solution viewing relationships in a new way. The solution provides an "aha!" or "Eureka" experience and, when found, suddenly becomes very "obvious."

Interest inventories. Psychological tests designed to assess the respondent's concerns, interests, and values.

Interference theory. In learning, the seemingly correct theory suggesting that responses are extinguished or "forgotten" only when a new response is learned that interferes with it.

Intergroup relations. The relations between two or more groups.

Intermittent reinforcement. Reinforcement following some, but not all, emissions of a "correct" response.

Internal consistency. In psychological testing, a form of reliability that expresses the extent to which the parts of a test of the same attribute intercorrelate. To the extent that a test is internally consistent, it is believed to assess one psychological attribute in a systematic way as opposed to a number of different attributes haphazardly.

Internalization. The process of incorporating social standards and rules into one's personality.

Internal stimuli. Sources of stimulation originating within the skin.

Internationalist. A person characterized by trust for the people of other nations, an interest in communication between nations, and preferences for friendly negotiated solutions to international conflicts.

Interpersonal attraction. The extent to which one person feels drawn toward another.

Introspection. The conscious analysis of experience.

Introvert. A person who is shy and withdrawn.

IQ tests. Ability tests that purport to measure the examinee's most general capacities for learning and performance.

Isolation. A defense mechanism that involves stripping painful experiences and desires of their strong emotional feelings. The unpleasant desire or memory may have access to awareness, but the associated painful emotions remain out of awareness.

Isolationist. A term used to designate a person characterized by a distrust for the people of other nations, a preference for minimizing communication between his own and potentially hostile nations, and a preference for forceful military solutions to international conflicts.

Kinesic communication. The transmission of information and affect through motions of the body and limbs.

Knowledge function. In attitude theory, the use of attitudes as aids for making sense out of the universe.

Latent stage. In psychoanalytic theory, the fourth psychosexual stage of development, supposedly characterized by quiescence, a lack of sexual concerns, and an absence of important personality-formative events. It is now believed that many important personality-formative events occur during this period of alleged "quiescence."

Laws of grouping. The principles that similar stimuli, stimuli close in space, stimuli that permit the smooth continuation of a line, curve, or contour, or stimuli moving in the same direction tend to be perceived as associated or "belonging together."

Leadership. The product of a two-way interplay between leader and followers such that the leader takes the initiative, plans and organizes action, and in doing so evokes cooperation.

Learning. Changes or modifications of behavior as a result of changing environmental conditions.

Level of analysis. A framework for approaching a problem. When a researcher bases an explanation of behavior on either biological, individual, or social variables, he is operating within the framework of a specific level of analysis. As he moves up the scale from smaller to larger units, he is, by convention, approaching the issue from a higher level of analysis.

Life-style. A person's characteristic patterns for living and meeting challenges.

Life themes. The major preoccupations and basic expectations of an individual, typically formed during the childhood years.

Low-talking seats. At a table, those positions where the occupants are likely to remain relatively quiet and not initiate many communications.

Manic-depressive psychosis. A form of psychosis characterized by extreme fluctuations in moods.

Manic reactions. When extreme, forms of psychosis characterized by an unwarranted elated mood.

Massed practice. Successive rehearsals of a response that are close together in time.

Matrix. (1) A mathematical table depicting interrelated numbers. (2) In economic models of social interaction, a table that shows the various response alternatives available to the participants and the various outcomes resulting from the various combinations of responses.

Maturation. Systematic changes in biological structure and functioning that result from normal, predetermined growth processes.

Maze. A series of interconnecting corridors or paths used for studying learning.

Medical model. An approach to understanding personal disorganization and deviance by considering it the product of a disease.

Membership group. A group to which the person belongs.

Mere exposure. Conditions that make a stimulus accessible to the individual's perception.

Method of concordance. A technique for investigating the effects of heredity through the inspection of family histories. The aim of this technique is to relate closeness in "family ties" (that is, presumed genetic similarity) to similarities of appearance or behavior.

Minor maladjustment. The least serious result of meeting new conditions in inefficient, ineffective ways. "Minor" indicates that this form of personal disorganization is likely to be transient, disrupt only a narrow band of the person's life, and not be reflected in dramatic behavior.

Mirror-image phenomenon. A tendency of the members of two conflicting social groupings to describe the members of their own groups as friendly, sincere, and trustworthy and the members of the other group as unfriendly, insincere, and deceitful.

MMPI. A personality test that utilizes the objective-report method to assess the ways in which the respondent's personality is similar to that of normal people and to that of patients in mental hospitals who have been diagnosed as falling into one of the categories describing personal disorganization.

Model. A person or animal that is imitated or that provides cues suggesting to observers how to behave.

Motivation. (1) The forces that instigate or impel behavior and lend it direction, strength, and persistence. (2) The study of the forces that instigate or impel behavior and lend it direction, strength, and persistence.

Motive. Preference for engaging in a class of behaviors, such as behavior related to success or behavior leading to association with others.

Multiple personality. A very rare form of personal disorder involving the same person's alternately displaying two or more different "personalities," each of which typically does not recognize the other "personality's" existence.

Need. Any biological or psychological deficit that the organism seeks to reduce.

Need achievement. A persistent preference for engaging in success-related activities.

Need affiliation. A persistent preference for being with other people.

Need for social approval. A condition of the organism which makes it sensitive to social approval.

Negative correlation. A relationship between two variables such that, as the magnitude of one variable increases, the magnitude of the associated variable decreases. For example, there is a negative correlation between the number of cigarettes consumed and life expectancy.

Neuroses. Personal disorders reflected in behavior that is more dramatic, less acceptable, and more pervasive than that reflecting minor maladjustment. The neurotic, however, is typically able to maintain social contacts, keep his job, and "get by" without proving too disruptive to others.

Normal. Anything that falls within the range of the appropriate and acceptable as defined by personal tastes and social standards.

Normative social influences. Social pressures to conform with the expectations of others.

Norm of reciprocity. In social relations, a norm holding that a person will act toward another in the same way that the other person acts toward him.

Norms. (1) Shared expectations concerning the standard and accepted forms of behavior or level of performance within a group. (2) In psychological testing, a set of scores with which individual or group performance is compared.

Obedience. Yielding to the authoritative demands of another.

Objective-report methods. Paper-and-pencil psychological tests of the "true-false" or "multiple-choice" variety. They are "objective" in that the questions are clearly stated and that the responses are easy to categorize.

Obsessive-compulsive neurosis. A form of neurosis characterized by recurrent thoughts and repetitive behavior.

Oceanic experiences. Term introduced by Maslow to refer to a "mystical" experience consisting of an impression of opening horizons, a feeling of timelessness, and a subsequent conviction that something very important happened.

Oedipus complex. Issues centering around the son's attachment to his mother and resentment of his father, which the psychoanalysts suggest originally occurs during the phallic stage of psychosexual development.

Omission. In open systems theory, a technique for coping with information overload by neglecting to process some of the potential input.

Open systems theory. A theory that attempts to integrate all behavioral sciences, from cellular biology through psychology to sociology and anthropology, by means of determining principles that apply for the cell, tissue, organ, person, group, organization, society, and organizations of society.

Opening new channels. In open systems theory, the process of readjusting the system to cope with information overload by means of establishing additional mechanisms for processing the potential input.

Operant conditioning. A form of learning in which a motivated organism responds until it emits a response that is strengthened through reinforcement.

Oral stage. In psychoanalytic theory, the first psychosexual stage of development. The mouth, lips, and tongue are believed to be highly sensitized during this stage, and the issues and concerns center around ingestion, love, and security.

Organic disorders. Unwanted forms of behavior believed to have their origin in specifiable physiological malfunctions, such as changes in blood chemistry, brain injury, and damage to the nervous or other vital systems.

Organic pathologies. Abnormalities in the biological apparatus due to heredity, nutritional deficiencies, disease, or injury.

Organizational psychologist. A psychologist who attempts to relate regularities in behavior to the person's position within a large and to some extent formalized group.

Organizations. General Motors, I.B.M., and other large groups of people who have formed an association for avowed purposes and who have formulated rules for working together.

Outcomes. (1) Results. (2) Consequences of an action, to which value is attached. (3) In the Thibaut-Kelley model, the consequences of social interaction.

Output. In open systems theory, information or material transmitted from the system after processing.

Overt communication. The transmission of information and affect through the culture's spoken and written language.

Paralinguistic communication. The transmission of information and affect through the manner of speaking.

Paranoia. A form of psychosis characterized by delusions ("I am being persecuted") that, on the surface, may appear to be logical and highly systematized.

Paranoid schizophrenia. A form of schizophrenia in which delusions are associated with disorganized and hard-to-decipher ways of thinking.

Penis envy. According to the psychoanalysts, a feeling of resentment experienced by girls during the phallic stage, when they discover that the male has a penis but they do not.

Perceiver variables. Contributants to perception that originate inside the perceiver.

Perception. (1) Inferred psychological processes by which the organism comes to organize, structure, and interpret incoming information. (2) The study of these processes.

Perceptual defense. A hypothesized process that keeps a perceiver from a full awareness of unpleasant stimuli.

Persona. The most peripheral part of the personality, which is very responsive to the immediate pressures of a social situation and is hence often described as a "facade" or "mask."

Personal consequences. Any result of the systematic forces that cast, shape, and temper the individual.

Personal disorders. The term used in this text to refer to what is often called "mental illness."

Personal growth theories. Humanistic theories of personality suggesting that people strive to exercise their abilities in such a way as to utilize to the utmost their psychological potentials.

Personality. All the internal qualities of the individual that contribute to his being in some ways like all other individuals, in some ways like some other individuals, and in some ways unique.

Personality tests. Psychological assessment devices designed to assess the ways in which the respondent is in some ways like all other individuals, in some ways like some other individuals, and in some ways unique.

Personal space. (1) An emotionally charged zone around each individual, sometimes described as a soap bubble or aura, which helps to regulate the spacing of individuals. (2) The processes by which individuals mark out and personalize the spaces they inhabit.

Phallic stage. In psychoanalytic theory, the third psychosexual stage of development, during which the genitals are highly sensitized. Boy-girl differences become apparent during this stage, and the main issues have to do with attachment to the opposite-sexed parent and a resentment of the same-sexed parent.

Phobias. Manifestations of neurosis characterized by strong, irrational fears.

Phonemes. Basic sound units of a language.

Physiological psychologist. A psychologist who attempts to relate regularities in behavior to internal, physiological processes.

Population. The entire group of people who could be measured or assessed. For example, in a presidential poll all registered American voters would constitute a population.

Pornography. Material that explicitly describes or depicts overt sexual activity.

Position. A location within a social unit such as a group, an organization, or a society.

Positive correlation. A relationship between two variables such that, as the magnitude of one variable increases, the magnitude of the associated variable also increases. For example, there is a positive correlation between shoe size and stocking size. (See *correlation; coefficient of correlation; negative correlation.*)

Positive habituation. A process whereby contact with a harmless stimulus leads to a reduction of uncertainty and conflict, resulting in a feeling of comfort.

Postdecisional dissonance. Cognitive dissonance arising following the choice of one of a number of about equally attractive alternatives. The bad features of the chosen alternative and the good features of the rejected alternatives will be dissonant with the knowledge of the choice.

Praegnanz. In Gestalt psychology, a term designating "good figures." The law of Praegnanz refers to the observation that the environment is often perceived in such a way as to make it seem as simple and orderly as possible.

Preconscious. That part of our psychological makeup of which we are not presently aware but which can be easily recollected or brought into awareness in an undistorted form.

Prediction. In psychology, a forecast that under stated conditions a certain form of behavior or level of performance is likely to result.

Preoperational thought period. According to Piaget, the second major stage of intellectual development (2–7 years) during which the child gains the ability to manipulate symbols.

Primary groups. Groups, such as families, in which the members relate to each other on an intimate basis and, in the course of their sustained relationship, remember that they are dealing with other people who have unique personalities.

Primary process. In psychoanalytic theory, the process of reducing tensions simply by fantasizing or imagining a wanted satisfier.

Primary reinforcers. Reinforcers such as food and water that are believed to strengthen the preceding response by reducing a physiological need.

Principles of behavior. Assertions that under specified conditions certain types of behavior are likely to occur.

Prisoner's Dilemma Game (PDG). A form of experimental game in which each of two players is allowed to make either a cooperative or a noncooperative response.

Prognosis. A statement about what is likely to happen under specified conditions.

Projection. A defense mechanism that involves attributing unacceptable characteristics of one's self to someone (or something) else.

Projective tests. Personality assessment devices that involve presenting the subject with vague, ambiguous stimuli or tasks and then observing the way in which he perceives the stimuli or completes the task, with the assumption that the way he performs will indicate something about his personality.

Propinquity. Closeness in physical space.

Proxemic communication. The transmission of information and affect via spatial arrangement.

Psychiatrist. A physician who practices psychiatry.

Psychiatry. (1) Literally, "healing of the mind." (2) A branch of medicine that deals with emotional and behavioral disorders. The title "psychiatrist" is reserved for professionals who have received an M. D. degree and specialized medical training in emotional and behavioral disturbances.

Psychoanalysis. The theory of personality and method of treatment originally proposed by Sigmund Freud.

Psychoanalyst. A practitioner with special training in the theory of personality and method of treatment originally formulated by Sigmund Freud. In the United States most psychoanalysts are psychiatrists who undertook this specialized training after qualifying as psychiatrists.

Psychogram. A chart or graph that shows at a glance how a respondent scored on the different parts of a test.

Psychological growth theories. Theories of personality suggesting that people seek to exercise their human abilities in such a way as to best fulfill their potentials.

Psychological processes. Mechanisms that serve as intermediaries between a set of specified antecedent conditions, on the one hand, and specific forms of behavior, on the other.

Psychological tests. Instruments for assessing the psychological qualities of people (such as intelligence, interests, personality, and so forth).

Psychologists. Professionals who follow special rules for trying to describe, understand, and explain what people think, say, and do and what animals do.

Psychology. Literally, the "study of the mind." Since the mind has proven to be quite elusive, psychology is now typically defined as the study of behavior.

Psychophysiologic disorders. Personal disorders in which problems of living are reflected in physical ailments such as skin eruptions and ulcers.

Psychoses. Extreme forms of personal disorders in which the discrepancy between inner resources and demands of living result in a loss of contact with reality. This loss of contact may appear in distorted perceptions, faulty reasoning, and inappropriate displays of emotion.

Psychosexual stages. In psychoanalytic theory, a series of developmental or "growth" stages characterized by different erotic interests and different problems to be solved.

Psychotherapy. A set of techniques by which a trained professional helps a "patient" or "client" to live a happier, more effective, more rewarding life.

Puberty. Biological maturity signified by the ability to reproduce.

Punishment. See *reinforcer.*

Punishment paradox. The finding that punishment following a response sometimes leads to the repetition of that response or even to performance of the response in a manner suggesting greater learning.

Queuing. In open systems theory, a technique for coping with information overload by means of delaying the processing of input.

Rationalization. A defense mechanism that involves unconsciously concocting an acceptable excuse for an evil wish, a shortcoming, or any display of inadequacy, incompetence, or unworthiness.

Reaction formation. A defense mechanism for handling incompatible feelings (such as love and hate) by relegating the unacceptable member of the pair to the unconscious and overemphasizing the acceptable member of the pair.

Receptors. Highly sensitive, specialized nerve endings that are activated by the changes in the physical energy of stimuli.

Recessive gene. A gene that does not produce an observable effect in the offspring but that is retained in the offspring's own genetic composition for transmission to its offspring. (See *gene.*)

Reference group. A group that provides standards in light of which the person evaluates his own actions, feelings, and beliefs. A *positive reference group* is one whose standards the individual subscribes to and attempts to live up to. A *negative reference group* is one whose standards the individual disavows and tries not to live up to.

Reflexes. Unlearned, automatic stimulus-response connections that are common to the members of a species.

Regression. The process of reverting to an earlier mode of existence.

Regression equation. Mathematical procedures for assisting in making a statement about the value of one variable given the value of a second, related variable.

Reinforcer. Thing or event that alters the probability of the response that it follows. *Positive reinforcers* (rewards) increase the probability of the response that they follow; *Negative reinforcers* (punishments) decrease the probability of the response that they follow.

Reliability. A desirable quality of observations and measurements that is roughly equivalent to "repeatability" and "verifiability." An observation or measure is reliable to the extent that it is the same when made by different people or on different occasions.

Repression. The basic process of shoving painful or unpleasant feelings out of awareness.

Reputational similarity. The degree to which two or more people are believed to be similar by associates who know them both. Reputational similarity may or may not correspond to the degree to which the rated people actually are similar.

Resistance to extinction. Durability of a learned response (1) in the absence of additional unconditioned stimulus/conditioned stimulus pairings, or (2) after the withdrawal of reinforcement following emission of the response.

Response. Behavioral reaction to a stimulus.

Response latency. Speed with which a response is emitted following presentation of the stimulus.

Response sets. Predispositions to respond to a psychological-test question in a certain way independent of the content of the question. (See *acquiescence; social desirability.*)

Rewards. See *reinforcers.*

Roles. A pattern of behavior prescribed for the occupants of positions within social networks.

Rorschach Inkblot Test. A projective technique for assessing personality by having the respondent make up stories about a series of inkblots.

Sample. A relatively small group of people singled out from a larger group for measurement or assessment.

Scatterplot. A graph in which the two axes or arms represent two variables. Observations take the form of points on the graph. The values of the observations can be determined by referring to the two axes.

Schizophrenia. A type of psychosis characterized by a sharp break with reality and strange, bizarre, incoherent thought processes.

Science. A set of rules of inquiry for understanding the regularities in the world about us.

Secondary group. A social grouping in which people relate to each other in impersonal, businesslike ways and do not recognize that they are dealing with other unique personalities.

Secondary process. In psychoanalytic theory, the psychological mechanisms that help the person experiencing a need to find or produce conditions that satisfy the needs.

Secondary reinforcers. Reinforcers such as money that are believed to strengthen behavior because they were earlier associated with primary reinforcers that directly reduced a physiological need.

Self. The part of the person roughly equivalent to what each person thinks of as "me" and that constitutes an object of awareness, a name, a set of bodily feelings, an axis of meaning, a controller of activity, and a product of social relations.

Self-actualization. Term introduced by Maslow to refer to the process of psychological growth. (See *psychological growth theories.*)

Self-esteem. Subjective feelings of adequacy and worth.

Self-fulfilling prophecy. The prediction of an event in such a way that the prediction causes the event.

Sensations. The immediate results of the stimulation of a receptor.

Sensitivity group. See *encounter group.*

Sensori-motor period. In Piaget's theorizing, the first stage of intellectual development, running from birth to about 2 years. This period is characterized by a lessening of reliance on instinctive, reflexive actions.

Sentiment relationships. In attitude theory, a relationship between people or cognitions that implies a state of liking or disliking.

Shaping. In operant conditioning, a procedure by which successively closer approximations of the desired response are reinforced.

Significant others. People whose evaluations carry a great deal of impact and weight for a given individual.

Significant results. Research findings that are not plausibly explained by chance.

Similarity hypothesis. In the study of interpersonal attraction, the well-supported hypothesis that people who are similar to each other will be attracted to each other.

Situational variables. Those forces contributing to behavior that are the product of the immediate environment, setting, or situation in which the behavior occurs. Situational variables help account for why different people often act in similar ways in the same situation and why the same person acts differently as he moves from place to place.

Small groups. Groups of sufficiently few people that each member has the opportunity for face-to-face contact with each and every other member.

Social control. Surveillance and pressures that keep the person from engaging in nonconforming or deviant behavior.

Social desirability. In psychological testing, a favorable-sounding quality of test items. Examinees have a strong tendency to check these desirable items as characteristic of themselves.

Social differentiation. The process by which people make themselves distinguishable from the other members of a group, organization, or society.

Social facilitation. A somewhat antiquated term remaining from the days when it was believed that the presence of passive spectators or coactors exerted a generally beneficial effect on learning and performance. Now used to refer to all coaction and spectator effects.

Social games. Ritualized ways of responding in a social situation that keep unpleasant issues in the background.

Social interaction. The process whereby two or more people affect each other's behavior.

Socialization. The social-learning procedures that form people into functioning members of groups, organizations, and societies.

Social learning. Learning contributed to by others. (See *imitation; social reinforcement.*)

Social network. A set of interrelationships among people.

Social psychologist. A psychologist who attempts to relate regularities in behavior to the relationships among individuals.

Social reinforcers. Reinforcers that are dispensed by others.

Social standards. Criteria for behavior maintained by a group.

Society. A large social grouping that attempts to articulate and coordinate all the people and groups with varied interests who are considered members of the society.

Socioemotional leader. In R. F. Bales' theorizing, the member of the group who assumes the responsibility for maintaining cordial relations within the group and smoothing over "ruffled feathers."

Socioemotionally oriented. In R. F. Bales' theorizing, a term used to refer to behavior in a group that is directed toward establishing and maintaining friendly and congenial social relations within the group.

Solipsist. Philosopher who believes that the only verifiable reality is that which he personally knows.

Standardized method. A method that involves a set series of tasks and items that are presented in an invariant order and under as uniform conditions as possible.

Standards. Criteria for evaluation.

Status. Esteem from others, reflected in many societies in the person's power, influence, and extent to which he enjoys the "good things in life."

Stereotype. A preformed idea triggered by cues such as skin color, glasses, blue uniforms, and badges.

Stigma. An unwanted personal attribute that serves as a sign to others that the person is inadequate, incompetent, guilty, or in some other way of low social worth.

Stimulus. A change in physical energy that impinges upon the individual, typically eliciting some sort of reaction or response.

Stimulus deprivation. Conditions that minimize the quality and quantity of sensory input.

Strain toward symmetry. In Newcomb's *ABX* theory, the balance principle suggesting that people who already have similar attitudes should find each other attractive and that people who already find each other attractive should develop similar attitudes.

Subidentities. Those parts of the personality that mediate between the innermost self and the demands of a social situation.

Subjects. People or animals that are observed in a study.

Superego. In psychoanalytic theory, the moral part of personality that makes judgments concerning "right" and "wrong" actions.

Superordinate tasks. Highly important tasks which require for completion the cooperation of two or more conflicting groups.

Superstitious. Having an unwarranted conviction that a certain action or set of conditions will produce a predictable outcome.

Survey research. A form of attitude study that involves obtaining estimates of the relative frequencies with which various kinds of attitudes are held.

T-group. See *encounter group.*

Task leader. The member of a group who assumes the responsibility for directing group activities toward accomplishing the objective task at hand.

Task oriented. A term used to refer to behavior in a group that is directed toward accomplishing the objective task at hand.

TAT. See *Thematic Apperception Test.*

Tedium. A quality of an "overfamiliar" or highly repetitive stimulus that makes it unpleasant.

Teleological explanations. In psychology, explanations of behavior that seek the cause of the behavior in the consequences of the behavior.

Tendencies. Predispositions to behave in a certain way.

Territorial defense. Techniques used for keeping others at a comfortable distance.

Test battery. A "package" or combination of psychological tests that have been selected to provide more information about the respondent than could be obtained by using one test alone.

Test norms. In psychological testing, a set of scores that provide standards for evaluating individual or group performance.

Test-retest stability coefficients. An estimate of reliability expressed as the correlation of the scores obtained on successive administrations of the same test.

Thematic Apperception Test (TAT). A projective technique for assessing personality by having the respondent concoct stories about a series of pictures similar to magazine illustrations.

Theory. A statement describing and explaining the relationship among variables.

Thinking. Internal processing of information when the procedures are neither instinctive nor reflexive.

Token economy. A form of the behavior-modification approach to psychotherapy that involves establishing special mental-hospital wards on which patients are given poker chips or tokens for behaving in acceptable ways. These tokens have positive-reinforcement value because they can later be exchanged for goods and services.

Traits. See *genotypic traits.*

Transference. In psychoanalysis, a process in which the patient begins responding to the analyst as he had earlier responded to his parents and other significant people in his life.

Transformation of identity. Term coined by Strauss to indicate the results of turning points in life at which the individual must stop, take stock of himself, say to himself "I am not the same person I used to be," and redefine himself accordingly.

Triadic relationships. (1) In group dynamics, relationships among three people. (2) In attitude theory, relationships among three elements or cognitions.

Trial. An opportunity or occasion to learn or perform.

Unconditioned response. In classical conditioning, a response reliably elicited by the unconditioned stimulus at the beginning of the conditioning procedures.

Unconditioned stimulus. In classical-conditioning procedures, a stimulus that reliably elicits a specific response at the beginning of the conditioning procedures.

Unconscious. That part of our psychological makeup that is inaccessible to awareness.

Undoing. A defense mechanism involving attempts to rub out wishes or memories as if they had never occurred.

Unfinished business. In Gestalt therapy, feelings such as anger, grief, and love that have never been appropriately expressed and are thought to drain energy away from creative living in the present.

Unit relationships. In attitude theory, a relationship between two elements or cognitions such that the two are seen as "belonging with" or "related to" each other.

Utilitarian function. In attitude theory, the use of an attitude for achieving personal ends.

Validity. Roughly synonymous with truthfulness. An observation is valid if it is an instance of that which it is supposed to be. There are several forms of validity. (See *construct validity; content validity; face validity.*)

Value-expressive function. In attitude theory, the use of an attitude for the purpose of expressing important underlying values.

Values. Judgments of attractiveness, desirability, and worth that are based on abstract concepts or broad classifications.

Variable. Something that varies or changes such as the causes or antecedents of behavior (independent variables) or behavior itself (dependent variables).

Veridical. In perception, a term used to describe a perception as accurate.

Yielding. In conformity research, abandoning one's personal judgment to make a judgment that conforms with that made by the other people in the group.

References

Abrahamson, M. L. *Interpersonal accommodation.* Princeton, N. J.: Van Nostrand, 1966.

Adams, J. S., & Hoffman, D. The frequency of self-reference statements as a function of generalized reinforcement. *Journal of Abnormal and Social Psychology,* 1960, **60,** 384–389.

Aderman, D. Effects of anticipating future interaction on the preference for balanced states. *Journal of Personality and Social Psychology,* 1969, **11,** 214–219.

Allee, W., & Masure, R. A. Comparison of maze behavior in paired and isolated shell-parakeets (*Melopsittacus undulatus Shaw*) in a two-alley problem box. *Journal of Comparative Psychology,* 1936, **22,** 131–151.

Allison, J., Blatt, S. J., & Zimet, C. N. *The interpretation of psychological tests.* New York: Harper & Row, 1968.

Allport, F. H. The influence of the group upon association and thought. *Journal of Experimental Psychology,* 1920, **3,** 159–182.

Allport, F. H. *Social psychology.* Cambridge, Mass.: Riverside Press, 1924.

Allport, F. H. *Theories of perception and the concept of structure.* New York: Wiley, 1955.

Allport, G. W. The historical background of modern social psychology. In G. Lindzey (Ed.), *Handbook of social psychology,* Vol. I. Reading, Mass.: Addison-Wesley, 1954.

Allport, G. W., & Odbert, H. S. Trait-names: A psycholexical study. *Psychological Monographs,* 1936, **47** (Whole No. 211), 1–171.

Allport, G. W., & Pettigrew, T. F. Cultural influence on the perception of movement: The trapezoid illusion among Zulus. *Journal of Abnormal and Social Psychology,* 1957, **55,** 104–113.

Allport, G. W., & Postman, L. *The psychology of rumor.* New York: Holt, 1947.

Allyon, T. Intensive treatment of psychotic behavior by stimulus satiation and food reinforcement. *Behavior Research and Therapy,* 1963, **1,** 53–61.

American Psychiatric Association, Committee on Nomenclature and Statistics. *Diagnostic and statistical manual: Mental disorders.* (2nd ed.) Washington, D. C.: American Psychiatric Association, 1968.

Amir, Y. Contact hypothesis in ethnic relations. *Psychological Bulletin,* 1969, **71,** 319–342.

Amsel, A. The effect upon level of consummatory response of the addition of anxiety to a motivational complex. *Journal of Experimental Psychology,* 1950, **40,** 709–715.

Anastasi, A. *Psychological testing.* (2nd ed.) New York: Macmillan, 1961.

Aronson, E., & Mills, J. The effect of severity of initiation on liking for a group. *Journal of Abnormal and Social Psychology,* 1959, **59,** 177–181.

Asch, S. *Social psychology.* Englewood Cliffs, N. J.: Prentice-Hall, 1952.

Asch, S. Effects of group pressure upon the modification and distortion of judgments. In D. Cartwright & A. Zander (Eds.), *Group dynamics: Research and theory.* (2nd ed.) Evanston, Ill.: Row, Peterson, 1960. Pp. 189–200.

References

Atkinson, J. W. (Ed.) *Motives in fantasy, action and society.* Princeton, N. J.: Van Nostrand, 1958a.

Atkinson, J. W. Toward expectancies and incentives. In J. W. Atkinson (Ed.), *Motives in fantasy, action and society.* Princeton, N. J.: Van Nostrand, 1958b. Pp. 288–305.

Atkinson, J. W. *An introduction to motivation.* Princeton, N. J.: Van Nostrand, 1964.

Atkinson, J. W., & McClelland, D. C. The projective expression of needs: II. The effect of different intensities of hunger drive on thematic apperception. *Journal of Experimental Psychology,* 1948, **38,** 643–658.

Azrin, N. H., Hutchinson, R. R., & Hake, D. F. Extinction induced aggression. *Journal of the Experimental Analysis of Behavior,* 1966, **9,** 191–204.

Back, K. Influence through social communication. *Journal of Abnormal and Social Psychology,* 1951, **46,** 9–23.

Backman, C. W., & Secord, P. F. Liking, selective interaction and misperception in congruent interpersonal relations. *Sociometry,* 1962, **25,** 321–335.

Bales, R. F. *Interaction process analysis: A method for the study of small groups.* Reading, Mass.: Addison-Wesley, 1950a.

Bales, R. F. A set of categories for the analysis of small group interaction. *American Sociological Review,* 1950b, **15,** 257–263.

Bales, R. F., & Strodtbeck, F. L. Phases in group problem solving. *Journal of Abnormal and Social Psychology,* 1951, **46,** 485–495.

Bandura, A. *Principles of behavior modification.* New York: Holt, Rinehart and Winston, 1969.

Bandura, A., Blanchard, E., & Ritter, B. Relative efficacy of desensitization and modeling approaches for inducing behavioral, affective and attitudinal changes. *Journal of Personality and Social Psychology,* 1969, **13,** 173–200.

Bandura, A., & Menlove, F. L. Factors determining vicarious extinction of avoidance behavior through symbolic modeling. *Journal of Personality and Social Psychology,* 1968, **8,** 99–108.

Bandura, A., Ross, D., and Ross, A. A comparative test of the status envy, social power, and secondary reinforcement theories of identificatory learning. *Journal of Abnormal and Social Psychology,* 1963, **67,** 527–534.

Bandura, A., & Walters, R. H. *Social learning and personality development.* New York: Holt, Rinehart, and Winston, 1963.

Barker, R., Dembo, L., & Lewin, K. Frustration and aggression: An experiment with young children. *University of Iowa Studies in Child Welfare,* 1941, **18** (1).

Barnum, P. T. *Struggles and triumphs: Or, forty years' recollections.* Buffalo, N. Y.: Warren, Johnson, 1872.

Baron, R. A. Attraction toward the model and model's competence as determinants of adult imitative behavior. *Journal of Personality and Social Psychology,* 1970, **14,** 345–351.

Baron, R. A., & Kepner, C. R. Model's behavior and attraction toward the model as determinants of adult aggressive behavior. *Journal of Personality and Social Psychology,* 1970, **14,** 335–344.

Bartlett, D. J., Hurley, W. R., Brand, C. R., & Poole, E. W. Chromosomes of male patients in a security prison. *Nature,* 1968, **219,** 351–354.

Baumrind, D. Child care practices anteceding three patterns of preschool behavior. *Genetic Psychological Monographs,* 1967, **75,** 43–88.

Baumrind, D., & Black, A. Socialization practices associated with dimensions of competence in preschool boys and girls. *Child Development,* 1967, **38,** 291–327.

Bavelas, A. A mathematical model for group structures. *Applied Anthropology,* 1948, **7,** 16–30.

Bavelas, A. Communication patterns in task-oriented groups. *Journal of the Acoustical Society of America,* 1950, **22,** 725–730.

Bavelas, A., Hastdorf, A. H., Gross, A. E., & Kite, W. R. Experiments in the alteration of group structure. *Journal of Experimental Social Psychology,* 1965, **1,** 55–71.

Becker, H. S. Becoming a marijuana user. *American Journal of Sociology,* 1953, **59,** 235–242.

Becker, H. S. *Outsiders: Studies in the sociology of deviance.* London: Free Press of Glencoe, 1963.

Becknell, J. C., Jr., Wilson, W. R., & Baird, J. C. The effect of frequency of presentation on the choice of nonsense syllables. *Journal of Psychology,* 1963, **56,** 165–170.

Bem, D. *Beliefs, attitudes and human affairs.* Belmont, Calif.: Brooks/Cole, 1970.

Berg, I. A. Deviant responses and deviant people: The formulation of the deviation hypothesis. *Journal of Counseling Psychology,* 1957, **4,** 154–161.

Berg, I. A. Measuring deviant behavior by means of deviant response sets. In I. A. Berg & B. M. Bass (Eds.), *Conformity and deviation.* New York: Harper & Row, 1961, Pp. 328–379.

Bergum, B. O., & Lehr, D. J. Efforts of authoritarianism on vigilance performance. *Journal of Applied Psychology,* 1963, **47,** 75–77.

Berkowitz, L. Group standards, cohesiveness and productivity. *Human Relations,* 1954, **7,** 509–519.

Berkowitz, L. The expression and reduction of hostility. *Psychological Bulletin,* **1958,** **55,** 257–283.

Berkowitz, L. The concept of aggressive drive: Some additional considerations. In L. Berkowitz (Ed.), *Advances in experimental social psychology,* Vol. 2. New York: Academic Press, 1965.

Berkowitz, L. *Roots of aggression: A reexamination of the frustration-aggression hypothesis.* New York: Atherton Press, 1969.

Berkowitz, L., & Geen, R. G. Film violence and cue properties of available targets. *Journal of Personality and Social Psychology,* 1966, **3,** 525–530.

Berkowitz, L., & LePage, A. Weapons as aggression-eliciting stimuli. *Journal of Personality and Social Psychology,* 1967, **7,** 202–207.

Berlyne, D. E. *Conflict, arousal and curiosity.* New York: McGraw-Hill, 1960.

Berlyne, D. E. Curiosity and exploration. *Science,* 1966, **153,** 23–33.

Berlyne, D. E. Novelty, complexity and hedonic value. *Perception and Psychophysics,* 1970, **8,** 279–286.

Berscheid, E., & Walster, E. H. *Interpersonal attraction.* Reading, Mass.: Addison-Wesley, 1969.

Bexton, W. H., Heron, W., & Scott, T. H. Effects of decreased variation in the sensory environment. *Canadian Journal of Psychology,* 1954, **8,** 70–76.

Birch, J. D., & Veroff, J. *Motivation: A study of action.* Belmont, Calif.: Brooks/Cole, 1966.

Bishop, F. V. The anal character: A rebel in the dissonance family. *Journal of Personality and Social Psychology,* 1967, **6,** 23–36.

Bixenstine, V. E., Potash, H. M., & Wilson, K. V. Effects of levels of cooperative choice by the other player on choices in a prisoner's dilemma game. *Journal of Abnormal and Social Psychology,* 1963, **66,** 308–313.

References

Blake, R. R., & Mouton, J. S. The intergroup dynamics of win-lose conflict and problem solving collaboration in union-management relations. In M. Sherif (Ed.), *Intergroup relations and leadership.* New York: Wiley, 1962.

Blake, R. R., Shepard, H. A., & Mouton, J. S. *Managing intergroup conflict in industry.* Houston: Gulf, 1964.

Blum, G. *The Blacky Pictures: A technique for the exploration of personality dynamics.* Ann Arbor, Mich.: Psychodynamic Instruments, 1950.

Blum, G. *Psychodynamics: The science of unconscious mental forces.* Belmont, Calif.: Brooks/Cole, 1969.

Blum, G., & Miller, D. R. Exploring the psychoanalytic theory of the "oral character." *Journal of Personality,* 1952, **20,** 287–304.

Bower, G. H., Fowler, H., & Trapold, M. A. Escape learning as a function of the amount of shock reduction. *Journal of Experimental Psychology,* 1959, **58,** 482–484.

Brady, J. V. Ulcers in the executive monkey. *Scientific American,* 1958, **199,** 363–404.

Brehm, J. W. Postdecision changes in the desirability of alternatives. *Journal of Abnormal and Social Psychology,* 1956, **52,** 384–389.

Brehm, J. W., & Cohen, A. R. Choice and chance relative deprivations as determinants of cognitive dissonance. *Journal of Abnormal and Social Psychology,* 1959, **58, 383–387.**

Brehm, J. W., & Cohen, A. R. *Explorations in cognitive dissonance.* New York: Wiley, 1962.

Brenner, C. *An elementary textbook of psychoanalysis.* Garden City, N. Y.: Anchor Books, 1957.

Bresler, D. E., & Bitterman, M. E. Learning in fish with transplanted brain tissue. *Science,* 1969, **163,** 590–592.

Broadhurst, P. L. Emotionality and the Yerkes-Dodson law. *Journal of Experimental Psychology,* 1957, **54,** 345–352.

Bronfenbrenner, U. The mirror image in Soviet-American relations—a social psychologist's report. *Journal of Social Issues,* 1961, **17,** 45–56.

Brophy, I. N. The luxury of anti-Negro prejudice. *Public Opinion Quarterly,* 1945, **9,** 456–466.

Brown, J. S. Gradients of approach and avoidance responses and their relation to motivation. *Journal of Comparative and Physiological Psychology,* 1948, **41,** 450–465.

Brown, J. S. *The motivation of behavior.* New York: McGraw-Hill, 1961.

Brown, J. S., Kalish, H. I., & Farber, I. E. Conditioned fear as revealed by magnitude of startle response to an auditory stimulus. *Journal of Experimental Psychology,* 1951, **41,** 317–328.

Brown, R. *Social psychology.* New York: Free Press, 1965.

Brown, R., & Bellugi, U. Three processes in the child's acquisition of syntax. In E. H. Lenneberg (Ed.), *New directions in the study of language.* Cambridge, Mass.: MIT Press, 1964. Pp. 131–161.

Brown, W. L. *The endless hours.* New York: Norton, 1961.

Broxton, J., A test of interpersonal attraction predictions derived from balance theory. *Journal of Abnormal and Social Psychology,* 1963, **66,** 394–397.

Bruner, J. S. Perceptual theory and the Rorschach test. *Journal of Personality,* 1948, **17,** 157–168.

Bryan, J. H., & Test, M. A. Models and helping: Naturalistic studies in aiding behavior. *Journal of Personality and Social Psychology,* 1967, **6,** 400–407.

Bugental, J. F. T. *Challenges of humanistic psychology.* New York: McGraw-Hill, 1967.

Buros, O. K. (Ed.) *The sixth mental measurements yearbook.* Highland Park, N. J.: Gryphon Press, 1965.

Buros, O. K. *Personality tests and reviews.* Highland Park, N. J.: Gryphon Press, 1970.

Byrne, D., & Blaylock, B. Similarity and assumed similarity of attitudes between husbands and wives. *Journal of Abnormal and Social Psychology,* 1963, **67,** 636–640.

Byrne, D., & McGraw, D. Interpersonal attraction towards Negroes. *Human Relations,* 1964, **17,** 201–213.

Byrne, D., & Nelson, D. Attraction as a linear function of proportion of positive reinforcement. *Journal of Personality and Social Psychology,* 1965, **1,** 659–663.

Campbell, D. A., & Kraeling, D. Response strength as a function of drive level and amount of drive reduction. *Journal of Experimental Psychology,* 1953, **45,** 97–101.

Campbell, D., Sanderson, R. E., & Laverty, S. G. Characteristics of a conditioned response in human subjects during extinction trials following a single traumatic conditioning trial. *Journal of Abnormal and Social Psychology,* 1964, **68,** 627–639.

Carlsmith, J. M., Collins, B. E., & Helmreich, R. L. The effect of pressure for compliance on attitude change. *Journal of Personality and Social Psychology,* 1966, **4,** 1–13.

Cartwright, D. The nature of group cohesiveness. In D. Cartwright & A. Zander (Eds.), *Group dynamics: Research and theory.* (3rd ed.) New York: Harper & Row, 1968.

Cartwright, D., & Zander, A. (Eds.) *Group dynamics: Research and theory.* (2nd ed.) New York: Harper & Row, 1960.

Cartwright, D., & Zander, A. (Eds.) *Group dynamics: Research and theory.* (3rd ed.) New York: Harper & Row, 1968.

Cattell, R. B., & Nesselroade, J. R. Likeness and completeness theories examined by sixteen Personality Factor Measures on stably and unstably married couples. *Journal of Personality and Social Psychology,* 1967, **7,** 351–361.

Centers, R. A laboratory adaptation of the controversial procedures for the conditioning of verbal operants. *Journal of Abnormal and Social Psychology,* 1963, **67,** 334–339.

Charters, W. W., Jr., & Newcomb, T. M. Some attitudinal effects of experimentally increased salience of a membership group. In E. E. Maccoby, T. M. Newcomb, & E. L. Hartley (Eds.), *Readings in social psychology.* (3rd ed.) New York: Holt, Rinehart and Winston, 1958. Pp. 276–280.

Chen, S. C. Social modification of activity of ants in nest building. *Physiological Zoology,* 1937, **10,** 420–436.

Child, I. L. The relation of somatotype to self-ratings on Sheldon's temperamental traits. *Journal of Personality,* 1950, **18,** 440–453.

Cialdini, R. B., & Insko, C. A. Attitudinal verbal reinforcement as a function of informational consistency: A further test of the two factor theory. *Journal of Personality and Social Psychology,* 1969, **12,** 342–350.

Clark, C. L. *Lockstep and corridor.* Cincinnati: The University of Cincinnati Press, 1927.

Clarke, J. *Man is the prey.* New York: Stein and Day, 1969.

References

Clausen, J. A. Mental disorders. In R. K. Merton & R. A. Nisbet (Eds.), *Contemporary social problems*. New York: Harcourt, Brace and World, 1961. Pp. 181–221.

Clausen, J. A. (Ed.) *Socialization and society*. Boston: Little, Brown, 1968.

Cleckley, H. *The mask of sanity*. St. Louis: Mosby, 1955.

Cohen, A. M., Bennis, W. G., & Wolkon, G. H. The effects of changes in communication networks on the behaviors of problem solving groups. *Sociometry*, 1962, **25**, 177–196.

Cohen, A. R. Experiment reported in J. W. Brehm & A. R. Cohen, *Explorations in cognitive dissonance*. New York: Wiley, 1962.

Collins, B. E. An experimental study of satisfaction, productivity, turnover, and comparison levels. Unpublished doctoral dissertation, Northwestern University, 1963.

Collins, B. E., & Raven, B. H. Group structure: Attraction, coalitions, communication, and power. In G. Lindzey & E. Aronson (Eds.), *The handbook of social psychology* (2nd ed.), Vol. IV. Reading, Mass.: Addison-Wesley, 1969. Pp. 283–322.

Coopersmith, S. *The antecedents of self-esteem*. San Francisco: W. H. Freeman, 1967.

Cottrell, L. S. The analysis of situational fields in social psychology. *American Sociological Review*, 1942, **7**, 370–382.

Cottrell, N. B. Social facilitation. In C. G. McClintock (Ed.), *Experimental social psychology*. New York: Holt, Rinehart, and Winston, 1972.

Couch, A., & Keniston, K. Yeasayers and naysayers: Agreeing response set as a personality variable. *Journal of Abnormal and Social Psychology*, 1960, **60**, 151–174.

Cowan, P. A., & Walters, R. H. Studies of reinforcement of aggression: 1. Effects of scheduling. *Child Development*, 1963, **34**, 543–551.

Cronbach, L. J. The two disciplines of scientific psychology. *American Psychologist*, 1957, **12**, 671–684.

Cronbach, L. J. *Essentials of psychological testing*. (2nd ed.) New York: Harper & Row, 1960.

Cronbach, L. J. *Essentials of psychological testing*. (3rd ed.) New York: Harper & Row, 1969.

Cronbach, L. J., & Meehl, P. E. Construct validity in psychological tests. *Psychological Bulletin*, 1955, **52**, 281–302.

Crowne, E. P., & Strickland, B. R. The conditioning of verbal behavior as a function of the need for social approval. *Journal of Abnormal and Social Psychology*, 1961, **63**, 395–401.

Crum, J., Brown, W. L., & Bitterman, M. E. The effect of partial and delayed reinforcement on resistance to extinction. *American Journal of Psychology*, 1951, **64**, 228–237.

Darley, J., & Latané, B. Bystander intervention in emergencies: Diffusion of responsibility. *Journal of Personality and Social Psychology*. 1968, **8**, 377–383.

Dashiell, J. F. An experimental analysis of some group effects. *Journal of Abnormal and Social Psychology*, 1930, **25**, 190–199.

Davis, K. Final note on a case of extreme isolation. *American Journal of Sociology*, 1947, **52**, 432–437.

Davitz, J. R. The effects of previous training in post-frustrative behavior. *Journal of Abnormal and Social Psychology*, 1952, **47**, 309–315.

Della Femina, J. *From those wonderful folks who gave you Pearl Harbor*. New York: Simon and Schuster, 1970.

Deutsch, M. The effect of motivational orientation upon trust and suspicion. *Human Relations*, 1960, **13**, 122–139.

Deutsch, M., & Gerard, H. B. A study of normative and informational social influences upon individual judgment. *Journal of Abnormal and Social Psychology*, 1955, **51**, 629–636.

Dollard, J., Doob, L., Miller, N., Mowrer, O., & Sears, R. *Frustration and aggression.* New Haven, Conn.: Yale University Press, 1939.

Douvan, E., & Adelson, J. *The adolescent experience.* New York: Wiley, 1966.

Douvan, E. L., & Gold, M. Modal patterns in American adolescence. In L. W. Hoffman & M. L. Hoffman (Eds.), *Review of child development research*, Vol. 2. New York: Russell Sage Foundation, 1966.

Dunnette, M. D., Campbell, J., & Jaastad, K. The effect of group participation on problem solving. *Journal of Applied Psychology*, 1963, **47**, 30–37.

Edwards, A. L. *The social desirability variable in personality assessment and research.* New York: Dryden, 1957.

Egan, G. *Encounter: Group processes for interpersonal growth.* Belmont, Calif.: Brooks/Cole, 1970.

Eisenstadt, S. N. *From generation to generation; age groups and social structure.* Glencoe, Ill.: Free Press, 1956.

Ekman, P. Body position, facial expression and verbal behavior during interviews. *Journal of Abnormal and Social Psychology*, 1964, **68**, 295–301.

Ekman, P. Differential communication of affect by head and body cues. *Journal of Personality and Social Psychology*, 1965, **2**, 726–735.

Ekman, P., & Friesen, W. V. Non-verbal leakage and clues to deception. *Psychiatry*, 1969, **32**, 88–106.

Elms, A. C. *Role playing, reward, and attitude change.* New York: Van Nostrand-Reinhold, 1969.

Elms, A., & Janis, I. Counter-norm attitudes induced by consonant versus dissonant conditions of role playing. *Journal of Experimental Research in Personality*, 1965, **1**, 50–60.

Erlenmeyer-Kimling, L., & Jarvick, L. F. Genetics and intelligence: A review. *Science*, 1963, **142**, 1477–1478.

Estes, W. K. An experimental study of punishment. *Psychological Monographs*, 1944, **57** (3).

Etzioni, A. Nonconventional uses of sociology as illustrated by peace research. In P. R. Lazarsfeld, W. H. Sewell, & H. L. Wilensky (Eds.), *The uses of sociology.* New York: Basic Books, 1967. Pp. 806–838.

Etzioni, A. Social psychological aspects of international relations. In G. Lindzey & E. Aronson (Eds.), *Handbook of social psychology* (2nd. ed.), Vol. V. Reading, Mass.: Addison-Wesley, 1969. Pp. 538–601.

Exline, R. V. Group climate as a factor in the relevance and accuracy of social perception. *Journal of Abnormal and Social Psychology*, 1957, **55**, 382–388.

Fauchaux, C., & Moscovici, S. Études sur la creativitie des groupes: I. Tâche, situation individuelle et groupe. *Bulletin Psychologie*, 1958, **11**, 863–874.

Faust, W. L. Group versus individual problem solving. *Journal of Abnormal and Social Psychology*, 1959, **59**, 68–72.

Felipe, N., & Sommer, R. Invasions of personal space. *Social Problems*, 1966, **14**, 206–214.

Festinger, L. *A theory of cognitive dissonance.* New York: Harper & Row, 1957.

Festinger, L., & Carlsmith, J. M. Cognitive consequences of forced compliance. *Journal of Abnormal and Social Psychology*, 1959, **58**, 203–211.

Festinger, L. S., Schachter, S., & Back, K. *Social pressures in informal groups: A study of human factors in housing.* New York: Harper & Row, 1950.

Flavell, J. H. *The developmental psychology of Jean Piaget.* Princeton, N. J.: Van Nostrand, 1963.

Forssman, H., & Hambert, G. Chromosomes and antisocial behavior. *Excepta Criminologica*, 1967, **7**, 113–117.

Fredenburg, N. C. Response strength as a function of alley length and time of deprivation. Unpublished master's thesis, State University of Iowa, 1956. (Reported in J. Brown, *The motivation of behavior.* New York: McGraw-Hill, 1961.)

French, J. R. P., Jr. The disruption and cohesion of groups. *Journal of Abnormal and Social Psychology*, 1941, **36**, 361–377.

French, J. R. P., Jr., & Raven, B. The bases of social power. In D. Cartwright (Ed.), *Studies in social power.* Ann Arbor, Mich.: Institute for Social Research, 1959.

Frincke, G., & Johnson, R. C. Word value and word frequency in homophone pairs. *Psychological Reports*, 1960, **7**, 470.

Gallo, P., & McClintock, C. G. Cooperative and competitive behavior in mixed-motive games. *Journal of Conflict Resolution*, 1965, **9**, 68-78.

Gardner, R. A., & Gardner, B. T. Teaching sign language to a chimpanzee. *Science*, 1969, **165**, 644–672.

Gates, M. G., & Allee, W. C. Conditioned behavior of isolated and grouped cockroaches on a simple maze. *Journal of Comparative Psychology*, 1933, **13**, 331–358.

Geen, R. G. Effects of frustration, attack and prior training in aggressiveness upon aggressive behavior. *Journal of Personality and Social Psychology*, 1968, **9**, 316–321.

Geiwitz, P. J. *Non-Freudian personality theories.* Belmont, Calif.: Brooks/Cole, 1969.

Gentry, W. D. Effects of frustration, attack and prior aggressiveness training on overt aggression and vascular processes. *Journal of Personality and Social Psychology*, 1970, **16**, 718–725.

Gerard, H. B., & Mathewson, G. C. The effect of severity of initiation on liking for a group: A replication. *Journal of Experimental Social Psychology*, 1966, **2**, 278–287.

Gesell, A., & Thompson, H. Learning and growth in identical infant twins. *Genetic Psychological Monograph*, 1929, **6**, 1–23.

Gibb, C. A. Leadership. In G. Lindzey & E. Aronson (Eds.), *The handbook of social psychology* (2nd ed.), Vol. 4. Reading, Mass.: Addison-Wesley, 1969. Pp. 205–282.

Glaser, B. G., & Strauss, A. L. *Time for dying.* Chicago: Aldine, 1968.

Glixman, A. F. Recall of completed and incompleted tasks under varying degrees of stress. *Journal of Experimental Psychology*, 1949, **39**, 281–295.

Glueck, S., & Glueck, E. *Unraveling juvenile delinquency.* New York: The Commonwealth Fund, 1950.

Goffman, E. *Stigma: Notes on the management of spoiled identity.* Englewood Cliffs, N. J.: Prentice-Hall, 1963.

Goldman-Eisler, F. Breast feeding and oral character formation. *Journal of Personality*, 1948, **17**, 83–103, 187–196.

Greening, T. (Ed.) *Existential humanistic psychology.* Belmont, Calif.: Brooks/Cole, 1971.

Greenspoon, T. The reinforcing effect of two spoken sounds on the frequency of two responses. *American Journal of Psychology*, 1955, **68**, 409–416.

Griffith, R., & Mayer, A. *The movies.* New York: Bonanza Books, 1957.

Haire, M. Projective techniques in marketing research. *The Journal of Marketing,* 1950, **14,** 649–656.

Hall, C. S. *A primer of Freudian psychology.* New York: Mentor Books, 1954.

Hall, C. S., & Van de Castle, R. L. An empirical investigation of the castration complex in dreams. *Journal of Personality,* 1965, **33,** 20–29.

Hanratty, M. A., Liebert, R. M., Morris, L. W., & Fernandez, L. E. Imitation of film-mediated aggression against live and inanimate victims. *Proceedings of the 77th Annual Convention of the American Psychological Association,* 1969, **4,** 457–458.

Harding, J., & Hogrefe, R. Attitudes toward Negro co-workers in an Eastern urban department store. *Journal of Social Issues,* 1952, **8,** 18–28.

Hare, H. P., & Bales, R. F. Seating position and small group interaction. *Sociometry,* 1963, **4,** 480–486.

Harris, P., & Nygaard, J. E. Resistance to extinction and number of reinforced trials. *Psychological Reports,* 1961, **8,** 233–234.

Harrison, A. A. Exposure, favorability, and item endorsement. *Psychological Reports,* 1968a, **23,** 1070.

Harrison, A. A. Response competition, frequency, exploratory behavior and liking. *Journal of Personality and Social Psychology,* 1968b, **9,** 363–368.

Harrison, A. A. Exposure and popularity. *Journal of Personality,* 1969, **37,** 359–367.

Harrison, A. A., & Crandall, R. Heterogeneity-homogeneity of exposure sequence and the attitudinal effects of exposure. *Journal of Personality and Social Psychology,* 1972, **21,** 234–238.

Harrison, A. A., & Hines, P. The effects of frequency of exposure at three short exposure times on affective ratings and exploratory behavior. *Proceedings of the American Psychological Association,* 1970, Pp. 391–392.

Harrison, A. A., Tutone, R., & McFadgen, D. G. The effects of frequency of exposure of changing and unchanging stimulus pairs on affective ratings. *Journal of Personality and Social Psychology,* 1971, **20,** 102–111.

Harrison, A. A., & Zajonc, R. B. The effects of frequency and duration of exposure on response competition and affective ratings. *Journal of Psychology,* 1970, **75,** 163–169.

Hatfield, J. S., Ferguson, L. R., & Alpert, R. Mother-child interaction and the socialization process. *Child Development,* 1967, **38,** 365–414.

Havighurst, R. J. Youth in exploration and man emergent. In H. Borrow (Ed.), *Man in a world at work.* Boston: Houghton Mifflin, 1964. Pp. 215–236.

Hayes, C. *The ape in our house.* New York: Harper & Row, 1951.

Hays, W. L. *Statistics for psychologists.* New York: Holt, Rinehart and Winston, 1963.

Heider, F. Attitudes and cognitive organization. *Journal of Psychology,* 1946, **21,** 107-112.

Heider, F. *The psychology of interpersonal relations.* New York: Wiley, 1958.

Heron, W. The pathology of boredom. *Scientific American,* 1957, **196,** 52–56.

Heron, W., Doane, B. K., & Scott, T. H. Visual disturbances after prolonged perceptual isolation. *Canadian Journal of Psychology,* 1956, **10,** 13–18.

Hildum, D. C., & Brown, R. W. Verbal reinforcement and interviewer bias. *Journal of Abnormal and Social Psychology,* 1956, **53,** 108–111.

Hope, K. The study of hostility in the temperaments of spouses: Definitions and methods. *The British Journal of Mathematical and Statistical Psychology,* 1969, 22(I), 67–95.

References

Hovland, C. I., & Sears, R. R. Minor studies in aggression: VI. Correlations of lynchings and economic indices. *Journal of Psychology*, 1940, **9**, 301–310.

Howes, D. H., & Solomon, R. L. A note on McGinnies' "Emotionality and perceptual defense." *Psychological Review*, 1950, **57**, 229–234.

Howes, D. H., & Solomon, R. L. Visual duration threshold as a function of word probability. *Journal of Experimental Psychology*, 1951, **41**, 401–410.

Hurwitz, J. I., Zander, A., & Hymovitch, B. Some effects of power on the relations among group members. In D. Cartwright & A. Zander (Eds.), *Group dynamics: Research and theory* (2nd ed.) New York: Harper & Row, 1960.

Hutt, P. J. Rate of bar pressing as a function of quality of food reward. *Journal of Comparative and Physiological Psychology*, 1954, **47**, 235-239.

Inkeles, A., & Levinson, D. J. National character: The study of modal personality and sociocultural systems. In G. Lindzey (Ed.), *Handbook of social psychology*. (1st ed.) Reading, Mass.: Addison-Wesley, 1954. Pp. 977–1020.

Inkeles, A., & Levinson, D. J. National character: The study of modal personality and sociocultural systems. In G. Lindzey & E. Aronson (Eds.), *The handbook of social psychology*, Vol. IV. (2nd ed.) Reading, Mass.: Addison-Wesley, 1969. Pp. 418–506.

Insko, C. A. Verbal reinforcement of attitude. *Journal of Personality and Social Psychology*, 1965, **2**, 621–623.

Isaacs, W., Thomas, J., & Goldiamond, I. Application of operant conditioning to reinstate verbal behavior in psychotics. *Journal of Speech and Hearing Disorders*, 1960, **25**, 8–12.

Ison, J. R. Experimental extinction as a function of the number of reinforcements. *Journal of Experimental Psychology*, 1962, **64**, 314–317.

Izard, C. E. Personality, similarity and friendship. *Journal of Abnormal and Social Psychology*, 1960, **61**, 47–51.

Janis, I. L., & Gilmore, J. B. The influence of incentive conditions on the success of role playing in modifying attitudes. *Journal of Personality and Social Psychology*, 1965, **1**, 17–27.

Jersild, A. Memory for the pleasant as compared with the unpleasant. *Journal of Experimental Psychology*, 1931, **14**, 284–288.

Johnson, R. C., Thomson, C. W., & Frincke, G. Word values, word frequencies and duration thresholds. *Psychological Review*, 1960, **67**, 332–342.

Jones, E. E. & Gerard, H. B. *Foundations of social psychology.* New York: Wiley, 1967.

Jordan, N. Behavioral forces that are a function of attitudes and of cognitive organization. *Human Relations*, 1953, **6**, 273–287.

Kalish, R. A. The aged and the dying process: The inevitable decisions. *The Journal of Social Issues*, 1965, **21**, 87–96.

Katz, D. The functional approach to the study of attitude change. *Public Opinion Quarterly*, 1960, **24**, 163–204.

Katz, D. Current and needed psychological research in international relations. *Journal of Social Issues*, 1961, **17**, 69–78.

Katz, D. Social psychology: A perspective. *Journal of Personality and Social Psychology*, 1967, **7**, 341–344.

Katz, D., & Kahn, R. L. *The social psychology of organizations.* New York: Wiley, 1966.

Kelley, H. H., & Thibaut, J. W. Group problem solving. In G. Lindzey & E. Aronson (Eds.), *Handbook of social psychology* (2nd ed.), Vol. IV. Reading, Mass.: Addison-Wesley, 1969. Pp. 1–101.

Kerckhoff, A., & Davis, K. E. Value consensus and need complementarity in mate selection. *American Sociological Review*, 1962, **27**, 295–303.

Kiesler, C. A., & Kiesler, S. B. *Conformity*. Reading, Mass.: Addison-Wesley, 1969.

Kleinmuntz, B. *Personality measurement*. Homewood, Ill.: Dorsey Press, 1967.

Klopfer, P. H. Influence of social interaction on learning rates in birds. *Science*, 1958, **128**, 903.

Knox, R. E., & Inkster, J. A. Post decision dissonance at post time. *Journal of Personality and Social Psychology*, 1968, **4**, 319–323.

Kogon, E. The theory and practice of Hell. New York: Berkley Books, 1960.

Kohler, I. Experiments with goggles. *Scientific American*, 1962, **200**, 84–99.

Komorita, S. S. Cooperative choice in the Prisoner's Dilemma Game. *Journal of Personality and Social Psychology*, 1965, **2**, 741–745.

Krasner, L., Knowles, J. P., & Ullmann, L. P. Effect of verbal conditioning of attitudes on subsequent motor performance. *Journal of Personality and Social Psychology*, 1965, **1**, 407–412.

Krushchev, N. *Krushchev remembers*. Boston: Little, Brown, 1970.

Kutner, B., Fanshel, D., Togo, A. M., & Langner, T. S. *Five hundred over sixty: A community survey on aging*. New York: Russell Sage Foundation, 1956.

Latané, B., & Darley, J. Bystander "apathy." *American Scientist*, 1969, **57**, 244–268.

Latané, B., & Rodin, J. A lady in distress: Inhibiting effects of friends and strangers on bystander intervention. *Journal of Experimental Social Psychology*, 1969, **5**, 189–202.

Lavin, N. I., Thorpe, J. G., Barker, J. C., Blakemore, C. B., & Conway, C. G. Behavior therapy in a case of transvestism. *Journal of Nervous and Mental Disorders*, 1961, **133**, 346–353.

Lawrence, D. H., & Festinger, L. *Deterrents and reinforcement*. Stanford, Calif.: Stanford University Press, 1962.

Lazarsfeld, P. The American soldier: An expository review. *Public Opinion Quarterly*, 1949, **13**, 377–404.

Leavitt, H. J. Some effects of certain communication patterns on group performance. *Journal of Abnormal and Social Psychology*, 1951, **46**, 38–50.

Leeper, R. W. A study of a neglected portion of the field of learning: The development of sensory organization. *Journal of Genetic Psychology*, 1935, **46**, 41–75.

Lessler, K. Sexual symbols, structured and unstructured. *Journal of Consulting Psychology*, 1962, **26**, 44–49.

Levinger, G., & Breedlove, J. Interpersonal attraction and agreement: A study of marriage partners. *Journal of Personality and Social Psychology*, 1966, **3**, 367–372.

Lewis, D. J. Partial reinforcement: A selective review of the literature since 1950. *Psychological Bulletin*, 1960, **57**, 1–28.

Lewis, D. J., & Duncan, D. P. Effect of different percentages of money reward on extinction of a lever pulling response. *Journal of Experimental Psychology*, 1956, **52**, 23–27.

Lieberman, S. The effects of changes in roles on the attitudes of role occupants. *Human Relations*, 1956, **9**, 385–402.

Likert, R. *New patterns of management*. New York: McGraw-Hill, 1961.

Lincoln, V. *A private disgrace*. New York: G. P. Putnam's Sons, 1967.

Lott, D. F., & Sommer, R. Seating arrangements and status. *Journal of Personality and Social Psychology*, 1967, **7**, 90–95.

Luce, R. D., & Raiffa, H. *Games and decisions*. New York: Wiley, 1957.

References

Luchins, A. S. Social influences on perception of complex drawing. *Journal of Social Psychology*, 1945, **21**, 257–273.

Lutzker, D. Internationalism as a predictor of cooperative behavior. *Journal of Conflict Resolution*, 1960, **4**, 426–435.

MacKenzie, B. K. The importance of contact in determining attitudes towards Negroes. *Journal of Abnormal and Social Psychology*, 1948, **43**, 417–441.

MacKinnon, D. W., & Dukes, W. F. Repression. In L. Postman (Ed.), *Psychology in the making*. New York: Knopf, 1962.

Maehr, M. L., Mensing, J., & Nafzger, S. Concept of self and the reaction of others. *Sociometry*, 1962, **25**, 353–357.

Maier, N. R. F. *Frustration: A study of behavior without a goal*. New York: McGraw-Hill, 1949.

Mallick, S. K., & McCandless, B. R. A study of catharsis of aggression. *Journal of Personality and Social Psychology*, 1966, **4**, 591–596.

Malpass, R. S., & Kravitz, J. Recognition for faces of own and other race. *Journal of Personality and Social Psychology*, 1969, **13**, 330–334.

Manis, M. *Cognitive processes*. Belmont, Calif.: Wadsworth, 1966.

Mann, J. H. The effects of interracial contact on sociometric choices and perceptions. *Journal of Social Psychology*, 1959, **50**, 143–152.

Marquis, D. G., Guetzkow, H., & Heyns, R. A social psychological study of the decision-making conference. In H. Guetzkow (Ed.), *Groups, leadership and men: Research in human relations*. Pittsburgh: Carnegie Press, 1951. Pp. 55–67.

Martens, R. Effect of an audience on learning of a complex motor skill. *Journal of Personality and Social Psychology*, 1969, **12**, 252–260.

Maslow, A. H. *Motivation and personality*. New York: Harper, 1954.

Maslow, A. H. Self-actualizing people: A study of psychological health. In C. E. Moustakas (Ed.), *The self*. New York: Harper & Row, 1956. Pp. 160–194.

Maslow, A. H. *Religions, values, and peak experiences*. Columbus: Ohio State University Press, 1964.

Maslow, A. H. Self-actualization and beyond. In J. F. T. Bugental (Ed.), *Challenges of humanistic psychology*. New York: McGraw-Hill, 1967. Pp. 279–286.

Matheson, R. *Shock waves*. New York: Dell, 1970.

Matlin, M. W. Response competition as a mediating factor in the frequency-affect relationship. *Journal of Personality and Social Psychology*, 1970, **16**, 536–552.

McClelland, D. C. *The achieving society*. Princeton, N.J.: Van Nostrand, 1961.

McClelland, D. C., & Atkinson, J. W. The projective expression of needs: I. The effect of different intensities of hunger drive on perception. *Journal of Psychology*, 1948, **25**, 205–232.

McClintock, C. G., Harrison, A., Strand, J., & Gallo, P. Internationalism-isolationism, strategy of the other player, and two-person game behavior. *Journal of Abnormal and Social Psychology*, 1963, **67**, 631–635.

McGinnies, E. Emotionality and perceptual defense. *Psychological Review*, 1949, **56**, 244–251.

McKeachie, W. J. Lipstick as a determiner of first impressions of personality. *Journal of Social Psychology*, 1952, **36**, 241–244.

McKeown, C. D., Gahagan, J. P., & Tedeschi, J. T. The effect of prior power strategy on behavior after a shift of power. *Journal of Experimental Research in Personality*, 1967, **2**, 226–233.

McNeil, E. B. *The concept of human development*. Belmont, Calif.: Wadsworth, 1966.

McNeil, E. B. *The quiet furies*. Englewood Cliffs, N.J.: Prentice-Hall, 1968.

McNeil, E. B. *Human socialization*. Belmont, Calif.: Brooks/Cole, 1969.

McWhirter, N., & McWhirter, R. *Guinness book of world records*. (10th ed.) New York: Bantam Books, 1971.

Medinnus, G. R., & Curtis, H. J. The relation between maternal self-acceptance and child acceptance. *Journal of Consulting Psychology*, 1963, **27**, 542–544.

Menninger, C. *Man against himself*. New York: Harcourt Brace Jovanovich, 1938.

Merton, R. K. Social structure and anomie *and* Continuities in the theory of social structure and anomie. In R. K. Merton (Ed.), *Social theory and social structure*. Glencoe, Ill.: Free Press, 1957.

Meumann, E. Haus-und Schularbeit: Experimente an Kindern der Volkschule. *Die Deutsche Schule*, 1904, **8**, 278–303, 337–359, 416–431.

Miles, W. R. Measures of human abilities throughout the life span. *Proceedings of the National Academy of Sciences*, 1931, **17**, 627–633.

Milgram, S. Behavioral study of obedience. *Journal of Abnormal and Social Psychology*, 1963, **67**, 371–378.

Milgram, S. Some conditions of obedience to authority. *Human Relations*, 1965a, **18**, 57–76.

Milgram, S. Liberating effect of group pressure. *Journal of Personality and Social Psychology*, 1965b, **1**, 127–134.

Millburn, T. W., Bell, N., & Koeske, G. F. Effect of censure or praise and evaluative dependence on performance in a free-learning task. *Journal of Personality and Social Psychology*, 1970, **15**, 43–47.

Miller, D. R. The study of social relationships. In S. Koch (Ed.), *Psychology: The study of a science*, Vol. 5. New York: McGraw-Hill, 1963. Pp. 639–737.

Miller, D. R., & Stine, W. The prediction of social acceptance by means of psycho-analytic concepts. *Journal of Personality*, 1951, **20**, 162–174.

Miller, J. G. Toward a general theory for the behavioral sciences. *American Psychologist*, 1955, **10**, 513–531.

Miller, J. G. Information input overload and psychopathology. *American Journal of Psychiatry*, 1960, **116**, 695–704.

Miller, N., Campbell, C. T., Twedt, H., & O'Connell, E. J. Similarity, contrast, and complementarity in friendship choice. *Journal of Personality and Social Psychology*, 1966, **3**, 3–12.

Miller, N., & Dollard, J. *Social learning and imitation*. New Haven, Conn.: Yale University Press, 1941.

Minani, H., & Dallenbach, K. M. The effect of activity on learning and retention in the cockroach. *American Journal of Psychology*, 1946, **59**, 1–58.

Minard, R. D. Race relations in the Pocahontas coal field. *Journal of Social Issues*, 1952, **8**, 29–44.

Mischel, W. *Personality and assessment*. New York: Wiley, 1968.

Mooney, C. M. Petty paranoia. In R. D. Baker (Ed.), *Psychology in the wry*. Princeton, N. J.: Van Nostrand, 1963.

Moore, H. T., & Gilliland, A. R. The immediate and long term effects of classical and popular phonograph selections. *Journal of Applied Psychology*, 1924, **8**, 309–323.

Morgan, W. J. *The O. S. S. and I*. New York: Norton, 1957.

Morissette, J. An experimental study of the theory of structural balance. *Human Relations*, 1958, **11**, 239–254.

References

Moustakas, C. *Loneliness.* Englewood Cliffs, N. J.: Prentice-Hall, 1961.

Moustakas, C. Heuristic research. In J. F. T. Bugental (Ed.), *Challenges of humanistic psychology.* New York: McGraw-Hill, 1967.

Mowat, F. *Never cry wolf.* New York: Dell, 1963.

Mull, H. K. The effect of repetition upon the enjoyment of modern music. *Journal of Psychology,* 1957, **43**, 155–162.

Murphy, G. *Personality.* New York: Harper & Row, 1947.

Murray, H. A. *Thematic Apperception Test.* Cambridge, Mass.: Harvard University Press, 1943.

Mussen, P., & Rutherford, E. Effects of aggressive cartoons on children's aggressive play. *Journal of Abnormal and Social Psychology,* 1961, **62**, 461–464.

Newcomb, T. M. *Personality and social change: Attitude formation in a student community.* New York: Holt, Rinehart, and Winston, 1943.

Newcomb, T. M. The prediction of interpersonal attraction. *American Psychologist,* 1956, **11**, 575–586.

Newcomb, T. M. *The acquaintance process.* New York: Holt, Rinehart and Winston, 1961.

Nuthmann, A. M. Conditioning of a response class on a personality test. *Journal of Abnormal and Social Psychology,* 1957, **54**, 19–23.

Olds, J. Differential effects of drives and drugs on self-stimulation at different brain sites. In D. E. Sheer (Ed.), *Electrical stimulation of the brain.* Austin: University of Texas Press, 1961.

Olds, J. The central nervous system and the reinforcement of behavior. *American Psychologist,* 1969, **24**, 114–132.

Olds, J., & Milner, P. Positive reinforcement produced by electrical stimulation of septal area and other regions of rat brain. *Journal of Comparative and Physiological Psychology,* 1954, **47**, 419–427.

Osborn, A. F. *Applied imagination.* New York: Scribner's, 1957.

Osgood, C. E. *An alternative to war or surrender.* Urbana: University of Illinois Press, 1962.

Oskamp, S. Attitudes toward U. S. and Russian actions: A double standard. *Psychological Reports,* 1965, **16**, 43–46.

Oskamp, S., & Perlman, D. Factors affecting cooperation in a prisoner's dilemma game. *Journal of Conflict Resolution,* 1965, **9**, 359–374.

Oskamp, S., & Perlman, D. Effects of friendship and disliking on cooperation in a mixed motive game. *Journal of Conflict Resolution,* 1966, **10**, 221–226.

O. S. S. Assessment Staff. *The assessment of men.* New York: Rinehart, 1948.

Paige, K. E. The effects of oral contraceptives on affective fluctuations associated with the menstrual cycle. Doctoral dissertation, The University of Michigan, 1969.

Paige, K. E. The effects of oral contraceptives on affective fluctuations associated with the menstrual cycle. *Psychosomatic Medicine,* 1972, in press.

Paige, K. E. *Women: Social, psychological and anthropological perspectives.* Stamford, Conn.: Sinauer Associates, 1972.

Pavlov, I. P. *Conditioned reflexes.* London: Oxford University Press, 1927.

Pepitone, A., & Reichling, G. Group cohesiveness and the expression of hostility. *Human Relations,* 1955, **8**, 327–337.

Perlman, D., & Oskamp, S. The effects of picture content and exposure frequency on evaluations of Negroes and whites. Paper read at the American Psychological Association Convention, Miami, 1970.

Perls, F. S. *Gestalt therapy verbatim.* Lafayette, Calif.: Real People Press, 1969.

Pessin, J. The comparative effects of social and mechanical stimulation on memorizing. *American Journal of Psychology,* 1933, **45,** 263–270.

Pigors, P. *Leadership or domination?* Boston: Houghton Mifflin, 1935.

Piliavan, I. M., Rodin, J., & Piliavan, J. A. Good samaritanism: An underground phenomenon? *Journal of Personality and Social Psychology,* 1969, **4,** 289–299.

President's Commission on Obscenity and Pornography. *The report of the commission on obscenity and pornography.* New York: New York Times and Bantam Books, 1970.

Price, K. O., Harburg, E., & McCleod, J. M. Positive and negative affect as a function of perceived discrepancy in *ABX* situations. *Journal of Personality and Social Psychology,* 1966, **3,** 265–270.

Price, W. H., & Whatmore, P. B. Behaviour disorders and patterns of crime among XYY males identified at a maximum security hospital. *British Medical Journal,* 1967, **1,** 533–536.

Reader, N., & English, H. B. Personality factors in adolescent female friendships. *Journal of Consulting Psychology,* 1947, **11,** 212–220.

Reynolds, E. L., & Wines, J. V. Individual differences in girls. *American Journal of Diseases of Children,* 1948, **75,** 329–350.

Richardson, H. M. Studies of mental resemblance between husbands and wives and between friends. *Psychological Bulletin,* 1939, **36,** 104–120.

Riesen, A. H. Stimulation as a requirement for growth and function. In D. W. Fiske & S. R. Maddi (Eds.), *Functions of varied experience.* Homewood, Ill.: Dorsey Press, 1961. Pp. 57–80.

Riley, M., Cohen, W. R., Toby, J., & Riley, J. W., Jr. Interpersonal orientations in small groups: A consideration of the questionnaire approach. *American Sociological Review,* 1954, **19,** 715–724.

Rodrigues, A. Effects of balance, positivity and agreement in triadic social relations. *Journal of Personality and Social Psychology,* 1967, **5,** 472–476.

Rogers, C. R. What it means to become a person. In C. E. Moustakas (Ed.), *The self.* New York: Harper & Row, 1956. Pp. 195–212.

Rogers, C. R. *On becoming a person.* Boston: Houghton Mifflin, 1961.

Rogers, C. R. The process of the basic encounter group. In J. F. T. Bugental (Ed.), *Challenges of humanistic psychology.* New York: McGraw-Hill, 1967. Pp. 261–278.

Rogers, C. R., & Dymond, R. F. *Psychotherapy and personality change.* Chicago: University of Chicago Press, 1954.

Rosenbaum, H. M., & Berger, M. M. (Eds.) *Group psychotherapy and group function: Selected readings.* New York: Basic Books, 1963.

Rosenbaum, M. E., & Tucker, I. F. Competence of the model and the learning of imitation and non-imitation. *Journal of Experimental Psychology,* 1962, **63,** 183–190.

Rosenberg, M. J. When dissonance fails: On eliminating evaluative apprehension from attitude measurement. *Journal of Personality and Social Psychology,* 1965, **1,** 28–42.

Rosenthal, R., & Jacobson, L. *Pygmalion in the classroom.* New York: Holt, Rinehart and Winston, 1968.

Rosenzweig, S. An experimental study of "repression" with special reference to need-persistent and ego-defensive reactions to frustration. *Journal of Experimental Psychology,* 1943, **32,** 64–74.

Rosenzweig, S. The investigation of repression as an instance of experimental idio-dynamics. *Psychological Review*, 1952, **59**, 339–345.

Rosenzweig, S., & Mason, G. An experimental study of memory in relation to the theory of repression. *British Journal of Psychology*, 1934, **24**, 247–265.

Ross, I., & Zander, A. Need satisfaction and employee turnover. *Personnel Psychology*, 1957, **10**, 327–338.

Saegert, S. C., & Jellison, J. Effects of initial level of response competition and frequency of exposure on liking and exploratory behavior. *Journal of Personality and Social Psychology*, 1970, **16**, 553–558.

Saegert, S., Swap, W., & Zajonc, R. B. Interpersonal attraction as a function of mere exposure. Paper presented at Midwestern Psychological Association, Detroit, 1971.

Salisbury, H. *The 900 days: The siege of Leningrad*. New York: Avon, 1969.

Salk, L. Mothers' heartbeat as an imprinting stimulus. *Transactions of the New York Academy of Sciences*, 1962, **24**, 753–763.

Sarnoff, I., & Zimbardo, P. Anxiety, fear and social affiliation. *Journal of Abnormal and Social Psychology*, 1961, **62**, 356–363.

Schachtel, E. G. *Metamorphosis*. New York: Basic Books, 1959.

Schachter, S. Deviation, rejection, and communication. *Journal of Abnormal and Social Psychology*, 1951, **46**, 190–207.

Schachter, S. *The psychology of affiliation*. Stanford, Calif.: Stanford University Press, 1959.

Schachter, S., Ellertson, N., McBride, D., & Gregory, D. An experimental study of cohesiveness and productivity. *Human Relations*, 1951, **4**, 229–238.

Scheflen, A. E., Quasi-courtship behavior in psychotherapy. In W. G. Bennis, E. H. Schein, F. I. Steele, & D. E. Berlew (Eds.), *Interpersonal dynamics*. Homewood, Ill.: Dorsey Press, 1968.

Schellenberg, J. A., & Bee, L. S. A re-examination of the theory of complementary needs in mate selection. *Marriage and Family Living*, 1960, **22**, 227–232.

Schjelderup-Ebbe, T. Beitrage zur soziale Psychologie des Haushuhns. *Zeitschrift Psychologie*, 1922, **88**, 225–252.

Scott, A. W. Cognitive complexity and cognitive balance. *Sociometry*, 1963, **26**, 66–74.

Sears, R. R., Hovland, C. I., & Miller, N. E. Minor studies of aggression. 1: Measurement of aggressive behavior. *Journal of Psychology*, 1940, **9**, 275–295.

Seashore, S. *Group cohesiveness in the industrial work group*. Ann Arbor, Mich.: Institute for Social Research, 1954.

Seligman, M. E. P., & Campbell, B. A. Effect of intensity and duration of punishment on extinction of an avoidance response. *Journal of Comparative and Physiological Psychology*, 1965, **59**, 295–297.

Sermat, V. Is game behavior related to behavior in other situations? *Journal of Personality and Social Psychology*, 1970, **16**, 92–109.

Severin, F. T. *Humanistic viewpoints in psychology*. New York: McGraw-Hill, 1965.

Shapiro, D. *Neurotic styles*. New York: Basic Books, 1965.

Shaw, M. E. Some effects of problem complexity upon problem solution efficiency in different communication nets. *Journal of Experimental Psychology*, 1954, **48**, 211–217.

Shaw, M. E. Communication networks. In L. Berkowitz (Ed.), *Advances in experimental social psychology*, Vol. I. New York: Academic Press, 1964. Pp. 111–147.

Sheldon, W. H., & Stevens, S. S. *The varieties of temperament*. New York: Harper & Row, 1942.

Sherif, M. *The psychology of social norms.* New York: Harper & Row, 1936.

Sherif, M., & Sherif, C. W. *Social psychology.* New York: Harper & Row, 1969.

Shirley, M. M. The first two years: A study of 25 babies. *Institute of Child Welfare Monograph Series,* No. 6. Minneapolis: University of Minnesota Press, 1931.

Sidowski, J. B., Wycoff, L. B., & Tabory, L. The influence of reinforcement and punishment in a minimal social situation. *Journal of Abnormal and Social Psychology,* 1956, **52,** 115–119.

Siegal, A. E., & Siegal, S. Reference group, membership groups, and attitude change. *Journal of Abnormal and Social Psychology,* 1957, **55,** 360–364.

Siegal, P. S. The relationship between voluntary water intake, body weight loss, and number of hours of water privation in the rat. *Journal of Comparative and Physiological Psychology,* 1947, **40,** 231–238.

Sigel, I. E. The attainment of concepts. In M. L. Hoffman & L. W. Hoffman (Eds.), *Review of child development research.* New York: Russell Sage Foundation, 1964.

Singer, R. D. Verbal conditioning and generalization of pro-democratic responses. *Journal of Abnormal and Social Psychology,* 1961, **63,** 43–46.

Skinner, B. F. *The behavior of organisms: An experimental analysis.* New York: Appleton-Century-Crofts, 1938.

Skinner, B. F. "Superstition" in the pigeon. *Journal of Experimental Psychology,* 1948a, **38,** 168–172.

Skinner, B. F. *Walden two.* New York: Macmillan, 1948b.

Skodak, M., & Skeels, H. M. A final follow-up of one hundred adopted children. *Journal of Genetic Psychology,* 1949, **75,** 185–215.

Smith, W. P. Power structure and authoritarianism in the use of power in the triad. *Journal of Personality,* 1967, **35,** 64–90.

Solomon, L. The influence of some types of power relationships and game strategies upon the development of interpersonal trust. *Journal of Abnormal and Social Psychology,* 1960, **61,** 223–230.

Solomon, R. L., & Howes, D. H. Word frequency, personal values and visual duration thresholds. *Psychological Review,* 1951, **58,** 256–270.

Solomon, R. L., Kamin, L. J., & Wynne, L. C. Traumatic avoidance learning: The outcomes of several extinction procedures with dogs. *Journal of Abnormal and Social Psychology,* 1953, **48,** 291–302.

Solomon, R. L., & Wynne, L. C. Traumatic avoidance learning: Acquisition in normal dogs. *Psychological Monographs,* 1953, **67** (354).

Sommer, R. Further studies of small group ecology. *Sociometry,* 1965, **28,** 237–248.

Sommer, R. Sociofugal space. *American Journal of Sociology,* 1967, **72,** 654–660.

Sommer, R. *Personal space.* Englewood Cliffs, N. J.: Prentice-Hall, 1969.

Sommer, R., & Becker, F. D. Territorial defense and the good neighbor. *Journal of Personality and Social Psychology,* 1969, **11,** 85–92.

Spitz, R. A. Hospitalism: An enquiry into the genesis of psychiatric conditions in early childhood. *Psychoanalytic study of the child,* Vol. 1. New York: International Universities Press, 1945. Pp. 53–74.

Spitz, R. A. Hospitalism: A follow-up report. *Psychoanalytic study of the child,* Vol. 2. New York: International Universities Press, 1946. Pp. 113–118.

Spitz, R. A. *The first year of life.* New York: International Universities Press, 1965.

Stagner, R. The reintegration of pleasant and unpleasant experiences. *American Journal of Psychology,* 1931, **43,** 463–468.

Staub, E. Effects of variation in permissibility of movement on children helping another child in distress. *Proceedings of the 77th Annual Convention, American Psychological Association, 1969,* **4,** 385–386.

Staub, E. A child in distress: The influence of age and number of witnesses on children's attempts to help. *Journal of Personality and Social Psychology, 1970,* **14,** 130–140.

Stone, L. J., & Church, J. *Childhood and adolescence.* New York: Random House, 1957.

Stouffer, S. A. An analysis of conflicting social norms. *American Sociological Review,* 1949, **14,** 707–717.

Stratton, G. M. Vision without the inversion of the retinal image. *Psychological Review,* 1897, **4,** 341–360.

Strauss, A. Transformations of identity. In A. Rose (Ed.), *Human behavior and social process.* Boston: Houghton Mifflin, 1962.

Strong, E. K., Jr. *Strong vocational interest blanks manual.* Palo Alto, Calif.: Consulting Psychologists Press, 1959.

Swingle, P. G., & Gillis, J. S. Effects of the emotional relations between protagonists in the Prisoner's Dilemma. *Journal of Personality and Social Psychology, 1968,* **8,** 160–165.

Sykes, G. M., & Matza, D. Techniques of neutralization. *American Sociological Review,* 1957, **22,** 664–670.

Szasz, T. S. *The myth of mental illness.* New York: Harper & Row, 1961.

Szasz, T. S. Moral man: A model of man for humanistic psychology. In J. F. T. Bugental (Ed.), *Challenges of humanistic psychology.* New York: McGraw-Hill, 1967. Pp. 45–52.

Taylor, D. W., Berry, P. C., & Block, C. H. Does group participation when using brainstorming facilitate or inhibit creative thinking? *Administrative Science Quarterly,* 1958, 3, 23–47.

Thibaut, J. W., & Kelley, H. H. *The social psychology of groups.* New York: Wiley, 1959.

Thigpen, C. H., & Cleckley, H. M. *The three faces of Eve.* New York: McGraw-Hill, 1957.

Thompson, D. F., & Meltzer, L. Communication of emotional intent by facial expression. *Journal of Abnormal and Social Psychology,* 1964, **68,** 129–135.

Thorndike, E. L., & Lorge, I. *The teacher's wordbook of 30,000 words.* New York: Teacher's College, Columbia University, 1944.

Travis, E. J. An investigation of the rational decision-making, cooperation, greed, punishment and withdrawal manifested by schizophrenics in several experimental conflict situations. *Dissertation Abstracts,* 1966, **26,** 7449.

Travis, L. E. The effects of a small audience upon eye-hand coordination. *Journal of Abnormal and Social Psychology,* 1925, **20,** 142–146.

Triplett, N. The dynamogenic factors in pacemaking and competition. *American Journal of Psychology,* 1897, **9,** 507–533.

Tuchman, B. *The proud tower.* New York: Bantam Books, 1966.

Tuddenham, R. C. Correlates of yielding to a distorted group norm. *Journal of Personality,* 1959, **27,** 272–284.

Turner, E. R. A. Social feeding in birds. *Behavior,* 1964, **24,** 1–46.

Veroff, J., Atkinson, J. W., Feld, S., & Gurin, G. The use of thematic apperception to assess motivation in a nationwide interview. *Psychological Monographs*, 1960, **94** (12, Whole No. 499).

Vinacke, W. E. Variables in experimental games: Toward a field theory. *Psychological Bulletin*, 1969, **71**, 293–318.

Von Senden, M. *Raum-und Gestaltauffassung bei operierten Blindgebornen vor und nach der Operation.* Leipzig: Barth, 1932.

Wagner, C., & Wheeler, L. Model, need and cost effects in helping behavior. *Journal of Personality and Social Psychology*, 1969, **12**, 111–116.

Wagner, R. V., & Sherwood, J. *The study of attitude change.* Belmont, Calif.: Brooks/Cole, 1969.

Walker, E. L. *Conditioning and instrumental learning.* Belmont, Calif.: Brooks/Cole, 1967.

Walker, E., & Heyns, R. *An anatomy for conformity.* Belmont, Calif.: Brooks/Cole, 1962.

Walker, R. N. Body build and behavior in young children: Body build and nursery school teachers' ratings. *Child Development Monograph*, 1962, **84**, 75–79.

Walster, E., Aronson, V., Abrahams, D., & Rottmann, L. Importance of physical attractiveness in dating behavior. *Journal of Personality and Social Psychology*, 1966, **4**, 508–516.

Watson, J. B., & Rayner, R. Conditioned emotional reactions. *Journal of Experimental Psychology*, 1920, **3**, 1–14.

Weintraub, D. J., & Walker, E. L. *Perception.* Belmont, Calif.: Brooks/Cole, 1968.

Wesman, A. G. Intelligent testing. *American Psychologist*, 1968, **23**, 267–274.

Whyte, W. H. *The organization man.* New York: Doubleday, 1956.

Wilner, D. M., Walkley, R. P., & Cook, S. W. Two studies of the effects of Negroes at varying distances from white neighbors in housing projects. *Journal of Social Issues*, 1952, **8**, 45–69.

Wilner, D. M., Walkley, R. P., & Cook, S. W. *Human relations in interracial housing.* Minneapolis: University of Minnesota Press, 1955.

Winch, R. F. *Mate selection: A study of complementary needs.* New York: Harper & Row, 1958.

Winch, R. F., Ktsanes, T., & Ktsanes, V. Empirical elaboration of theory of complementary needs in mate selection. *Journal of Abnormal and Social Psychology*, 1955, **51**, 508–514.

Wolowitz, H. Lectures delivered at the University of Michigan, Fall, 1963.

Wrightsman, L. (Ed.) *Contemporary issues in social psychology.* Belmont, Calif.: Brooks/Cole, 1968.

Wrightsman, L. S. Wallace supporters and adherence to "law and order." *Journal of Personality and Social Psychology*, 1969, **13**, 17–22.

Wylie, R. *The self-concept.* Lincoln: University of Nebraska Press, 1961.

Wylie, R. The present status of self theory. In E. F. Borgatta & W. W. Lambert (Eds.), *Handbook of personality: Theory and research.* Chicago: Rand-McNally, 1968. Pp. 728–772.

Zajonc, R. B. Some effects of the "space" serials. *Public Opinion Quarterly*, 1955, **18**, 367–374.

Zajonc, R. B. *Social psychology: An experimental approach.* Belmont, Calif.: Brooks/Cole, 1966.

References

Zajonc, R. B. Attitudinal effects of mere exposure. *Journal of Personality and Social Psychology Monograph Supplements*, 1968a, **9** (2), Part 2, 1–27.

Zajonc, R. B. Conformity. In *The international encyclopedia of the social sciences.* New York: Macmillan, 1968b.

Zajonc, R. B., & Burnstein, E. The learning of balanced and unbalanced social structures. *Journal of Personality*, 1965a, **33,** 153–163.

Zajonc, R. B., & Burnstein, E. Structural balance, reciprocity and positivity as sources of cognitive bias. *Journal of Personality*, 1965b, **33,** 570–583.

Zajonc, R. B., Heingartner, A., & Herman, E. M. Social enhancement and impairment of performance in the cockroach. *Journal of Personality and Social Psychology*, 1969, **13,** 83–92.

Zajonc, R. B., & Sales, S. Social facilitation of dominant and subordinate responses. *Journal of Experimental Social Psychology*, 1966, **2,** 160–168.

Zajonc, R. B., Swap, W., Harrison, A. A., & Roberts, P. Limiting conditions of the exposure effect: Satiation and relativity. *Journal of Personality and Social Psychology*, 1971, **18,** 384–391.

Zeigarnik, B. Uber das Behalten von erledigten und unerledigten Handlungen. *Psychologische Forschuung*, 1927, **9,** 1–85.

Zeller, A. F. An experimental analogue of repression. II. The effect of individual failure and success on memory measured by relearning. *Journal of Experimental Psychology*, 1950, **40,** 411–422.

Author Index

Subject Index

515